KU-205-978

GUTENBERG AND THE IMPACT OF PRINTING

STEPHAN FÜSSEL

Gutenberg

AND THE IMPACT OF PRINTING

TRANSLATED FROM THE GERMAN BY
DOUGLAS MARTIN

ASHGATE

The translator acknowledges the willing and expert help of Hans Eckert, librarian, of Rüsselsheim. He would also like to thank Erika Gaffney at Burlington, VT, and Kirsten Weißenberg at Aldershot for valued advice and encouragement.

This book was first published in German in 1999 under the title *Gutenberg und seine Wirkung* by Insel Verlag Frankfurt am Main and Leipzig
The English edition first published 2003 by
Scolar Press, Ashgate Publishing Limited
Gower House, Croft Road, Aldershot, Hampshire GU11 3HR
and Ashgate Publishing Company
Suite 420, 101 Cherry Street, Burlington, Vermont 05401-4405

The German text copyright © Stephan Füssel 1999, 2005
The English translation copyright © Douglas Martin 2005

All rights reserved. No part of this publication may be reproduced, stored in a retrieval system, or transmitted in any form or by any means, electronic, mechanical, photocopying, or otherwise without the prior permission of the publisher.

The publisher acknowledges a grant for the translation from Stiftung Moses

Designed and typeset in dfTYPE Rialto by Douglas Martin
Printed and made in Great Britain by MPG Books, Bodmin, Cornwall

British Library Cataloguing-in-Publication Data
Füssel, Stephan
Gutenberg and the impact of printing
1. Gutenberg, Johann, 1397?–1468. 2. Printers – Germany – Biography.
3. Printing – History – Origins and antecedents
I.Title
686.2'092
ISBN 0-7546-3537-6

Library of Congress Cataloging-in-Publication Data
Füssel, Stephan
[Gutenberg und seine Wirkung. English]
Gutenberg and the impact of printing / Stephan Füssel;
translated from the German by Douglas Martin – English ed.
Originally published in German under the title: Gutenberg und seine Wirkung.
Frankfurt am Main: Insel 1999.
Includes bibliographical references and index.
ISBN 0-7546-3537-6 (alk. paper)
1. Gutenberg, Johann, 1397?–1468. 2. Printers – Germany – Biography.
3. Printing – History – Origin and antecedents.
I. Title
Z126.Z7F9613 2005 686.2'092–dc22
2004001759

WITHDRAWN
Undergraduate Lending Library

Contents

WITHDRAWN

Foreword

Johann Gutenberg was voted "man of the millennium" by an American team of journalists (see Agnes Hooper Gottlieb, Henry Gottlieb, Barbara Bowers, Brent Bowers: *1000 Years, 1000 People: Ranking the men and women who shaped the millennium*. New York, Tokyo, London, 1999). In their reasoning it was stressed that Gutenberg had created, by means of his invention, the conditions for all other intellectual, political or religious changes in the centuries ahead. The exceptional story of Gutenberg's influence lay at the heart of their final decision, based not on a single timely invention, but rather on his fundamental significance for the global history of human communication.

We know that methods also existed in the Far East from as early as the eighth century for the multiplication of texts from woodcuts, from 1100 using clay letters, and after 1377 by means of the sand-casting process; but it was Gutenberg's related sequence of inventions involving casting and setting single metal types and printing from them in a press, that first created texts which were comparable in beauty to the finest manuscripts, and at the same time distributed them in unprecedented quantities. The possibilities opened up by printing supported the educational trends of the late Middle Ages that had launched the aspiring European universities of the fourteenth and fifteenth centuries, promoted the spread of the ideas of the Italian humanists with their belief in a universal human capacity for education, whilst at the same time bringing about the preconditions for the Reformation of the Church and the popularisation of the contents of faith in the vernacular languages. Printing also heralded the birth of public opinion mediated through newspapers and the press, and prepared the way by circulating factual information as well as agitation and propaganda through pamphlets and broadsides.

It is the interaction between technological history and intellectual history which makes the study of early printing history so fascinating. This shows that the new medium did not take over from what had gone before with a bang, but rather that for quite some time the old contents continued to be handed down in their familiar external forms.

Thus the page layout, choice of letter-form and format for early printed books followed directly from that of similar manuscripts, and it was those same grammars and textbooks that had proved themselves over the centuries that were selected for wider distribution in print. The true nature and potential of the new medium came to light at first little by little: a title page was grafted on at the front, more convenient formats were developed, the vernacular gained ground alongside the learned Latin tongue, and all this encouraged the habit of personal reading.

Epics in verse form – an outward indicator of public reading – were no longer published, their place being taken by pocket editions of prose romances for private reading; and the first factual books on medicine and natural history, printed maps of Europe and the world, calendars and almanacks were circulated. Only fifty years after the invention, more than a thousand printing offices using the new technology were at work in some 350 towns right across Europe, and between 1450 and 1500 about 30,000 titles were published with a total estimated output of 9 million volumes. Contemporaries rejoiced that it was now possible for "everyone of moderate means to acquire a higher education."

The technical essentials of Gutenberg's invention remained unchanged for 350 years. The first modifications came in the nineteenth century with steam-driven cylinder presses, mechanical composition and manufacture of paper in continuous reels, but metal composition and the letterpress process held out until the middle of the twentieth century. Filmsetting and the offset process took over from that point until the scope of present-day electronic publication created a new technological environment. The communication revolution associated with Gutenberg's name, however, continues on its way.

Gutenberg – his life and work

In May 1451 the papal legate Nicholas of Cues, known as Cusanus, took part in the fourteenth general chapter of the Benedictines in Mainz, which dealt with the adoption of monastic reforms, and which also looked into the resources of monastic libraries and their central importance for the monastic community. In an earlier work *De concordantia catholica* (1434), written during his visits to the Council of Basle (1431–48), he had already spoken out for a correct and reliable edition of the text of the missal for use throughout the Catholic world, for only a standardised text could ensure that mass would be performed in the same fashion everywhere. On the tours of visitation he made after 1450, Cusanus must have seen for himself that the basic prayers of the faith were insufficiently familiar to the parish priests, let alone to the congregation. And so in order to improve popular religious education in the churches he had wooden or stone tablets set up on which the Lord's prayer, the creed, the "Hail Mary" and the ten commandments were inscribed. Whilst Cusanus was still hoping that the reforms so urgently needed in the Church could be brought about – as in former centuries – through religious knowledge put across by stained glass, murals or suchlike one-off inscriptions; Gutenberg was sitting just a few yards away from Mainz's cathedral square in his workshop in the Humbrechthof, cutting punches for the successful casting of metal types.

THE COURSE OF GUTENBERG'S LIFE

The fifteenth century was an age of stagnation in politics and Church affairs; the emperor stood opposed to the imperial hierarchy, of whom the electors formed a particularly factious element. The imperial diet which met at irregular intervals revealed the emperor's dependence on the princes when it came to the Hussite and later the Turkish campaigns. The territorial overlords gained an ever more commanding position, and the free cities frequently invoked their special status under the law. Learning flourished, leading to changes in higher education and the foundation of universities in Cologne and Erfurt in 1389, Würzburg in

1402, Leipzig in 1409 and Louvain in 1425; jurisprudence and mathematical sciences were strongly promoted. The dominant intellectual current of the age was humanism, with its belief in universal educability and a new spiritual openness that tried to bring together Platonism and Christianity. Although only about six per cent of the population lived in towns, these grew in importance with the introduction of simple industries such as cloth and linen production, whilst the agricultural economy was in slow decline. The old Hansa privileges were being lost and new methods of trading were taking their place, which benefited the international trade fair centre of Leipzig and made use of merchant and private banking houses, particularly those of Augsburg and Nuremberg in southern Germany.

At the beginning of the fifteenth century, the city of Mainz had about 6000 inhabitants. At this time of radical upheaval the city council enacted a new constitution, which was more strongly weighted in favour of the right of the guilds to be informed and to participate at the expense of the old patrician class. In the quarrels between patricians and guilds the families of the "ancients" were several times forced to leave the city, and at other times they absented themselves in protest. The financial situation of the city developed so catastrophically during the 1540s that it had to borrow massively from the surrounding towns, and above all from Frankfurt. By 1456 the city was literally bankrupt and more or less in pawn to Frankfurt. At the same time Mainz, however, still retained its legal status as an imperial free city, whereas after the archbishops' war of 1462 it became a dependency of its archbishop and elector. The economic position of Mainz – which had been such a prosperous city in the fourteenth century – became ever more critical until it went into recession around 1450 with a drastic population decline. Immigrants were welcomed because of this underlying problem, and in 1436 new citizens were solicited with the offer of a ten-year break from taxes and levies. The local trades and occupations included woodworking and the timber-trade, river transport, farming and viticulture, and also cloth-weaving, wrought-iron and non-ferrous metal crafts as well as goldsmithing.

No certain date of birth has been handed down for Gutenberg. In connection with the division of his father's estate in 1420, he was considered to have come of age, and – on the basis of different arguments – researchers have settled for various years from the range between 1393 and 1403. Since the turn of the century was accepted as the token year by international consensus in 1900, then this traditional argument allowed his 600th birthday to be celebrated in the year 2000. And as it was not uncommon at the time to name someone after the patron saint of their date of birth, then traditionally 24 June (St John's Day) has been the accepted birthday; but it is very probable – as the name Johann (or Johannes, or in Mainz dialect of the fifteenth century Henchen, or Hengin or Henne) was so popular and widespread – that the name-day connection is tenuous indeed. His father, Friele Gensfleisch zur Laden, born in about 1350 and a Mainz citizen from 1372, married Elsa Wirich in 1386 as his second bride. A Mainz patrician, he was by occupation a merchant, probably in the cloth trade; he belonged to the companionship of the mint and served for a time as one of the masters of accounts for the city. During his lifetime he never used the surname "zum Gutenberg"; this additional family name was only taken up by his relatives in the 1520s. Ever since the early fourteenth century the Hof zum Gutenberg had belonged in the family. This house, which stood at the corner of Schustergasse and Christophstrasse, no longer exists. It was a two-storey Gothic building with room for a number of families and most probably for a composing room and a press room as well.

We can only speculate about Gutenberg's childhood and youth. At best we may suppose from his good grasp of Latin and his technical knowledge that he was well educated in a monastic school, probably followed by a spell at university. It has been suggested, and also disputed, that he may have attended the monastery of St Victor (south of the city near Weisenau) and acquired Latin and the rudiments of learning there, since at an advanced age he can be traced as a member of the brotherhood of St Victor. Whilst still quite young, Gutenberg probably had to leave Mainz with his family as yet another dispute between patricians and guilds came to a head in August 1411, leading to the withdrawal from the city of 117 patricians who were seeking by this strategy to protect their privileged exemption from tax and tolls. In all probability they moved at short notice to Eltville, where Gutenberg's mother had inherited a house on the town walls (in the Burghofstrasse). Once again in 1413 his father had to leave Mainz hurriedly on account of hunger rioting and once more the family members would have accompanied him. An equally good schooling could have been had in Eltville at the "community school" attached to St Peter's church, for grammar was taught there from Aelius Donatus's textbook, and rhetoric through readings from the leading Latin writers. We find one "Johannes de Alta villa" enrolled for the summer semester of 1418 and winter semester of 1419 at the University of Erfurt (which fell within the diocese of Mainz), which provides a clue that might encourage us to identify this "John from Eltville" with Johann Gutenberg. But just as we are unable to find more evidence for this theory, so we lack information about possible further training in the 1420s. The few documentary records confine themselves to inheritance settlements and the payment of life annuities. His immediate neighbour in the Gutenberghof was Heinz Reyse, who was a companion of the mint and probably an active coin-maker. Heinz Reyse and "Henchin zu Gudenberg" were among those who once again left the city as its finances were threatened with bankruptcy and the guilds took command. We know for certain from a further document that Gutenberg was no longer resident in Mainz after 16 January 1430.

Four years later, we pick up his trail in the Strasbourg suburb of St Arbogast. He had caused the city clerk of Mainz Niklaus Wörstadt, who was passing through Strasbourg, to be imprisoned for debt, because the city of Mainz had not yet paid him 310 Rhenish gulden due on an annuity from the division of his late mother's estate. More important for us than sketchy personal suggestions of an engagement and the breaking off of an engagement in Strasbourg, are those sources which reveal Gutenberg as an entrepreneurial businessman, as an experienced inventor, and as a master-craftsman. Since 1437 he had taught the Strasbourg citizen Andreas Dritzehn the "cutting and polishing of precious stones", that is to say, he had offered a kind of apprenticeship in the coin-maker's or goldsmith's crafts. Now, as on several occasions later in his career, he set up a financing consortium with various associates to put up the capital for a project which involved both a technical process and the production of wares. On the next big pilgrimage to Aachen for the display of the relics, visitors would want to buy mirrors as souvenirs, and because it was deeply rooted in popular devotion that something of the beneficial radiation from the relics could be captured in these mirrors and carried home. These much-loved mirrors were made from an alloy of lead and tin, and – although we can only speculate about the exact production method – were turned out in great numbers by a casting process. The consortium threatened to fall apart on discovering that it was mistakenly producing for 1439, whereas the Aachen pilgrimage with its marketing opportunity would not in fact take place until the following year, 1440. We know about this through an action brought by one of the brothers of the deceased associate and former apprentice Andreas Dritzehn. From this lawsuit it emerged that Gutenberg acted as master in teaching goldsmithing, that they worked together in manufacturing the mirrors, and that a further, third project was planned.

A great deal of speculation has been caused by the secretive sounding phrase "Aventur und Kunst" which occurs several times in the documentation. A glance at the contemporary contexts in which the word is used, however, will show that "Aventur" does not indicate some colourful adventure from knightly romance, but rather a risky business "venture" in the modern sense. And similarly the term "Kunst" stood for skilful knowledge of handicrafts. Gutenberg is revealed here and in the following years as an inventive entrepreneur and technologist.

Other intriguing terms from the documents of the Strasbourg period that are hard to pin down include the "Pressen" (presses), the "Form" (forme), and the "Gezeug" (tool, instrument). These could be used to describe either coin stamping or perhaps an experiment in letterpress printing, the latter more likely as one of the associates was the co-owner of a papermill. Strasbourg was a world trading city, with connections to the south of France and Italy, but also via Nuremberg and Prague to the Orient. In Strasbourg, the use of high relief stamps for bookbinding had been developed, for example, and it was the leading city for bell-founding. It is interesting that paper currency notes, which had been produced by a printing process in the Far East, were known about there in Gutenberg's day. Since the early seventh century in China and Korea, and somewhat later in Japan, Confucian and Buddhist texts had been written on wood and circulated. These written *Sutras* (doctrines) were cut into the woodblock to prevent changes or wear, so reproducing them by inking and rubbing onto paper was at first an incidental use. In many instances only two to five copies would be taken, but in contrast the original woodblocks were kept safely and many Korean examples still survive. Experimentation with ceramic types took place in China from the eleventh century, and with types cast in various metal alloys in Korea from the fourteenth century. If at first the huge number of over 10,000 signs required was an obstacle to casting and printing from moveable types, then the introduction of the Hangul-alphabet in about 1444 should have given the Koreans an opportunity to develop more practical casting methods. Castings were made from sand-moulds, which could not give a sharp-edged quality to the types to compare with Gutenberg's later developments. Furthermore it was not permissable at the time to use this alphabet for general purposes. Experiments with composition from single types in the Far East are clearly attested, but despite much reflection there are still no routes by which information about them could have reached Strasbourg by 1440.

Paper, which had been developed in China by the second century, did, on the contrary reach Baghdad and Cairo along the Silk Road by the tenth century, and with the expansion of Islam, extended over North Africa, Sicily and Gibraltar to reach Europe in the twelfth century. The first papermill in German lands was set up by Ulman Stromer in Nuremberg in 1390 and with it one of the essential preconditions for Gutenberg's invention fell into place, and an early instance of mass production was created.

Similarly woodcutting, which originated in the Far East, can be shown to have reached central Europe by the early fifteenth century. The earliest woodcuts were used to produce playing cards and devotional images. The latter noted miraculous events or special pilgrimages, and often contained a few woods of text which also had to be cut into the woodblock. So the means of providing large numbers of single-sided sheets of paper by this method was common knowledge by 1440, but it was not very practical since a woodblock could not be re-used once a particular text or image had been cut.

We simply do not know what Gutenberg did between 1444 and 1448; but there is evidence to show that he was back in Mainz by 17 October

1448. On that day he took out a loan of 150 gulden at 5 per cent interest from his cousin Arnold Gelthus. Just as in Strasbourg, Gutenberg sought business relationships with bankers and merchants with whose financial support he could put his new technical developments into practice. By 1450 his experiments had reached the stage that he could go ahead with the setting and printing of broadsides and extensive books.

BRINGING THE TECHNICAL INVENTIONS TOGETHER

Gutenberg's invention is as simple as it is ingenious: texts were broken down into their smallest components, i.e. into the 26 letters of the Roman alphabet, and from placing single letters in the right order the new text required would result time and again. Texts had been copied over the centuries by writing them out completely and sequentially, or by cutting them equally completely in wood (text and illustrations were being cut in wood for such contemporary "blockbooks" as prayers, *ars moriendi* or cribs for sermons), but now only the letters of the alphabet had to be cut and supplies cast and they would always be available for setting up whatever text was chosen. His second brain-wave was in effect as simple as it was technologically revolutionary: instead of transferring the ink to the paper by rubbing as had been done for 700 years in Asia, Gutenberg used the physical action of the paper- or wine-press to transfer the ink from typematter to dampened paper with one even and forceful impression (see Plate 2, the first contemporary woodcut to show a press, dating from 1499).

Very many stages were naturally called for in the development of this apparently obvious and straightforward procedure. Punches for individual letters, skilfully cut by goldsmiths, had been around for some time, and the engraving of sacred artefacts such as chalices and monstrances was a widespread technique. Casting methods were in use whether for bellfounding or coinmaking. It was a question of realising the idea by bringing together individual letters, and casting techniques, and finding the appropriater constituents of the typemetal. At the heart of Gutenberg's discovery stands the development of a casting instrument which allowed the casting void to be precisely adjusted so that identical supplies of each type could be cast. No original instruments have survived from the fifteenth century, and the so-called adjustable hand mould shown in the textbooks only reached that precise form some two centuries later, but the earliest types which do survive and the quality of Gutenberg's impression make it evident that some comparable casting instrument must have been part of the original invention.

To start with a letter was engraved on the top of a tall steel bar or cube. This bar carried a single character in deep relief and in mirror image; it was then struck by a hammer into softer copper so that a right-reading, deeply sunken letter resulted. This was now the matrix, which had to be correctly fitted into the casting instrument. Molten metal was poured in, and a single type cast, with the letter at its head in relief but again in mirror-image. As the casting matrix in harder metal could be used again and again, a theoretically endless supply of identical types of the same letter and shape could be cast. The exact constitution of the first alloys is not known but may be inferred from later discoveries to have been about 83 per cent lead, 9 per cent tin, 6 per cent antimony and 1 per cent each of copper and iron; this compares with an actual find from the mid-seventeenth century in Mainz, where the lead content was markedly lower at 73 per cent and tin and antimony totalled 25 per cent (a composition which would have had the advantage of cooling more rapidly, allowing a higher rate of production).

Supplies of these singly cast types were then placed in compartmented cases where an ergonomic principle operated, in that the most frequently used letters had larger, well-positioned compartments close to the compositor's hand. The individual letters were then assembled in a composing stick, in which the lines could be "justified". For this purpose metal spacing material that was blind (i.e. below printing height) was introduced to equalise the space between the words and bring the lines out to equal length. These composing sticks were at first made of wood and later replaced by metal. Small groups of completed lines were transferred to a galley, a stable wooden tray in which they could be made up into column or page depths. These could be brought out to the correct depth if needed by "leading", or adjusting the space between lines, using further strips of blind spacing material. The finished pages were placed in correct relationship to each other, and locked up into a "forme" or frame to fit the bed of the press.

The typesetting was then inked using mushroom-shaped leather balls (the printing ink developed by Gutenberg was made from soot from lamps, varnish and egg-whites). The paper to be printed had been dampened so that it would take the impression from the type better, and was positioned on a number of pins within a hinged tympan. A frisket, which in turn hinged over that, had a cut-out corresponding to the type area, and otherwise protected the margin of the paper from coming into contact with the forme and possibly being soiled. The frisket was closed and then the tympan with the frisket and paper was folded above the forme which rested on the bed of the press. The bed was drawn in under the platen, which was brought down by a heavy pull on the lever to take an impression. This first impression was "backed-up" on the other side of the sheet, with the pin-holes keeping the registration exact so that the lines of type on both sides of the sheet corresponded. Sheets of various sizes could be printed, in the early days a page at a time, and later two, four or eight pages together, and allowed to dry before the other side could be printed, and later folded into sections. Careful "imposition" ensured that the pages fell in the right order when folded into 16-page sections for sewing.

Early printing was produced in black only as a rule, and all special features such as illuminated initials, coloured page headings, illustrations, as well as rubrication (lit. writing in red) had to be added later by hand. As a result many early printed books can be mistaken for manuscripts at first glance, since their decoration was added individually by hand. None of the 49 surviving copies of the *Gutenberg Bible* resembles another, for each has its own illumination and finishing touches. At first woodcuts were not printed together with typematter, as it was difficult to get the inking and impression right for printing from wood and metal at the same time. In the earliest instances, text and illustrations were usually printed in two separate operations, although this could bring its own problems when it came to register. This is well illustrated in *Der Edelstein*, the fable collection printed by Albrecht Pfister in Bamberg in 1461 (see Plates 42/43).

Whereas it would have been theoretically possible to make do with two sets of 26 characters – one each for the capitals and lower case – Gutenberg was evidently concerned to imitate the manuscript as faithfully as possible, in that he reproduced double-column setting and the same marginal proportions and went to great trouble to match the look of the page *en masse*. To that end he cut and cast a total of 290 different characters: 47 capitals, 63 lower case, 92 abbreviations, 83 ligatures or combined letters and 5 punctuation marks (see Plate 3). The ligatures, such as **ff**, **ſi**, **ffi**, **ſt**, saved space by being cast on a single body. Abbreviations and contractions taken over from Latin manuscript usage for prefixes (pro, prae, per), case-endings (um, am, as) and doubled letters (mm, nn), were also great space savers. All these, and the width variants available for many lower-case letters, helped the skilled compositor to produce evenly spaced lines and a wonderfully close and evenly spaced page. At the same time it becomes apparent what high demands were placed on the compositor's knowledge of Latin. Some 100,000 types would have had to be cast for the compositors' work on the *Gutenberg Bible*. This allowed every detail of a manuscript text to be followed, whilst surpassing it in accuracy and quality. The first experiments and attempts at printing in this typeface must have related solely to Latin texts, for many of the abbreviations provided were only called for in Latin.

THE "WORK OF THE BOOKS": THE 42-LINE BIBLE

Those early pieces of printing which we can confidently attribute to Gutenberg fall into two main groups, on the one hand jobbing printing such as indulgences, calendars and vocabularies, and on the other hand that great masterpiece of 1282 printed pages, the Latin *Bible*. Gutenberg chose for this the *Vulgate* of St Jerome, the definitive textual basis for all theological work and religious instruction during the Middle Ages. It is most probable that he would have taken a handwritten *Bible* available in Mainz as his example from which to set the text. That same copy has never been rediscovered, but then it is likely to have been little short of worn out by the treatment it would have received. However, there is a manuscript *Bible* preserved in the Library of Congress that was written in Mainz in 1450 and which must come close to the model Gutenberg in fact used (see Plate 4). It is striking to note that it contains illuminated pages by the same artist who decorated the printed copy of a *Gutenberg Bible* to be found today in Göttingen University Library.

Gutenberg imitated the manuscript in all its aspects, so he adopted the division into columns, and the massed look of the text panel – which he was able to improve upon through typesetting – and that placing of the columns on the page which yielded ideal margin proportions. The missal type he used was a textura, that gave a very dense type area, in which individual letters had a perpendicular emphasis and produced a latticed effect so that the finished page resembled a woven textile (Lat. *textura*).

In his *Chronik der Stadt Köln* of 1499, Johann Koelhoff has this to say about our *Bible*: "In the year of our Lord which one wrote as MCCCCL (1450) – that was a golden year – printing began. And the first book to be printed was the *Bible* in Latin which was printed in a large type of the kind only used nowadays for printing missals." The chronicler not only places the beginning of printing in elevated conjunction with a holy year, but also sets it in the right liturgical context. These missal letter-forms were relatively large on the manuscript page – and consequently on the printed one – so that they would be readable from the lectern in dark church or refectory interiors. The *Gutenberg Bible* is set in a choral type of 4.2 mm (x-height), and it followed that in this fairly large size the extensive text would occupy 1282 printed pages in large folio format. In order to use paper economically, Gutenberg experimented with the number of lines per column. For the initial setting trial he started with 40 lines to the column (fols. 1–5r and fols. 129–132r), increased to 41 lines (fol. 5v only), and then to the 42 lines with which he decided to stay (from fol. 6 and throughout). He evidently had the faulty pages set again at 42 lines per column depth. Examples of both setting variants are to be found among the surviving copies.

For the first pages to come off the press, Gutenberg had also made the experiment of taking over the work of the rubricator, so on leaves 1, 4, 5, and 129 and 130 the headings of the chapters are printed in red. Thereafter he gave up on this red printing, and it was omitted when it came to reprinting sheets from the second typesetting. It is obvious that two-fold inking and problems with impression were holding up the work-rate and giving unsatisfactory visual results, so he left further rubrication in the hands of the professional scribes as hitherto in the manuscript era. The Vienna and Munich copies of B42 still contain their complete *Tabula Rubricarum*, or printed list of headings to be inserted in red with instructions on where they are to appear.

On the final folios of both volumes of the copy on paper at the Bibliothèque Nationale in Paris, there is a handwritten note from Heinrich Cremer, vicar of St Stephan's in Mainz, stating that he completed the work of rubricating, illuminating and binding these volumes by 24 August 1456. This gives us a useful guide as to when the finished printed books must have been available.

Close textual analysis and the study of individual habits in handling abbreviations let us conclude that there were four different compositors at work when typesetting began, and six as production reached a more advanced stage. Examination of inks through electron spectrography has confirmed these numbers. At least half a year has to be allowed for the casting of a supply of 100,000 types, and the typesetting would have extended over about two years. At the height of production at least twelve printers would have been teamed with the compositors to keep six presses busy, and other helpers would have been needed for inkmaking and paper handling. To print 180 copies of 1282 pages would have involved 230,760 passes through the press, which in turn would require at least 330 working days. Allowing for the fact that the medieval working year had only about 200 days (because of the large number of religious festivals) and that only four presses were operated to start with and that there were bound to have been teething troubles, it is certain that typesetting and printing would have taken more than two years. Whereas a scribe would have worked a whole three years on a single copy of the *Bible*, it was now possible to produce 180 copies in the same time, 40 on vellum and 140 on paper. The paper imported from Italy would have cost about 600 gulden, the vellum (i.e. the skins of 3,200 animals) perhaps 400 gulden.

Such high charges, not to speak of the development costs, were beyond Gutenberg's personal means. As we have already seen him do in Strasbourg, he set about finding partners with capital to invest in his technically innovative and commercially bold enterprise as soon as he was back in Mainz in 1448. He borrowed 150 gulden from his cousin Arnold Gelthus straight away and took out a loan from Johann Fust (c.1400–66) in each of the years 1449 and 1452. Fust placed the initial loan of 800 gulden at Gutenberg's free disposal against the security of the equipment to be produced with the money. The second advance was specifically intended as working capital for their joint "work of the books". These arrangements show both of them as financial partners in the process of developing their business collaboration. From their legal dispute of 1455, for which only part of the proceedings has come down to us (in the legal instrument named after the lawyer Helmasperger, see Plate 10), we learn that Fust accused Gutenberg of having paid no interest (Gutenberg's counter-argument was that Fust had told him that no interest would be due), and of Fust's further charge of embezzlement, namely that the money had not been applied to their joint project.

After simple and compound interest had been added, Gutenberg was faced with paying back 2026 gulden, the equivalent in purchasing power to about four houses. A valuable letter of 1455 from Enea Silvio Piccolomini, who later became Pope Pius II but was still at that time secretary to emperor Friedrich III, tells us that the *Bible* was already finished by autumn 1454 and had already found buyers. Piccolomini wrote from Wiener Neustadt to the Spanish cardinal Juan de Carvajal in Rome on 12 March 1455, reporting an interesting encounter when in Frankfurt (probably for the Reichstag held there in October 1454). There he had met a "remarkable man" (*vir mirabilis*) who had shown him quinternions (sections of five folded sheets) of a Latin *Bible* that could be read without difficulty and "without spectacles". What is more some sheets had already been sent to the emperor in Vienna. Piccolomini was able to ascertain that the edition (and this consisted either or 158 or of 180 copies) had sold out before printing had been completed. This would suggest that the business had run its profitable course, if we had not heard arguments to the contrary in the Helmasperger legal instrument. We can only suppose that, because of the customary trading practice whereby payment only became due when the next fair was held, or perhaps as a result of further delays in finishing the work, Gutenberg was in no position to pay Fust back in the autumn of 1454. Another possibility is that Gutenberg had proceeded to tie up the incoming funds in new projects.

Forty-nine copies have survived to the present day, of which a few were apparently placed with rubricators, illuminators and binders through the agency of Fust and Schoeffer. Each of these copies is unique, as has been said, on account of its individual rubrication and illumination. The rubricator's main job entailed underlining *Nomina Sacra* with fine red strokes or bringing out individual capitals at the start of sentences to ease the reader's task. The illuminator provided the printed text with decorated initials, and in certain cases, with further marginal scroll-work. According to the importance of the context, blank spaces of two, three, four or even as many as ten lines' depth were left for these initials. This left the purchasers free to determine what decoration should be added to their copies according to personal, regional or contemporary taste. As with high and late medieval manuscript illumination, so in the practice of illuminating printed books that persisted for at least thirty or forty years we can recognise schools with distinct characteristics of region and period. Two outstanding illuminated *Bibles* that are to be found in Göttingen University Library and in the Biblioteca Pública Provincial in Burgos, Spain, will repay closer scrutiny.

The Burgos copy of the Bible

The first page of the second volume of the Burgos copy (see Plate 5) has three lines handwritten in red: two lines preceding the initial "I" which occupies the left-hand margin, and a single-line heading in the right column above the ornamented six-line initial "P" for the opening word *Parabolae* of the Wisdom of Solomon. This distinguished letter "P" with its slender tendrils fits compactly into the space between the columns, whereas the initial "I" extends into the outer margins where it links up with more fanciful scrollwork richly embellished with gold leaf. These floral elements are not taken from nature but spring from the illuminator's creative imagination and twine playfully around both columns.

The colours, as in the volume as a whole, are well attuned to each other; light pastel shades, often mixed with white, which go together admirably. Light greens, pale blues, and a variety of reds and ochres make up a harmonious whole. The eye is caught by the two crossed knotty branches in the centre of the lower margin, from which fresh foliage appears to grow. These remarkable crossed branches are to be found in other books as well, amongst them an incomplete *Gutenberg Bible* belonging to the Pierpont Morgan Library in New York. It is true that the foliage in this New York copy is differently intertwined and the colouring also differs, nevertheless the same painter's hand is unmistakable, particularly in this central motif of the crossed branches. We encounter this same hand again in a copy of the *48-line Bible* (1462) of Fust and Schoeffer, in a Cicero edition of 1465, a *Constitutiones* of Clement V (1460), and in all illuminated copies of the *Rationale divinorum officiorum* by Guillelmus Durandus (1459) and the *Liber sextus Decretalium* of Boniface VIII (1465). Since all these works came from the Mainz printing office of Fust and Schoeffer, and as the Latin surname *fustis* means "Knotenstock" (knotty stick), it was soon conjectured that these branches symbolised Fust's name. The conclusive evidence is provided by the familiar partnership mark of Fust and Schoeffer which shows their arms hanging from such a branch (see Plate 18). The Berlin art historian Eberhard König has shown that this illuminator was already at work in Upper Austria during the manuscript era; and that he was based in Mainz from the mid-1450s to the mid-1460s, where he decorated numerous works for the Fust and Schoeffer workshop, probably on a commission basis. This workshop had added to Gutenberg's purely black and white process that intricate technique for printing two-colour decoration from metalcuts to be seen in the *Mainz Psalter*, and, on the publishing side, had apparently specialised in the sale of ready-illuminated printed books.

The Göttingen copy of the Bible

The illumination of one of the rare complete examples on vellum, belonging to Göttingen University Library, leads us to another school of Mainz book decoration and reveals how the artist adhered strictly to the rules to be found in a copy book. Once again further examples of this illuminator's work are to be found in manuscripts at Frankfurt University Library, in the *Giant Bible* at the Library of Congress in Washington (see Plate 4), and also in the *Gutenberg Bible* from Cardinal Mazarin's Library that is to be found today in the Bibliothèque Nationale in Paris.

The Göttingen copy is one of only four complete vellum copies in the world and is uniformly rubricated throughout its 1282 pages and illuminated to a high standard. The remaining complete copies printed on vellum are to be found in the British Library (probably from the Charterhouse in Mainz), the Library of Congress (from the Benedictine monastery of St Blasius in the Black Forest) and in the Bibliothéque Nationale (from the Benedictine monastery of St James in Mainz).

The Göttingen example has running titles writtten in red in a missal hand (matching the text face), the chapter numbering is in red, but the opening initials alternate between red and blue, giving the pages a stately look. All the required initials have been inserted, some with finely drawn flourishes, the larger ones rich with gold, colour and ensuing scrollwork. The opening page of the *Bible* and those of the individual books are framed with colorfully designed scrollwork of acanthus, fern or thorn. (see Plates 6 and 7).

The design is the outcome of following a mid-fifteenth-century pattern book which has survived by pure chance and is housed today in the same Göttingen library. This copy book is of exceptional interest for us in that it provides not merely the range of colours to be used and the painting method, but shows the juxtaposition of the colours in detail. It starts with colour samples for scrollwork, and then for the square or lozenge-shaped backgrounds or "fields", and finally for a few ornamental initials and flowers. The successive stages in painting foliage and these various chequered fields in paint are comprehensively explained. It provides guidance – using in each case a standard outline for the foliage – on how different colourways may be used: a soft raspberry red on one side of the leaf and a complementary slate green on what the writer calls the "turnover" side; alternatively a light blue may be paired with a deep minium red or a rather powdery-looking gold colour (see Plate 8). The dark red was obtained from ground brazilwood to which lye, chalk and alum were added. This is brighter than the carmine in use in the high Middle Ages which had a heavier consistency. The green hues such as mountain green or slate green were derived from malachite, and shaded down to a sap green with a vegetable varnish of uncertain constituency. The gold coloured tint was achieved through a mixture of mercury, tin, sal-ammoniac and sulphur. This gold colour is more reserved in effect than the genuine gold leaf or powder used where boldness and contrast were required instead. Fine brush shadings and accents in lead white conveyed modelling and surface detail.

Besides the manufacture of colours, the copy book describes how to use them and build up the painting in layers. To produce the "third chequered background" (see Plate 9, folio 8v), one is shown how to draw the outlines of the field, plan the gold and red squares with a brush, cross through with the black lines and add the gold, then build up the blue, red and green squares. One heightens the florets in the blue squares with lead white, and then the green and red squares are finished with white and yellow dots. A comparison of these colours and painting methods demonstrates conclusively that this pattern book served as the actual model for the illumination of the Göttingen B42. A micro-photographical analysis confirms that the assembly of the colours and their layer by layer application follows the instructions to the letter.

This outstanding copy originally belonged to a monastery, as the handwritten marginal notes reveal. It entered the Wolfenbüttel Library in 1587, which placed it at the disposal of Helmstedt University Library in 1614. After the dissolution of Helmstedt University in 1812, it found its way to Göttingen.

Since we have already found a comparable painting technique and approach in the manuscript *Giant Bible* of Mainz (1450), it may at the very least be suggested that both could have been illuminated in Mainz. It must be borne in mind, however, that it was still rather the exception in the incunabula period for a publisher to burden himself with the final decoration. And so it became possible, as far afield as Scandinavia and Britain, Italy and Poland, for regional and local traditions to come into play to create unique works of art.

JOBBING PRINTING IN LONG RUNS

Indulgences and propaganda against the Turks

Fust alleged in 1455 that Gutenberg had not put the loans made to him exclusively into their joint "work of the books" but had also used them to finance other projects. And there are a whole series of minor publications such as broadsides, indulgences, short grammars and calendars that can be dated to the very years which saw the emergence of the *Gutenberg Bible*. It is interesting that these texts are set in a different type to that reserved for the *Bible*, in fact in Gutenberg's original typeface, known for the uses to which it was put as the Donatus and *Kalender* or DK-type. This is similarly a textura, although cruder in cut and larger in point size than the B42-type. Again a multitude of abbreviations, ligatures and variants were cut for it, so that the reconstructed fount consists of 202 individual characters. After several stages of improvement it served for printing the *36-line Bible* (probably in Bamberg, c.1458–60, see Plate 14).

Unquestionably one of the most lucrative commissions for early jobbing printing was to print massive numbers of indulgences for the Church. These indulgences, which became such a bone of contention for the Reformers, played a material role in fifteenth-century religious practice and were extensively circulated in manuscript. Such certificates of indulgence were issued against an individually assessed contribution, and could be presented at the next confession in order to obtain a full remission of the temporal penalities for sin. The text was formally laid down, and wanted only for a name, date and signature to be added to the single-sided printed sheet. The new printing process was ideally matched to such an opportunity for mass production, for once a single page had been set in type it could be run off in a massive edition. Both of the earliest printed indulgences survive in several editions. In the years which followed we learn of print-runs ranging from several thousands to – in one exceptional case – 190,000 copies. The significance the recipients attached to these indulgences is to be measured by the fact that all early surviving letters of indulgence are printed on vellum.

The grounds for issuing these indulgences lay in the very real fear of further advances by the Ottoman empire which coloured the fifteenth century. When Constantinople fell to Sultan Mahommed II on 29 May 1453, a hitherto unfocussed danger drew menacingly closer. This dread of the "Turks", everywhere understood to mean Ottoman invasion and the expansion of Islam, was widespread. Pope Nicholas V had earlier granted the King of Cyprus the right to issue a plenary indulgence to run from 1 May 1452 to 30 April 1455. The Cypriot agent Paulinus Chappe arranged for such indulgences to be printed in Mainz from the late summer of 1454 onwards. The earliest surviving example carries the handwritten date 22 October 1454.

It is however possible that indulgences had been printed in Mainz two years earlier than that, as on 2 May 1452 Nicholas of Cues had authorised the prior of St James on to sell two thousand indulgences to Frankfurt citizens. Since Cues, in his licence to produce these forms, uses the un-usual word *expressio*, it is reasonable to conjecture that this word had been pressed into service to refer to the new printing process (otherwise we find *imprimere* rather than *exprimere* used at the time for "to print"). But as no example of this edition has so far been found, we must return to the above-mentioned letters of indulgence of 1454–55. The example in the possession of Göttingen University Library (see Plate 11) uses for its text face a printed bastarda, a letter form which copies a hand in which legal documents were written. The DK-type is used for the two headings. The copy reproduced comes from the fourth edition of this item in 1455, is printed on vellum and has the date 26 February 1455 inserted by hand.

There is a parallel 30-line setting of this indulgence which uses the B42-type for the displayed headings. This leads us to conclude that it appeared from the same printing office as the B42, whereas the 31-line version came from the jobbing printing works.

One of the most active champions of a Turkish crusade was the imperial secretary Eneo Silvio Piccolomini, who addressed the imperial assembly in Frankfurt am Main on 15 October 1454 (when he was apparently able to examine printed sections from the *Gutenberg Bible*). On that occasion the crusading preacher Johann Capistrano, one of the most eloquent of anti-Turkish agitators, also spoke. Therefore it is not surprising, given these proximities of time and place, that the first surviving pamphlet from Gutenberg's office should deal with the Turkish crisis. It took the form of a calendar for the year 1455 entitled *Eine Mahnung der Christenheit wider die Türken* (A warning to Christendom against the Turks). A unique but complete copy of this six-leaved publication set in the DK-type survives in the Bavarian National Library in Munich (see Plate 12). The types in evidence from the setting include 93 lower case characters, abbreviations and punctuation marks, and 15 capitals. We may assume that these type were originally produced for setting Latin texts, because the capitals K, W, X, Y and Z are missing. In the German-language *Türkenkalender* there is a makeshift use of lower case in place of these missing capitals. This fount already appears to have been in use for some time as signs of wear are evident. Under the guise of a calendar for the year 1455 – which offers the dates of twelve new moons as its sole concession to the kind of information expected of a calendar – a rhetorically impressive piece of propaganda has found its way into print:

> Almighty king on heaven's throne [. . .]
> help us prevail in parlous times
> against our foes the Turks and heathen,
> let them suffer for their evil acts of violence,
> committed against many a Christian mortal
> at Constantinople on Grecian soil . . .

In the twelve "months" which follow at first the pope, then the emperor, the European monarchs, the German nation, the free imperial cities, and eventually the whole of Christendom are exhorted to rise up against the Turks:

> Germania, proud teutonic nation,
> who chooses through the seven electors,
> the king who wears the Roman crown by right;
> so shall your admirable and cheerful might
> willingly help combat the armed aggressor
> with all your lordships, counts and knights,
> for Christian faith and lasting salvation.

We may conclude that printing took place in Mainz during the second half of December 1454; that is to say between receiving news of the Turkish war which was made known in Frankfurt on 6 December 1454 and the calendar coming into operation on 1 January 1455.

The lines are run-on although the piece is written in rhymed couplets, and so at first glance it looks as though one is dealing with a text in prose. Apparently this was done to save space, but at the same time the lines have not been justified and retain a ragged right hand edge. The author of the *Türkenkalender* is unknown, but its language is a mixture of Middle Rhenish and Alemannic dialects. It is therefore quite possible that the manuscript originally came from Strasbourg or Alsace before being set up by a Mainz compositor. Attempts to attribute this text have so far remained unconvincing.

In a solemnly promulgated bull of 29 June 1455, pope Calixtus III (successor to Nicholas V) exhorted the whole of Christendom to join in a crusade against the Turks. Everyone was called upon either to take part personally in this crusade, which was set to begin on 1 May 1456, or to support it through prayers and cash donations. The printing of the German translation of this bull must accordingly have taken place between June 1455 and April 1456. The Koblenz-born bishop of Trondheim, Heinrich Kalteisen, who was responsible for propaganda within the German empire, translated the bull himself: "This is the bull and indulgence which our holy father and ruler pope Calixtus has sent and given us against the evil and accursed Turks, anno MCCCCLVI . . ." This pamphlet of 14 leaves with 25 printed pages survives in a complete and unique copy at the Berlin State Library, and was facsimilied at the beginning of the twentieth century. An edition of the same date in Latin is to be found in the Scheide Library, Princeton, USA.

To judge from the condition of the types, the *Provinciale Romanum* – a listing in Latin of all the bishoprics and archiepiscopal sees – must date from 1457. A substantial fragment, comprising leaves 2 to 9 of what would originally have been ten printed leaves, is housed in the Library of the Academy of Sciences, Kiev.

Once again, in the case of another piece of early printing, the *Aderlass- und Laxierkalender* for the year 1457 (GW 1286), only a fragment (January to June) survives in Paris. Its none-too-accurate dates for new moons were apparently calculated by the same author as those for the *Türkenkalender*. Typical of the popular medical literature of the period (as evidenced in manuscripts after 1439), advice was given on the days best for bloodletting and those most propitious for taking laxatives.

A fragment of a further broadsheet from the same period is preserved in Cambridge University Library, the so-called *German Cisianus* (GW 7054), from which the calendar of feast days could be learned by heart and which was named after the opening words of the (Latin) edition:

"Cisio-*Janus*" (*circumcisio Januarius* = 1 January). As German versions of these mnemonic rhymes, known since the fourteenth century, were not linked to any specific year, this fragment is difficult to date precisely. The types in use point to the second half of the 1450s.

School books

Alongside those writings needed for use in religious connections – the *Bible*, indulgences, and the Turkish ephemera with their dual spiritual and worldly propaganda appeal – educational books offered by far the most rewarding texts for the early printers to call upon. The Latin grammars of the late Roman writer Aelius Donatus (*c.*310–380), the teacher of St Jerome, were particularly widely distributed both in manuscript and in print. His *Ars minor* for beginners served throughout the Middle Ages as the most important introductory textbook, and was printed over 350 times during the fifteenth century, including several editions by the blockbook process; i.e. where the entire text had to be cut letter-by-letter in wood and impressions taken from the woodblock by rubbing. This universally popular textbook quickly established itself as a bread-and-butter item for Gutenberg's earliest workshop. In Mainz during Gutenberg's lifetime at least 24 different editions have been identified, most of them set in his proto-typeface, which has been named after this text as the Donatus and *Kalender* or DK-type. Despite this high number of editions for which there is evidence, not a single complete example has survived from the printing office of Gutenberg or his immediate successors, merely such fragments as have been found in bookbindings, etc. Apparently such schoolbooks were little short of worn to death, but with their relatively small compass of 28 pages they were quick to set up and print.

In order to teach the pupils their five declensions and four conjugations, these were not yet set out in tabular form to give a schoolmasterly overview, but simply given through run-on examples. The only organisational feature was that a space was left at each section opening for a two-line initial to be added by hand. The verbs chosen as examples for conjugation were – then as nowadays – *legere* and *docere*. Our specimen page (a fragment belonging to the Gutenberg Museum and set in the

B36 state of the typeface, see Plate 13) teaches the participles of *docere*. All the fragments which have been recovered are printed on vellum, indicating that they were destined to pass through many hands in the classroom. The 24 distinct editions in the DK-type can be divided into 26-, 27-, 28- or 30-line Donatuses. The 27-line Donatus fragments are considered to be the earliest and to date from the early 1450s. The 26-line versions were printed in the 1460s. There are also editions set in the polished form of the DK-type – as it was used for the *36-line Bible* – and thus likely to have been printed in Bamberg at the beginning of the 1460s.

The Donatus had served as an instructional work throughout the Middle Ages, but it was printing, together with the revival of the linguistic sciences and the cultivation of classical Ciceronian Latin by the humanists, that put paid to it in the sixteenth century; it was supplanted by more sophisticated and voluminous grammars.

Further ephemera

In 1909 a fragment of an *Astronomical Calendar* was discovered in Wiesbaden, that showed the position of the planets for the year 1448 and then again for 1467, etc. The state of the DK-type clearly indicated that printing must have taken place after that of the *Turkish Bull* of 1456. A proof sheet later found in the Jagiellonian Library in Kraków confirmed this typographic discovery, especially since the reverse of this proof contained a trial page for a *40-line Bible* in the type later used for the B36. This appears to be a trial proof relating to the pre-history of that *Bible*, which was probably printed in about 1458. It is possible to conclude from both these fragments that the astronomical data would have occupied six pages which would have been pasted together to give an imposing broadside of 65 x 75 cm. This evidently constituted an early poster for casting and interpreting horoscopes.

There is a single-sided print using the same typographic material which contains a Latin prayer: *Respice, domine sancte pater* from the pen of Ekbert von Schönau in the twelfth century. This broadside measures 20.5 x 29.5 cm, and survives in a unique copy belonging to the University Library in Munich.

Controversy surrounds the dating of a small fragment from the *Sibyllen-Buch*. This scrap of paper is printed on both sides with 'dancing' lines of unevenly impressed types, and little attempt at justification. The fact that the edges of the types are so unclear has to be put down to inadequate casting or even to the suggestion that the casting instrument was still at an experimental stage. But the fact that the fragment is printed on both sides with consecutive texts rather rules out the suggestion that it is just a proof. Far-reaching speculations falter when confronted by the slight extent of a mere 11 lines on each side of the fragment. The text goes back to the corpus of *Sibylline Prophesies* from the fifth century AD, which had been translated into German in Thuringia in 1361. It was repeatedly republished towards the end of the fifteenth and beginning of the sixteenth centuries, and enjoyed great popularity. Since, as we have seen, the DK-type was initially cut and cast with the characters necessary for setting Latin texts, in the *Sibyllen-Buch* (also known as the *Fragment vom Weltgericht* or Fragment of the World Judgment) we are unlikely to be dealing with the earliest surviving piece of printing, as has been variously claimed. Insofar as the wretched condition of the fragment permits an overall assessment, it belongs to the second half of the 1450s.

Alongside the central enterprise of the "work of the books", numerous bread-and-butter titles were set and printed – such as school books, calendars and indulgences – that found a ready market and led to a dependable cashflow during the long drawn-out production of the *Bible*. Simultaneously, alongside the qualitative aspect – the intention to surpass the manuscript book with the *Gutenberg Bible* – the quantitative aspect of the new invention also became apparent; it was those very school books or indulgences in greatest demand which, by virtue of the minimal amount of typesetting involved, could be produced in the hugest editions and against the clock.

THE 36-LINE BIBLE

On the back of the proof sheet containing the Kraków fragment of the *Astronomical Calendar* we find an impression of a 40-*line Bible* page set in a developed form of the DK-type. As a larger body was eventually used,

Plate 1: Fictional portrait of Gutenberg. After the copper engraving by André Thevet (1584), *this version by* Nicolas de l'Armesin, *c.* 1660. Mainz, Gutenberg Museum.

Plate 2: *Danse macabre* (*The Lyons dance of death*), Lyons, Matthias Hus, 1499. *The first representation of a printing press (showing setting cases, inking balls, and adjacent bookbindery).*

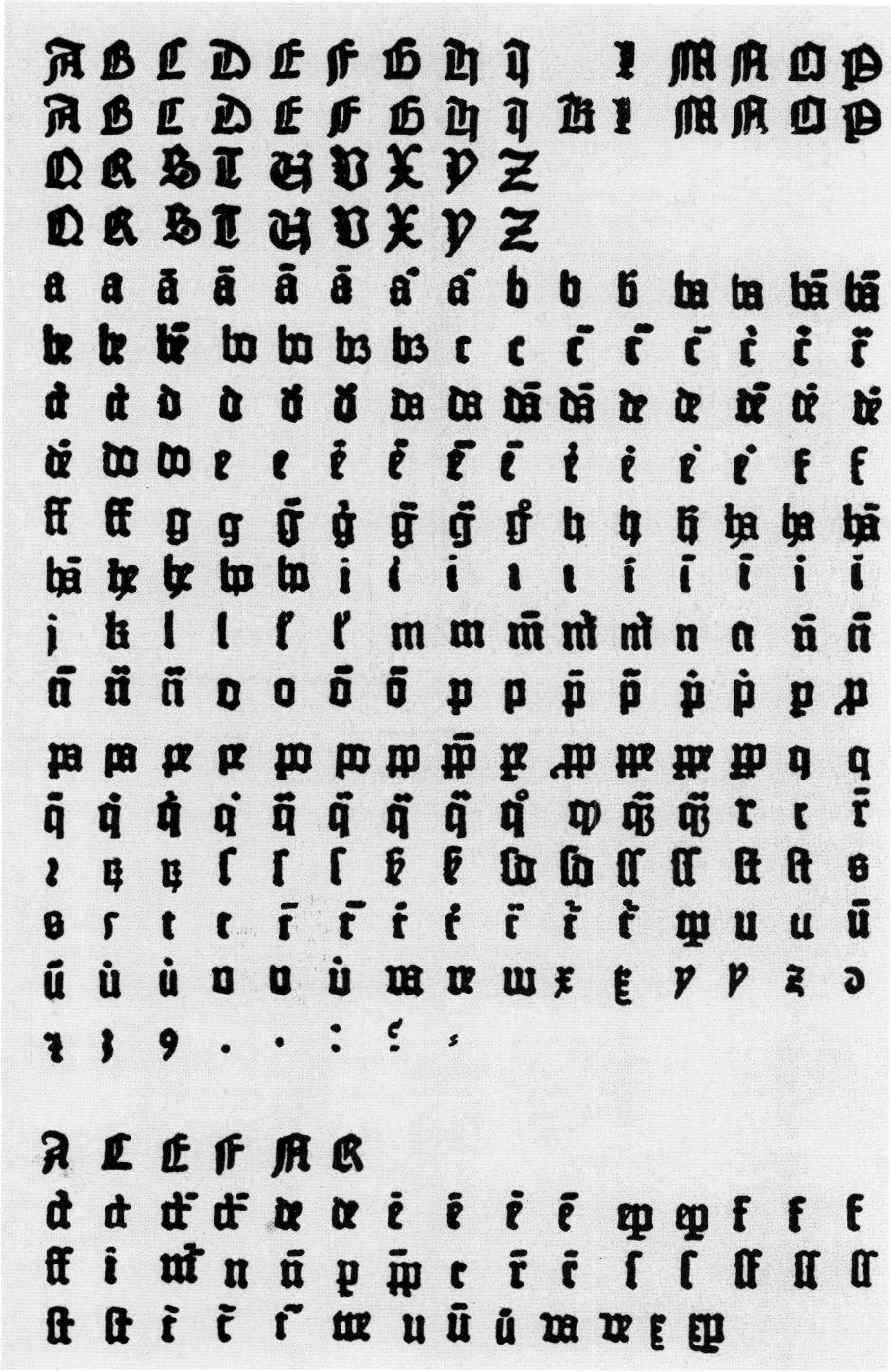

Plate 3: Synopsis of the B42-types.
The bottom 4 lines show characters added later.

Plate 4: Latin Bible, the so-called "Giant Bible of Mainz", fol 2v. Mainz manuscript of about 1500. Washington, Library of Congress.

Epl'a sci iheronimi p̄sbri ad chromaciũ
et eliodorũ ep̄os de libris salomonis
Iungat epistola quos iũgit sacerdoti-
um: immo carta non dividat: quos
xp̄i nectit amor. Cõmẽtarios in osee-
amos. et zachariã malachiã. quoq;
poscitis. Scripsissẽ: si licuisset pre vali-
tudine. Mittitis solacia sumptuum
notarios nr̄os et librarios sustenta
tis: ut vobis potissimũ nr̄m desudet
ingeniũ. Et ecce ex latere frequẽs turba
diũsa poscẽtiũ: quasi aut equũ sit me
vobis esurientibz aliis laborare: aut
in racione dati et accepti. cuiq; preter
vos obnoxi9 sim. Itaq; lõga egrota-
tione fractus. ne penitus hoc anno re-
ticerẽ et apud vos mutus essem. tridui
opus nomini vr̄o consecraui. interp̄-
tacionẽ videlicet triũ salomonis vo-
luminũ: masloth qd̄ hebrei parabolas.
vulgata edicio pũbia vocat: coeleth.
quẽ grece ecclesiasten. latine cõcionatorẽ
possum9 dicere: sirasirim. qd̄ ĩ linguã
nr̄am vertit̃ canticũ cãticoꝝ. Fertur et
panaretos. ihesu filii sirach liber: et ali9
pseudographus. qui sapiencia salomonis inscribit̃. Quoꝝ priorẽ hebra-
icum rep̄ri. nõ ecclesiasticũ ut apud latinos: sed parabolas pn̄otatũ. Cui iũcti
erãt ecclesiastes et canticũ canticoꝝ: ut
similitudinẽ salomonis. nõ solũ nu-
mero librorũ: sed eciã materiaꝝ genere coequaret. Secũdus apud hebreos
nusq; est: quia et ipse stilus grecam
eloquẽciã redolet: et nõnulli scriptoꝝ
veteꝝ hũc esse iudei filonis affirmãt.
Sicud ergo iudith et thobie et macha-
beoꝝ libros. legit quidẽ eos ecclia. sed
inter canonicas scripturas nõ recipit:
sic et hec duo volumina legat ad edi-
ficationẽ plebis: nõ ad auctoritatem
ecclesiasticoꝝ dogmatũ cõfirmandam.
Si cui sane septuaginta interpretum
magis edicio placet: habet eã a nobis
olim emendatã. Neq; enĩ noua sic cu-
dim9: ut vetera destruam9. Et tamẽ cũ
diligẽtissime legerit. sciat magis nr̄a
scripta intelligi: que nõ in tertiũ vas
transfusa coacuerit: sed statim de prelo
purissime cõmendata teste: suũ saporẽ seruauerit. Expl' epl'a. Incip' liber prouerbioꝝ.
Parabole salomonis A
filii david regis isrl̄:
ad sciendã sapienti-
am et disciplinã: ad
intelligenda verba
prudentie et suscipi-
endã eruditationẽ doctrine: iusticiã
et iudiciũ et equitatẽ: ut detur paruulis
astucia: et adolescenti sciencia et intel-
lectus. Audiens sapiens sapiencior erit: et
intelligens gubernacula possidebit. Ani-
aduertet parabolam et interpretacio-
nem: verba sapienciũ et enigmata eoꝝ.
Timor dñi principiũ sapiencie. Sapien-
tiam atq; doctrinam stulti despiciunt.
Audi fili mi disciplinã pr̄is tui et ne
dimittas legem matris tue: ut addatur
gracia capiti tuo: et torques collo tuo.
Fili mi si te lactauerint peccores: ne ac-
quiescas eis. Si dixerint veni nobiscũ. B
insidiemur sãguini. abscõdam9 tendi-
culas cõtra insontem frustra. deglutia-
mus eũ sicud infernus viuentẽ et inte-
grum. quasi descẽdentẽ in lacũ: omnẽ
p̃ciosã substanciã reperiem9. implebim9
domus nr̄as spoliis. sortem mitte no-
biscum. marsupiũ sit unum omniũ
nr̄m: fili mi ne ambules cũ eis. Pro-
hibe pedem tuũ a semitis eoꝝ. Pedes
enĩ illoꝝ ad malũ currũt: et festinãt ut
effundant sãguinem. Frustra autem
iacit̃ rete ante oculos pennatoꝝ. Ipi q;
contra sanguinẽ suũ insidiantur: et

Plate 5: The 42-line or Gutenberg Bible, c.1454.
Example belonging to the Biblioteca Pública in Burgos, Spain.

Epl'a

Incipit epl'a sancti ieronimi ad paulinũ
presbiterũ de oĩbꝫ divine historie libris.
Capitlm primũ

Frater ambrosius
tua michi munuscu-
la perferens · detulit
simul ⁊ suavissimas
litteras: que a prin-
cipio amicicia꜠ fidẽ
probate iam fidei et veteris amicicie
p̃ferebant. Vera enĩ illa necessitudo ẽ.
et xp̄i glutino copulata: quã nõ utilitas rei familiaris · non p̃sentia tantũ
corporũ · nõ subdola ⁊ palpãs adulatõ:
sed dei timor · et divinarũ scripturarũ
studia conciliant. Legimꝰ in veteribꝫ
historijs · quosdã lustrasse p̃vincias ·
novos adijsse p̃plos · maria transisse:
ut eos quos ex libris noverãt: coram
q̃ꝫ viderent. Sic pitagoras memphiticos vates · sic plato egiptum · ⁊ architam tarentinũ · eamq̃ꝫ orã ytalie · que
quondã magna grecia dicebat̃ : laboriosissime peragravit: et ut qui athenis
mḡr erat · ⁊ potens · cuiusq̃ꝫ doctrinas
achademie gignasia p̃sonabãt · fieret
peregrinus atq̃ꝫ discipulus: malens a-
liena verecunde discere: q̃ꝫ sua impudenter ingerere. Deniq̃ꝫ cum litteras
quasi toto orbe fugientes persequitur ·
captus a piratis et venũdatus · tyranno crudelissimo paruit · ductus captivus vinctꝰ et servus: tamen quia philosophus: maior emente se fuit. Ad ty-
tumliviũ · lacteo eloquentie fonte manantem · de ultimis hispanie galliarũ
q̃ꝫ finibus quosdam venisse nobiles
legimus: et quos ad cõtemplatõnem
sui roma non traxerat: unius hominis fama perduxit. Habuit illa etas
inauditum omnibus seculis · celebrã-
dumq̃ꝫ miraculum: ut urbem tãtam
ingressi: aliud extra urbem quererent.
Apolloniꝰ sive ille magꝰ ut vulgus
loquitur · sive phũs ut pitagorici tradunt · intravit p̃sas · p̃transivit caucasũ ·
albanos · scithas · massagetas · opulentissima indie regna penetravit: et
ad extremum latissimo physon amne
trãsmisso p̃venit ad bragmanas: ut
hyarcam in throno sedentẽ aureo · ⁊ de
tantali fonte potantem · inter paucos
discipulos · de natura · de moribꝫ ac de
cursu dierũ ⁊ siderũ audiret docentem.
Inde p̃ elamitas · babilonios · chaldeos · medos · assirios · parthos · syros ·
phenices · arabes · palestinos · reversus ad alexandriã · perrexit ad ethiopiam: ut gignosophistas ⁊ famosissimam solis mensam videret ĩ sabulo.
Invenit ille vir ubiq̃ꝫ quod disceret: ⁊
semp̃ proficiens · semper se melior fieret. Scripsit super hoc plenissime octo
voluminibus · phylostratus. Cap̃ · ij.

Quid loquar de seculi hominibꝫ:
cum apostolus paulus · vas e-
lectionis · et magister gentium · qui de
consciencia tanti in se hospitis loque-
batur · dicens. An experimentum que-
ritis eius qui in me loquitur cristus.
post damascum arabiãq̃ꝫ lustratam ·
ascenderit iherosolimã ut videret petrũ
et mãserit apud eum diebus quindecĩ.
Hoc enim misterio ebdomadis et o-
gdoadis: futurꝰ gentium predicator
instruendus erat. Rursumq̃ꝫ post annos quatuordecim assumpto barna-
ba et tyto · exposuit cum apostolis eu-
angelium: ne forte ĩ vacuum curreret
aut cucurrisset. Habet nescio quid la-
tentis energie vive vocis actus: et in
aures discipuli de auctoris ore transfusa: fortiꝰ sonat. Unde et eschines cũ
rodi exularet · et legeretur illa demostenis

Plate 6: *The 42-line or Gutenberg Bible, c. 1454, vol 1, fol 1r.*
Complete example on vellum at Göttingen State and University Library.

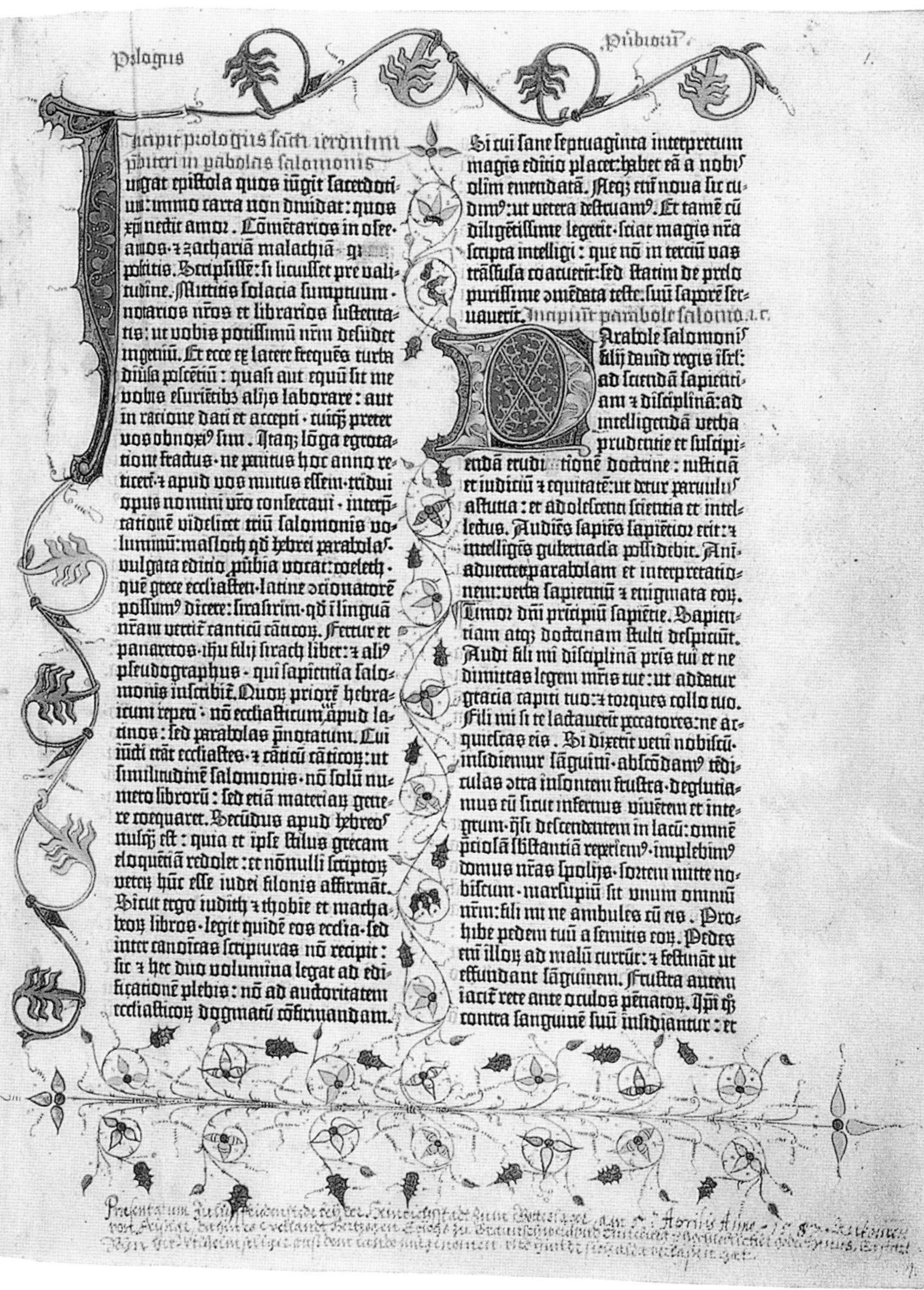

Incipit prologus sancti ieronimi
presbiteri in parabolas salomonis
Iungat epistola quos iungit sacerdoci-
um: immo carta non dividat: quos
xpī nectit amor. Cōmētarios in osee.
amos. z zachariā malachiā. q̄ poscitis. Scripsisse: si licuisset pre vali-
tudine. Mittitis solacia sumptuum.
notarios nr̄os et librarios sustenta-
tis: ut vobis potissimū nr̄m desudet
ingeniū. Et ecce ex latere frequēs turba
diversa poscētiū: quasi aut equū sit me
vobis esurientibȝ aliis laborare: aut
in racione dati et accepti. cuiq̄ꝫ preter
vos obnoxi⁹ sim. Itaqȝ lōga egrota-
tione fractus. ne penitus hoc anno re-
ticerē z apud vos mutus essem. tridui
opus nomini vr̄o consecravi. interp̄-
tatione videlicet triū salomonis vo-
luminū: masloth q̄d hebrei parabolas.
vulgata editio p̄ūbia vocat: coeleth.
q̄ grece ecclesiasten. latine contionatorē
possum⁹ dicere: sirasirim. q̄d i linguā
nr̄am vertit canticū cāticoꝝ. Fertur et
panaretos. ihū filii sirach liber: z ali⁹
pseudographus. qui sapientia salomonis inscribit. Quoꝝ priorē hebra-
icum reperi: nō ecclesiasticum ut apud latinos: sed parabolas p̄notatum. Cui
iūcti erāt ecclesiastes. z cāticū cāticoꝝ: ut
similitudinē salomonis. nō solū nu-
mero librorū: sed etiā materiaꝝ genere coequaret. Secūdus apud hebreos
nusq̄ꝫ est: quia et ipse stilus grecam
eloquētiā redolet: et nōnulli scriptoꝝ
veterū hūc esse iudei filonis affirmāt.
Sicut ergo iudith z thobie et macha-
beoꝝ libros. legit quidē eos ecclesia. sed
inter canonicas scripturas nō recipit:
sic z hec duo volumina legat ad edi-
ficationē plebis: nō ad auctoritatem
ecclesiasticoꝝ dogmatū cōfirmandam.
Si cui sane septuaginta interpretum
magis editio placet: habet eā a nobis
olim emendatā. Neqȝ enī nova sic cu-
dim⁹: ut vetera destruam⁹. Et tamē cū
diligētissime legerit. sciat magis nr̄a
scripta intelligi: que nō in terciū vas
trāsfusa coacuerit: sed statim de prelo
purissime cōmēdata teste: suū saporē ser-
vaverit. Incipiūt parabole salomonis. i. c.
Parabole salomonis
filii david regis isrl̄:
ad sciendā sapientī-
am z disciplinā: ad
intelligendā verba
prudentie et suscipi-
endā erudi tionē doctrine: iusticiā
et iudiciū z equitatē: ut detur parvulis
astutia: et adolescenti scientia et intel-
lectus. Audiēs sapiēs sapientior erit: z
intelligēs gubernacula possidebit. Ani-
madvertet parabolam et interpretatio-
nem: verba sapientū z enigmata eoꝝ.
Timor dn̄i principiū sapientie. Sapien-
tiam atqȝ doctrinam stulti despiciūt.
Audi fili mi disciplinā pr̄is tui et ne
dimittas legem m̄ris tue: ut addatur
gracia capiti tuo: z torques collo tuo.
Fili mi si te lactaverit peccatores: ne ac-
quiescas eis. Si dixerit veni nobiscū.
insidiemur sāguini. abscōdam⁹ tedi-
culas contra insontem frustra. deglutia-
mus eū sicut infernus viventem et inte-
grum. q̄si descendentem in lacū: omnē
preciosā substantiā reperiem⁹. implebim⁹
domus nr̄as spoliis. sortem mitte no-
biscum. marsupiū sit unum omniū
nr̄m: fili mi ne ambules cū eis. Pro-
hibe pedem tuū a semitis eoꝝ. Pedes
enī illoꝝ ad malū currūt: z festināt ut
effundant sāguinem. Frustra autem
iacit rete ante oculos pēnatoꝝ. Ipsi q̄ꝫ
contra sanguinē suū insidiantur: et

Plate 7: The 42-line or Gutenberg Bible, Göttingen copy, vol 2, fol 1r.
Handwritten ownership entry in lower margin.

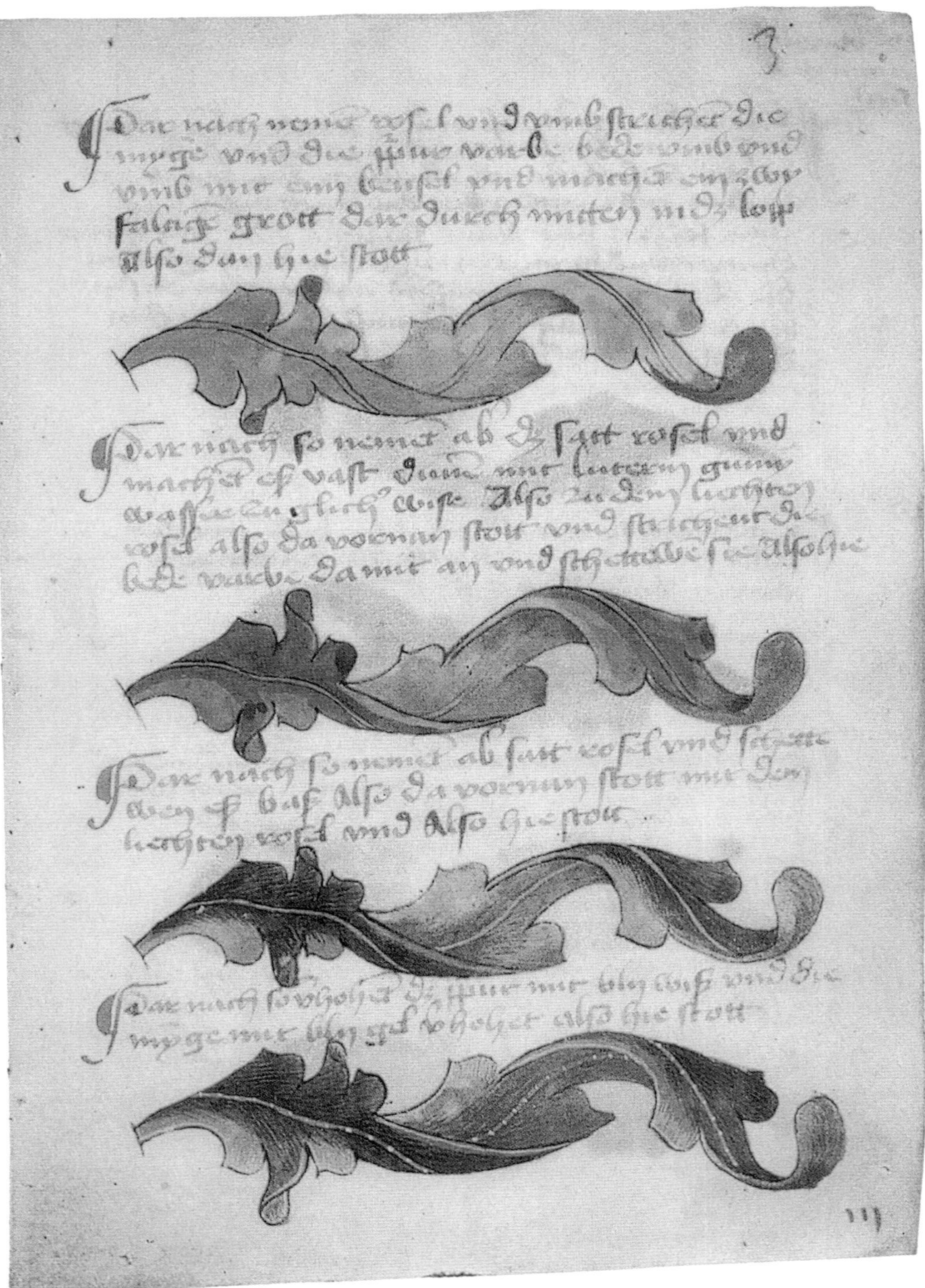

Plate 8: The Göttingen Pattern Book. Manuscript on vellum of about 1450, fol 3r. Göttingen State and University Library.

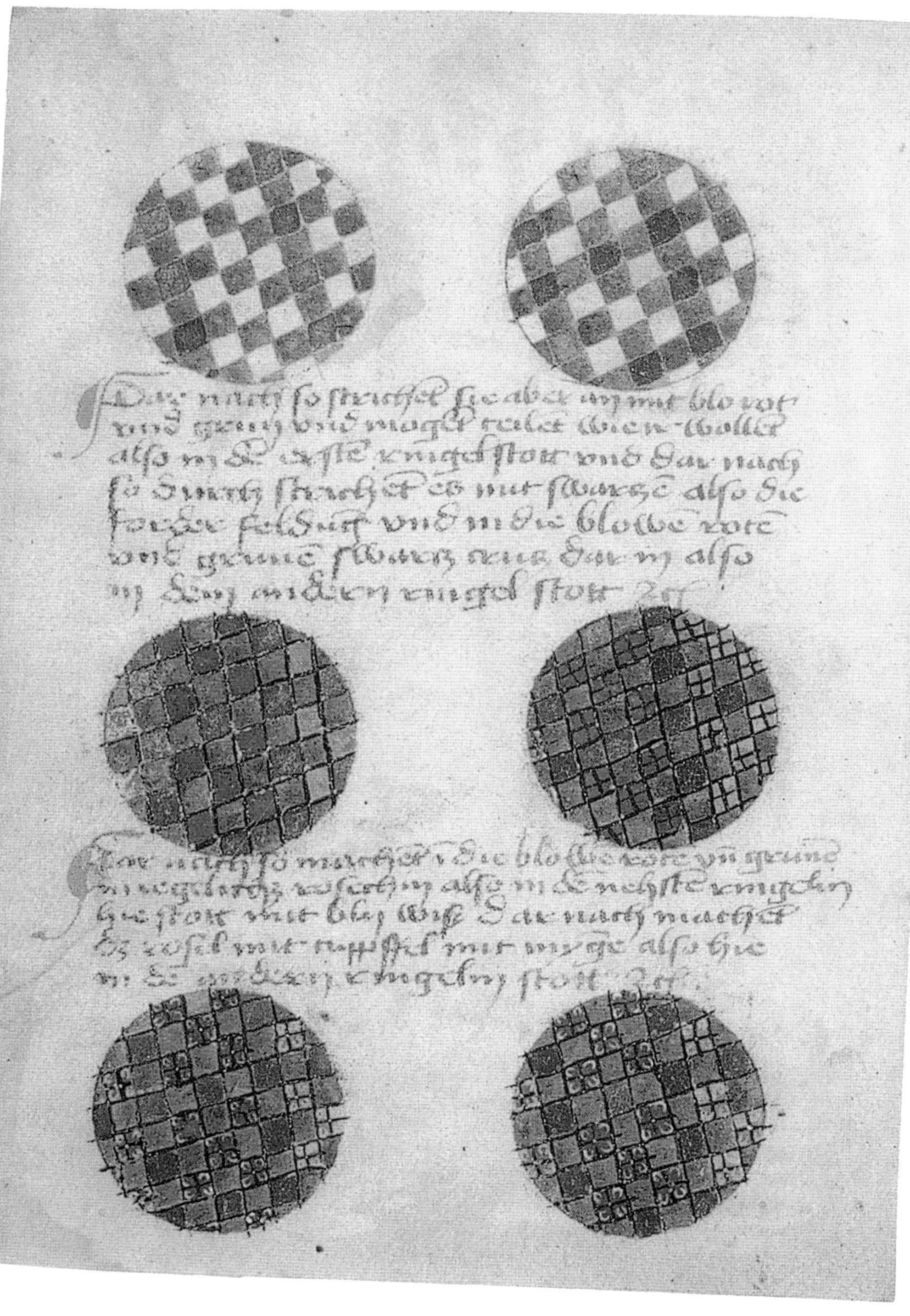

Plate 9: The Göttingen Pattern Book. fol 8v.

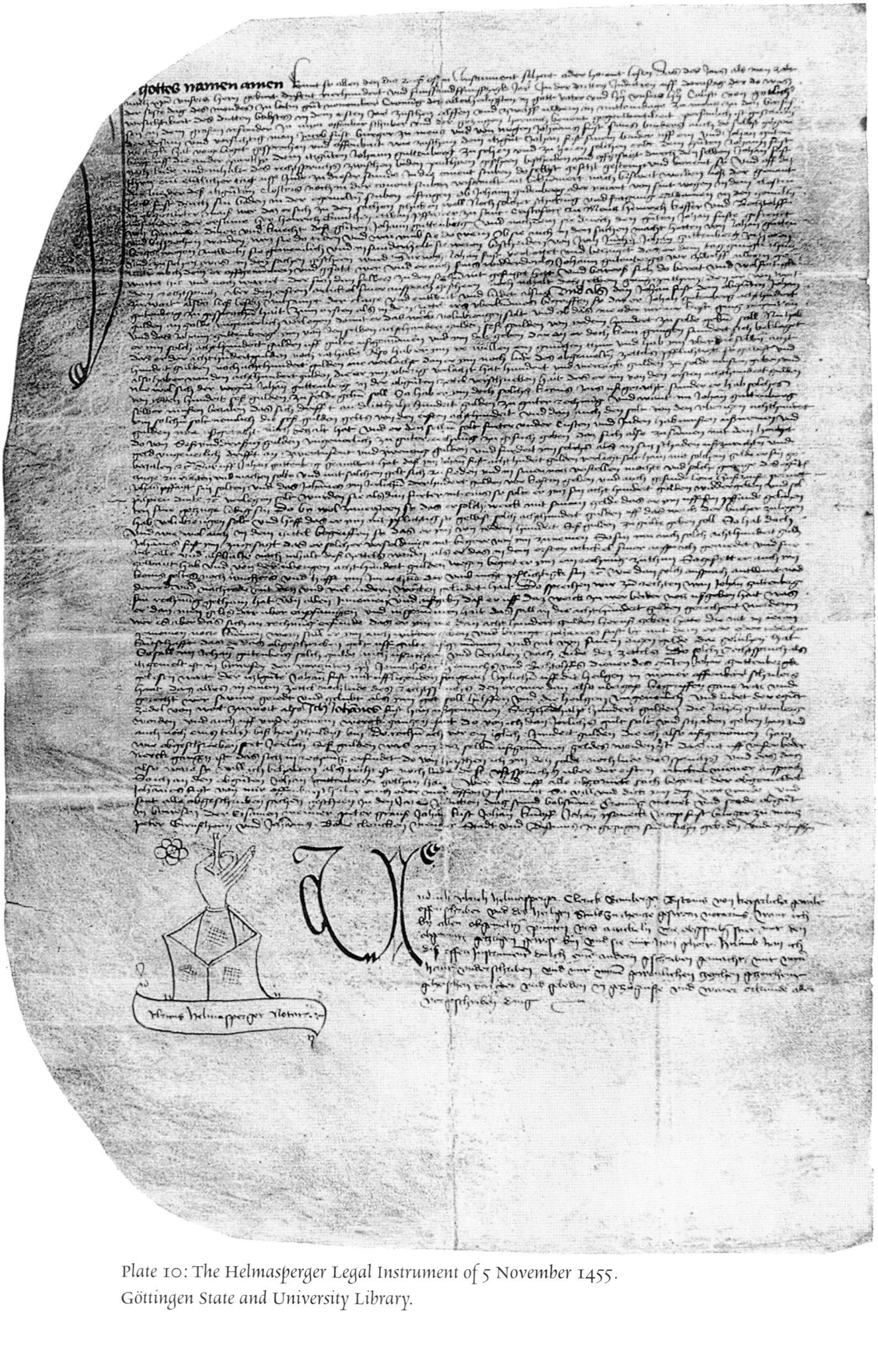

gottes namen amen

Plate 10: The Helmasperger Legal Instrument of 5 November 1455.
Göttingen State and University Library.

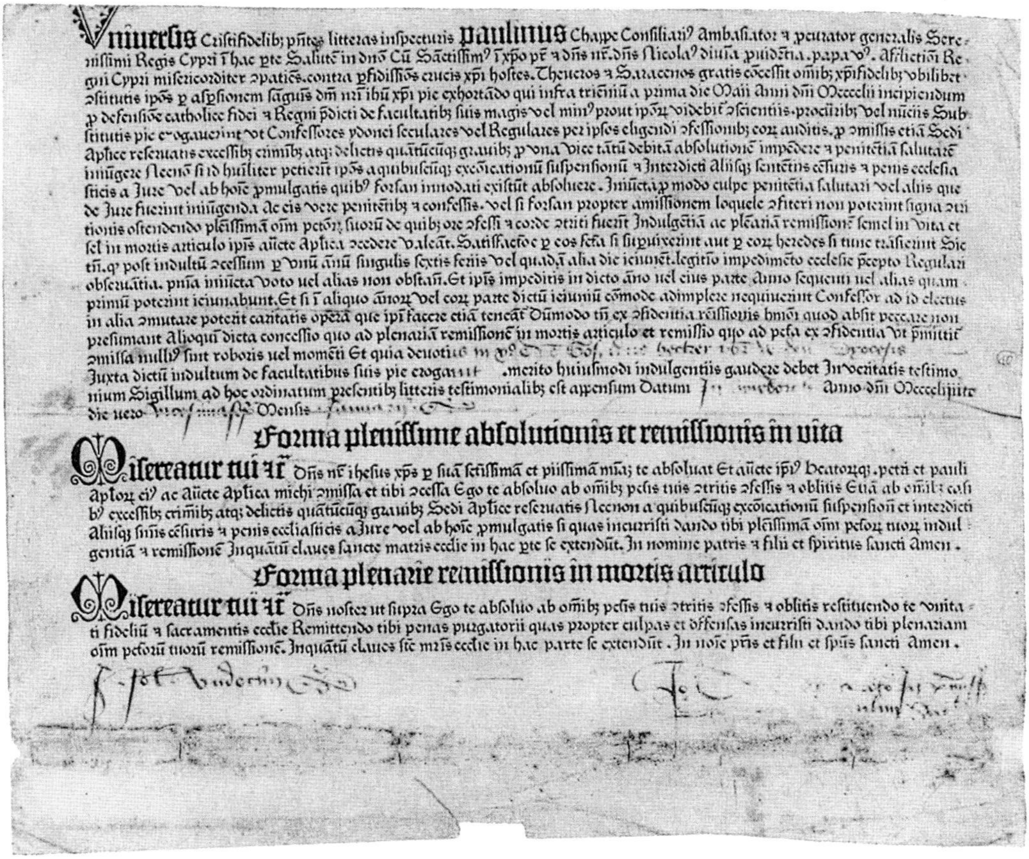

Plate 11: Paulinus Chappe: 31-line Indulgence for Cyprus, fourth edition 1455 (GW 6556). Göttingen State and University Library.

Eyn manūg d' cristēheit widd' die durkē

O Almechtig könig in himels tron
Der uff ertrich ein dorne crone Vñ
sin streijt baner vō blude roit Das heilge
cruze in sterbendē not Selb' hat getragē
zu d' mart' grois Vñ dē bittrn dot nacket
vñ blois Dar an umb menschlich heil
gelittē Vñ uns do mit erloist vñ erstrittē
Vñ den bosē fyant ub' wūden Hilff uns
vorbas in allē stūden widd' unser fynde
durcken vñ heiden Mache en yren bosen
gewalt leidē Den sie zu cōstantinopel in
kriechē lant An manchē cristē menschē
begangē hant Mit fahen martrī vñ dot
slagē vñ ūsmehē Als den aposteln vor
zijtē ist gescheen Umb die xij stucke des
heilgen glaubē gut Halt xij die gulden
zale in hut Auch werden dis iar xij nu-
wer schin Visiteren die xij zeichē des him
mels dun Als mā zelet noch dīn geburt
uffenbar M · cccc · lv · iar Siebē wochē

Liber Eximiae Raritatis et inter Cimelia
Bibliothecae asservandus. F. G.

Plate 12: *Eine Mahnung der Christenheit wider die Türken* (*A warning to Christendom against the Turks*), Mainz 1454 (H 10741). Bavarian State Library, Munich. *Reproduced from the facsimile with commentary by* Ferdinand Geldner, Wiesbaden, Reichert 1975.

Plate 13: Aelius Donatus: *Ars minor, fragment,* B36-*type, c.* 1460–62. Mainz, Gutenberg Museum. *Reproduced from facsimile print of the* Gutenberg-Gesellschaft *no.* 1.

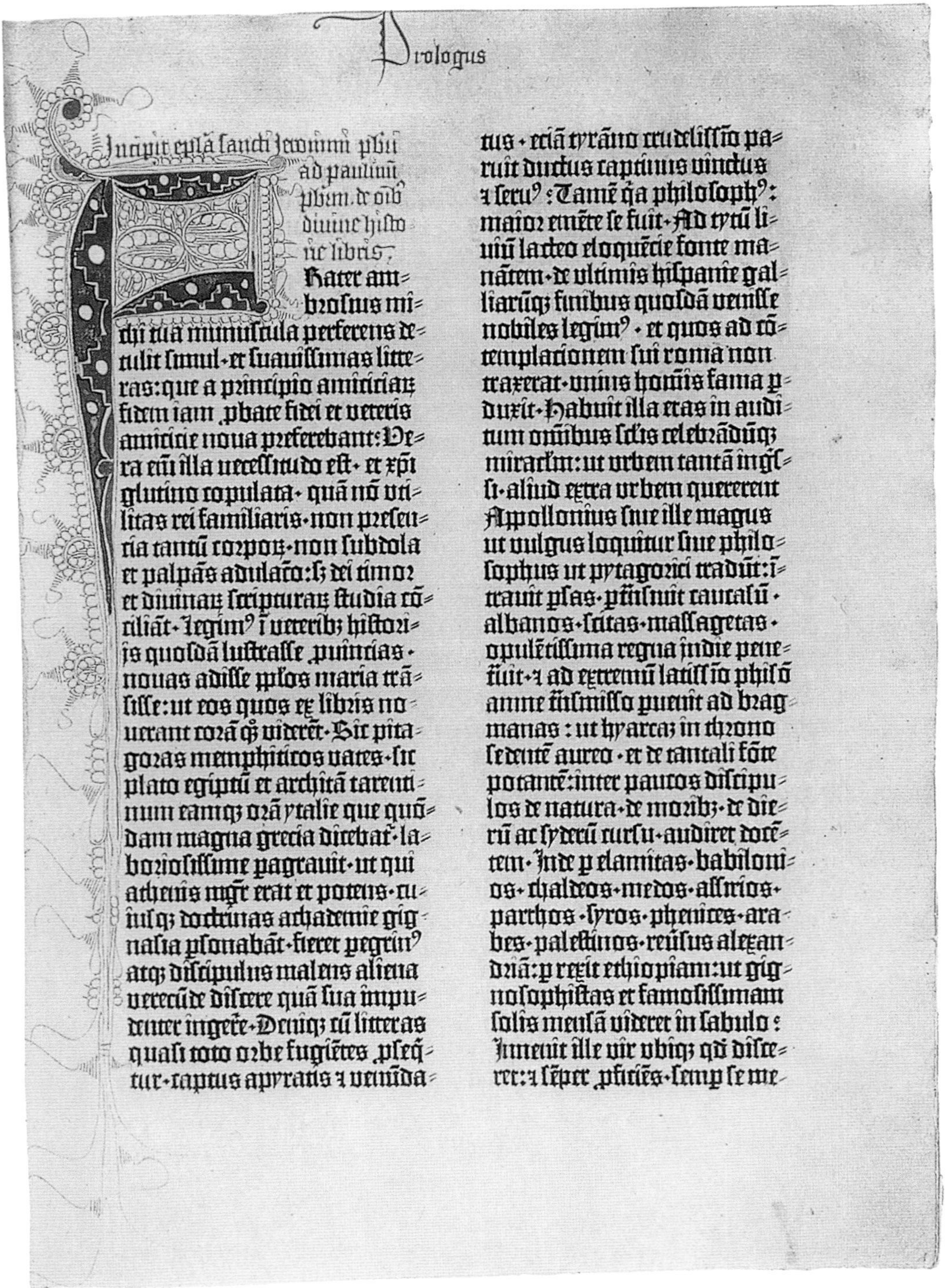

Prologus

Incipit epistola sancti Jeronimi presbiteri ad paulinum presbiterum de omnibus divine historie libris.

Frater ambrosius michi tua munuscula perferens detulit simul et suavissimas litteras: que a principio amicitiarum fidem iam probate fidei et veteris amicicie noua preferebant: Vera enim illa necessitudo est et christi glutino copulata quam non utilitas rei familiaris non presentia tantum corporum non subdola et palpans adulacio: sed dei timor et divinarum scripturarum studia conciliant. Legimus in veteribus historiis quosdam lustrasse provincias novos adisse populos maria transisse: ut eos quos ex libris noverant coram quoque viderent. Sic pitagoras memphiticos vates. sic plato egiptum et architam tarentinum eamque oram ytalie que quondam magna grecia dicebatur laboriosissime peragravit: ut qui athenis magister erat et potens cuiusque doctrinas achademie gignasia personabant fieret peregrinus atque discipulus malens aliena verecunde discere quam sua impudenter ingerere. Denique cum litteras quasi toto orbe fugientes persequitur captus a piratis et venundatus etiam tyranno crudelissimo paruit ductus captivus vinctus et servus: Tamen quia philosophus: maior emente se fuit. Ad tytum livium lacteo eloquencie fonte manantem de ultimis hispanie galliarumque finibus quosdam venisse nobiles legimus. et quos ad contemplacionem sui roma non traxerat unius hominis fama perduxit. Habuit illa etas inauditum omnibus seculis celebrandumque miraculum: ut urbem tantam ingressi aliud extra urbem quererent. Apollonius sive ille magus ut vulgus loquitur sive philosophus ut pytagorici tradunt: intravit persas. pertransivit caucasum. albanos. scitas. massagetas. opulentissima regna indie penetravit: et ad extremum latissimo phison amne transmisso pervenit ad bragmanas: ut hyarcam in throno sedentem aureo et de tantali fonte potantem: inter paucos discipulos de natura de moribus de dierum ac siderum cursu audiret docentem. Inde per elamitas babilonios chaldeos medos assirios parthos syros phenices arabes palestinos reversus alexandriam: perrexit ethiopiam: ut gignosophistas et famosissimam solis mensam videret in sabulo: Invenit ille vir ubique quod disceret: et semper proficiens semper se me-

Plate 14: The 36-line Bible, Bamberg (?), Albrecht Pfister (?), c. 1460, fol 1r. Wolfenbüttel, Herzog August Library.

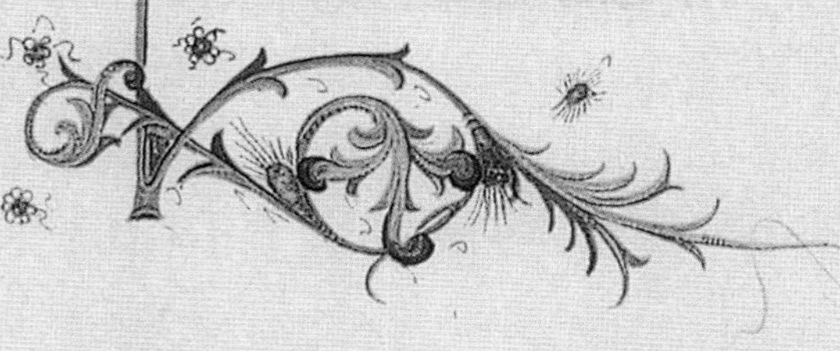

Plate 15: *Johann Balbus: Catholicon*, Mainz, c. 1460 (GW 3182). *Göttingen State and University Library.*

EX
BIBLIOTHECA
UNIVERSITATIS
MOGUNTINAE

Beatus vir a Seruite dño· Euouae·
qui nõ abiit in cõsilio im=
pioȝ: ⁊ in via pccatoȝ nõ
stetit: et in cathedra pestilẽ=
tie nõ sedit. Sed in lege
dñi volũtas eius: ⁊ in lege ei⁹ meditabit̃ die
ac nocte. Et erit tanq̃ȝ lignũ qd̃ plantatũ est
secus decursus aqrũ: qd̃ fructũ suũ dabit in
tpe suo. Et foliũ ei⁹ nõ defluet: ⁊ oĩa quecũq̃ȝ
faciet psperabunt̃. Non sic impii nõ sic: sed
tanq̃ȝ pulvis quẽ proicit ventus a facie terre.
Ideo nõ resurgẽt impii in iudicio: neq̃ȝ pccõ=
res in cõsilio iustoȝ. Qm̃ novit dñs viã iu=
stoȝ: et iter impioȝ pibit. Gl̃ia pri. Ps dd
Quare fremuerũt gẽtes: ⁊ ppl̃i meditati
sũt inania. Astiterũt reges t̃re: et prin=
cipes cõvenerũt in vnũ: adũsus dñm ⁊ adũsus
xpm ei⁹. Dirũpam⁹ vincla eoȝ: ⁊ piciam⁹
a nobis iugũ ipoȝ. Qui habitat in celis irri=
debit eos: et dñs subsannabit eos. Tũc lo=
quet̃ ad eos in ira sua: et in furore suo cõtur=
babit eos. Ego aũt cõstitutus sũ rex ab eo

EX
BIBLIOTHECA
UNIVERSITATIS
MOGUNTINAE

Plate 16: Psalterium Moguntinum (Mainz Psalter), Mainz, Johann Fust and Peter Schoeffer, 1457. Mainz, Gutenberg Museum.

the decision came down in favour of having 36 lines to the column. (see Plate 14). This increased the extent of the *Bible* appreciably so that, at 1768 pages, it made almost 500 pages more than the B42. Through a rubricator's entry on a single leaf held by the Bibliothèque Nationale we learn that the work of rubrication was finished in 1461. Accordingly printing would probably have taken place between 1458 and 1460. Careful textual examination has shown that the opening 12 pages follow an unknown manuscript source, but thereafter it is continuously set up from a copy of the B42. The B36 is considerably rarer than the B42, only 13 copies and a few fragments have survived. There is no information whatever concerning the size of edition. The *Bible* also lacks any printer's imprint, leaving both printer and place of printing wide open to speculation. Since once again we are confronted by a masterpiece in the setting and printing of the B36, we must assume experienced compositors and pressmen.

The Bamberg printer Albrecht Pfister was printing with these same B36-types by no later than 1461, so he has often been proposed as the actual printer of the B36. But as Pfister's first dated piece, Boner's *Der Edelstein* of 1461, fails to exhibit the same mastery of typesetting, this suggestion does not altogether hold water. More compelling is the evidence that all ten of the sorts of paper used are drawn from mills in the vicinity of Bamberg and that most of the surviving copies were once owned by monasteries close to Bamberg. This raises the question of whether around 1458 it may have been possible for some of Gutenberg's fellow craftsmen to have taken this typographic repertoire with them on their travels and to have set up a new works in Bamberg, with which Albrecht Pfister became associated from about 1460. As Heinrich Keffer, who is named in the Helmasperger legal instrument as Gutenberg's co-worker, set up in business in Nuremberg a decade afterwards, it has often been asked whether Keffer may not have been the B36 printer, very possibly in Bamberg. Albrecht Pfister was formerly secretary to Georg I von Schaumberg, who was chosen as prince-bishop of Bamberg in 1459. Pfister can be shown to have published mostly popular vernacular texts over the next decade, such as the fable collection *Der Edelstein* which has already been mentioned, or the early humanistic tract *Der Ackermann aus Böhmen* by Johann von Tepl.

An electron-spectrographic examination and comparison of the ink of the unique surviving copy of *Der Edelstein* with that of the B36 could shed light here, but the library concerned has up to now refused permission.

THE CATHOLICON

Whereas all the books so far considered have been set either in the B42-type or the DK-type (forerunner of the B36-type), a new typeface in a much smaller size is found in the *Catholicon* of 1460 (see Plate 15). This belongs to the Gothic-roman (or *fere-humanistica*) class of typefaces, since it looks back to humanistically influenced Italian models whilst at the same time combining with them features from the Germanic tradition. Roman type with its excellent legibility evolved swiftly – and primarily in Italy – from the current humanist writing hand, which was in turn a revival of the Carolingian minuscule hand of the eighth century. Most of the writings of classical antiquity had been transmitted in this script, so imitation of the spirit and ideas of the ancients in the content of humanist writings found an external parallel in this attachment to humanist handwriting. (For Italian examples of typefaces see Plates 22 and 23.) But a different Gothic-roman was in use in the Fust and Schoeffer workshop, to be seen in the *Rationale* of Durandus (1459) and the 48-*line Bible* of 1462. The fact that Fust and Schoeffer were in possession of this other Gothic-roman typeface makes the theory that only Gutenberg could have printed the *Catholicon* in about 1460 all the stronger. And Gutenberg had entered into a new business partnership, this time with the Mainz patrician and scholar Konrad Humery.

The *Catholicon* had been compiled in 1286 by the Dominican, Johann Balbus de Janua (of Genoa) as an aid to clerics studying the Latin *Bible*, and it had already enjoyed wide circulation during the manuscript era. It contained a Latin grammar, and a dictionary which offered encyclopaedic information throughout with a full explanation of terms. The title *Catholicon* indicates the comprehensive scope of the work. Despite its small typesize and double-column setting the work calls for no less than 726 printed pages. In consequence, it placed considerable demands on the learning and skill of the compositors and the astuteness of its printer-publisher. The colophon presents a self-confident appraisal of the art of printing and of the city of Mainz, which in English translation reads as follows:

> By the help of the most high, at whose bidding the tongues of children become eloquent, and who often reveals to the lowly what he conceals from the wise; the noble book, *Catholicon*, in the year of our Lord's incarnation, 1460, in the mother city of Mainz of the renowned German nation (which the clemency of God has deigned with so lofty a light of genius and free gift to prefer and render illustrious above all other nations of the earth), without help of reed, stylus or quill, but by a wonderful concord, proportion and measure of punches and formes has been printed and finished. Hence to thee, holy Father, thyself, the Son together with the Holy Spirit, praise and glory be rendered, the triune Lord and one; and thou, devout believer in the universe, who never ceasest to praise the blessed Mary; join your approval with tribute to the Church for this book. Thanks be to God.

Unfortunately this colophon does not divulge the name of the printer, but only the place of printing. Its theologically well-versed author may well have been the actual publisher or supervisor of the enterprise, who allowed the quotations from the Book of Wisdom and the Gospels of Matthew and Luke to find their own resonances. The printing history of the *Catholicon* is still the subject of debate, as three distinct variants on different paper sorts have been identified. Although watermark research may argue for a later dating, the year 1460 (in roman numerals) is plainly given in the colophon. According to an ownership entry, a *Catholicon* was in any case sold to the Marienkloster in Altenburg in 1465.

GUTENBERG'S FINAL YEARS

Traces of Gutenberg's existence after he had handed over his share in the partnership to Fust are slight indeed; in 1458 his name appears as a debtor in the account books of the St Thomas Chapter in Strasbourg. He never repaid the principal sum he had borrowed there in 1442, and the debt was only written off in 1474, some years after his death.

The archbishops' war of 1462 between Adolf von Nassau and Diether von Isenburg which weighed so heavily on the history of Mainz was not without its consequences for Gutenberg. After the sack of the city on 28 October, Adolf von Nassau expelled many Mainz citizens, among them bakers, butchers and the majority of craft workers. In all probability Gutenberg was among this number. It is possible that at this time he retreated to Eltville for a while. But in any case, by 1465 he was back in favour and appointed a courtier by Adolf von Nassau, receiving each year clothing and a generous fixed allowance of grain and wine to be delivered to him at his Mainz residence. He was further released from taxation and other obligations, and the archbishop expressly thanked him for "the agreeable and willing service he had rendered and may or shall render in future time". The delivery of basic commodities tells us that Gutenberg was not at court in Eltville but living and working once more in Mainz. Provision of foodstuffs on this scale was intended in compensation for the "free table" that would otherwise have been open to him at Eltville. The extent to which Gutenberg may have been at the service of Adolf von Nassau in matters to do with print either in Mainz or Eltville may never be known. The fact some of his own typographic material shows up in the first printing works of the brothers Heinrich and Nikolaus Bechtermünze in 1467 in Eltville has led to the suggestion of a communal workshop. And in Mainz too it is apparent that Gutenberg may not have been financing his own activities independently, for after his death Konrad Humery retrieved from the workshop certain equipment that he had loaned to Gutenberg.

Gutenberg died in Mainz on 3 February 1468 and was buried in the church of St Francis. Two subsequent remodellings of the church amounted to its destruction in the sixteenth century and again in the eighteenth, and no kind of inscription or direct evidence of his resting place survives.

THE SUCCESSOR WORKSHOP OF FUST AND SCHOEFFER

A verse colophon to an edition of Justinian's *Institutiones* printed in 1468 by Peter Schoeffer states that he, Peter, had excelled both the Johanns as an expert in metal cutting (*sculpendi lege sagetius*). Thus Schoeffer embarks on his distinguished career as master printer, whilst paying tribute to his predecessors Johann Fust (d. 1466) and Johann Gutenberg (d. 1468). The same point is made in the colophon to the *Annales Hirsaugiensis* (1515) of Abbot Johann Trithemius, namely that Schoeffer had been the one who improved typefounding. Peter Schoeffer from Gernsheim on the Rhine is known to have been a cleric and a calligrapher at the University of Paris in 1449. The Helmasperger Legal Instrument has him as "Peter Girnssheim, cleric of the city and bishopric of Mainz." Only Trithemius records him as the "adoptive son" of Johann Fust, but it is well established that Schoeffer later married Fust's daughter Christine.

Because the partners Fust and Schoeffer furnished their editions with a printer's imprint and mark, their work is plainly identifiable; consisting for the most part of masterpieces of the printer's art, which extend and excel Gutenberg's work in the areas of typographic repertoire, metal-cut embellishment and colour printing. On 14 August 1457 their first magnificent folio appeared: the *Psalterium Moguntinum* (Mainz Psalter) on vellum. It contained, for the first time in printing history, a colophon and a printer's device. The imprint reads: "The present book of psalms . . . is achieved through the ingenious invention of printing and letter forms without any use of the pen, and to the worship of God has been diligently brought to completion by Johann Fust, a citizen of Mainz, and Peter Schoeffer of Gernsheim in the year of the Lord 1457, on the vigil of the Feast of the Assumption."

The new art was described in Latin terms as *Ars imprimendi ac caractericandi*. In classical usage *imprimere* denoted an impressing process, thus Suetonius speaks of a coin or a ring with a stamped out image using this verb. Virgil also speaks in the *Aeneid* of a jug with impressed pictures, and Tacitus of wooden rods into which signs had been impressed or cut. This term for the new printing process was reinforced by a second: *caractericare*. Of Greek derivation this time, it meant to incise, to engrave, to sink (a hole) in, or to imprint. A die used in striking coins was called a "character", so in time this notion was transferred to the product so impressed. Whereas *imprimere* denoted the printing process itself, *caractericare* described the types themselves or the typefounding method. *Imprimere* has survived as *imprimerie*, the French word for printing office, and in the English word "print"; we still use the *Impressum* (Ger.) or imprint for the legally required printer's details, or

Imprimatur “Let it be printed” for a (mainly) religious printing permit.

With the *Psalter*, Fust and Schoeffer elevated the basic idea of reproducing the manuscript as closely as possible to a new level of quality. Whilst a mere handful of trial lines of red printing are to be found in the sheets of the *Gutenberg Bible* to be printed first, Fust and Schoeffer used red printing throughout the *Psalter*; supplying the red uncial initials that would normally have been added by a rubricator, and eliminating the illuminator’s work as well by means of large metal-cut initials printed in both red and blue. These initials came in three sizes, our illustration (see Plate 16) shows the largest, the magnificent “B”, designed on an 8.8 x 8.8 cm square corresponding to the depth occupied by six lines of the large Psalter-type. Then there are 4-line initials for C, D, E and S to be found, and numerous 2-line initials (see the letter “Q” in our illustration). Each of these was produced from metal printing plates; it seems that each initial with its surrounding scrollwork was supported on a type-high wooden block – just as a woodcut would have shared the same standard height from the bed of the press to paper as its surrounding text. The printing sequence would have been as follows: first a page with all its type and ornamental blocks would have been composed, locked up, and inked in black; then the printer would remove those units to be printed in colour, clean and re-ink them in red or blue respectively (the shallow initial plate fitted into a recess in the deeper ornamental block) and replace everything in position to take a three-colour print with a single pull of the press. This was certainly a very tedious process, yet it offered the best guarantee of maintaining register and preventing erroneous overprintings. A few smeared Lombardic initials show that these were transposed or reinserted into the final forme with difficulty. This first example of multi-colour printing in the history of the craft does, however, merit further superlatives: the type repertoire included a large Psalter-type (*c.* 39 pt) of 210 individual characters and a smaller Psalter-type (*c.* 32 pt) of 185 characters to which must be added totals of 53 related uncial initials and 228 initials for colour printing in three different sizes. The design of the type and ornamental elements, casting and typesetting must have taken a considerable time, so that preparations would certainly date back to 1453 or 1444, that is to say, to a time when Gutenberg was still in charge of the printing office.

All of the ten surviving copies, each of 340 folio pages, are printed on vellum, testifying once again to their predominant use in liturgical service. The psalms, canticles, hymns, antiphons and responses included are arranged in the order needed by a breviary. Since this *Psalter* was prepared according to the usage of Mainz – the hymns for religious festivals had a special Mainz flavour, for example – it was only valid within that diocese. In the same year a second edition of only 246 pages appeared which was suitable for sale outside the diocese. Another issue appeared in 1459, the *Psalterium Benedictinum* (H 13480), this time revised to suit the requirements of the Bursfeld Congregation of Benedictines. As a larger, paper format was adopted this time, the generous margins gave its pages a more harmonious effect. It is likely that this edition was produced in response to a direct commisssion from the Benedictine order.

Several of the ten surviving *Mainz Psalters* were originally owned by Mainz monasteries, by that of St Victor – with its close Gutenberg connections – for example, or that of St John. A copy from the Ursuline Convent in Hildesheim belonged for a time in the library of Göttingen University, from whence it was presented to George III. It is now in the Royal Library at Windsor Castle.

Besides these Psalter-types, the Fust and Schoeffer workshop made use of a really small but quite legible Gothic-roman for Latin texts. It was first used for a *Rationale divinorum officiorum* of Guillelmus Durandus (6 October 1459, GW 9101), and works of canon law were also set in these same types: such as the *Constitutiones* of Pope Clement V (GW 7077) in 1460 and the *Liber sextus decretalium* of Pope Boniface VIII in 1465 (GW 4848). The outstanding 48-*line Bible* followed from the same workshop, and this was set in a newly-cut Gothic-roman. The use of a smaller size of type may be taken as an indication that these *Bibles* were intended more for personal reading than for use during services, for reading the lessons or teaching. Fust and Schoeffer were able to draw on their experience of red printing for the *Psalter* and as a rule to print display lines such as chapter openings in red. But one can tell from a copy in the Göttingen University Library what problems printing in red could present even to such experienced printers in these early days. It is evident from the page reproduced (Plate 17) that the incipit of the Letter to the

Hebrews has been set in red, but that the incipit for the Letter to Philemon and other copy was left off and had to be inserted by a scribe. The scribe went to pains to imitate the typeface, but lacked finesse when it came to the spacing and contractions. The running headlines have been added by hand in red throughout, but even here the flowing script follows the printed letter forms closely. In the colophon to this volume as well (see Plate 18), Fust and Schoeffer relate, in what is rapidly becoming a formula, that this book has been produced "by the new art of printing and without help of the pen" in the city of Mainz by Johann Fust and Peter Schoeffer in 1462. This *48-line Bible* belongs to those masterpieces of early printing that were already finding their way to a growing educated public, regardless of the directives of the Church.

After the death of Johann Fust in Paris in 1466, Peter Schoeffer, married to Fust's daughter Christine, became sole heir to the printing and publishing house. From the 1470s onwards he took an interest in book illustration, and in 1484 and 1485 respectively brought to the market a Latin *Herbarius* and his *Gart der Gesundheit* (Garden of Health), two important and richly illustrated plant books and guides to herbal medicine. Herbalism can be traced back to the philological work of the humanists, who edited the Latin texts of classical antiquity which contained many translations from Greek. The writings of Theophrastus – pupil of Aristotle and founder of botany – had been re-discovered and debated in this way. Theological, philosophical, medical, folkloric and natural scientific treatises and interpretations found their way into these books that conveyed the sum of medical knowledge in the classical age. When Peter Schoeffer issued his Latin *Herbal* in 1484, using his Psalter-types for the headings, no author's name was mentioned – but then there was nothing unusual in that. It set out to be a compilation of basic instruction about medicinal herbs, intended for the widest popular audience. A total of 150 plants are depicted, mostly in outline, by woodcuts in its 348 pages (see Plate 19). Hatched shadings are used sparingly, and most of the surviving copies have been fully coloured. Because the plants are represented so stiffly, it has been suggested that most of them may have been drawn from pressed flowers.

This edition caused such a stir that pirated copies appeared in the same year from the brothers Hist in Speyer and a year later from Johann Petri in Passau. As no protection existed for originator's rights, this practice went on for many years to come, and, with all its disadvantages, it contributed massively to the spread of knowledge.

In March 1485 Peter Schoeffer brought out a still more popular version in the vernacular under the title *Gart der Gesundheit*. He prepared 378 new woodcuts to illustrate its 720 large-format pages. Here again the author's name was only to be found hidden away in the text, but it was clearly the work of Johann Wonnecke from Kaub. In contrast to the *Herbal*, this text was not extracted from classical sources but offered a state-of-the-art summary of fifteenth-century knowledge of medicinal herbs. One of the main sections gave an account of the pharmacological properties of plants, and also of animal and inorganic materials. A second section dealt systematically with laxatives, fragrances, gums, fruits, seeds, roots, gemstones and animals. A short section was given over to the urine. A form of index gave catchwords for a total of 313 illnesses, recommending the relevant herbs to use.

The *Cronicken der sassen* by Konrad Bote (or Botho, fl. 1475–1501) is worthy of note as a further important vernacular publication from Schoeffer's office (see Plate 20). This much-read Middle Low German "Saxon Chronicle of the World" dating from 1490 gives an annalistic account from the creation of the world to 1489. With numerous woodcut illustrations, coats of arms and decorative initial types, it was printed in Mainz by Peter Schoeffer in 1492 (GW 4963).

Thus Peter Schoeffer became heir in Mainz to Gutenberg, whose invention he improved upon in many technical details, also transforming the trade structures he had inherited with a true publisher's acumen. In 1479 he obtained citizenship of Frankfurt-am-Main, making it more convenient to have a presence at the book fair there and to participate in the international market in books in Latin which had grown up so rapidly.

Of the few further Mainz printers whose work has lasting significance, mention should be made of Erhard Reuwich, painter and maker of preliminary drawings on woodblocks. He accompanied Bernhard von Breydenbach, dean of Mainz Cathedral, on his travels to the Holy Land in 1483 and sketched the most important cities, islands and landscapes. The completed woodcuts made from his drawings formed large format folding plates to the report of Breydenbach's journey; to this day a key source for geographical history as well as a landmark in the art of the woodcut. In the years which followed, these detail-packed illustrations were frequently recut, and they still form an outstanding source for the contemporary appearance of Venice, the island of Rhodes or Jerusalem. The first Latin and German editions (GW 5075, 5077) appeared in 1486, and a Low German one (GW 5081) in 1488. The printer's imprint in the German edition states that Erhard Reuwich has printed these books "at his house". But as the types used are those of Peter Schoeffer, it is more likely that this exceptional printing task was a joint enterprise between workshops. Further editions were printed using the original woodblocks in Lyons and Speyer in 1490 and by Paul Hurus in Saragossa in 1498.

After Peter Schoeffer's death in 1503 his son took over his office, in which his first concern became printing classical Latin texts to meet university requirements. In 1509 he published the first German translation of Livy, which he decked out with 214 woodcuts and had to reprint seven times in his own workshop. In his first publication of 1505, he paid homage to Gutenberg and to his own father, and evaluated their respective contributions: "In Mainz the sagacious Johann Gutenberg discovered the wonderful art of printing, thereafter it was improved and perfected thanks to the industry, outlay and efforts of Johann Fust and Peter Schoeffer in Mainz."

The spread of printing

Part and parcel of the phenomenon of Gutenberg's invention was the incredible speed with which it spread throughout Europe, whilst achieving astonishing quality in the earliest printing to come from each and every centre. At first the new technology was free to develop without regulation by governments, princely houses or the Church, nor is there any evidence that any restrictions were imposed by the guilds or others. A *Bible* with 36 lines (B36, see Plate 14) had been printed before the close of the 1450s in Bamberg, from which city Ulrich Boner's *Der Edelstein* carries a firm completion date of 14 February 1461. Its printer Albrecht Pfister issued the most significant document of early humanism in Germany, Johann von Tepl's *Der Ackermann aus Böhmen* (see Plate 21), from the same workshop. Johann Sensenschmidt was at work in Bamberg by no later than 1481, printing a *Missale Benedictum* (31 July 1481) and further liturgica.

Printing was already taking place in Strasbourg at roughly the same time as in Bamberg; a copy of a 49-*line Bible* printed there by Johann Mentelin is undated, but was rubricated in 1460. Mentelin (*c*.1410–78) used his own typefaces, a Gothic-roman and further purely roman founts. In general he dispensed with fitted initials or woodcuts and concentrated on textually accurate editions of the fathers of the Church, of Augustine, Aquinas, Jerome and Albertus Magnus, in parallel to the *Opera* of Virgil and the *Comoediae* of Terence. He was responsible for printing the *First German Bible* (GW 4295, see Plate 54), which, despite its antiquated language, formed a not insignificant basis for further biblical versions in the vernacular until Luther's translation appeared. He picked up a few tips from the experienced manuscript manufacturer and distributor Diebold Lauber of Hagenau in Alsace and printed medieval court poetry, including Wolfram von Eschenbach's *Parzifal* (H 684) and the *Jüngeren Titurel* (H 6683) in 1477. He was also engaged in bookselling, as a list of his – one of the earliest sales advertisements of its kind – testifies.

But the first journeymen printers of all were active not only in Bamberg and Strasbourg, but also in the commercial metropolis of Cologne. The first printer there, Ulrich Zell from Hanau (*c.*1435–1503), could claim direct links with the birthplace of printing, having learned his craft from Fust and Schoeffer in Mainz before setting up at Cologne in 1464. It is probable that his edition of Cicero's *De officiis* was ready for publication by 1465; the start of an extensive output of some 140 titles, 95 per cent of which were in Latin (theological works for the most part, but also humanistic texts). In terms of the number of titles printed, Cologne soon outranked the other German printing centres. It demonstrated that commercial centres offered the best conditions for the new trade to flourish. Whilst Mainz and Bamberg could only muster small production totals for the decades which followed, those for printing offices situated in major trading centres such as Augsburg (1468), Nuremberg (1470) and Lübeck (1475) continued to soar.

ROME

The route over the Alps to the south was crucial in the spread of printing, and to the outstanding and artistically independent art of printing in Italy which was soon to stimulate the whole of Europe. The German printers Konrad Sweynheym (d. 1477) and Arnold Pannartz (d. 1477) were working in the Benedictine monastery of Sancta Scholastica at Subiaco in the Sabine hills west of Rome as early as 1465. Their first publication, dated 29 October 1465, was an edition of Lactantius, active at the start of the fourth century (H 9806). This father of the Church played only a marginal role in late antiquity and the Middle Ages, but he was rediscovered by the humanists on account of his Ciceronian style and promoted as the "Christian Cicero". A further 14 editions followed this *editio princeps* in the incunabula period alone.

That same year saw Sweynheym and Pannartz's printed edition of Cicero's *De oratore* (GW 8742), and Augustine's *De civitate* (GW 2874) followed in 1467. This last apparently proved to be big business for the monastery, as the earliest customs document that we possess for the book trade records that the monastery had sent 60 copies of this title to Rome. In the following year as well books to the value of 1400 to 3000 ducats at a time were supplied from Subiaco to Rome.

Sweynheym and Pannartz themselves had moved to Rome in 1467; where Ulrich Han (d. 1479) from Ingolstadt was already at work. He had published the *Meditationes* of Cardinal Juan de Torquemada (H 15722) in 1466 and was to issue classical authors over the next few years, before concentrating on canonical works and papal bulls and addresses. A petition addressed to Sixtus IV in 1472 by Giovanni Andrea Bussi, Bishop of Aleria, requesting support for Sweynheym and Pannartz in view of their unsold stocks, sheds light on their further activities and their close association with the Curia. This letter shows than a typical print run would be 275 copies, and that an extensive backlist had built up. The only item to have sold out was a *Donatus* with which they had launched their publishing activity back in Subiaco. Early printers at a variety of locations found by bitter experience that Latin grammars and school books continued to sell like hot cakes, but that the market for the wealth of Roman classics which had survived in manuscript was soon satisfied and that it was necessary to move on to new outlets with new wares. Sweynheym appears to have used his contacts with the Curia in 1496 to obtain a five-year monopoly to print an indulgence for his home parish of St Michael in Schwanheim in the diocese of Mainz.

We may infer the close relations between the Curia and the German dioceses, or rather between a handful of prominent representatives of the Church, from a dedication from Giovanni Andrea Bussi to Pope Paul II which appears in the *Epistolae* of St Jerome printed by Sweynheym and Pannartz in Rome in 1468. In it Bussi, who later became the Vatican's first librarian, praises the importance of printing and the special significance of the invention for Germany and names Nicholas of Cues above all others as the great patron of the new art: "Germany is in fact worthy, privileged, and to be praised for centuries to come, as the inventor of this beneficial art . . . It is that which the soul, rich in honours and meriting heaven, of Nicholas of Cues, Cardinal of St Peter in Vinculis, so fervently desired; that this holy art, whose shoots became visible at that time in Germany, should be transferred to Roman soil. May this wish . . . find fulfilment during your pontificate."

Nicholas of Cues (d. 1464), who had apparently turned to Mainz in the matter of having an indulgence printed as early as 1452, and who had stood up for the free dissemination of knowledge and religious doctrine during his lifetime, is here openly spoken of as the middleman between printing in Germany and the development of those techniques in Italy. This encourages the speculation that after journeymen printers were forced to leave Mainz in consequence of the archbishops' war of 1462, they may possibly have found a home in Rome – or more specifically in Subiaco – through his intervention. Although there is no supporting evidence for this in detail, the continuity between the theological interests of Nicholas of Cues and his support for printing is striking.

Sweynheym and Pannartz, and Ulrich Han as well, found a further religious patron in the abbot of Subiaco, Cardinal Juan de Torquemada (a relative of the Spanish inquisitor). His *Meditationes* having formed Ulrich Han's first Rome publication of 1466, Han became a papal *familiare* that same year, and was thus able to lobby the pope directly for a chaplaincy of the church of St Ulrich, Vienna.

Among Sweynheym and Pannartz's productions was an edition of Cicero's De *officiis* (GW 6924, see Plate 22) which was completed on 24 January 1469. The handsome, wide-margined copy at Göttingen University Library with its pleasing roman typeface is surrounded by an interlaced border, showing northern Italian influence, incorporating an initial "Q" in gold, a portrait of the author to the right and an empty wreath into which the owner's arms might be set at the foot. This volume contains interesting signs of use in its underlinings and copious marginal annotations. Rome remained the most important centre of Italian printing throughout the incunabula period, with evidence for over forty printing houses, of which about twenty-five were operated by German printers.

VENICE

Italian-German cultural and academic connections increased markedly in the second half of the fifteenth century, and quite a few patricians' sons from Nuremberg or Augsburg studied the humanities or medicine and law in Italy. But we also find numerous craftsmen, architects and master builders on their travels south of the Alps. The rich interchange of scholarly printers between Germany and Italy in these decades simply formed part of a prevailing cultural scene. Venice's first German printer, Johann von Speyer, puts these matters into perspective in the colophon to his edition of Cicero's *Epistolae ad Familiares* (GW 6800) of 1469:

> Each German once brought home a book from Italy
> For which a German would pay as much again today.
> Since Hans von Speyer shows how to write books better,
> Whom none surpasses in these arts with brazen letter.

Johann von Speyer's origins are unknown, but since one "Hans von Spyre" surfaces as witness to a Mainz document, it has repeatedly been suggested that he may have learned typesetting and presswork there in Gutenberg's day. In 1469, he was awarded a monopoly of printing in Venice for five years by the *collegio* (an organ of Venetian government). However, he had died by 1470, and the business was continued by his brother Wendelin. As in other Italian cities it was the classical Latin writers and legal works that were printed most frequently. The Speyer brothers' printing house was responsible for the first *Bible* in Italian (1471, GW 4311), and for an important product of Italian humanism in the vernacular, the *Canzoniere* of Petrarch in 1470 (GW 12753). A clear, robust roman type is typical of Venetian printing in these early years.

Venice's next printer of importance, Nicholas Jenson from Sommevoire near Troyes, had in all probability also learned his craft in Mainz. He was master of the mint to Charles VII of France, and had been sent to Mainz in order to discover the secrets of printing. From 1470 he began to issue the Latin classics and Church fathers in Venice in a particularly well-cut and harmonious roman type (see Plate 34, showing his 1472 edition of the Elder Pliny's *Naturalis historia*). Jenson ran his office as a syndicate with two German merchants at the Fondaco dei Tedeschi. He was made a papal count in Rome in 1480 and was highly honoured at the time of his death.

There was yet a further German printer active in Venice at this time, Erhard Ratdolt from Augsburg. He had earlier spent some time working with the Nuremberg astronomer and printer Johann Regiomontanus, whose *Calendarium* he printed in an elegant Venetian roman with decorated initials and borders in both Latin and Italian editions (H 13776, H 13789). The actual initials used (white-line capitals and scrollwork out of black) had previously only been used by Regiomantanus himself in Nuremberg. Ratdolt refined these in his Venetian office, and added to them with further decorative strips and borders in the Italian style. One of his finest achievements was Euclid's *Elementa geometriae*, finished on 25 May 1482 (GW 9428). Not only are his deeply-cut white-line borders seen here to fine effect, but geometrical diagrams are printed from woodcuts for the first time (see Plate 35).

The next phase of Venetian printing is dominated by the Italian Aldus Manutius (1449–1515), who opened a printing house there with the express intention of publishing editions of the Latin and Greek classics (see pp. 75–6) One of his loveliest and best-known books is the *Hypnerotomachia Poliphili* (The strife of love in a dream of Poliphilo) of 1499; its Italian text illustrated by 172 woodcuts (GW 7223, see Plates 24 and 25). Its author, Fra Francesco Colonna (whose true identity is still hotly debated), guides the reader with his sleep-walking hero Poliphilo through a fantastic world of mythological riddles and allusions. The printing of this at once obscure and fascinating text presented Aldus with formidable challenges. And if it is universally regarded as the "most beautiful printed book of the Renaissance" then this is not on account of its light and regular typeface alone, but for the careful shape given to each individual page, and the way in which the delicate woodcut illustrations with their wealth of iconographical playfulness fall inevitably into place. Illustration and type areas find a perfect harmony here, perhaps for the first time, and on many pages the text terminates in a tapering inverted pyramid that supports the allegorical illustration placed above. For all the lightness of the typography, many lines are set in the capitals of the text with the formality of Roman lapidary inscriptions. The careful composition of the woodcuts is matched by the elegance of their cutting which puts them in a different class from earlier woodcuts, which were still dependent on hand colouring for their effect, or from contemporary work north of the Alps. These illustrations are no mere afterthought or addenda, but a creative component in the presentation of a literary text. In its travels from Germany to Italy, printing had undergone transformation and acquired autonomy in matters of design and typography. Towards the end of the century this flow was reversed, and journeymen and master printers returned from Italy bringing fresh thinking to German book design. Amongst these was Erhard Ratdolt, who, after some ten years of forward-looking work in Venice, returned to set up his press in Augsburg in 1486 and produced a specimen sheet which showed as well as rotunda types, three sizes of roman and a Greek typeface.

Johann Numeister (*c.*1435–1512) returned to Mainz where in all probability he had learned to print in 1457, from Foligno in Italy where he had been one of the earliest printers of the Italian humanists, incidentally printing the first edition of Dante's *Divina comedia* in 1472. (GW 7958). In 1479 he printed Juan de Torquemada's *Meditationes*, probably after he was back in Mainz (H 15726). This edition contains 34 metalcuts, which copy the woodcuts from Ulrich Han's Rome edition of 1466. Numeister's travels led him further to Albi and Lyons, where he became one of France's earliest printers as well.

PARIS

It is not possible to cover the spread of printing within individual European countries in any detail in this study. A couple of examples from France and England must suffice to show the close links between the German art and its further development in Europe. The advantages of printing for the spread of ideas and instruction were soon grasped by the universities. Accordingly the first printing office in France was set up within the University of Paris in 1470. The prior of the Sorbonne, Johann Heynlin (1435–96) and the rector and university librarian Guillaume Fichet (1433–96) charged Ulrich Gering (d. 1510) from Constance, Martin Cranz (1440–*c.*1480) from Strasbourg and Michael Friburger (d. after 1477) from Colmar with printing classical and humanist writings, for which they used a fairly large roman type. In 1473 the three printers set up on their own account in the rue Saint-Jacques and began to publish those standard theological works which had already brought the best returns to Mainz's proto-typographers: a *Vulgata* in 1476 (GW 4225) and the *Rationale divinorum officiorum* of

Guillelmus Durandus in 1475 (GW 9108). Lyons followed Paris as a further major French printing city in 1473, Albi in 1475 and Toulouse in 1476.

Within a decade of Gutenberg's death in 1468, his technology had spread right across Christian Europe, attracting resourceful followers and specialists, who made improvements to the process itself as well as reorganising the channels of book distribution. Gutenberg and Schoeffer had begun by closely aligning themselves to the tradition of manuscript production within a framework of learning dominated by the Church, and had printed the Latin *Vulgate* and familiar liturgical books as well as indulgences, linguistic reference works, grammars and the like; all aimed at a Europe-wide, Latin-reading market. In Italy, apart from the Curia, it was the humanists first and foremost who adopted the new technology and printed – in line with their belief in a universal human capacity for education – the venerated Latin texts of Roman antiquity and the neo-Latin output of their contemporary literary successors. In France, besides Latin *bibles*, it was those texts needed for teaching purposes by the University of Paris that found their way into print.

THE BOOK IN BRITAIN

The introduction of printing to England followed an independent course, in that it took place relatively late on and was concerned almost exclusively with English literature in the vernacular produced solely for an internal book market. This situation also reflected the insular nature of England's cultural outlook in the fifteenth century, which was not as receptive towards the new ideas of Renaissance humanism as were more southern lands. Likewise the Pope was far enough away in Rome for independent and national religious usages to be cultivated. So it is not possible to trace the spread of printing to England back to Church or university roots, but rather to the activities of an erudite merchant, who in the second half of his life brought his rich business experiences as a wool trader – and at the same time his predilictions as a translator and promotor of literature in English – to bear on this novel enterprise.

The history of the book, and equally the history of literature and education, in England is crucially determined by William Caxton (c.1422–

1491). This learned cloth merchant moved to the Netherlands whilst young and rose to eminence as a businessman in Bruges; from time to time he undertook diplomatic assignments for the Crown, becoming Head of the Guild of the Merchant Adventurers and Governor of the English Nation at Bruges. He was active in the Netherlands, based in Flanders, Bruges and Ghent, for more than thirty years. His mercantile prominence made him a kind of Minister of Foreign Affairs for Britain and brought him into personal contact with the King and also with the King's sister Margaret of York, Duchess of Burgundy, and other members of the royal entourage.

Margaret of York was herself greatly interested in literature and manuscripts, and Caxton repeatedly procured manuscripts for her and translated Raoul Lefèvre's *Receuils des histoires de Troye* into English at her behest. He completed the work of translation on 19 September 1471 during a stay in Cologne, as he writes himself in the prologue to the printed version (Bruges 1474): "And ended and fynisshid in the holy cyte of Colen the XIX day of septembre the yere of our sayd lord god a thousand four honderd sixty and enleuen." This statement establishes Caxton's residence in Cologne in 1471, and further documents found in the archives of that city confirm his presence in the following year.

His successor as printer at Westminster, Wynkyn de Worde, later asserted that Caxton had first printed the encyclopedia *De proprietatibus rerum* (1472) by the Franciscan friar, Bartholomaeus Anglicus, in Cologne at this time; but it is probable that Caxton merely sponsored the publication of this encyclopaedia by his fellow countryman, also known as Bartholomew de Glanville. But it was apparently then that he learned to print in the workshop of the typefounder and master printer Johann Veldener.

Together with Veldener, he left Cologne at the end of 1472 and they moved to Bruges, where Veldener let Caxton print vernacular titles for the English market, amongst them his own translation of *The Recuyell of the Historyes of Troye* (c.1473, H 7048). This is considered to be the first printed book in the English language, and its idiosyncratic bastarda typeface from Veldener's workshop was to become typical for his subsequent publications.

After he had printed a further four titles, he returned to England in 1475/6 and set up his own workshop in the precincts of Westminster

Abbey. There he began straightaway to print Chaucer's *Canterbury Tales*, dividing the work between two presses. In between he produced indulgences, just as Gutenberg had done, as a profitable side-line bringing rapid returns. He further attuned his publishing programme towards the English-speaking market, leaving liturgical and theological tomes in Latin and the works of classical authors to the continental incunabula printers. Amongst some one hundred volumes, he offered *The Chronicles of England*, *The Mirrour of the World* (the first English book with woodcuts), *The Golden Legend* and *The Dictes and Sayengs of the Philosophers* (c. 1477, see Plate 26). This last leans heavily on a manuscript by Guillaume de Tignoville entitled *Les ditz moraulz des philosophres* which had been translated into English by Anthony Woodville, second Earl Rivers. Caxton writes in an epilogue that for some incomprehensible reason Rivers had omitted to translate Socrates's statements about women, so that he had translated these himself and reinstated them. Twenty of his publications were translated into English by Caxton himself. Amongst these were assorted commissions from the English king, including the *Fayttes of Armes and of Chyualrye* (Westminster 14 July 1489, GW 6648) translated from Christine de Pisan's *Faits d'armes et des chevalerie*. The French writer Christine de Pisan (1365–1430) was born at Venice and became celebrated for her allegorical fiction. Her political and historical record of Charles V and his court (1405) was also translated by Caxton. Henry VII placed his own manuscript of this work, still to be found in the British Library, at Caxton's disposal for the purposes of his translation. Such close connections with the royal house doubtless made the successful marketing of these titles easier to accomplish.

With the *Statutes* of Henry VII of 1490, Caxton published the first work of jurisprudence in English. His numerous prologues and postscripts to his books reveal his close contacts with the highest circles in Westminster and London and his privileged access to the monarchy. That so many of his works evidently went through second and later editions suggests that in all probabilty he achieved considerable financial success as well. After his death in 1491, the workshop "at the sign of the Red Pale" near Westminster Abbey continued to flourish under his colleague Wynkyn de Worde.

With the exception of Caxton the other early printers in England were foreigners who were nevertheless expressly encouraged in their activities through an act of parliament of Richard III in 1484. Not until the very different political climate of 1534 were foreign printers and booksellers prohibited from pursuing their occupations in England. Apart from Caxton, his colleague and successor, the Dutchman Wynkyn de Worde, who relocated the press to London's Fleet Street in 1500, is worthy of mention, as is Richard Pynson (d. 1530). From 1490 onwards Pynson, who came from Normandy, printed in a most agreeable typeface and from skilful woodcuts. Among his successes was the translation of Giovanni Boccaccio's *De casibus virorum illustrium* by John Lydgate (c. 1370–1450) entitled *The Fall of Princes* (London 1494, GW 4431).

Smaller printing offices were set up after about 1477 in nearby St Albans and at Oxford, where Theodoric Rood came from Cologne and printed some twenty classical and patristic texts with no great success; or as early as 1480 in the City of London itself, where John Lettou, a Lithuanian who had studied printing at Rome in about 1478/9, and William de Machlinia (i.e. Malines), practised together until 1482.

William Caxton occupies a significant place in the history of printing and literature, but even this is outweighed by his contribution to the emergence of a standard English which overrides the various dialects. So Caxton serves as a significant promoter of a universal English literary language, to be compared in terms of the history of language to Martin Luther and the tremendous impact on the German language of his *Bible* translation. Lutheran writings were at first banned in England, and in the 1520s they were publicly burned. The first translations of the *Bible* into English by William Tyndale (1490–1536) had to be printed in Antwerp, Cologne, Mainz and Worms. and then smuggled into England. The theologian Tyndale visited Luther in Wittenberg in 1524 and resided in the Netherlands after 1529. Closely following Luther's procedure for his German vernacular *Bible*, he translated first the New Testament and then the Old Testament in parts between 1525 and 1534. Arrested and executed under the Inquisition, he was unable to finish the work of translation. His *New Testament*, translated into English with marginal notes by William Tyndale assisted by William Roye, was published in Cologne in 1525, with a second edition appearing from Worms in the following year. The Pentateuch was published in Antwerp in 1530, as *The firste Boke of Moses called Genesis Newly correctyd and amendyd by* W.T., and a new edition of the New Testament: *The newe Testament, dylygently corrected and compared with the Greke by Willyam Tyndale* appeared there in 1534. Tyndale's translation had a significance for the English language and the course of theology in England which corresponded to the impact of Luther's translation on the German language and continental theology.

After England, printing reached Stockholm in 1483, Istanbul in 1503, Salonika in 1515 and Moscow in 1553. Printing can be shown to have taken place in Goa (India) by 1556 and in Kazusa (Japan) by 1590. Although texts had been multiplied by taking rubbings since the eighth century in the Far East, it was not for a further eight centuries that Gutenberg's method of printing by means of a press became known to the advanced cultures in these parts of the world.

Printing and humanism

It is thanks to a son of the city of Mainz, wrote the German "arch-humanist" Conrad Celtis (1459-1508) at the end of the fifteenth century in an ode, that the Germans may no longer be ridiculed for the intellectual laziness attributed to them by the Italians. For the art of printing had made the great minds of classical antiquity accessible. And, just as Virgil in his *Georgics* had once postulated the migration of the Greek muses to Italy, so Celtis now expressed the desire to transfer the muses, and therewith the gift for true poetry and learning, over the Alps to German lands. Already in 1486, the year of Maximilian's election as German king, Celtis prayed, in another of his odes, to Apollo, patron of poets, that he should come with his lyre from Italy to Germany: "Come then, so we plead, to our coasts, as once you visited Italy's lands; may barbaric tongues then take flight and all darkness be dispersed".

Celtis stressed the difference between uncultivated barbarians, with their awkward speech, and the educated, well-bred Romans. He equated this language deficiency with a cultural one. In doing so he allied himself intellectually with the leading Italian humanists Francesco Petrarch (1304–74) and Lorenzo Valla (1406–57), who insisted on the function of Latin in providing a basis for culture. They valued Latin as the universal language of civilisation and as the language of scholarship and the liberal arts in general. In their view, however, language was not only the medium, but at the same time the source (*semen* = seed) and even the object, of scholarly communication. The Latin tongue became the badge of each true *eruditus* and each *civilitas*, and thus for any social life worthy of mankind. The close identity of Latin with legal parlance and the language of the Church served as proof for crediting Latin with a fundamental character as the defender of a fixed social and spiritual outlook. Through mastering this language one could share in the wisdom it encapsulated. Conversely, the decay of language may be seen in the overall intellectual decadence and the expulsion from Asia and Africa at the end of the Roman empire. Therefore, as the cultivation of Latin became a national task for the Italian humanists – as a stratagem for re-establishing contact with the former greatness of Rome – so Celtis also hoped that it would fall to him to convey the erudition contained within Latin to the German realm, and so equip scholars there to attain proud equality with cultured peoples. In the ode mentioned earlier, Celtis describes how it would be possible to make up for Germany's intellectual backwardness: solely through Gutenberg's technical invention, which allowed, "fixed types to be formed from metal, and the art of writing with reversed letters to be taught" – this is a scant but equally a sensible description of the new technology. It facilitated:

- The issue of classical texts in editions and anthologies which enabled their implicit "wisdom" to be shared.
- The spread of knowledge (as an educational task) through affordable and accurate texts in convenient format.
- A sound basis for university teaching and research.
- The preservation of international and national manuscript treasures.

RENAISSANCE HUMANISM

By Renaissance humanism we understand the deeper engagement with classical and Christian antiquity, a cultural movement aiming at their ideals, shaping religious, political and social life and soon making itself independent as an educative force and embracing the whole wealth of existence. Antiquity came to be seen as a measure of human conduct, and its aesthetic and stylistic categories were taken over as well. A new breed of poets asserted themselves, the *poeta doctus*, or "scholastic poets", taking up a middle position amongst philosophers, scholars and writers and displacing more naturally gifted poets. Their highest aspiration was stylistic mastery after the model of Cicero, whose rhetorical treatises and letters were far more widely received than his philosophical writings. The return to the Greek classics as well was encouraged through the setting up of the first university chair for Greek language and literature at Florence in 1397. Early Christianity, chiefly transmitted through the Church fathers (and above all by Augustine) was naturally equally close to the humanists. Nineteenth-century researchers in the wake of Jacob Burckhardt had left a one-sided picture of a Renaissance humanism with secular, anti-religious and anti-clerical tendencies, in which criteria such as individualism, atheism and immorality were over-emphasised. More recent research has shown, on the contrary, a fruitful alliance between humanism and theology, not only in philosophical questions, but also in forming a view of the human condition. The "humanistic theology" of an Erasmus of Rotterdam (1466–1536) can accordingly be regarded as a connecting link between medieval and reformational theology.

There had already been weighty voices opposed to a stylistic purism devoid of content, notably those of the Florentine politician and humanist Coluccio Salutati (1331–1406) and the Roman rhetorician Lorenzo Valla in Italy. In German-speaking lands it was Erasmus of Rotterdam above all who, in his polemical letters, reprimanded with biting satire a new generation of scholastics who had failed to encounter the classics on creative terms or to understand the enlightened impulse that lay behind *humanitas*. Alongside Cicero, he promoted Horace, Plutarch and Lucian as intellectual models. According to a definition by the authority on humanism Dieter Wuttke, the point at issue for the humanists – in resorting to the priority of ancient classical learning whilst being aware of the dignity and obligation of mankind as the image of God – was to produce new knowledge, new consciousness and new wisdom that would make humanity more ethically mature and bring it closer to God. The unity of the arts and the natural sciences was obvious to the humanists. Beyond the close circle of *studia humanitatis*, which comprised grammar, rhetoric, dialectics, history, poetry and moral philosophy, lay the challenge to engage with the mathematical arts of the *quadrivium*: arithmetic, geometry, astronomy and music. The most evident token of this interplay was the establishment of a "Collegium poetarum et mathematicorum" at the University of Vienna in 1502 by Emperor Maximilian at the suggestion of Conrad Celtis. In his programmatical introductions and illustrated broadsides, Celtis had defined the ideas of Renaissance humanism as an "integrative force" for the whole of thought and action. The woodcut *Philosophia* by Albrecht Dürer which Celtis initiated for his own *Amores* (1502) depicts philosophy as the sum of all spheres of nature and the intellect. The caption within this print summarizes: "What the nature of heaven, earth, air and water stipulates, and what human life comprises, as well as what the fiery God creates throughout the globe: I, philosophy, carry in my breast."

The importance the humanists attached to their own creative task in the educational field led them to ask a lot from the illustration and technical presentation of the printed works they published. These had not only to be textually accurate but also to correspond in outward appearance to their inner worth. This requirement placed great demands on the training of compositors, proof-readers and publishers. A large number of testimonies from printer-publishers have come down to us pointing out how much care has been lavished on the faultless printing of a text. But typography and page layout attracted the attention of the publisher and before long that of the purchaser as well. The selection of the right size of type, or suitable inter-linear spacing, or the use of a fine, smooth paper came to be extensively debated, as did the fundamental preference for roman types as those most appropriate for setting texts of the classics. These types were adapted for printing from the humanistic minuscule, which in turn imitated the Carolingian minuscule in which numerous Roman writers had been handed down. The roman letter was revived from this earlier hand in the course of reproducing classical sources, and was adopted for contemporary humanist writings inspired by the classics. The earliest printing from a true roman typeface on German soil was produced by the mathematician and astronomer Regiomontanus (Johann Müller from Königsberg, 1436–76) at his printing office in Nuremberg from 1474. This type also became the trademark of Johann Amerbach (1443–1513) of Basle, who in 1486 used it to set the *Epistolae* of Francesco Filelfo (1391–1483).

Erasmus of Rotterdam expressed similar views to Celtis on the prospects printing offered for popular education. In a letter to the Alsatian theologian Johann Botzheim (c.1480–1524) he lamented the intellectual time-lag north of the Alps: "Whilst I was a child, the "liberal sciences" began to flourish again in Italy. But whether it was because printing had not yet been invented or because it was still so little known, no books reached us, and everywhere those who wielded the sceptre held forth on the least informed teachings with never a murmer of discontent." After the spread of printing the Italians used the new technology to more appropriate and telling effect in Erasmus's view, and in consequence he appealed – in his *Adagia* – for public support north of the Alps as well: "Were our princes' [. . .] endeavours on behalf of scholarship as generous-minded as those of the Italians, then the snakes of Froben would not fall behind the dolphin of Aldus in book trade success. Under his motto *Festina lente* ("hasten slowly"), Aldus earned money no less than fame, and both deservedly. But Froben – who always held the staff upright and had no other end in sight than the common good – would not swerve from the innocence of the dove, and displayed the cunning of snakes more in his printer's mark than in his dealing methods, and so became celebrated but not rich."

Erasmus is making a play on the well-known printer's marks of the eminent printers Aldus Manutius (*c*.1451–1515) in Venice and Johann Froben (1460–1527) of Basle, both of whom did so much to spread his own writings as well as for the diffusion of classical texts in the spirit of Renaissance humanism.

Aldus Manutius produced texts of the Roman and Greek classics set in roman type in swift succession. To this day these "Aldine" editions are regarded as masterpieces of printing. After his studies in Rome and Ferrara and at the recommendation of Pico della Mirandola, Manutius the classical scholar was appointed tutor to the young princes of Carpi (near Modena), Alberto and Lionello Pio. In 1490 he began to set up a printing office in Venice with the support of his pupils and with the express purpose of helping to disseminate the works of Roman and Greek authors. He surrounded himself with linguists and learned editors, took pains to obtain suitable handwritten examplars for printing and provided his own introductory commentaries. His trademarks became the pocket-sized octavo format and the italic text face which Francesco Griffo of Bologna had cut for him by 1501. Aldus also attracted favourable attention with 28 first editions of Greek classical writers, for which he had special types produced that closely followed good calligraphic models (see Plate 36). Aldus corresponded throughout scholarly Europe. Amongst his authors and correspondents was Erasmus, who frequently enthused over his work. In discussing the proverb *Festina lente* in his *Adagia*, for example, Erasmus digresses to praise Aldus Manutius: "Venice is a most illustrious city, but principally it owes its fame to the printing house of Aldus."

This high regard for the productions of his press is clear from a letter making an offer to Aldus dated 1507: "I am sending you two tragedies which I have been bold enough to translate, whether with success you may judge for yourself. Badius [Ascensius, 1461–1535, printer and publisher in Paris from 1503] has already printed them, so he writes, and he thinks with great success since he has evidently sold practically all the copies. But he takes my reputation rather too lightly into account, for everything is crawling with mistakes, and Badius has offered to repair the damage by issuing a second, improved edition. Yet I am afraid of his mending ill with ill, as the Sophoclean saying goes. I should consider my labours to have been immortalised if they could be printed in your smaller types, the most beautiful of all."

Erasmus strove for a typographic handsomeness appropriate to the text, but also for the literal correctness of his works. Like other scholars of his day he maintained a close relationship with his printer-publishers and worked with them not only on questions of which other titles to publish and how many copies to print but also on matters of content and appearance (illustrations, special spacing for schoolbooks, etc.) and correction for the press.

In his collaboration with Johann Froben of Basle, known as the "second Aldus" because he had introduced the use of roman type to that town, Erasmus went so far as to live in the publisher's household whilst his writings were going to press, and to carry out his own proofreading. He supervised there in part the reprinting of his *Adagia*, the Greek *New Testament* and the *Praise of Folly*. He often mentions this occupation in his letters, full of complaints about his "forced labour in Basle". This symbiosis of author and scholarly publisher also accounts to some extent for the miserly honorariums he was paid. On the one hand a writer's scholarly sense of duty does not lend itself readily to the idea of direct payment for intellectual work, whilst on the other hand authors often received no more than shelter and free copies in settlement for their pains.

Erasmus let his *Moriae encomium* or *Praise of Folly*, which was to become the most brilliant example of satire for the sixteenth century, be printed in Paris in 1511. In it Moria, Dame Folly herself, ascends the pulpit and rebukes the scholars, theologians, judges and high officials. With its dazzling word play, classical allusion and literary genius, this satire, which emulates Lucian, has remained popular to the present day. On a different plane it follows on from *The Ship of Fools* (*Das Narrenschiff*, 1493) of Sebastian Brant (1457–1521). In a sequence of 112 illustrated poems, Brant deals with all kinds of human foolishness including the vices, the absurdities of life, professional peculiarities, fashionable sillinesses and religious aberrations. The image of the ship brings all these frailties of human nature together for a voyage around the human condition. Brant intended the destination of this world of fools to be the recognition of folly and insight into true wisdom. Brant's masterpiece was eagerly taken up by his contemporaries and by the time of his death in 1521, 17 editions had been brought out in the German language and 18 of the Latin version (*Stultifera navis*) by Jakob Locher (1471–1528). This Latin translation, published by Bergmann von Olpe (c.1460–1532) in 1497, secured Europe-wide circulation for *The Ship of Fools* and surely it can not have failed to have influenced Erasmus.

EDITIONS OF CLASSICAL AUTHORS

The most frequently printed classical texts during the incunabula period were the writings of Cicero (GW 6708–7023). Half the 316 known editions come from Italy, from the great printing towns of Rome, Venice, Milan but from Parma as well (see Plates 22, 23 and 27). Predominant among these editions were the letters and rhetorical works, which became celebrated as artistic and stylistic models. Of the Roman writers, more than 80 Ovid editions are to be found, of which more than half are of the *Epistolae heroidum*, which came to be used as a school textbook.

The comedies of Terence were close to these in popularity, and were circulated in Germany after 1470 through Johann Mentelin. Johann Grüninger (1455–1533) brought out a Latin edition in 1496, and in 1499 a richly-illustrated German Terence (H 15431 and 15434). This last was preceded by a Terence with 159 woodcuts printed in Lyons in 1493 by Johann Trechsel (d. 1498), which is a notable achievement in French book art (H 15424). Grüninger's edition is of great importance not only for its critical text and the history of printing, but also in the fields of theatrical and costume history. The woodcut on the titlepage (see Plate 28) shows for the first time a contemporary "Terence stage", and the full-width stage settings at the head of each comedy depict dramatic characters for the first time in the history of book illustration. Text and accompanying commentary are set in double-column and graphically illustrated with 158 woodcuts in the text (see Plate 29).

Jacob Locher's edition of Horace, richly decorated with woodcuts, appeared from Johann Grüninger in 1498 (H 8898). Petrarch numbered the poet of the *Odes* among his favourite writers. Landino had published a humanistic commentary to Horace in 1482, the first of several. Conrad Celtis discovered Horace for the German humanists when, in 1486, he introduced the Horatian metre in his *Ars versificandi*.

Virgil's writings occupy a special position quantitatively speaking; at the end of his lifetime they were widely circulated on papyrus rolls – at the express wish of Emperor Augustus – and subsequently transcribed to parchment codices in the fourth century AD. Eight of these codices, more than for any other classical writer, have been preserved from late antiquity. After some fifty generations in which these texts had been copied and recopied by hand, the first printed edition appeared in 1469 in Rome. Hardly a year has gone by since without at least one of Virgil's works appearing, and there were 81 impressions of the *Opera omnia* alone between 1469 and the end of the incunabula period. Giovanni Andrea Bussi, bishop of Aleria, prepared the *editio princeps* for the German printers Conrad Sweynheym and Arnold Pannartz in Rome; it contained the additional material that had become customary in medieval manuscript transmission: the *Vita* of Donatus, the poems of the *Appendix Vergiliana* and further loosely ascribed *Opuscula*, and after 1475 the commentary of Servius was generally printed with it. The typographic layout of this commentary took its bearings from manuscript precedents, as so often in these matters. The main text was framed by the commentary, which was set in a smaller size (see Plate 30 which shows a double-page spread with the opening lines of the *Aeneid* surrounded by Servius's commentary). The modern convention of placing the commentary at the foot of the text page did not come in until the seventeenth century.

The first illustrated edition of Virgil's *Opera* was printed in 1502 by Johann Grüninger in Strasbourg with 214 large format woodcuts. Grüninger maintained a printing office in Strasbourg from 1482 and put out German prose tales (among them *Till Eulenspiegel* in 1515), but above all he issued numerous generously illustrated classics in Latin and German. Beside the Terence already mentioned he published the *Carmina* of Horace in 1498, the *Golden Ass* of Apuleius in 1499, *De consolatione philosophiae* of Boethius in 1501, Virgil in 1502 and Livy and Caesar in 1507/8.

Sebastian Brant edited the text for Grüninger's Virgil but he was also at hand to advise on the selection of themes for the illustrations (see Plate 31). These pictures called for a sound knowledge of the Latin text, and of the commentary and classical mythology (the attributes of the Gods, and so forth). The classical settings reflect a German setting of about 1500: timber-framed houses, churches with bells in Troy, Emperor Octavian wearing the German imperial crown, etc. Nor were the draughtsmen and wood cutters – or their advisor in particular – unacquainted with Christian iconography; realism and vividness prevail in the representation. The actual artists are unknown, but we do know that Grüninger's press made use of Hans Baldung Grien, Hans Leonhard Schäufelein and Urs Graf among others.

However it was not only the works of classic authors which appeared, but also works of jurisprudence and the natural sciences. On 24 May 1468 Peter Schoeffer finished printing the *Institutiones Justiniani* (GW 7580); its page layout freshly and sympathetically adapting manuscript models, with the commentary surrounding and set in a smaller size of type than the text (see Plate 32, a later example of this typical arrangement). Of some two hundred editions of the *Corpus iuris civilis* (GW 7581–7777) catalogued in the *Gesamtverzeichnis der Wiegendrucke*, the majority come from Venice, although Heinrich Eggestein (c.1420–88) in Strasbourg and Anton Koberger (d. 1513) in Nuremberg printed editions of Roman law.

The *Historia naturalis* of Gaius Plinius Secundus (23–79 AD), a compendium of classical physics, mathematics, medicine, zoology, geography and astronomy first appeared in 1469 from John of Speier in Venice and was reprinted fifteen times up to 1500 (H 13087–13106); a richly illuminated copy of Nicolas Jenson's 1472 Venetian edition is shown (see Plate 34). This encyclopaedia of natural history was ever present during the Middle Ages and more than 200 manuscripts have come down to us.

The medical writings of the Greek doctor Galen (129–199 AD) found particular favour in Italy: a few works appeared in Latin translation in the collection *Articella* (GW 26783) and a larger selection in 1490 in Venice (GW 10481), as did a Greek edition of the *Therapeutica* (H 74260) in 1500. These publications led to the establishment in the sixteenth century of a classically-based but "humanistic medicine" that took the motto *ad fontes* and sought to turn the medical wisdom of the ancients, in particular that of Greek antiquity, to the advantage of the present.

Euclid's *Elementa geometriae* of 1482 ranks as one of the most important astronomical and astrological incunabula. Euclid (365–300 BC) brought the entire mathematical knowledge of the Greeks into a logical system in his *Elementa*; accordingly it represents the oldest mathematical textbook in the world. Through an Arabic translation it reached Europe in the twelfth century, where it became known once it had been translated into Latin. The basis of Erhard Ratdolt's Venetian first edition of 1482 was a revision made in 1260 by Johannes Campanus (GW 9428). Ratdolt operated one of the leading printing offices in Venice from 1476. The first page of the *Elementa* (see Plate 35) displays the high quality of his workshop, which featured magnificent initials and borders (with letters and scroll-work in white line on a black ground). In addition to these we find here for the first time geometrical diagrams – which up to this point would have been inserted by hand – printed from woodcut with the text.

One of the last celebrated classical men of learning, Ptolemy (active between AD 125 and 151), was chiefly known during the Middle Ages for his astronomical writings. His *Geographia* (or *Cosmographia*) was first translated into Latin at the start of the fifteenth century. The first edition still contained no maps, but instead only his table of over 8000 place entries with indications of latitude and longitude. Six editions with maps appeared from 1477 onwards. The *Geographia* printed in 1482 in Ulm by Lienhart Holl is the first world atlas to be printed north of the Alps. The maps have a trapezoidal projection and were carefully hand-coloured before leaving the publisher. Holl had a special large roman type made for this edition. Plate 37 shows a double-page spread of Italy that comprised one of five modern, that is to say contemporary, maps, together with maps of Spain, France, Palestine and the Northern Lands.

et nos insipiētes increduli errātes servientes
desiderijs et voluptatibus varijs: et malicia et
inuidia agētes: odibiles. odientes inuicē.
Cū aūt benignitas et humanitas apparuit
saluatoris nostri dei nō ex operibus iusticie q
fecimus nos sed scdm suā misericordiam saluos
nos fecit p lauacrū regnacōis et renouacōis
spūs sancti quē effudit in nos abūde p ihesum xpm saluatorem nrm: vt iustificati gratia ipsius heredes simus scdm spem vite e-
terne. Fidelis sermo est. Et de hijs volo te cō-
firmare: ut curent bonis operibus pesse q cre-
dunt deo. Hec sunt bona et vtilia hominibus.
Stultas aūt questiōes. et genealogias et
cōtentiones et pugnas legis deuita. Sunt
enim inutiles et vane. Hereticū hominē p9
vnam et scdam correptionē deuita: sciens q
subūsus est qui eiusmodi est: et delinquit cū
sit pprio iudicio condemnatus. Cū misero ad
te arteman aut thychicū: festina ad me ve-
nire nicopolim. Ibi enim statui hyemare.
Zenam legisperitū et appollo sollicite pmit-
te: ut nichil illis desit. Discant aūt et nrī bonis operibus preesse ad vsus necessarios:
vt non sint infructuosi. Salutāt te qui mecum sūt omnes. Saluta eos qui nos amāt
in fide. Gratia dei cum omnibus vobis amē.
Explicit epla ad thytū Incip argumētū in
epistolam ad philemonē.
Philemoni familiares lras facit pro onesimo seruo eius:
scribens ei ab vrbe roma de
carcere per suprascriptum o-
nesimū. Explic. argumentū Incip epla
Paulus ad philemonē.
vinctus cristi ihesu et
thimotheus frater: phi-
lemoni dilecto adiu-
tori nostro. et appie so-
rori carissime et arcippo
cōmilitoni nostro: et
ecclesie que in domo tua est. Gratia vobis
et pax a deo patre nostro: et domino ihesu
cristo. Gratias ago deo meo semp memori-
am tui faciens in orōnibus meis audiens cari-
tatem tuam et fidem quā habes in dño ihū
et in omēs sanctos: ut cōmunicacō fidei tue
euidēs fiat in agnicōne omīs opis boni in
ihū xpo. Gaudiū enim magnum habui et
consolacōnem in caritate tua: q viscera san-
ctorum requieuerūt per te frater. Propter qd
multā fiduciam habens in cristo ihesu impe-
randi tibi qd ad rem ptinet: pter caritatē
magis obsecro cū sis talis vt paulus senex
nūc aūt et vinctus ihesu xpi: obsecro te p meo
filio quē genui in vinculis onesimo qui tibi
aliquādo inutilis fuit: nūc aūt et michi et tibi
vtilis: quē remisi tibi. Tu aūt illū ut mea viscera suscipe. Quē ego volueram mecū detine-
re: ut p te michi ministraret in vinculis euan-
gelij. Sine osilio aūt tuo nichil volui facē:
vti ne velut ex necessitate bonū tuū esset. s
volūtariū. Forsitan enī ideo discessit ad ho-
rā a te. vt eternū illū reciperes: iā nō vt seruū
s p seruo carissimū frēz: maxīe michi. Quanto autē magis tibi: et in carne et in dño. Si
ergo habes me socium: suscipe illū sicut me.
Si aūt aliquid nocuit tibi aut debet: hoc michi imputa. Ego paulus scripsi mea manu.
Ego reddam: ut nō dicā tibi q et teipsum michi debes. Ita frater ego te fruar in dño: re-
fice viscera mea in cristo. Confidens in obe-
diencia tua scripsi tibi: sciens qm et super id
qd dico facies. Simul et para michi hospici-
um: nam spero p orationes vrās donari me
vobis. Salutat te epafras ocaptiuus meus
in xpo ihesu: marcus aristarchus demas et
lucas adiutores mei. Gratia domini nostri
ihesu cristi cum spiritu vestro amen.
Explicit epistola ad philemonem. Incipit
argumentum in epistolam ad hebreos.
In primis dicendū est cur apostolus paulus
in hac epistola scribendo nō seruauerit morē
suū: ut vel vocabulū nominis sui vel ordinis
describeret dignitatē. Hec causa est: q ad e-
os scribens qui ex circūcisione crediderant
quasi gentiū apostolus et non hebreorum: sciens q eorum superbiā suamq humilitatē ipe
demōstrans: meritū officij sui noluit anteferre.
Nam simili modo etiam iohannes apls
pter humilitatē in epla sua nomen suū ea-
dem racōne non ptulit. Hanc ergo eplam
fertur apostolus ad hebreos oscriptā hebraica ligua misisse: cuius sensū et ordinē retinēs
lucas euangelista post excessum apli pauli
greco sermone composuit. Expl. argumētū.

Plate 17: The 48-line Bible, Mainz, Fust and Schoeffer workshop, 1462 (GW 4202), fol 21r.
Göttingen City and University Library.

singulas. Et singl'e porte erant ex singulis
margaritis: et platea ciuitatis aurū mūdū:
tanq̄ vitrū pluciđū. Et templū non vidi in
ea. Dn̄s enim deus omīpotens templū illius
est: et agnus. Et ciuitas non eget sole neq3
luna: ut luceant in ea. Nam claritas dei il-
luminabit eam: et lucerna eius est agnus.
Et ambulabunt gentes in lumine eius: et
reges terre afferent gloriam suam ꝛ honorem in illam. Et porte eius non claudentur
per noctem. Nox enim nō erit illic. Et afferent gloriam ꝛ honorem gentium in illam:
nec intrabit in ea aliquid coinquinatū aut
abominationem faciens et mendaciū: nisi
qui scripti sūt in libro vite agni. XXII

ET ostendit michi fluuiū aque viue.
splendidum tanq̄ cristallum: proce-
dentem de sede dei ꝛ agni. In medio platee
eius ꝛ ex vtraq3 parte fluminis lignū vite
afferens fructus duodecim: per menses sin-
gulos reddens fructum suū: et folia ligni
ad sanitatem gentiū. Et omne maledictū
non erit amplius: ꝫ sedes dei et agni in illa
erunt: et serui eius seruient illi. Et videbūt
faciem eius: et nomē eius in frontibꝫ eoꝝ.
Et nox vltra nō erit: et nō egebūt lumīe lu-
cerne neq3 lumīe solis qm̄ dn̄s deus illumīabit
illos: et regnabunt in secula seculoꝝ. Et dixit michi. Hec verba fidelissima sunt ꝛ vera.
Et dominus deus spirituū pphetaꝝ misit angelum suū: ostendere seruis suis que oportet fieri cito. Et ecce venio velociter. Beatus
qui custodit verba pphetie libri huius. Et
ego iohānes q̄ audiui et vidi hec. Et post-
q̄ audissem et vidissem cecidi ut adorarē
ante pedes angeli qui michi hec ostende-
bat. Et dixit michi: Vide ne feceris. Con-
seruus enim tuus sum ꝛ fratrum tuoꝝ pphe-
tarū: et eoꝝ qui seruant verba pphetie libri
huius. Deum adora. Et dixit michi: Ne si-
gnaueris verba pphetie libri huius. Tempus enim prope est. Qui nocet noceat adhuc: et qui in sordibꝫ est sordescat adhuc.
Et qui iustus est iustificetur adhuc: et san-
ctus sanctificetur adhuc. Ecce venio cito: et
merces mea mecum est: reddere vnicuiq3
secundum opera sua. Ego sum alpha et o:
primus et nouissimus: principium et finis.
Beati qui lauant stolas suas in sanguine a-
gni: ut sit potestas eoꝝ in ligno vite: et per
portas intrent ciuitatem. Foris autē canes
et venefici et impudici et homicide et ydolis
seruientes: et omnis qui amat et facit men-
dacium. Ego ihesus misi angelum meum te-
stificari vobis hec in ecclesijs. Ego sū radix
et genus dauid: stella splendida et matuti-
na. Et spiritus et sponsa dicunt veni. Et qui
audit: dicat veni. Et qui sitit veniat: et q̄ vult
accipiat aquā vite gratis. Contestor enim
omni audienti verba pphetie libri huius. Si
quis apposuerit ad hec: apponet deus super
illū plagas scriptas in libro isto: et si quis
diminuerit de verbis libri pphetie huius: au-
feret deus partē eius de libro vite et de ciuitate sancta: et de hijs que scripta sunt in libro isto. Dicit qui testimoniū phibet istoꝝ.
Etiam: Venio cito amen. Veni dn̄e ihesu.
Gr̄a dn̄i nr̄i ihesu cristi cū omibꝫ vobis amē.
Explicit liber apocalips beati iohānis apli.

Pn̄s hoc opusculū Artificiosa adinuētione
imprimendi seu caracterizandi: absq3 calami
exaracōn in ciuitate Moguntin sic effigiatū
ꝗ ad eusebiā dei industrie per Johēz fust ciuē
et Petrū schoiffher de gernshem clericū di-
ocesis eiusdem est consummatū. Anno dn̄i. M.
cccc.lxij. In vigilia assumpcōis virg. marie.

Plate 18: The 48-line Bible, Mainz, Fust and Schoeffer workshop, 1462, fol 239r, with the colophon of Fust and Schoeffer and their printer's mark.

Cxxviij

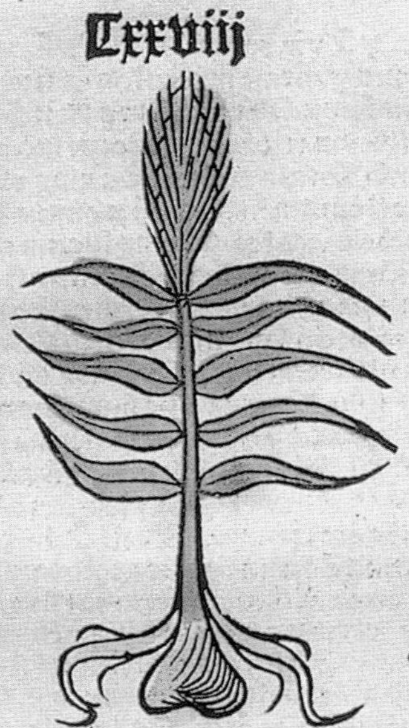

Satirion | stendelwortz

Satirion.i.testiculus vulpis est calidus et humi-
dus in primo.habet folia similia foliis lilij albi et
etiã in floribꝫ cõuenit.et qd de ipsa administrat
est radix que dulcis est. Et in humiditate eius
est inflatio supflua gratia cuius incitat ad libi-
dinem.Et vinũ decoctionis radicis eius incitat
ad libidinẽm.Et radix eius elixata cum carnibꝫ
recentibus vel assata magis conuenit ad car-
nis libidinem.Et diascorides dicit ca.orchis.i.

Plate 19: *Herbarius* (*Latin Herbal*), Mainz, Peter Schoeffer, 1484 (HC 8444).
Leipzig University Library.

Plate 20: Konrad Bote: *Chroniken der sassen* (Saxon world chronicle), Mainz, Peter Schoeffer, 1492 (GW 4963). Leipzig University Library.

Plate 21: Johann von Tepl: *Der Ackermann aus Böhmen* (*The ploughman from Bohemia*), Bamberg, Albrecht Pfister, c. 1470. From a facsimile.

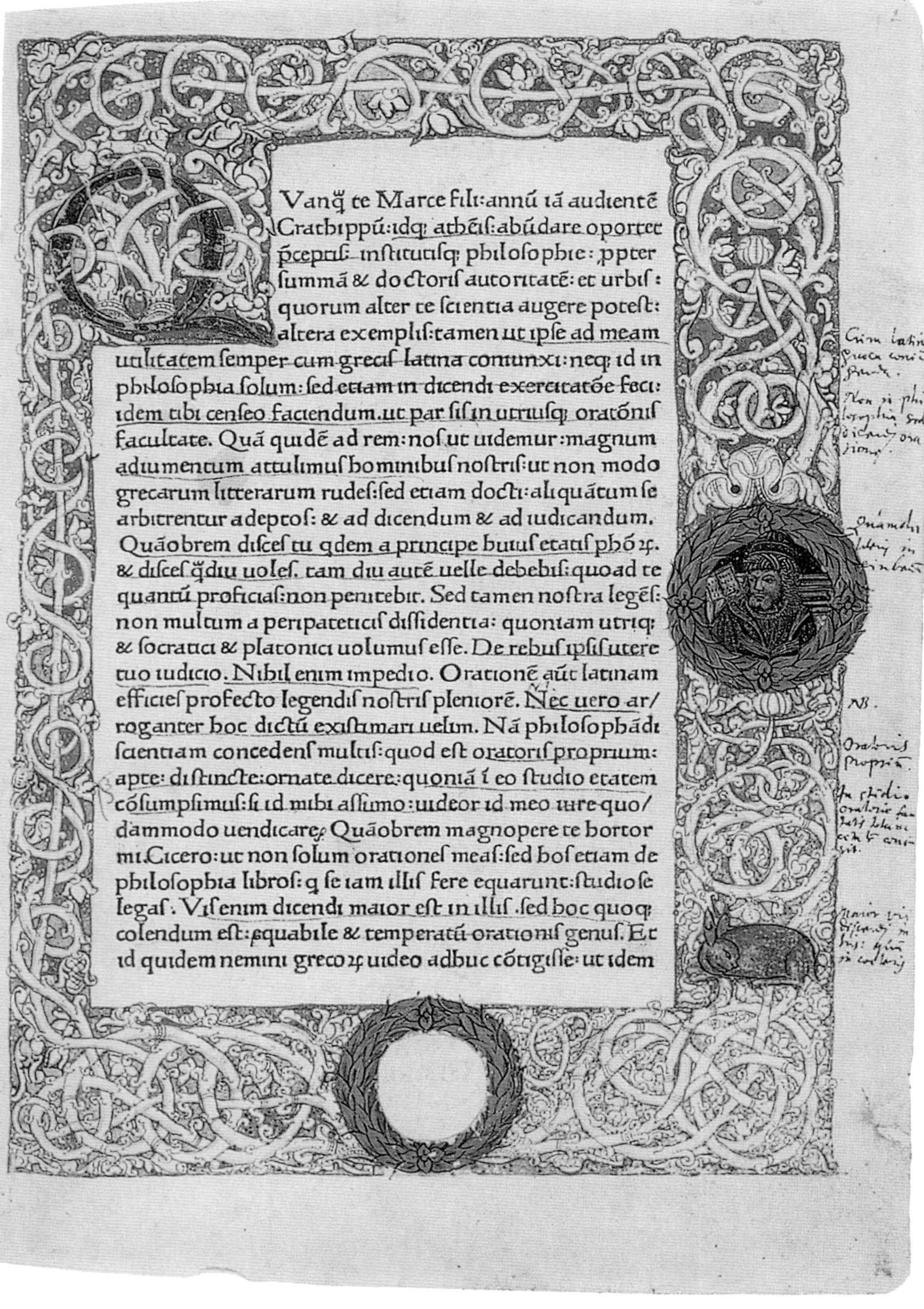

Vanq̄ te Marce fili: annū iā audientē
Cratbippū: idq; athenis: abūdare oportet
p̄ceptis institutisq; philosophie: ꝓpter
summā & doctoris autoritatē: et urbis:
quorum alter te scientia augere potest:
altera exemplis: tamen ut ipse ad meam
utilitatem semper cum grecis latina coniunxi: neq; id in
philosophia solum: sed etiam in dicendi exercitatōe feci:
idem tibi censeo faciendum, ut par sis in utriusq; oratōnis
facultate. Quā quidē ad rem: nos ut uidemur: magnum
adiumentum attulimus hominibus nostris: ut non modo
grecarum litterarum rudes: sed etiam docti: aliquātum se
arbitrentur adeptos: & ad dicendum & ad iudicandum.
Quāobrem disces tu q̄dem a principe huius etatis phōꝝ.
& disces q̄diu uoles. tam diu autē uelle debebis: quoad te
quantū proficias: non penitebit. Sed tamen nostra legēs:
non multum a peripateticis dissidentia: quoniam utriq;
& socratici & platonici uolumus esse. De rebus ipsis utere
tuo iudicio. Nihil enim impedio. Orationē aūt latinam
efficies profecto legendis nostris pleniorē. Nec uero ar/
roganter hoc dictū existimari uelim. Nā philosophādi
scientiam concedens multis: quod est oratoris proprium:
apte: distincte: ornate dicere: quoniā i eo studio etatem
cōsumpsimus: si id mihi assumo: uideor id meo iure quo/
dammodo uendicare. Quāobrem magnopere te hortor
mi Cicero: ut non solum orationes meas: sed hos etiam de
philosophia libros: q se iam illis fere equarunt: studiose
legas. Vis enim dicendi maior est in illis. sed hoc quoq;
colendum est: equabile & temperatū orationis genus. Et
id quidem nemini grecoꝝ uideo adhuc cōtigisse: ut idem

Plate 22: Cicero: De Officiis, Rome, Konrad Sweynheym and Arnold Pannartz, 1469 (GW 6924), fol 2r. Göttingen State and University Library.

2

MARCI TVLLII CICERONIS TVSCVLA-
NARVM QVAESTIONVM LIBER PRIMVS.

Vm defenſionũ laboribus: ſenatoriiſq;
muneribus aut omnino: aut magna ex
parte eſſẽ aliquãdo liberatus: rettuli me
Brute te hortante maxime ad ea ſtudia:
quæ retenta animo: remiſſa tẽporibus:
longo interuallo intermiſſa reuocaui.
Et cum omnium artium: quæ ad rectam uiuendi uiam
pertinerent: ratio & diſciplina ſtudio ſapientiæ: quæ philoſophia dicitur: contineretur: hoc mihi latius litteris
illuſtrandum putaui: non quia philoſophia græcis & lr̃is
& doctoribus percipi non poſſet: Sed meũ iudiciũ ſemper
fuit: omnia noſtros aut ĩueniſſe per ſe ſapiẽtius q̃ græcos:
aut accepta ab illis feciſſe meliora: quæ quidem digna
ſtatuiſſent: in quibus elaborarent. Nam mores & ĩſtituta
uitæ: reſq; domeſticas: ac familiares nos profecto melius
tuemur: & lautius. Rem uero publicã noſtri maiores certe
melioribus temperauerunt: & inſtitutis: & legibus. Quid
loquar de re militari? in qua cum uirtute noſtri multum
ualuerũt: tũ plus etiam diſciplina. Iã illa quæ natura non
litteris aſſecuti ſunt: neq; cum græcia: neq; ulla cũ gente
ſũt conferenda. Quæ.n. tanta grauitas: quæ tãta cõſtãtia:
magnitudo animi: probitas: fides: quæ tam excellens in
omni genere uirtus in ullis fuit: ut ſit cum maioribus
noſtris cõparanda? Doctrina græcia nos & omni litterarũ
genere ſuperabat: ĩ quo erat facile uĩcere nõ repugnãtes.
Nam cum apud græcos antiquiſſimum e doctis ſit genus
poetarum: ſiquidem Homerus fuit: & Heſiodus ante
romam conditam: Archilochus regnante Romulo: ſerius
poeticam nos accepimus. Annis fere.cccc.x. poſt romam
conditam Liuius fabulam dedit Caio Claudio Cæci filio

EX
BIBLIOTHECA
REGIA ACAD.
GEORGIÆ
AUG:

a 2

Plate 23: Cicero: *Tusculanae disputationes*, Venice, Nicolas Jenson, 1472 (GW 6890), fol 2r. Göttingen State and University Library.

POLIPHILO QVIVI NARRA, CHE GLI PARVE ANCORA DI DORMIRE, ET ALTRONDE IN SOMNO RITROVARSE IN VNA CONVALLE, LAQVALE NEL FINE ERA SERATA DE VNA MIRABILE CLAVSVRA CVM VNA PORTENTOSA PYRAMIDE, DE ADMIRATIONE DIGNA, ET VNO EXCELSO OBELISCO DE SOPRA. LAQVALE CVM DILIGENTIA ET PIACERE SVBTILMENTE LA CONSIDEROE.

LA SPAVENTEVOLE SILVA, ET CONSTIpato Nemore euaſo, & gli primi altri lochi per el dolce ſomno che ſe hauea per le feſſe & proſternate mẽbre diffuſo relicti, me ritrouai di nouo in uno piu delectabile ſito aſſai piu che el præcedente. El quale non era de monti horridi, & crepidinoſe rupe intorniato, ne falcato di ſtrumoſi iugi. Ma compoſitamente de grate montagniole di non tropo altecia. Siluoſe di giouani quercioli, di roburi, fraxini & Carpini, & di frondoſi Eſculi, & Ilice, & di teneri Coryli, & di Alni, & di Tilie, & di Opio, & de infructuoſi Oleaſtri, diſpoſiti ſecondo laſpecto de gli arboriferi Colli. Et giu al piano erano grate ſiluule di altri ſiluatici

Plate 24: Francesco Colonna: *Hypnerotomachia Poliphili*, Venice, Aldus Manutius, 1499 (GW 7223). Göttingen State and University Library.

EL TERTIO cæleſte triumpho ſeguiua cum quatro uertibile rote
di Chryſolitho æthiopico ſcintule doro flammigiante, Traiecta per el-
quale la ſeta del Aſello gli maligni dæmonii fuga, Alla leua mano gra-
to, cum tutto quello cħ di ſopra di rote e dicto. Dapoſcia le aſſule ſue in
ambito per el modo compacte ſopra narrato, erano di uirente Helitro-
pia Cyprico, cum potere negli lumi cæleſti, el ſuo geſtãte cœla, & il diui-
nare dona, di ſanguinee guttule punctulato.

Offeriua tale hiſtoriato inſculpto la tabella dextra. Vno homo di regia maieſtate iſigne, Oraua in uno ſacro templo el diuo ſimulacro, quel
lo che della formoſiſſima fiola deueua ſeguire. Sentendo el patre la eie-
ctione ſua per ella del regno. Et ne per alcuno fuſſe pregna, Fece
una munita ſtructura di una excelſa torre, Et in quella cum
ſolẽne cuſtodia la fece inclauſtrare. Nella quale ella ceſſabonda aſſedẽdo, cum ex-
ceſſiuo ſolatio, nel uirgi
neo ſino gutte do
ro ſtillare
uede
ua.

*

Plate 25: Francesco Colonna: *Hypnerotomachia Poliphili, liber secundus.*

Sedechias was the first Philosophir by whom
thorugh the wil and pleaser of oure lorde god
Sapience was understande and lawes resceyv-
ued. whiche Sedechias saide. that every creature of good beleue ought to haue in hym sixtene vertues
¶ The first vertue is to drede and knowe god and his 1
angellys ¶ The seconde vertue is to haue discrecion to dis 2
cerne the good from the badde and to vse vertu and fle
vices ¶ The thirde vertue is to obeye the kynges or princes 3
that god hath ordeyned to reygne vpon hym and that
haue lordship and power vpon the people ¶ The fourthe. 4
vertue is to worship hys fadre & hys modre ¶ The fyfthe 5
vertue is to do. Justely and truely to every creature aftir
his possibilite ¶ The sixte vertue is to distribute his al- 6
mes to the pore people. ¶ The seuenthe vertue is to kepe 7
and defende straungers and pilgrymes ¶ The eyght ver 8
tue is to bynde and determine him self to serue our lorde
god ¶ The nynthe vertue is to eschewe fornicacion ¶ The 9 10
tenthe vertue is to haue paciencè ¶ The enleuenth vertue 11
is to be stedefast and true ¶ The twelfthe vertue is to 12
be peasible and attemperate and shamfast of synne ¶ The 13
thertenthe vertue is to loue Justice ¶ The fourtenthe ver- 14
tue is to be liberal and not couetous ¶ The fyftenthe ver- 15
tue is to offre sacrifices to our lord god almyghty for the
benefices and gracis that he sheweth hym dayly ¶ The 16
sixtenthe vertue is to worship god almyghty and to put
hym holy in his protection and defence for resistence of the
in fortunitees that dayly falles in thys worlde ¶ The saide
Sedechias saide that right as it apparteineth to the people

EX BIBLIOTHECA REGIA ACAD. GEORGIÆ AUG:

Plate 26: The Dictes and Sayengs of the Philosophers, Westminster, William Caxton, second edition 1479 (GW 8322). Göttingen State and University Library.

¶Marci. T. C. de natura deorum ad. M. Brutum liber primus.

QVum multæ res ĩ philoſophia nequaq̃ ſatis adhuc explicatæ ſint:
tũ pdifficilis Brute quod tu minime ignoras: & perobſcura quæ-
ſtio eſt de natura deorũ: quæ ad agnitionẽ animi pulcherrima eſt:
& ad moderandã religionẽ neceſſaria. De qua tam uariæ ſunt do-
ctiſſimorũ hominum tamq; diſcrepãtes ſentẽtiæ: ut magno argu
mento eſſe debeat: cauſam ideſt principiũ philoſophiæ eſſe ſcien-
tiam: prudẽterq; Academicos a rebus incertis aſſenſionem cohi
buiſſe. Quid enim temeritate fortius? aut quid tã temerariũ: tamq; idignũ ſapiẽtis gra
uitate atq; cõſtantia: q̃ aut falſum ſentire: aut quod nõ ſatis explorate pceptum ſit & co-
gnitũ: ſine ulla dubitatione defendere. Velut in hac quæſtione pleriq; quod maxĩe ueri
ſimile eſt: & quo omnes duce natura uehimur: deos eſſe dixerũt. Dubitare ſe pithagoras
nullos eſſe omnino. Diagoras melius: & Theodorus Cyrenaicus putauerũt. Qui uero
deos eſſe dixerũt tanta ſunt in uarietate: ac diſſenſione cõſtituti: ut eorũ moleſtum ſit an
numerare ſententias. Nã & de figuris deorũ & de locis atq; ſedibus & actiõe uita multa
dicũtur: deq; his ſũma philoſophorum diſſenſione certatur. Quod uero maxime cauſã
rem q; cõtinet eſt: utrũ nihil agant: nihil moliantur: an ab omni curatione & adminiſtra-
tione rerum uacent: an contra ab his & a principio omnia facta & conſtituta ſint: & ad in
finitũ tẽpus regnantur: atq; moueãtur. Imprimiſq; magna diſſenſio eſt: eaq; niſi diiudi-
catur: in ſũmo errore neceſſe eſt homines atq; in maximarũ rerũ ignoratõne uerſari. Sũt
enim philoſophi & fuerũt: qui omnino nullã habere cẽſerent rerũ humanarũ pcuratio-
nem deos: quorũ ſi uera ſententia eſt: quæ poteſt eſſe pietas quæ ſanctitas? quæ religio?
Hæc enim omnia pure ac caſte tribuenda deorũ numina ita ſunt: ſi animaduertantur ab
his: & ſi eſt aliquid a diis immortalibus hominũ generi tributũ. Sin aũt dii neq; poſſunt
iuuare: nec uolũt: nec omnino curant: nec quid agamus aĩaduertunt: nec eſt quod ab his
ad hominũ uitã permanere poſſit: quid eſt quod ullos deis immortalibus cultus: hono-
res: preces adhibeamus? In ſpecie autẽ fictæ ſimulationis ſicut reliquæ uirtutes: ita pietas ineſſe nõ poteſt: cũ qua ſimul & ſanctitatem & religionẽ tolli neceſſe eſt: quibus ſub
latis pturbatio uitæ ſequitur & magna cõfuſio. Atq; haud ſcio an pietate aduerſus deos
ſublata fides etiã & ſocietas generis humani & una excellẽtiſſima uirtus iuſtitia tollat.
Sunt autẽ alii philoſophi: & hi quidẽ magni atq; nobiles: qui deorum mẽte atq; ratione
omnem mundũ adminiſtrari & regi cenſeant: neq; uero id ſolũ ſed etiã ab eiſdẽ uitæ hominum conſuli & puideri. Nam & fruges & reliqua quæ terra pariat: & tempeſtates ac
temporũ uarietates cæliq; mutationes: quibus omnia quæ terra gignat: maturata pube
ſcentia diis immortalibus tribui generi humano putãt: multaq; quæ dicent in his libris
colligũt: quæ talia ſunt: ut ea ipſa dii immortales ad uſum hominũ fabricare pene uideã
tur. Contra quos Carneades ita multa diſſeruit: ut excitaret homines nõ ſocordes ad ue
ri inueſtigandi cupiditatẽ. Res enim nulla eſt: de qua tantopere nõ ſolum docti ſed etiã
indocti diſſentiant: quorũ opiniones quũ tam uariæ ſint: tanq̃ inter ſe diſſidentes: alterũ
pfecto fieri poteſt ut earũ nulla alterũ certæ non poteſt: ut plus una uera ſit. Qua quidem in cauſa & beniuolos obiurgatores placare: & inuidos uituperatores confutare poſ
ſumus: ut alteros repræhẽdiſſe pæniteat: alteri ſed didiciſſe gaudeant. Nam qui admo-
nent amice docendi ſunt: qui inimice inſectantur repellẽdi. Multum autem fluxiſſe ui-

a

EX BIBLIOTHECA REGIA ACAD. GEORGIÆ AUG:

Plate 27: Cicero: de Natura deorum, Venice, Philippus Pincius, 1494 (GW 6904), fol 1r. Göttingen State and University Library.

Plate 28: *Terence: Comoediae, Strasbourg, Johann Grüninger, 1496 (HC 15431), fol 1r. Göttingen State and University Library.*

MENEDEMVS. CHREMES.
SOSTRATA. CLITIPHO.

ENimuero Chremes nimis grauiter cruciat adolescentulũ: nimisq; inhumane: exeo ergo vt pacem conciliem. optime ipsos video. CHRE. Ehem menedeme. cur nõ accersi iubes filiam: & q̃d dotis dixi firmas? Sostr. Mi vir obsecro te ne facias. CLI. Pater obsecro vt mihi ignoscas. MENE. Da veniam chreme. sin te exorem CHRE. Egone mea bona vt dem Bachidi dono sciens? non faciã. ME. At id nos nõ sinemus. CLITI. Si me viuũ vis pater ignosce. Sost. Age chremes. MENE. Age queso ne tam obfirma te chremes. CHRE. Quid istuc? video nõ licere mihi: vt coeperam: hoc pertendere. MENE. Facis vt te decet. CHRE. ea lege hoc adeo faciam: si id faciat: quod ego hunc æquum censeo. CLI. Pater omnia faciam. impera. CHRE. Vxorem vt ducas. CLITI. Pater. CHRE. Nihil audio. ME. Ad me recipio: faciet. CHRE. Nihil etiã audio ipsum. CLI. Perij. SOSTRA. An dubitas Clitipho? CHRE. Immo vtrũ vult. MENE. Faciet omĩa. SOST.

In hac scena. XXII.

Interuenit persona cuius gratia pax concilietur ita vt omnia tranquilla sint. & composita prout comedie finis postulat.

a Enimuero. Hoc loquitur Menedemus solus apud se. Enimuero nonnunq̃ principium est aliquid per iram dicturi. b Hem. Interiectio percipientis eum quem volebat. c Accersi. Bene accersi quia proprie accersitur vxor dũ ad virũ ducitur. d Mi vir, te. Putat sostrata id quod erat fictum esse verum timebatq; ne pater penitus exhereditaret filium omnia tribuens filie. e Obsecro. Nil significantius. Nam orare ẽ placidos petere. Obsecrare vero iratos rogare. f Ne facias. Hec timebat ne omnia bona illi traderet. g Sciens. Quod peius esset q̃ si nesciret h Age. Vt sit aduerbium hortantis. q.d. age ignosce ei i Ne tam obfirma te. Id est noli te tam obstinatum ostẽdere. Ille enim dicitur se affirmare in aliquo proposito qui obstinate ac pertinaciter in illo perseuerat tanq̃ immobilis truncus. & est translatio sumpta a repagulo, offirmando. k Pater. Tantum dicit hoc verbum non statim volens dare responsum tanq̃ prius deliberatur l Ad me recipio. Hoc dicendi genere sæpius. Cicero vtitur in suis epistolis. & precipue commẽdaticiis vt cerne facile est nemo enim negat recipere interdum sumi pro promittere.

Plate 29: Terence: Comoediae, Strasbourg, Johann Grüninger, fol 85r.

Arma : Multi uarie dixerunt cur ab armis Virgilius coeperit : omnes tamen in hanc sententiam as
sentire manifestum est : quum eum constet aliunde sumpsisse principium : sicut in pręmissa eius
uita monstratum est . Per arma autem bellum significat : et est tropus metonymia. Nam arma qui
bus in bello utimur pro bello posuit : sicut toga qua in pace utimur : pro pace ponitur : Vt Cicero:
Cedant arma togę : idest bellum paci . Arma uirumque: figura usitata est : ut non eo ordine respõ
deamus : quo proposuimus : nam prius de erroribus Aeneę dixit : post de bello. hac autem figura etiam
in prosa utimur . Sic Cicero in uer
rinis : Nam sine ullo sumptu no
stro coriis tunicis frumentoque sup
peditato maximos exercitus nostros
uestiuit: aluit: armauit . Virum
quem non dicit : sed ex circunstan
tiis ostẽdit Aeneam . Cano : po
lysemus sermo est Tria enim signi
ficat : aliquando laudo : ut Regem
que canebant . Aliquando diuino :
ut Ipsa canas oro . Aliquando can
to : ut hoc loco . Nam proprie can
to significat : quia cantanda sunt
carmina . Troię : Troia regio ẽ
asię : Ilium ciuitas est Troię . Plerũ
que tamen usurpant poetę . et pro ci
uitate uel regionẽ uel prouinciam po
nunt . Iuuenalis : Et flammis asiã
ferroque cadentem . Qui prius:

ARMA : VIRVMQVE
CANO : TROIAE
QVI PRIMVS
AB ORIS
Italiam fato profugus lauinaque uenit
Littora : multũ ille et terris iactatus et alto

Quęrunt multi cur Aeneam primum ad italiam uenisse dixerit : cum paulo post dicat Antenorem an
te aduentum Aeneę fundasse ciuitatem . Constat quidem : sed habita temporum ratione perite Virgi
lius dicit . Namque illo tempore quo Aeneas ad Italiam uenit finis erat italię usque ad Rubiconem
fluuim : Cuius rei meminit Lucanus : ut Et gallica certus Limes ab ausoniis disterminat arua colonis
Vnde apparet Antenorem non ad Italiam uenisse : sed ad Galliam cisalpinam : in qua Venetia est.
Postea uero promotis usque ad alpes Italię finibus nouitas creauit errorem . Plerique tamen quęstionẽ
hanc uolunt ex sequentibus solui : ut uideatur ob hoc addidisse Virgilius ad lauina littora : ut non
significaret Antenorem . Melior tamen est superior expositio . Italiam : Ars quidem hoc exigit :
ut nominibus prouinciarum prępositionem addamus : ciuitatum nunquam : Tamen plerunque peruer
so ordine lectum est . Nam ecce hoc loco detraxit prouincię pręposttionem dicens : Italiam fato uenit:
pro ad italiam uenit . Tulius in uerrinis : Ea die Veres ad messanam uenit. Sane sciendum est usur
pari ab auctoribus : ut uel addant : uel detrahant pręposttiones . Nanque ait Virgilius : Siluis te tyr
rhene feras : pro in siluis . Vt ergo illic detraxit loco pręposttionem : sic hic prouincię : et est figura.
Italia autem pars Europę est . Italus enim rex siculorum profectus de Sicilia uenit ad loca quę st
iuxta tyberim : et ex nomine suo appellauit Italiam . Ibi autem habitasse siculos : ubi Laurolauini
um est: manifestum est : Sicut ipse alio loco dicit : Siculi ueteresque sicani . Item Et gentes uenere sica
nę. Fato profugus : Fatum ad utrunque pertinet : et ꝙ fugit : et ꝙ ad Italiam uenit . et bene addi
dit fato : ne uideatur aut causa criminis patriam deseruisse : aut noui imperii cupiditate. Profugus
autem proprie dicitur qui procul a sedibus suis uagatur : quasi porro fugatus . Multi tamen ita diffini
unt : ut profugos esse dicant eos : qui exclusi necessitate de suis sedibus adhuc uagantur et simulac in
uenerint sedes non dicantur profugi : sed exules . Sed utrunque falsum est : Nam et profugus lectus est :
qui iam sedes locauit : Vt in Lucano : Profugique a gente uetusta Gallorum celtę miscentes nomen
iberis : et exules qui adhuc uagantur : Vt in Salustio : qui nullo certo exilio uagabantur : adeo exili
um est ipsa uagatio . Lauinaque uenit littora : hęc ciuitas tria habuit nomina . Nam prius Laui
num dicta est a Lauino Latini fratre . Postea Laurentum a lauro inuenta a Latino : dum adepto im
perio post fratris mortem ciuitatem augeret . Postea Lauinium a Lauinia uxore Aeneę . Ergo Lauina
legendum est ; non Lauinia . quia post aduentum Aeneę Lauinium nomen accepit . Ergo aut Laui
num debuit dicere : sicut dixit : aut Laurentum : quamuis quidam superflue esse prolepsim uelint: Lit
tora : Laurolauinium constat . viii . miliaribus amari remotum . Nec nos debet fallere quia dixit lauia
littora . Littus enim dicitur terra queq; mari uicina: sicut ipse Virgilius in quarto: Cui littus arandũ : quũ
per naturam littus arari non possit. Ergo sciendum est littus uocari et terram. Multum ille: collisio est .
et ille hoc loco abundat. Est enim interposita particula propter metri necessitatem: ut stet uersus nam si de
trahas ille stat sensus. qui primus enim ad omnia possumus trahere: sic alio loco: Nunc dextra ingeminãs
ictus : nunc ille sinistra. Est autem archaismos. Et terris iactatus: fatigatus est enim apud thraciã mon
stro illo: quod e tumulo Polydori sanguis emanauit: apud cretam pestilentia: apud strophadas insulas har
pyiis . Tempestate uero et in primo: et in tertio : et proprie locutus: nam iactamur in mari fluctibus: fatiga
mur in terris . et bene duorum elementorum mala uno sermone conclusit . Et alto: modo mari. Altum
tamen sciendum est ꝙ et superiorem ; et inferiorem altitudinem significat. Nãq; mensure nomẽ altitudo .

Plate 30: Virgil: Opera, with the commentary of Servius, Venice, Antonio Miscomini, misdated 1486 for 1476 (Copinger 6044).

V i superum: seuæ memorem iunonis ob iram:
M ulta quoque et bello passus dũ cõderet urbẽ:
I nferetque deos latio: genus unde latinum
A lbanique patres atque altæ mœnia romæ
M usa mihi causas memora quo numine læso

Vi superum: uiolentia deorum secundum Homerum qui dicit a Iunone rogatos esse deos in odium troianorum: quod et Virgilius tetigit dicens: Vos quoq; pergameę iã fas ẽ parcere genti Diiq;: Deęq; omnes. Latenter autem defendit hac ratione troianos ꝙ non suo merito eos insequebantur numina: sed Iunõis impulsu. Sęuę: Cum a iuuando dicta sit Iuno: quęrunt multi cur eam dixerit sęuã. et putant temporale esse epithethon quasi sęuam contra troianos: nescientes ꝙ sęuam dicebant ueteres magnam: ut Ennius: Inducta fuit sęua stola: scilicet magna: Item Virgilius quum ubiq; pium inducat Aeneam ait Maternis sęuus in armis Aeneas: idest magnus. Memorem Iunonis ob iram: constat multa in auctoribus inueniri per contrarium significantia: pro actiuis passiua: ut Pictis bellãtur amazones armis pro passiuis actiua: ut Populatq; ingentem farris aceruum. Et hęc uarietas uel potius cõtrarietas inuenitur etiam in aliis partibus orationis: ut sit pronomen pro aduerbio: ut ẽ hoc tũc ignipotẽs cęlo descẽdit ab alto: pro huc. Et i pricipio ut Et qua uectus abas: pro uehebatur et i nomine: ut Memorem Iunonis ob iram: Non quę meminerat: sed quę in memoria erat: nam ira non meminit. De his autem hęc tantum quę lecta sunt ponimus: nec ad eorũ exẽplum alia formamus. Multa quoq; et bello passus: duas coniunctiones sęparatas naturaliter nemo coniungit. Sed hoc plerumq; a poetis causa metri fit: ergo hic una uacat. Sicut alio loco: Dixitq; et pręlia uoce diremit. Bello passus: quod contra Turnum gessit. Dum conderet urbem: Tres hic sunt significationes. Aut enim Troiã dicit: quam ut primum uenit in Italiã fecit Aeneas: de qua ait: Castrorum in morem pinnis atq; aggere cingit. et alio loco Mercurius: Nec te troia capit. Troiam autem dicit: quam primum fecit Aeneas. Et Liuius in primo et Cato in originibus testãtur: Dum enim hęc fieret ab agrestibus ob uulneratum regium ceruum commota sunt bella: Aut laurolauinium. et significat dum donec. tam diu enim dimicauit quã diu tempus faciendę ciuitatis ueniret: idest donec Turnus ocumberet: Aut romam significat. et ẽ sensus dummodo ergo conderet urbem: aut troiam: aut Laurolauinium: aut Romam significat. Inferretq; deos latio: latium duplex est: unum a tyberi usq; ad fundos: Aliud inde usq; ad uulturnum: Latium autem dictum est ꝙ illic Saturnus latuerit. Inferretque deos latio: hoc est latium. et est usitata figura apud Virgilium. Quod enim cum pręposítione per accusatiuum dicimus: ille per datiuum ponit sine pręposítione. sic alibi: It clamor cęlo pro ad cęlum. Genus unde latinum: Si iam fuerunt latini: et latium dicebatur: contrarium est quod dicit ab Aenea latinos originem ducere. prima est iocunda absolutio: ut unde non referas ad personã sed ad locum: Nãq; unde aduerbiũ ẽ de loco: nõ deducto ad persona. Tamen Cato in originibus dicit hoc: cuius autoritatem Salustius imitatur i bello Catilinę: primo Italiam tenuisse quosdã qui appellabãtur aborigines: hos postea aduentu Aeneę phrygibus iunctos latinos uno noie nũcupatos. Ergo descẽdũt latini nõ tãtum troianis: sed etiã ab originibus. Est autem uera expositio hęc: nouimus ꝙ uicti uictorum nomẽ accipiũt: potuit Ergo uictore Aenea perire nomẽ latinum. Sed uolẽs sibi fauorẽ latii cõciliare nomẽ latium nõ solum illis nõ sustulit: Sed etiam troianis imposuit. Merito ergo illi tribuit quod i ipo fuerat ut posset perire: Vnde et ipe iducit i .xii: libro rogãtẽ Iunonem ne pereat nomẽ latinũ. itẽ iexacratõe Didõis legimus Nec cũ se sub leges pacis iiquę Tradiderit. Iniqua eis pax ẽ i qua nomẽ amittit ille qui uicit. Albãiq; pẽes: Albã ab Ascanio cõditam fuisse cõstat: sed a quo icertum utrũ a Creusę an a lauinię filio: de qua re etiam Liuius dubitat. Hãc ãt quũ euertisset Tullus Hostilius: omẽs nobiles familias romã trãstulit. Et sciẽdum bene hũc ordiem sẽper seruare Virgiliũ: ut ãte dicat latiũ: de ide albã: post romã: Quod et i hoc loco fecit: et i .v. libro: Priscos docuit celebrare latinos: Albani docuere suos: nũc maxima porro Accepit roma: et patriũ seruauit hõrem. Itẽ i. vii. libro: Mos erat hespio i latio quẽ protius urbes Albanę coluere sacrũ: nũc maxia rerũ Roma colit. Altę męnia romę: aut propter gloriam: aut propter ędificia: aut quia in mõtibus collocata ẽ. Musa mihi cãs memora: Poetę i tres ptes diuidũt carmẽ suũ: proponũt: iuocãt: narrãt. plerũq; tamẽ duas res faciũt: et ipas propositões miscẽt iuocatõi: qđ i utroq; ope Hõerus fecit: Nãq; hoc melius ẽ. Lucãus tamẽ ipus ordinẽ uertit. prio eis proposuit: deide narrauit: postea iuocauit: ut ẽ Nec si te pectoꝛ uates accipiã. Sãc obseruãdũ ẽ i oibs carmibs ne numẽ aliqđ iuocetur: nisi aliquid ultra hũanã possibilitatẽ requirimus: hic i arte poetica Hor: Nec deus itersit nisi dignus iudice nodus Inciderit. Bẽe ergo iuocat Vir: nõ eis poterat ꝑ se irã nuis nosse. Itẽ i. viiii. libro nisi addret Iũo uires aiusq; mistrat: quis crederet Turnũ euasisse d castris? Quo nuie lęso quo i quo i qua cã. et ẽ. vii. casus: et cõis elocutõ. dicius. n. quo te lęsi ẽ et alia expositõ: nãq; Iũo multa hẽt nuia ẽ Curretis ꝗ utitur curru: et hasta: ut ẽ hic illius arma Hic currus fuit: ẽ Lucia ꝗ partubus ꝑest: ut Iũo Lucia fer opẽ. ẽ regia: ut Quę diuũ icedo regia. Sũt et alia eius nuia. Merito ergo dubitat qđ numẽ eius lęserit. Alii tamẽ dicũt separãdũ ẽẽ: ut de odio Iũonis nõ dubitet: quęrat ãt qđ aliud numẽ ẽ lesũ. Quo nuie lęso: ideo trahitur i ãbiguitatẽ: et requirit i quo Iunonis numen lęsit Aeneas: quia in ipsum certa non erant odia sed igentem propter causas paulo post dicendas.

·g·

Fols 60v/61r (opening of the Aeneid). Göttingen State and University Library.

Plate 31: Virgil: *Opera*, edited by Sebastian Brant, Strasbourg, Johann Grüninger, 1502. Wolfenbüttel, Herzog August Library.

German humanism came about through direct encounter with the Italian humanism of the mid-fifteenth century in various places, at courts and government offices, schools and universities. It appealed to rank-conscious nobility, patricians and persons of lower birth for whom education opened the path of advancement. At first it was taken up by the secular intelligentsia, but then found a response in so-called "monastic humanism" and in the renewal of Christian training (especially in the Upper Rhineland).

The frequently cited "early humanism" of around 1400 at the Prague court of Charles IV influenced art and architecture, but initially it had little literary resonance. The reception of its most important literary document, the *Ackermann aus Böhmen* (1400) by Johann von Tepl (c. 1350–1415), a disputation between the ploughman of the title and Death, only really began seventy years later with its appearance in print: it came out as one of the first books in the vernacular, with woodcuts illustrating key scenes printed together with Albrecht Pfister's text in Bamberg in about 1470, and was followed by 16 further reprintings in rapid succession in Bamberg, Strasbourg, Basle, Augsburg and Heidelberg. In 32 conversational exchanges, Johann von Tepl keeps before our eyes man's rebellion against the inevitable fate of death; the elements of medieval dialectics are retained throughout the debate, but humanistic overtones are present in a new evaluation of the relationship of man to his creator. This many-faceted text from a transitional period is of fundamental importance for the development of prose style in the German language. Its wide reception in printed form shows its popularly instructive character for a lay readership and its use as edifying monastic reading matter as well.

Just as Rudolf Agricola (1444–85), Conrad Celtis or Peter Luder (1415–72) were moulded through their personal experiences of Italy into protagonists of humanist ideas and neo-Latin literature – which they spread within the "sodalities" they founded in German lands – so the earliest representatives of humanistic literature in the vernacular became confirmed in their approach through personal contacts with Italian humanists. Two scholars who propagated humanistic ideas in German – each in his specific way – in the second half of the fifteenth century, were the Ulm doctor and writer Heinrich Steinhöwel (1411–79) and the Chancellor to Count Ulrich of Württemberg, Niclas von Wyle (1415–79). As contemporaries, they became the first major literary translators at work in the German-language area. Steinhöwel methodically brought out all his works in print from 1471 with Günther Zainer in Augsburg, and from 1475 onwards with that printer's brother Johann in Ulm. Steinhöwel's Latin and German *Aesop* (1476) from Zainer in Ulm (see Plate 44) has as an appendage the short story *Guiscardus und Sigismunda* translated at second hand by Niclas von Wyle from a translation into Latin by Leonardo Bruni (1369–1444) from the Italian of the *Decameron* by Giovanni Boccaccio (1313–75).

With the publication of his *Translationen oder Tütschungen* in Esslingen in 1478, Niclas von Wyle turned to the literary public with new humanistic role models: the prince qualified through learning and the noble lady who was also his equal in erudition took centre stage in his translations. Niclas von Wyle's close personal relationship and correspondence with Enea Silvio Piccolomini during the latter's occupation in the service of Frederick III in Vienna (before he was elected to the papacy as Pius II in 1458) was to prove formative for him. Piccolomini's letters and discourses were regarded by his contemporaries as examples of style just as much as for the intellectual stimulation and analysis of Italian Renaissance humanism they provided. Niclas von Wyle was bilingual like all the scholars of his age, although he used Latin only in his letters: one can best describe him as a propagator of the fund of humanist ideas in the German language. He laboured over his principal work, the *Translatzen*, between 1461 and 1478; it consists of a collection of eighteen different tales by the Italian humanist writers Poggio (Giovanni Bracciolini), Enea Silvio Piccolomini, Leonardo Bruni, Francesco Petrarch, Nicolosia Sanuda, Gasparino Barzizza and Buonaccorsa da Montemagno. These tales had circulated widely in manuscript, but thanks to their translation and issue as single printed texts they came into great demand as reading matter. The translator did his best to make German correspond to the stylistic ideals of Latin and to imitate his Latin copy as exactly as possible. The resultant German conformed so closely to Latin syntax and word order that it could only be understood by those educated in Latin. Some of the translations contain a special humanistic agenda, especially the tenth *Translatze*, a treatise on upbringing, which Eneo Silvio Piccolomini had composed in 1443 for the 16-year-old Duke Sigmund of the Tyrol. On his own part, Niclas von Wyle dedicated this exhortatory letter and mirror for princes to Margrave Karl of Baden, and recommended it for bringing up his three sons. They should address themselves to studying the classics, and make positive use of the theoretical and practical wisdom they conveyed.

The sixteenth *Translatze* is a panegyric on women, whose virtues and wisdom he praises, and in doing so adopts the examples of the wisest, most learned and cultivated women given by his author Nicolosia Sanuda, and nominates as his own example of a remarkable contemporary woman the Countess Palatine Mechthild.

In his documented collaboration with the printers Günther and Johann Zainer in Augsburg and Ulm respectively from 1471 onwards, the Ulm city physician Heinrich Steinhöwel planned the publication of his translations in a more organised way than Niclas von Wyle had done. Steinhöwel had urged Johann Zainer to set up a press in Ulm and supported him financially for life whilst at the same time retaining a say in his publishing programme. Among his most successful translations is the tale *Griseldis* from Boccaccio's *Decamerone*; Steinhöwel knew it from a Latin reworking by Francesco Petrarch under the blunt title *De oboedientia et fide uxoris* (1373). This widely circulated tale tells of a poor man's daughter who is married by a prince who subjects her to almost unendurable trials. Steinhöwel's very free translation was printed in 1471 by Günther Zainer in Augsburg (H 12817) and twice reprinted in that same year; an illustrated edition came from Johann Zainer in Ulm in 1473, followed by a further ten new editions by 1500.

Steinhöwel's most extensive publication was a Latin-German edition of the late-classical Aesop's *Fables* which he brought out as a richly illustrated folio with Johann Zainer in 1476 (GW 351; see Plate 44). This composite volume contained Aesop as handed down through the Middle Ages, enriched from a newer fable collection by Rinuccio da Castiglione issued from Milan in 1471 and some of Poggio's *Facetiae*. Steinhöwel alternates these Latin texts with his own free prose renderings in German. This bilingual edition is decorated with over two hundred woodcuts which make it a particularly fine example of the reception of late classical and humanistic fables in print (see Plates 42–4).

A third early humanist calls for mention, who, besides translating into the vernacular, engaged in the the gathering and restoration of classical Latin poetry and instructional writings: Albrecht von Eyb (1420–75). The intellectual cast of mind of this Eichstätt canon had been formed during a 14-year stay in Italy, where he had become acquainted with the *studia humanitatis*. By 1459 he had compiled a floreligium of rhetorical, poetical and historical writings which Johann Sensenschmidt of Nuremberg first printed in 1472 under the title *Margarita poetica*. He intended this anthology as a book of samples of classical rhetoric, letter-writing and poetry. The lengthy extracts from the works of Virgil, Juvenal, Ovid, Statius, Prudentius as well as Cicero, Valerius Maximus and Apuleius and the newer Italian humanists Petrarch and Poggio pursued the twin aims of making rhetoric native to Germany and so improving its use there, whilst encouraging the wisdom implicit in these texts to be applied in relevant areas of life, thereby contributing to an intellectual renewal. Albrecht von Eyb's compilation has its own specific character and a particular linguistic and philosophical cast that merits closer analysis: but no doubt his contemporaries for the most part regarded it as a straightforward anthology of extracts from classical and humanistic texts not yet available complete in individual editions. The *Margarita* went through at least fifteen editions between 1472 and 1503. In his epilogue, Albrecht von Eyb explained the need to be familar with classical poetry, for only he with such knowledge possessed "the education worthy of a free man".

The *Ehebüchlein*, or "Little Marriage Book" – to take a single example from von Eyb's tracts in German which display his erudition and familiarity with classical, medieval and humanist writers – was issued in 1472 by Anton Koberger in Nuremberg under the explicit title *Ob einem Manne sey zu nehmen ein eheliches Weib oder nicht* (whether a man should marry or not). Apart from the theological context, he stresses the importance of marriage for society and the well-being of the partners. In parallel to this re-evaluation of marriage, the status of women and their cultural significance is seen from a fresh angle with reference to important women in history.

Albrecht von Eyb's translations are distinguished from those of Niclas von Wyle by their livelier prose and a freer handling. He does not translate from Latin slavishly, but "according to the sense and meaning of the material". Albrecht von Eyb belongs accordingly not only to the mediators of classical literature and culture from the Latin, but also to the early creators of literary German.

PRINTING IN GREEK AND HEBREW

Greek texts were only rarely printed in their entirety during the incunabula period, and at first only Greek grammars and dictionaries were typeset in that language (GW 7812–18). The first edition of Homer in Greek appeared in Florence in 1488 (H 8772). This picture changes only after 1495, when Aldus Manutius began to print with Greek types in Venice: by 1498 we find him with Theocritus and Hesiod and nine comedies by Aristophanes in his programme. Prior to this, most Greek authors were known only in Renaissance Latin translation, and this applies to Herodotus and Thucydides or Plutarch (1470, H 13125). The *Iliad*, for example, had been twice printed in Lorenzo Valla's translation. In 1495 Aldus was ready – in his initial year as publisher – with the first in a five-volume edition of Aristotle (GW 2334; see Plate 36), and in the following ten years he brought out Thucydides, Herodotus, Sophocles, Euripedes, Demosthenes and Plutarch's *Moralia*. He had his own Greek types cut for this purpose in close imitation of fine calligraphic models. Aldus had to close down his printing office between 1509 and 1512 on account of the war against Venice by the League of Cambrai; but in the final three years of his life to 1515 he published Pindar, Plato, Hesychius, Athenaeus and the Attic orators.

Through establishing the "New Academy", a learned society for Greek studies in 1500 in Venice, attracting the best Greek scholars, and making a critical selection of the most suitable texts, Aldus contributed significantly to the textual history of the ancient Greeks. His "head readers" were the Cretans Markos Musurus (Professor of Greek at the

University of the Venetian State in Padua) and Johann Gregoropulos. A great many manuscripts which served Aldus as printer's copy are preserved in the Bibliothèque Nationale in Paris and in the Library of Beatus Rhenanus in Sélestat, and these, taken together with the printed books, are important testimony in the history of text transmission.

There were a number of universities in Italy where Greek studies had been possible since the mid-fifteenth century, including Florence, Rome, Bologna, Ferrara, Pavia and Padua. In addition to that, Greek was also taught at Latin schools in Italy. But the situation was altogether different in German-speaking lands, where reservations concerning the Greek language (and the intellectual outlook associated with it) were manifold. As late as 1521, a monk had cautioned from the pulpit that one should beware this newfangled tongue known as Greek as it was the mother of all heresies, that at that very time a book in that language, calling itself the New Testament, was to be found in many hands, and that this was full of thorns and snakes!

This warning concerned the *Novum Testamentum Graece* of Erasmus of Rotterdam, which had been published by Johann Froben in Basle in the spring of 1516 in two folio volumes, containing the original Greek text with its Latin translation and surrounding commentary. Four further printings of this important edition, which was to form the basis for Luther's *Bible* translation, appeared in 1519, 1522, 1527 and 1535, each time with textual changes and additional notes. In a preamble, Erasmus explained his hermeneutical principles and his future intention of making the *Bible* accessible to ordinary people in the vernacular. This Greek New Testament was the first integral Greek printing in German-speaking lands. In 1515 the first chair in classical Greek was established at Leipzig University. Up until then, interested humanists had had to choose either between an education in Italy or private studies with a scholar such as Conrad Celtis in Vienna.

The Nuremberg patrician and autodidact Willibald Pirckheimer (1470–1530) made himself proficient in Greek from grammars and dictionaries and acquired the Greek writers little by little. Pirckheimer constantly stepped up his efforts to master Greek, and with such success that he is still regarded today as one of the leading intermediaries between Greek literature and Germany. Lucian's treatise *How to write history* was among his first renderings into Latin, and this translation was printed in 1515 in Nuremberg by Friedrich Peypus (1485–1535) so that it could be held up as a model to German humanists to spur them on to greater historical labours. Not by chance did he dedicate this work to the emperor Maximilian I, who was eager to record the history of the empire and of the Habsburgs for posterity. He undertook several literary projects for Maximilian I, including the *Ehrenpforte* and *Triumphzug*, on which he worked between 1515 and 1517 together with his friend Albrecht Dürer, who produced the monumental woodcut plates.

A translation of Lucian's *Piscator seu reviviscentes* printed by Friedrich Peypus in Nuremberg in 1517 carried a dedicatory preface, the *Epistola apologetica*. In it, Pirckheimer drew an idealized picture of the modern theologian, who should have a comprehensive grasp of all the sciences; he should be well versed in grammar and Latin, Greek and Hebrew letters, know both Aristotelian and Platonic philosophy, and be at home with the quadrivium and the writing of history. The close connection between theology and humanistic studies is clearly apparent from this curriculum drawn up by Pirckheimer.

Among Pirckheimer's most significant translations for the history of learning are Plutarch's *Moralia*, issued in 1513 by Friedrich Peypus in Nuremberg, and Ptolemy's *Geographia* of 1525, with large-scale illustrations, from Johann Grüninger in Strasbourg in co-operation with Anton Koberger in Nuremberg.

The medieval rediscovery of the classical languages was accompanied by that of Hebrew, which had largely lain buried. At the end of the fifteenth century, Hebrew manuscripts were brought together and edited in Italy: Avicenna's *Canon medicinae*, for instance, printed in Naples in 1491 by Azriel ben Joseph Ashkenazi Gunzenhauser (GW 3113). The first Hebrew professorships in Germany date from 1518 in Wittenberg, Erfurt and Leipzig, 1520 in Rostock, 1521 in Greifswald, 1522 in Heidelberg, and 1525 in Tübingen and Freiburg. The Reformation initially encouraged Hebrew studies, but these were soon scaled down to become a mere adjunct to theology. Printing in Hebrew is to be found from the begining of the century in the works of assorted humanists, and the first attempt to expound the Hebrew language from the Christian standpoint came in 1506 with the *Rudimenta hebraica* of Johann Reuchlin, printed in Pforzheim by Thomas Anshelm (see Plate 38). An abridged Hebrew grammar had appeared in the anthology *Margarita philosophica* by Gregor Reich (1467–1525) from Johann Grüninger in Strasbourg in 1503. The *Margarita* covered a compendium of book learning, and this reference work went through numerous editions between 1503 and 1517.

VADIAN AND THE PROVISION OF TEACHING TEXTS

The demand for reliable texts to work from in academic teaching can be explored through the example of the humanist Vadian (Joachim von Watt, 1484–1551) from St Gall, who taught philosophy and poetics in Vienna in the footsteps of Conrad Celtis after 1508. He particularly emphasised the need for good school editions in the dedication to his pupil Christophorus Crassus (*c*.1490–1549) which appears in his edition of Sallust's *De coniuratione Catalinae et bello Iugurthino historiae* (Vienna, 1511). Vadian published these texts in connection with his lectures on the historical writings of Sallust. He had observed whilst preparing these, as he put it in his dedicatory letter, in what a sorry state the available editions of Sallust, Lucretius and Pliny were to be found. He took particular exception to an edition which Pomponius Laetus, a pupil of Lorenzo Valla and founder of the Accademia Romana in Rome, had provided in Rome in 1490. In language bristling with metaphor, Vadian describes how in his need he had sought refuge in the new text edited by Aldus Manutius, and compared this resource – in Homer's words in the *Odyssey* – with a "rescue from a great disaster at sea". Vadian had a thousand copies of Aldus's edition reprinted by the printer-publishers Hieronymus Vietor (1480–1546) and Johann Singrenius (*c*.1480–1545) in Vienna in 1510.

The Elder Pliny's *Praefatio* to his *Naturalis historia*, dedicated to the emperor Vespasian, should be mentioned as one of Vadian's most important editions (Vienna, 1513). In his own dedication to his colleague Georg Collimitius (1482–1535), Vadian gives a detailed account of the only available, and in his opinion inadequate, editions from the Italian humanists. He intends to make his a reliable version that will safeguard the text for the benefit of students.

One of Vadian's mathematical and astronomical editions was of the *Sphaera* attributed to Proklos Diadochus (410–485 AD), which had also appeared in Latin translation in a collection of *Scriptores astronomici veteres* published by Aldus Manutius in 1499. Vadian had this printed and published on its own in 1511 by his friends Vietor and Singrenius. Here, once again he gave prominence in his introduction to protecting the text as the basis for future commentary, and to making classical texts available for the "less well-to-do young". Students were also well served by further reference works, dictionaries and collections of historical documents which were entrusted to him. In this way Vadian edited in 1513 a small publication with glosses (ascribed to Luctatius Placidus) to Ovid's *Metamorphoses*, and dedicated it to his younger brother Melchior as he felt himself "responsible for his intellectual development". And as the writings of Ovid could shape mental aptitudes, he wanted to do all he could to contribute to their spread.

The special role of classical texts in learning and the instruction of pupils becomes apparent from Vadian's dedicatory epistle to the Vienna Boys' Choir. He had dedicated his edition of the seventh book of the Elder Pliny's *Naturalis historia* to them. Calling upon Plato – and in close accord with the ideas of Pico della Mirandola – Vadian wrote that a good knowledge of human nature should be the basis for all debates on philosophy and natural history.

Vadian translated not only classical writings, but also those of Italian and German humanists such as Lorenzo Valla or Conrad Celtis. He issued Celtis's poetical works (*Odes*, *Epodes*, *Carmen saeculare*) in 1513 through his Viennese publisher Lukas Alantsee (d. 1522) in an edition printed by Matthias Schürer of Strasbourg. Here, once again he underlined in his preface that these texts should serve not only for the cultivation of the young, but for the promotion of virtue in general. However, the theological faculty in Vienna did not see it that way, and summoned the publisher Alantsee in 1514 to defend himself on account of the immoral and unchristian content detected by some religious orders.

For the Viennese university professors, and their printers in turn, it became apparent how interdependent were scholars, with their concern for the best textual foundations, and publishers, who counted on the scholars for advice.

The procurement of Greek and Hebrew texts for teaching purposes remained difficult for a long time. Reuchlin complained in 1520 that he had found no single printed Greek or Hebrew book available during his lectureship in those subjects at Ingolstadt. Two years later, Reuchlin reported from his position at the University of Tübingen that he had obtained several hundred Hebrew *Bibles* from Venice, mainly for use as teaching material. He had furthermore only imported editions of Xenophon at his disposal. In 1524 Melanchthon had access to just a single copy for his lectures on Demosthenes, from which he had to dictate a few lines at the start of each lecture in order to be able to comment on them. It is true that printing was up and running to provide great numbers of cheap books, but it took a long time before all scholars and students could be furnished with texts in Greek and Hebrew typography.

Nevertheless, it is possible to confirm that Latin teaching texts had been available in appropriate numbers since about 1480. Outwardly, by this date book design had broken away from manuscript production, the title page and colophon had developed, and octavos and quartos were largely supplanting folio formats. The individual illumination of copies was being replaced by woodcut illustrations printed with the text. Book prices sank during the 1470s to between a half and a quarter of their starting level. Above all, a change came about in the titles on offer: after the *Bible* editions, liturgical and simple instructional texts, grammars and dictionaries which dominated the early years, it was now the writings of the humanists and editions of the classics which found favour with the printer-publishers.

Printing made possible the transmission of knowledge through affordable text editions which combined literary accuracy with suitable appearance. The advancement of philology through the possibilities opened up by printing and the necessity of teaching from reliable texts were emphatically proclaimed above all by Joachim Vadian, in an introductory poem to a Viennese impression by Vietor and Singrenius in 1511. Because Vadian here goes beyond contemporary topicality and places the invention of printing in a world historical context, and characterises it as a cultural quantum leap that is only to be compared with the discovery of writing by the ancients, it is worth giving the full text in the original Latin and in translation:

In artis Impressoriae meritam laudem
Scazon Iochimi Vadiani

Aegiptii quos fertilis fovet Nilus.
Hermem suum subinde laudibus tollunt
Quod litterarum primus ipse repertor
Dederit Nepotibus scientiae lumen.
Agenoris natum vigil beat Graecus
Cadmum / figurae cultioris auctorem:
Phoenice dum suis refert Characteres:
Quos Atticus coluit lepor bona fruge
Dum posteris tam digna lectu compegit.
Latina lingua gloriatur Carmentem
Quae mater et nutrix veteris est Euandri
Cum patriam linguens novas sedes quaerit
Latio attulisse formulas: quarum est usus
In litteris politioribus. Verum
Germanus is qui litteras fudit Stanno
Docuitque tantum comprimi semel praelo
Quantum celerrimae manus die longo
Scribunt: beatus et perennitur foelix
Praecellit Hercle cuncta priscorum inventa
Quanto melius animum polire quam corpus.
Iam Chalcitypus humanus est: siquidem scribit:
Iam quod legas praestat benignitas aeris:
Et quo frequenter percolas diam mentem.
Si vivat Hermes gratias ageret Rheno:
Et Cadmus ipse si rederit ex umbris:
Carmentis ipsa / si veniret ex Orco
Cum Graeca cernerent rudi imprimi plumbo.
Hebraeque et quaecunque sunt prius scripta:
Tam insigniter quam nunc latina cuduntur.

An iambic by Joachim Vadian
on the well-deserved praise of printing

The Egyptians showered with favours from the fertile river Nile never tired of extolling their god Hermes, for as the prime

> inventor of letters he had bestowed the light of knowledge on posterity.
>
> The Greeks praised Cadmus, son of Agenor, for his attention as creator of a more developed form of writing. The characters which he caused his brother Phoinix to bring home to his countrymen raised Attic sensibilities to a higher plane and combined them with literature worthy to be handed down to future generations. Latinists attribute to Carmenta, mother of the ancient Evander, the honour of bringing to Latium those characters employed in polite letters, when she left her native land in search of a new residence.
>
> The Germans, however, cast single letters from metal and showed that through a single pull of the press the highest daily output of the nimblest scribe could be exceeded, thus outshining all the inventions of the ancients put together; praise and glory to them!
>
> And how much more highly are mental labours to be valued than physical ones? Even if a man still writes (by hand) today, he is in a sense already a printer. For what one reads and by what means one's god-given brains are fed will be attended to from now onwards by the quality of metal alloy.
>
> If Hermes still lived, so would he thank the Rhine, as would Cadmus returned from the realm of shades or Carmenta back from the underworld, if all were able to see how Greek, Hebrew and everything that was earlier written by hand now gets printed metallically just as excellently as does Latin.

The national argument most frequently used in praise of the invention of printing – that Gutenberg's invention now enabled the Germans to share in the intellectual world of the classics – was placed by Vadian in a world historical context. In the form of a four-stage progression which culminated in Gutenberg's invention of moveable letters, the Egyptian god Toth (re-cast as the mythological Hermes), who was looked upon as the inventor of written signs, is first recalled. Then Cadmus, descendant of the progenitor of the Phoenicians, Agenor, and considered since Herodotus to be the inventor of the Greek alphabet and thus father of Western culture. The Arcadian naiad Carmenta, who migrated to Italy with her son

Evander, finally serves as the inventor of the earliest Latin alphabet, which had 15 letters. With his word-play on *litterae politiores*, Vadian alludes not only to the cultivated Latin of classical literature, but also to the neo-Latin humanistic poetry of his own day which was also described by those same words. Vadian intended to bridge the gap between the works of Roman antiquity and the present in using this term, but he further plays on *litterae politiores* to refer to the use of roman type (as opposed to black letter) for the works of his contemporaries.

Gutenberg cumulated all mankind's former advances through his invention, which now made it possible in a single printing operation to publish many times more than any diligent copying could yield. It was not these new quantities alone, but above all the quality and accuracy of publication, that vouched for the fact that education could now shed a universal light.

Vadian shows how in the year 1511 printing had not only spread right across Europe, but that it was already possible to set and print with Greek or Hebrew types. The extremely close bond between technical history and intellectual history is tersely expressed in Vadian's poem: only through the discovery of letter forms and the new scope to multiply them endlessly could knowledge and culture be globally disseminated.

A FEW DISSENTING VOICES

The arguments brought on the humanist side were almost exclusively in favour of printing, but there were isolated voices opposed to it. The verdict of Abbot Johannes Trithemius in a publication descriptively entitled *De laude scriptorum* (1515) is well known. He begins with the question of durability, since for him the manuscript still remains associated with vellum, but printing with that relatively new material, paper:

> Writing, if set down on vellum, will last for a millennium; however printing is on paper, and so how long will it last? It would be much if printing in a paper volume were to survive for two hundred years in the opinion of many by reason of the material on which it is printed. Let the future decide that. But even if many printed books shall become available, yet they

will never be printed to the extent that one can't easily find something to copy that has not already been printed [. . .] He who gives up the occupation of writing for the sake of printing, is no true friend of manuscript transmission: since at best he fixes his gaze on the present and takes no pains to provide for future generations [. . .] When compared to the handwritten book, the printed one can never be placed on the same level. The printer generally takes little care over the spelling and layout of his books. But he who transcribes, goes to much trouble in these matters.

The scholarly contention that insufficient care is exercised in the composing room is widely shared by the humanists. Their general concern is expressed in a complaint which Erasmus of Rotterdam makes in his introduction to Lorenzo Valla's *Annotationes* to the Latin translation of the New Testament, namely that: "in earlier times a single writing mistake would only affect one copy, but now it appears in an edition of thousands".

The printer-publishers acknowledged this danger, and that is why Peter Schoeffer reassures his customers in a list advertising books in stock of 1472: "No one should refrain from purchasing these books on the grounds that they may be disfigured through slipshod workmanship or downright errors [. . .]. All may see with what care and attention and how much mental and physical labour the texts of these books have been read and revised." But the very fact that the correctness of the text needed to be emphasised in this way shows clearly how prevalent this criticism had become.

Theological suspicions were directed not against printing as such, but rather against the translation of the "holy" Greek and Latin tongues into German and against possible misuse. In one of the first censorship pronouncements, on 22 March 1485, the Archbishop of Mainz, Berthold of Henneberg, gave his views on translations from Greek or Latin into German:

Although people may come to acquire erudition thanks to the so-called divine art of printing by turning to the books of the various sciences which are readily available in ample measure, we

> have nevertheless heard how certain men, tempted by greed after fame and fortune, have misused this art and steered that which had been given to mankind for the cultivation of life into the paths of corruption and falsification. Then we had to see books containing the order of the Mass, and sundry others, that were written on divine matters and the cardinal issues of our religion, translated from Latin into German and falling into the hands of common folk, not without bringing dishonour to religion.

The respectability of printing is not in question, but care has to be taken that:

> the unsullied purity of godly writings shall be preserved. And so we command that no work, whatever its kind and to whichever science, art and knowledge it refers, that has been or shall be translated from Greek, Latin or any other language into German, publicly or secretly, directly or indirectly, shall be printed or such printing offered for sale, without the appointed doctors and masters of the university of our city of Mainz or such in our city of Erfurt respectively, being allowed to examine it and issue a permit for it to be printed or offered for sale.

The threatened penalty was excommunication, forfeiture of the books and a fine of 100 gold gulden. A proper concern for textual accuracy in translation has here become confused with the prevalent fear of theological texts in the vernacular.

In a papal bull – dated two years before Luther's first reformatory stirrings of 1515 – Leo X brought this concern to the point where he denounced anew the spread of texts in the vernacular. He had this to say about translations: "Errors of faith just as pernicious contain teachings contrary to Christian religion and matters aimed at the reputation of high-ranking dignitataries, so that to risk printing and selling writings, from the reading of which no edification is to be derived, will lead readers instead into the gravest errors in faith as well as in their lives and morals. Out of this, as teachers' experience proves, manifold troubles issue forth which it is to be feared will grow worse from day to day." Accordingly, censorship was enacted to the greater glory of God, and for the welfare of the faithful the supervision of the printing of books was instituted, "so that in future thorns may not grow together with the good seeds nor poison be mixed with medicines".

Despite the high-flown language, the fear of the Church establishment that it will lose power and influence with the spread of theological and religious knowledge in the vernacular is evident. By contrast, the only arguments raised by their humanisic contemporaries against printing were bibliophilic ones relating to the aesthetics of handwriting and a literary reminder that the mass production of texts in a printing office must be at least as well controlled as in a scriptorium. But beyond that, all the evidence from letters, introductions and the published books themselves speaks for the fact that printing clearly corresponded to the educational endeavours of the humanists.

Popular instruction in the vernacular

POPULAR BOOKS

From the first books of Gutenberg up until 1500 – the year laid down on purely bibliographical grounds for the end of the incunabula (Lat. *incunabula*, cradle) period – some 30,000 different publications appeared that are still traceable today. Eighty per cent of these were written in Latin, the obligatory European language of the Church and the learned community. Naturally, this had one tremendous advantage for the many printing offices spread right across Europe, in that their marketing area was not confined to a single narrowly encircled territory. That is why the Frankfurt book fair, for example, developed at so early a date into an emporium for books from France, the Netherlands and Italy.

Only the remaining 20 per cent of printing was in the vernacular, although this share was to continue to rise. Early romances for light reading were published in German, alongside short dogmatic writings, herbals and guides to living. The domination of the book market by Latin was not broken until the end of the seventeenth century, with the Reformation in Central Europe during the sixteenth century playing no inconsiderable part in this.

But the circulation of narrative fiction in the German language may be dated back to the manuscripts of the late Middle Ages. The circumstances surrounding its reception began to alter, and this new readership was no longer exclusively made up from ecclesiastical and titled circles; it came from crafts and tradespersons in the towns and from lay intellectuals at the courts of the nobility. An outward sign of this steady rise in reading numbers is offered by the late-medieval manuscript workshop of Diebold Lauber of Hagenau in Alsace, in which up to five scribes and sixteen illustrators were active at times between 1427 and 1467. From "publisher's advertisements" and numerous surviving manuscripts we are very well informed about his publishing repertoire of 38 titles. Lauber manufactured his manuscripts on a production line, down to their pen-drawn decoration. We find him offering "typological" *Bibles*, courtly and heroic epics, religious and instructional texts, juristic and natural historical writings. Eighteen manuscript copies of the "typological *Bible*" alone have survived: a popular, vernacular pairing of texts, in which stories from the Old Testament are supported and enriched by tales from apocryphal and secular history, omitting the prophetical books. Konrad von Mengenberg's *Buch der Natur* belongs to the natural history category, and the *Schwabenspiegel* or *Belial* are legal texts. Knightly epics are represented by Wolfram von Eschenbach's *Parzival* and Gottfried von Strassburg's *Tristan*. Lauber was equally successful at marketing an "art of dying", prayer books, the *Zehn Gebote* or ten commandments with commentary, the *Legende der heiligen drei Könige* or the *Pfaffen Amis* by Der Stricker. Lauber produced stock in advance, and so needed to advertise his wares. His texts were always clearly set out, and came complete with table of contents, headings and, of course, pictures. The coloured pen-drawings were executed on a production line as well, making use of multi-functional picture types.

These titles satisfied the prevailing public taste very well, which explains why light reading in the vernacular found its way into print so early on. The works of Wolfram von Eschenbach came out in 1477 from Johann Mentelin in Strasbourg, as did Gottfried von Strassburg's *Tristan*. The early Augsburg printer Günther Zainer had learned his skills from Mentelin in Strasbourg, from whence he returned to Swabia with both the technology and a successful publishing plan. Augsburg became a publishing centre for the German prose romance in the 1470s and 1480s; besides Zainer, Johann Bämler, Anton Sorg and Johann Schönsperger the elder devoted themselves to this genre. Anton Sorg printed *Tristrant* in 1484 and *Wilhelm von Österreich* in 1481 and 1491. From 1483 onwards, Schönsperger printed the romance *Pontus und Sidonia* (the translation is attributed to Eleonore of the Tyrol) at least four times, the *Alexander* romance at least nine times from 1472, and the story *Griseldis* again on nine occasions. Texts frequently reappeared in pirated editions from Strasbourg; thus we find a printing dating from *c.*1489 of the *Troja* (Troy) romance that had already appeared from Bämler, Sorg and Schönsperger from 1474 onwards. In addition to the literature of the late Middle Ages in German, translations of popular works from the Italian fifteenth century were undertaken, such as the above-mentioned Petrarch romance *Griseldis*, or *Florio und Biancefora* after Boccaccio. Favourites among romances modelled on French tales included *Melusine* by Thüring von Ringoltingen alongside *Pontus und Sidonia* or the *Ritter von Turn* in Marquart von Stein's translation.

Since the early nineteenth century these texts have come under the general heading of "chapbooks", but modern literary criticism prefers to call them "prose romances". In his study *Der Mythos vom Volksbuch* (1977), Joachim Kreuzer concludes that the term "Volksbuch" (popular or chapbook), which dates back to the romantic era, evokes the wrong connotations with reference to the conditions in which these texts came into being as well as those under which they were distributed and read. The more neutral description "prose romance" makes it clear that these texts are no longer in verse form (and thus for recitation), but rather in prose, which indicates that they were meant for the private reader. Quite a number of the Middle High German epics were rendered from verse into prose after the invention of printing. The contemporary term for these texts was "Historia", which denoted romance-like tales that hopefully would be taken for true. The connecting element was the notion of truth in popular historiography and the edifying character of these credited stories. In support of this feigned writing of history, sources of evidence were cited, eyewitness reports in the case of *Alexander des Großen Historie* by Johann Hartlieb, or biographical references and alleged surviving documents for *Eulenspiegel* or for *Doktor Faustus*. Taken as a group, "Historia" represents an attempt to combine truths and what might pass for truth into a credible didactic message, for instance in *Melusine* the warning of the fragility of human happiness, or with *Fortunatus* the moral: "wisdom instead of riches". Actual places, dates and distance measurements contribute to the air of authenticity.

These Augsburg editions were provided as a rule with powerfully stated woodcuts that illustrated the narratives in a lively manner. The representation of emotions through stereotypes, frequent enough in the storytelling, was repeated in the woodcuts: as a sign of love, a box containing a heart would be presented, and farewells and welcomes would take place at a town wall or by the sea shore. The woodblocks themselves were often sold on, crudely sawn down to fit new formats, and used again in different contexts. A moral exhortation accompanied the earliest of these histories ("Here ends the book and history of how the rich, delightful and mighty city of Troy was destroyed through the destiny of God. As an example to the whole world"), but this was soon replaced by an emphasis on entertainment value ("Hereinafter follows the history of Lord Tristan and the fair Isolde of Ireland, which history well merits an opening speech, though it be unused, since readers and listeners are vexed by long preambles . . .").

The vernacular prose romance of the fifteenth century in German is inconceivable without the translated output, or rather the stimulus to translate, provided by two ladies of the German-Austrian higher nobility: Elisabeth of Nassau-Saarbrücken (1393–1456) and Eleonore of the Tyrol (1430–80). Both were politically active and were deeply involved with French and Latin literature. One of the translations of *Pontus und Sidonia*, a prose romance originating in France around 1400, can be traced back to Eleonore. It describes the flight of the king's son Pontus, driven from his native Spain by the Moors, who foils many plots and in the end wins the favour of the princess Sidonia of Britain through heroic deeds. Johann Schönsperger printed this "fair history" in 1483, 1485, 1491 and 1498. Plate 39 is taken from the 1498 edition and depicts the wedding of Pontus and Sidonia. This woodcut is still crude in style, with no attempt to achieve spatial recession or represent the landscape, and with only the simplest shadings, but it is enlivened by the contemporary colouring, which was probably added in the printer's workshop.

Whilst the framing story runs along the classical lines of a journey in search of a bride, with the overcoming of various dangers and the testing of the hero through adversities, Sidonia represents an emergent type of self-confident heroine who behaves autonomously within the personal and political scope available to her.

Similarly, Elisabeth of Nassau-Saarbrücken succeeded in carrying the knightly romantic style over into a realistic treatment of contemporary themes with her translation of a French *chanson de geste* into a German prose romance. She translated *Huge Scheppel* into German in 1437. The titular hero is Hugo Capet, son of a prince and a butcher's daughter. Great heroic exploits win him the hand of the daughter of Ludwig, last of the Carolingians (here put forward as the son of Charlemagne). In a second part, which only survives in the German version, the hero has to fend off many envious persons. Because of his lowly origins and unfeigned honesty, the hero of the title became well known and achieved widespread popularity. *Hug Schapler*, the first of Elisabeth's translations, appeared as a "truthful historie" in a re-working by

Konrad Heindörffer from the Strasbourg printing office of Johann Grüninger in 1500. Grüninger printed and published liturgical and theological texts as his main line of business, alongside numerous editions of the classics. His German-language publications are distinguished by their magnificent woodcut illustrations (see Plate 40). Lively depiction and an effect of recession are due to the fine hatchings, reminiscent of copper engraving, which make any kind of colouring superfluous. The publicity value of the narrative illustration underlines a new function for the title page, which gives a short and sharp summary of the contents in five lines, and advertises in a single size of type that this "true history" will prove a "good read" (*"lieplich lesen"*).

Alongside these translations from French and Italian, and the renderings of Middle High German epics into early New High German prose form, there are "original romances" in the vernacular to be met with increasingly after 1500, such as *Fortunatus* (1507), the *Eulenspiegel* (c. 1510), or the *Historia von D. Johann Fausten* (1587). Besides their issue as individual titles, collections of these tales and novelettes began to appear in the sixteenth century, like, for instance, the enormous compendium *Das Buch der Liebe* which Sigmund Feyerabend brought out in Frankfurt in 1587.

However, the favourite prose for German readers was not drawn from this fictional literature alone, but from instructional matter in the form of fables and early textbooks. Herbals, medical guides and encyclopaedias reached out to a new public in the towns.

ENCYCLOPAEDIAS

Take your way, oh book, and soar swiftly through the air;
Never was anything printed to compare with you.
A thousand hands grasp out for you with eager love,
You are constantly read with busy purpose.
In you, human affairs follow the deeds of the gods,
Each page is adorned with splendid decoration.
You report the primal dawn and creation of matter,
All that has ever happened, you make completely known.

In this bookseller's advertisement (the original is in Latin) from the year 1493, a masterpiece of book art is being launched with a poem: a chronicle of the world from the pen of the Nuremberg town physician Hartmann Schedel. With humanistic erudition, a compendium of received and contemporary knowledge is provided in word and picture, and made further accessible through extensive and detailed indexes. Relating to actual events in time, whether warlike threats or natural disasters, this work is recommended as a comprehensive manual for any educated person prepared to read not just the orthodox theological interpretation, but also empirically based knowledge when this is reliably presented. The totality of scientific culture, for which the antique world had already coined the term "encyclopaedia", is contained in this monumental work, which above all possesses great clarity and vitality through its illustrations.

Some 1400 copies of the Latin version and about 800 copies of the German edition of the *Weltchronik* were produced in 1493 in Nuremberg by Anton Koberger's large enterprise there. The *Nuremberg Chronicle* has remained famous to this day for its numerous woodcut views of towns, sometimes the earliest ones extant. It is true that only a small proportion of these are authentic: for instance, one and the same woodblock does duty for Mainz, Naples, Aquila, Bologna and Lyons, for – according to the medieval tradition of praising towns – they all had to be protected by high walls, situated on a river to facilitate trade and close to a mountain range to ensure a good climate. But other views, such as those of Regensberg or Nuremberg, are still highly regarded for their faithful recording of detail. A consortium was formed in Nuremberg for this production. Michael Wolgemut and his stepson Wilhelm Pleydenwurff created the woodcuts in their workshop, and since Albrecht Dürer was a pupil with them from 1486 to 1489, this has led to much speculation as to whether the young Dürer may have been involved in the preliminary drawings for these woodblocks.

The impetus for the project came from two Nuremberg citizens known to be patrons, Sebald Schreyer and Sebastian Kammermeister. The wealthy dealer Schreyer was a councillor and master of St Sebald's church between 1482 and 1503. Together with his brother-in-law, the mining entrepreneur Kammermeister, he carried the financial risk of this book.

Hartmann Schedel, who had been commissioned by them, divided his chronicle into seven "ages of the world" in accordance with the story of the Creation. And when he presents different creation myths at the outset, he nevertheless leaves us in no doubt about the scriptural dimension: “But all these things were not made by Jupiter, but by the architect of the world, the source of redemption, whom we call God.” The first age interprets the Creation story (see Plate 41), and the second age begins with the building of Noah’s ark and ends with the departure of Lot and the destruction of Sodom. The third age contains the stories of Abraham, Moses, Joseph and King Saul. Here, wide-ranging accounts of the history of Greece and the ancient gods are introduced, as well as descriptions of the cities of Paris, Mainz, Venice and Padua, since Schedel traces their respective foundations back, directly or indirectly, to the Trojans.

The fourth age starts with King David and Solomon, and ends with the destruction of Jerusalem. Rome’s history is slipped in here, with further digressions on ancient poets and philosophers. The fifth age extends from the Babylonian captivity as far as the beheading of John the Baptist, although Persian history, Alexander’s campaigns and a further stretch of Roman history engage the author’s special interest as well.

The sixth age takes us from the birth of Christ to the present, thus comprising some 1500 years; it also makes the longest chapter, with over 300 pages. The next few pages are left blank to give each reader the chance to write up entries which will carry the chronicle forward with events taking place during his or her lifetime. In this chapter, most of the authentic townscapes are to to be found in the order of their foundation dates: Regensburg, Vienna, Nuremberg, Metz, Geneva, Constantinople, Budapest, Strasbourg and so forth.

The seventh age once again contains scriptural meditations on the end of the world, corresponding to the opening chapter. The map of Germany included at the end of the book is the first map of Central Europe to appear in print, and is a reworking of the so-called Cusanus Map of 1439 by the Nuremberg cosmographer Hieronymous Münster (1437–1508).

This encyclopaedia is of the greatest interest to us on book historical grounds, since the handwritten layouts for both the Latin and German versions have been preserved in their entirety in Nuremberg City Library. These let us follow the preparatory writing out of the text and the preliminary sketches for the illustrations as well. Anton Koberger had to raid the riches of his previous book production, and especially his German *Bibles*, in order to make up the huge number of 645 woodblocks that were called upon for the 1809 illustrations.

Hartmann Schedel put together his text from various sources; in another of his books he states his working principle: *Colligite fragmenta, ne pereant* ("Gather up the fragments that remain, that nothing be lost"), in the words of the miracle of loaves and fishes. By these means, the encyclopaedia offered a comprehensive synthesis of the state of knowledge of its time, still framed in theological modes of thinking, but alert to contemporary experience. Consequently, we find all sorts of matter being extracted from this printed chronicle throughout the sixteenth century, as often in other historical-geographical descriptions of the world such as Sebastian Münster's *Cosmographey* (Basle, 1550) as in current collections of tales for which it provides the basis for fictional travel descriptions. For instance, Dr Johann Faust (when his legend first assumed a fixed literary form in 1587) took an unusual route for his journey through the air on a winged horse; he went from Trier to Paris and thence by way of Mainz to reach Naples. This lets us glimpse how the still unknown author of the *Historia von D. Johann Fausten* made up this early flight plan at his writing desk whilst leafing through the pages of the *Schedelsche Weltchronik* (fols 23–42). In other words, the itinerary follows the sequence of the woodcuts exactly. The author of this story, written a full century later and published in 1587, took over not just the order of the woodcuts, but relied on the chronicle for factual data on various large European towns, their trading structure and the local etymology for place names. This prominent example makes clear the importance of this vast Nuremberg book enterprise for the cultural, intellectual and book history of the early modern period.

It is also possible to trace Anton Koberger's far-flung trading connections, with copies sold to Florence, Venice, Bologna, Milan and Lyons and, perhaps less predictably, to Graz, Vienna and Buda or to Breslau, Krakow and Danzig. The final account of sales which has survived shows that besides his own business partners, there were booksellers, booktraders and bookbinders, and merchants and traders involved in this distribution, among them factors of the Fugger trading and banking houses in Augsburg and Nuremberg, and individual clerics and academics who acted as agents.

It was natural enough for Gutenberg's invention to be honoured in such an encyclopaedia. Schedel praises it for its capacity to mediate, and counts it among mankind's greatest advances:

> The art of printing first took place in the city of Mainz on the Rhine in AD 1440, from whence it spread to all parts of the world. By its means the riches of literature and wisdom contained in the books of the ancients – long unknown to the world and buried in the grave of ignorance – have again been brought to light [. . .]. If this art had been discovered and employed sooner, undoubtedly many books of Livy, Cicero or Pliny and other highly learned men would not have been lost through the ravages of time. And as the inventor of that art and craft of printing now merits no small amount of praise, who can say with what measure of praise, honour or renown are to be esteemed those Germans who, through their enlightened, ingenious and apt knowledge of printing have discovered how the long closed fountains of untold wisdom, whether human or divine in origin, can be made to flow forth to all mankind.

FABLES

The fable is particularly suited to conveying the basic constants of human behaviour, ethical standards and the practical conduct of life. Already in his *Rhetoric*, Aristotle thinks highly of the fable as a means of convincing through a contrived example. The fable belongs on the one hand to animal literature, on the other hand to instructive literature which gives advice through disguising truth as fiction. This fictionality is asserted by protagonists drawn predominantly from the animal kingdom, which from time to time behave like humans; by constructing particularly compelling examples which relate to the human condition, the didactic aspect of this modest literary form is predetermined. It follows that these pointed exemplary tales may be prefaced or concluded by spiritual, moral or political advice at some length: "And the moral of this story . . .".

So it is not surprising that among the few early German-language texts of the incunabula period, editions of fables should be repeatedly encountered. A mere six years after the invention of printing, the first vernacular text – and the earliest illustrated book – was printed by

Pfister in Bamberg: Ulrich Boner's collection of fables, *Der Edelstein*. Another collection appeared fifteen years later, the Latin-German edition known as the *Ulm Aesop* compiled by Heinrich Steinhöwel.

The fable collection *Der Edelstein* by Ulrich Boner, a Dominican from Berne, was completed in 1349 and strove to be a "mirror of life's wisdom". The hundred examples from Aesop are drawn from the world of animals and plants, and only to a limited extent from human life. The rhymed Middle High German fables are so grouped that a natural progression through the morals can be followed. Often morals are juxtaposed in pairs, so that each enhances the other's effectiveness: kernel and shell, faithful and unfaithful spouses, deserved and undeserved ridicule, treachery and uprightness, success and failure, greed and contentment. Moral teaching is opposed to "deceit, trickery, underhandedness, hypocrisy, envy, avarice, miserliness, bickering, violence, vanity", and argues instead for "freedom, honour, and skill". The title comes from a fable which tells of a cock who finds a precious stone in the dirt but does not recognise its worth and asks a grain of seed in exchange for it, for that at least he can eat. Just like this precious stone, the poem is meant only for prudent and sensible folk, and not for fools who lack proper insight. The same moral is pointed out in a second fable, with which this printed book starts out. It tells of apes who only long for the sweetness of the nut kernel, as the shell is too hard and bitter for them. This can be seen in Plate 42, and the book opens on to this page without any preamble, since most early editions were printed without any title page in the modern sense.

Boner states in his epilogue that his work has been "zu tütsche bracht von latein", that is, taken from Latin into German. This should not be taken as meaning a literal translation, but rather that the originals have served him as a general source. He names his authorities for some of the examples in the text, and in Fable 55 he mentions Aesop as the begetter of the genre in antiquity.

Boner takes over pre-existing content, and paraphrases it for his readership. He clothes familiar material in the costume of the age for the instruction and entertainment of his public, and to make it accessible to them. He treats his sources very freely for the most part, and writes at length, occasionally using pentameters in verse in contrast to his patterns. A constant in fable writing is that animals embody human attributes and characteristics: the lion is proud, the fox is cunning, the ass is stupid, etc. People and animals are representatives of a type, bearers of a projected character. Boner generally uses rhyming couplets of four metrical feet. This is not apparent from the look of the page, as the text is not set as verse, but run-on in a justified measure to save space. Reading is not easy, not just because of this typesetting convention, but on account of the author's clumsy versifying. Beauty of language and elegance of expression generally elude him. Add to this the fact that a printed version of the second half of the fifteenth century has been based on a manuscript exemplar that was already more than a century old and thus out of fashion.

Nevertheless, one can speak of a vogue for manuscripts of the *Edelstein* in the fourteenth and early fifteenth centuries, as a good two dozen copies and additional fragments are extant. So it is not surprising that early printing seized upon *Der Edelstein*, since it generally took its cue from the "bestsellers" of the manuscript era. Early printing in Bamberg is linked to the name of Albrecht Pfister. He brought out some nine titles between 1460 and 1464, among which are the *Vier Historien* (free adaptations of the Old Testament stories of Joseph, Daniel, Judith and Esther), a German and a Latin *Biblia Pauperum*, and the *Belial* of Jacobus de Theramo; and then in about 1470 there came Johann von Tepl's *Der Ackermann aus Böhmen*. All Pfister's publications are set in large missal-type, and he printed almost exclusively in German. Furthermore, all his works contain woodcut illustrations, and this was something quite new in the early days of printing. The Boner edition is preserved in a unique and complete copy in the Duke August Library at Wolfenbüttel. It was completed – so the colophon tells us – on St Valentine's Day 1461: "At Bamberg is this little book finished after the birth of our Lord Jesu Christ in the years that are numbered 1400 and in the 61st, it is true, on St Valentine's Day. God protect us from his plague. Amen."

Der Edelstein is printed in the B36 types (those of the 36-*line Bible*), which in their monumentality suit neither the text nor the illustrations. The font available for typesetting comprised 192 letters, punctuation marks, contractions and ligatures. Following a manuscript tradition that was still very much alive, a rubricator has marked the opening capital of each verse line and added large initials in red to enhance readability. Otherwise, capitals are only used at the beginning of lines of verse, and then only in so far as typographic sorts were provided: "W" and "Z" are missing altogether, which can be taken as an indication that this fount was originally cast for setting Latin texts. In the same way, the lower-case "w" is missing, and Pfister gets round this by setting an unpointed "ı" against a "v" as a makeshift "w", but since there is no linking stroke between these characters the deception is easily spotted. Each sheet was passed through the press three times: first for the text, then for the woodcut showing the main scene, and finally for the woodcut with the figure of the narrator. This can be seen from Plate 43, where the pictorial woodcut has fallen below its allotted space and overprinted the text, so that the narrator block has had to be repositioned to overprint both. It would require further technical experimentation before the leaden type material and the wooden illustrations could be transferred to paper in the same impression.

The woodcuts in the single surviving copy were hand-coloured at the time. They are simple in style, and do not show any interiors or detailed representations of architecture or landscape. The animal drawing is crude: it is hardly possible to tell a wolf from a dog, or a horse from a donkey. The lion is closer to a heraldic beast, and unlikely to scare anyone.

The figures of the narrators are recurrent leitmotifs, and we find this tradition in the earlier Boner manuscripts. A few of the pictorial subjects are derived from these medieval manuscripts, although we are not able to point to one particular manuscript which may have served as the model for this edition.

THE ULM AESOP

Printing came to Ulm on the direct initiative of the humanist and city physician Dr Heinrich Steinhöwel, who lived there from 1450 until his death in 1478. His extensive literary activity centred on making humanist texts available in translation for a German public. His first opus was a translation of a Latin prose romance dating from late antiquity which he completed in 1461, and which he published as *König Apollonius von Thyrus* with the Augsburg printer Günther Zainer in 1471.

His next work was to become one of the key publications of early humanism in South Germany, his famous translation of Petrarch's Latin reworking of the *Griseldis* story from Boccaccio's *Decameron*. The first edition appeared, also in 1471, from Zainer in Augsburg, and went through two new impressions within a year. Steinhöwel got to know Günther Zainer's younger brother Johann through this involvement, and persuaded him to move to Ulm, promising to support him financially in setting up a printing office. On 11 January 1473 the first dated edition left the new press at Ulm. It was a work of Steinhöwel's from his main professional field of activity: *Das büchlein der ordnung der pestilenz*, the first printed book about the plague by a contemporary writer, and one of the earliest of all medical texts in German.

Although the *Aesop* edition contains a printer's mark, there is no date given, but a comparison of the typefaces used allows it to be reliably assigned to the winter of 1476/7. The *Aesop* became his most successful book. This Latin-German volume comprises 171 chapters in eight parts, starting with a novelistic *Vita Aesopi* and followed by the body of the text, which divides 80 fables of similar extent but different provenance into four books. As in the remainder of his translated output, Steinhöwel makes very free use of the source material. By inserting proverbs, rhymes, popular sayings and allusions to real events, he often makes his versions half as long again as the originals and adapts the book for a broader reading public. It is clear how much interest this compilation generated from the fact that it ran through about twenty editions before 1500, for which the woodcuts were taken, directly or indirectly, from the Ulm edition. The book's European reputation, however, was based on a Latin version produced by Anton Sorg of Augsburg in 1480. In Zainer's edition, after an initial woodcut portrait of the author, we find 190 woodcuts which in their diversity of subject matter provide a panorama of late medieval life. People are shown in modern costume, and detailed information is given for the furniture and interiors. Animal scenes are enacted in front of landscape backdrops, although these are still formally simplified. Differentiated colouring of the various picture planes manages to convey an effect of spatial recession (see Plate 44). For most of the fables, no pictorial references would have been needed, nor anything that would have been difficult for the artist who drew on the blocks or the woodcutter to have found in Ulm. An exception has to be made for the Bamberg edition of Ulrich Boner's *Der Edelstein*, from which we can detect a few borrowings, as for example in the fable of the wolf and the crane, with its lateral reversal of the woodcut from Boner's fable of the wolf and the stork. The two surviving copies of this book – equally popular and valuable on account of its decoration - are hand-coloured throughout: even the hundred initials (outline Lombardics) have been coloured in. It is highly probable that this work was carried out in Ulm, perhaps even to the printer's commission and in the workshop responsible for the illustrations.

PRACTICAL BOOKS

It is of great interest for the history of science that, thanks to printing, technical literature was not only disseminated in Latin for theoretical teaching purposes within the universities, but that the literature of the seven free arts – grammar, rhetoric, dialectics, astronomy, geometry, arithmetic and music – appeared in large print runs in the German vernacular for an educated urban public. Peter Schoeffer published a *Herbarius* in Mainz in 1484 (probably in imitation of the first herbal produced in Rome in 1483), and stated in a preface that it was expressly intended for the general public. The sole concession to those ignorant of Latin was that the German names appeared in the captions to 150 woodcuts of plants, otherwise the text was kept in Latin throughout. In the following year, though, he did bring out in German a more elaborately designed *Gart der Gesundheit* with 381 woodcut illustrations. Next to woodcuts in simple outline are to be found blocks with lively hatching and three-dimensional effects. The hand-colouring, typical for the period and probably organised by the publisher, gives the pictures clarity and vitality. The relation of this extensive text to numerous illustrations makes this herbal a masterpiece of layout (see Plate 45). This 'garden of health' describes 382 plants, 25 animals and 28 minerals under their Latin names in its total of 435 chapters. The author, the Frankfurt city physician Johann Wonnecke of Kaub, falls back on German sources from the twelfth to the fourteenth centuries. Starting with an Augsburg reprint in its year of first publication, 1485, the *Gart der Gesundheit* met with a tremendous reception that continued with 15 further incunabula editions and 55 others through to the eighteenth century. The Mainz printer-publisher Jacob Meydenbach translated it in 1491 and published it in that same year as his *Hortus Sanitatis*, a volume of more than 900 pages containing 1073 woodcuts. Copiously illustrated herbals were also printed in Italy and France during the incunabula period.

Plants were the the focus of attention, not for themselves, but for their healing properties, and similar success was to attend books of popular medical advice. The Augsburg physician Bartolomäus Metlinger published his *Kinderbüchlein* in 1473 with Günther Zainer, and it went into more than thirty printings by 1571. Metlinger had studied in Padua – as was the general custom – and had learned the anatomical presentation of clinical pictures from his teacher there, Paulo Bagellardi. Beyond that, the text offered instruction on baby care and tips for bringing up children. His introduction is expressly addressed to "fathers and mothers".

Hieronymus Brunschwig (c.1450–1512) turned to the practical side of medicine with *Dis ist das Buch der chirurgia. Hantwirkung der wund artzeney* (1497). This first medical text book in German and with clear illustrations was intended for doctors, medical students and nurses. An experienced publisher was found in Johann Grüninger of Strasbourg, who had already introduced a variety of large-format woodcuts of the best quality in his publications. The 61 woodcuts are printed from only 18 different blocks. Two equally large blocks predominate, which yield several pictorial variants when combined with others. We have already noted the successful hatchings in his woodcuts for Terence (Plate 28) and the *Hug Schapler* romance (compare Plate 40). They gain their effect from black and white contrast and from the grey values achieved by hatchings, so that additional colouring may be dispensed with. This medical textbook was also reprinted many times. Grüninger himself reissued it in 1513 with 60 new woodcuts.

Even more strongly practical in orientation was a guide to midwifery by the city physician of Frankfurt and Worms, Eucharius Rösslin, published by Martin Flach in Strasbourg in 1513. As a scholar concerned with the theoretical aspects of medicine, this doctor wrote a compendium on childbirth for lay persons. Doctors or surgeons seldom took the trouble to attend births, which were left almost exclusively to "wise women". This manual in German enjoyed enormous success, and over a hundred editions are known over the following decades. Because Rösslin put this guide together from many sources, and had little or no practical experience of his own, it contains a mass of false information. Thus he writes that it is normal for the baby to emerge head first, "its face bent backwards so that it is looking towards the heavens or towards the navel of its mother". In reality, the normal presentation of the back of the head is such that the face is aligned straight downwards. In this matter Rösslin follows the Church father Albertus Magnus, who is equally unlikely to have had any personal experience. His book advises on the conduct of the mother during pregnancy, on nutrition and childcare. A birthstool is recommended, and clearly shown as a diagram and in use, normal and abnormal fœtal positions are discussed in detail, and the necessary actions of the midwife explained. Our Plate 46 shows two contingencies, in one of which the misplacement of a single baby in the uterus (drawn as a bottle-shape) calls for the midwife's intervention: "You should straighten up the child and set all to rights." In the case of the correctly aligned twins, the midwife should: "draw them out one after the other". All possible complications of the birth are fully debated, including miscarriages and Caesarean sections.

The final chapter concerns the nursing of healthy and sick-born children, and recommends breast-feeding. A Latin-German glossary rounds things off, so that the many Latin technical terms in use can be easily followed by the German reader.

Other texts were devoted to the specialised subjects of pure and applied mathematics, such as Adam Riese's *Rechenung auff der Linihen* (1518), or a *Geometria deutsch* (Nuremberg, 1498) by the master of the cathedral works at Regensburg, Matthäus Roritzer. Albrecht Dürer's writings on art theory hold a prominent position for their application of mathematics to the pictorial arts, above all his *Underweyssung der messung* (Nuremberg, 1525) and his *Vier Bücher von menschlicher Proportion*, published in 1528 by Hieronymus Andreae in Nuremberg. These last became a milestone in the literature of art, for they put the teaching of human anatomy on a systematic basis, clearly exemplified in words and pictures. We owe the coinage of many new words to his striving after a precise technical vocabulary. These treatises on proportion were distributed throughout Europe in the Latin translation of Joachim Camerarius

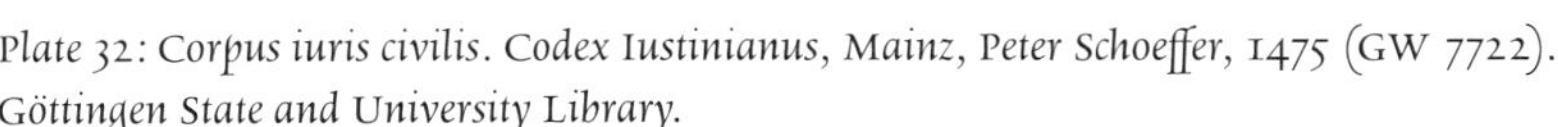

Plate 32: *Corpus iuris civilis. Codex Iustinianus*, Mainz, Peter Schoeffer, 1475 (GW 7722). Göttingen State and University Library.

BEATISSIMO PATRI PAVLO SE
CVNDO PONTIFICI MAXIMO.
DONIS NICOLAVS GERMANVS

On me fugit beatiſſime pater. Cūq; ſummo

Plate 33: Ptolemy: *Geographia*, Ulm, Lienhart Holl, 1482.
The enlarged initial shows Nicholas Germanus, an unknown Benedictine monk from the circle of Nicholas of Cues presenting the volume to Pope Paul II.
Leipzig University Library.

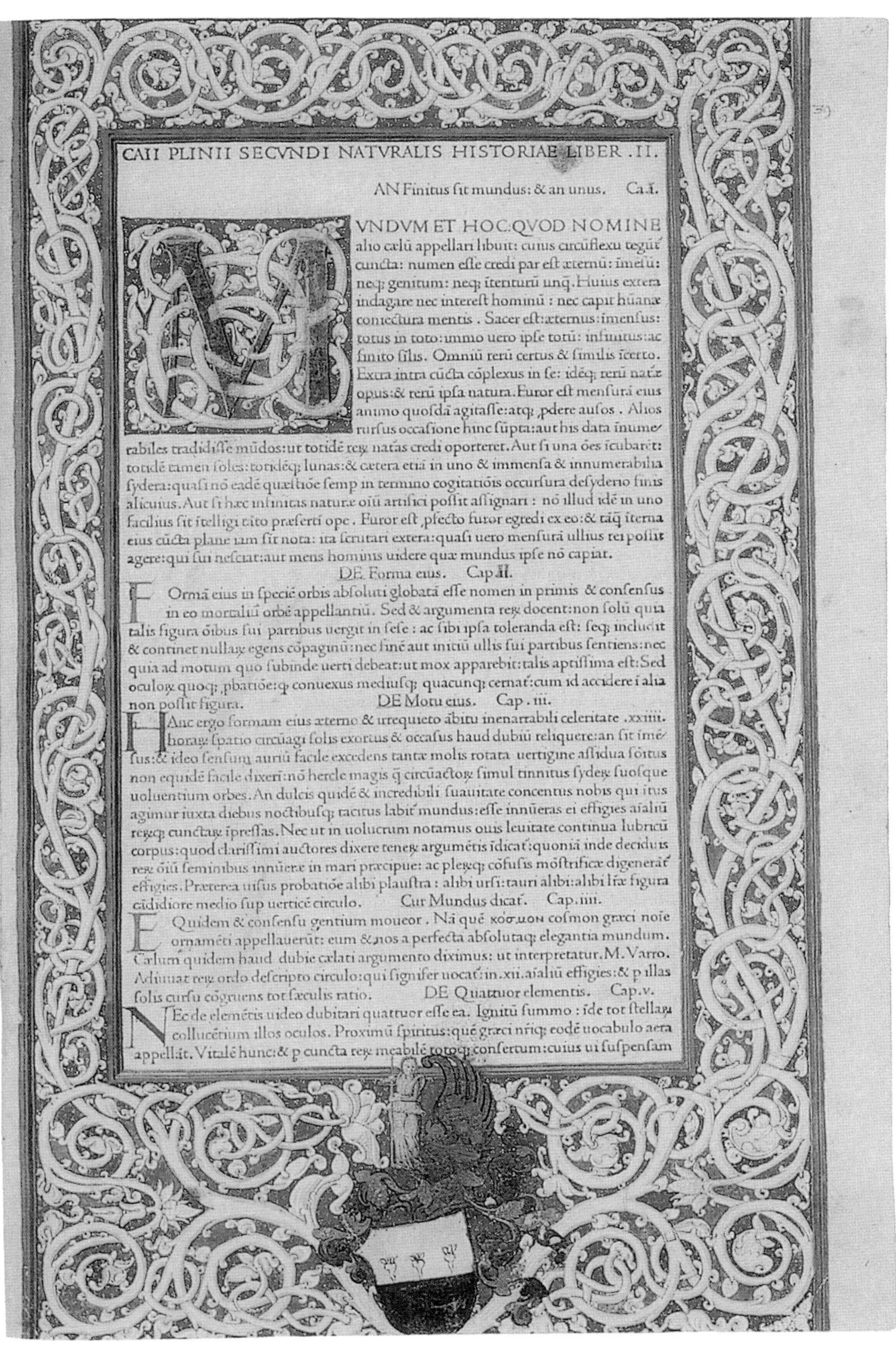

CAII PLINII SECVNDI NATVRALIS HISTORIAE LIBER .II.

AN Finitus sit mundus: & an unus. Ca.i.

MVNDVM ET HOC QVOD NOMINE alio cælũ appellari libuit: cuius circũflexu tegũt cuncta: numen esse credi par est æternũ: imẽsũ: neq; genitum: neq; iteriturũ unq̃. Huius extera indagare nec interest hominũ: nec capit hũanæ coniectura mentis. Sacer est: æternus: imensus: totus in toto: immo uero ipse totũ: infinitus: ac finito silis. Omniũ rerũ certus & similis icerto. Extra intra cũcta cõplexus in se: ideq; rerũ naturæ opus: & rerũ ipsa natura. Furor est mensurã eius animo quosdã agitasse: atq; ꝓdere ausos. Alios rursus occasione hinc sũpta: aut his data inumerabiles tradidisse mũdos: ut totidẽ rerũ naturas credi oporteret. Aut si una oẽs icubaret: totidẽ tamen soles: totidẽq; lunas: & cætera etiã in uno & immensa & innumerabilia sydera: quasi nõ eadẽ quæstiõe semp in termino cogitatiõis occursura desyderio finis alicuius. Aut si hæc infinitas naturæ oĩũ artifici possit assignari: nõ illud idẽ in uno facilius sit itelligi tãto præsertĩ ope. Furor est ꝑfecto furor egredi ex eo: & tãq̃ iterna eius cũcta plane iam sit nota: ita scrutari extera: quasi uero mensurã ullius rei possit agere: qui sui nesciat: aut mens hominis uidere quæ mundus ipse nõ capiat.

DE Forma eius. Cap.II.

FOrmã eius in speciẽ orbis absoluti globatã esse nomen in primis & consensus in eo mortaliũ orbẽ appellantiũ. Sed & argumenta rerũ docent: non solũ quia talis figura oĩbus sui partibus uergit in sese: ac sibi ipsa toleranda est: seq; includit & continet nullarũ egens cõpaginũ: nec finẽ aut initiũ ullis sui partibus sentiens: nec quia ad motum quo subinde uerti debeat: ut mox apparebit: talis aptissima est: Sed oculorũ quoq; ꝓbatiõe: q͂ conuexus mediusq; quacunq; cernat: cum id accidere i alia non possit figura.

DE Motu eius. Cap.iii.

HAnc ergo formam eius æterno & irrequieto ãbitu inenarrabili celeritate .xxiiii. horarũ spatio circũagi solis exortus & occasus haud dubiũ reliquere: an sit imẽsus: & ideo sensum aurĩũ facile excedens tantæ molis rotata uertigine assidua sõitus non equidẽ facile dixeri: nõ hercle magis q̃ circũactorũ simul tinnitus syderũ suosque uoluentium orbes. An dulcis quidẽ & incredibili suauitate concentus nobis qui itus agimur iuxta diebus noctibusq; tacitus labit mundus: esse innũeras ei effigies aĩaliũ rerũq; cunctarũ ĩpressas. Nec ut in uolucrum notamus ouis leuitate continua lubricũ corpus: quod clarissimi auctores dixere terrenũ argumẽtis ĩdicat: quoniã inde deciduis rerũ oĩũ seminibus innũeræ in mari præcipue: ac plerũq; cõfusis mõstrificæ digenerat effigies. Præterea uisus probatiõe alibi plaustra: alibi ursi: tauri alibi: alibi lræ figura cãdidiore medio sup uerticẽ circulo.

Cur Mundus dicat. Cap.iiii.

EQuidem & consensu gentium moueor. Nã quẽ κόσμον cosmon græci noĩe ornamẽti appellauerũt: eum & nos a perfecta absolutaq; elegantia mundum. Cælum quidem haud dubie cælati argumento diximus: ut interpretatur M. Varro. Adiuuat rerũ ordo descripto circulo: qui signifer uocat: in .xii. aĩaliũ effigies: & p illas solis cursu cõgruens tot sæculis ratio.

DE Quattuor elementis. Cap.v.

NEc de elemẽtis uideo dubitari quattuor esse ea. Ignitũ summo: ĩde tot stellarũ collucẽtium illos oculos. Proximũ spiritus: quẽ græci nr̃iq; eodẽ uocabulo aera appellãt. Vitalẽ hunc: & p cuncta rerũ meabilẽ totoq; consertum: cuius ui suspensam

Plate 34: Gaius Plinius Secundus: *Naturalis historia*, Venice, Nicholas Jenson, 1472 (HC 13089), fol 4r. Göttingen State and University Library.

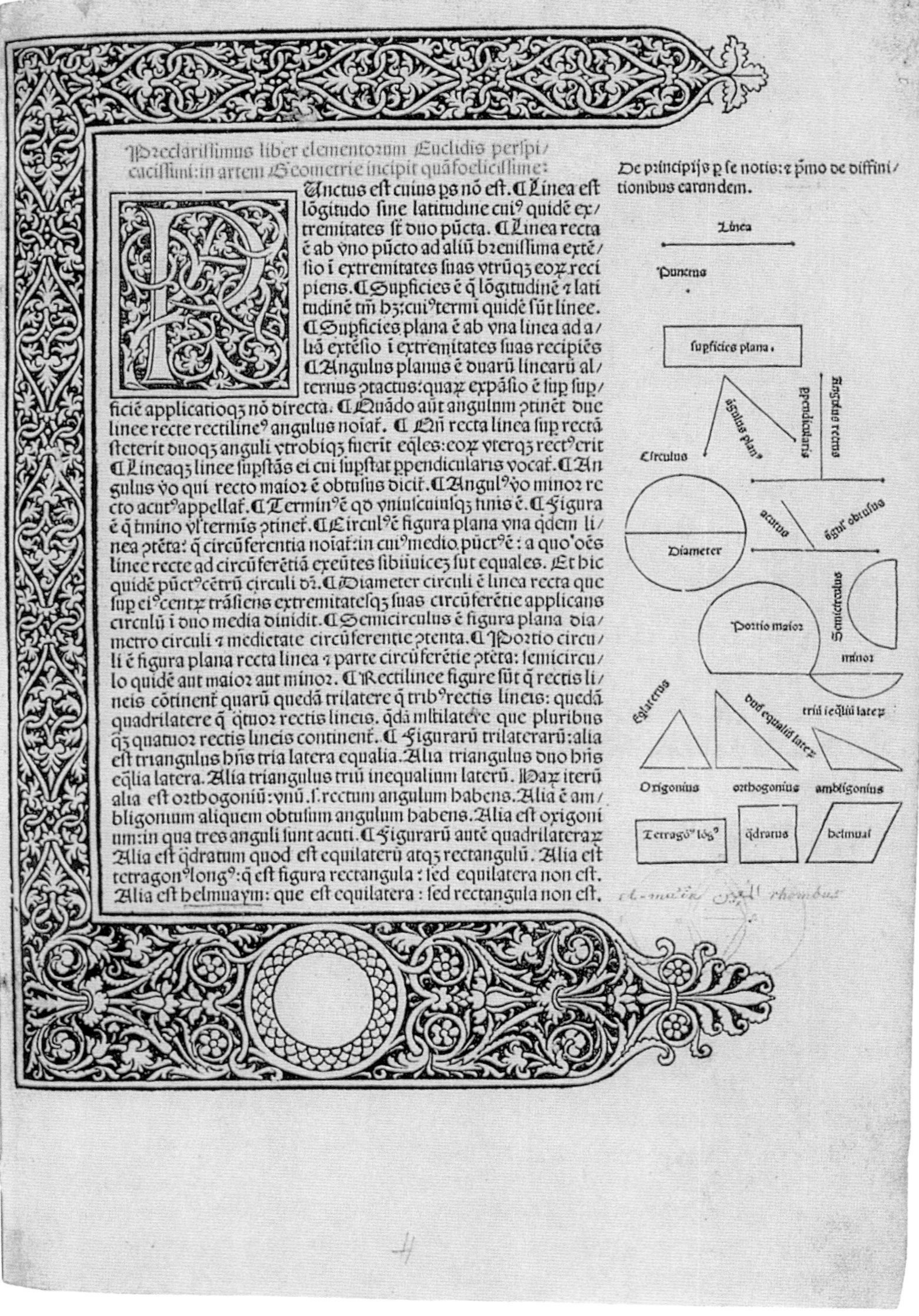

Preclarissimus liber elementorum Euclidis perspi/cacissimi: in artem Geometrie incipit quā foelicissime:

Punctus est cuius ps nō est. Linea est lōgitudo sine latitudine cuiꝰ quidē ex/tremitates sūt duo pūcta. Linea recta ē ab vno pūcto ad aliū breuissima extē/sio i extremitates suas vtrūq3 eorū reci/piens. Superficies ē q̄ lōgitudinē 7 lati/tudinē tm̄ h3: cuiꝰ termi quidē sūt linee. Superficies plana ē ab vna linea ad a/liā extēsio i extremitates suas recipiēs. Angulus planus ē duarū linearū al/ternus ɔtactus: quarū expāsio ē sup sup/ficiē applicatioq3 nō directa. Quādo aūt angulum ɔtinēt due linee recte rectilineꝰ angulus noiat. Qn̄ recta linea sup rectā steterit duoq3 anguli vtrobiq3 fuerit eq̄les: eorū vterq3 rectꝰ erit. Lineaq3 linee supstās ei cui supstat ppendicularis vocat. Angulus vo qui recto maior ē obtusus dicit. Angulꝰ vo minor recto acutꝰ appellat. Terminꝰ ē qd vniuscuiusq3 finis ē. Figura ē q̄ tmino vl terminis ɔtinet. Circulꝰ ē figura plana vna q̄dem linea ɔtēta: q̄ circūferentia noiat: in cuiꝰ medio pūctꝰ ē: a quo oēs linee recte ad circūferētiā exeūtes sibiiuicē sūt equales. Et hic quidē pūctꝰ cētrū circuli dr. Diameter circuli ē linea recta que sup eiꝰ centrū trāsiens extremitatesq3 suas circūferētie applicans circulū i duo media diuidit. Semicirculus ē figura plana diametro circuli 7 medietate circūferentie ɔtenta. Portio circuli ē figura plana recta linea 7 parte circūferētie ɔtēta: semicirculo quidē aut maior aut minor. Rectilinee figure sūt q̄ rectis lineis cōtinent quarū quedā trilatere q̄ tribꝰ rectis lineis: quedā quadrilatere q̄ q̄tuor rectis lineis. q̄dā mltilatere que pluribus q3 quatuor rectis lineis continent. Figurarū trilaterarū: alia est triangulus hn̄s tria latera equalia. Alia triangulus duo hn̄s eq̄lia latera. Alia triangulus triū inequalium laterū. Harū iterū alia est orthogoniū: vnū .s. rectum angulum habens. Alia ē amblygonium aliquem obtusum angulum habens. Alia est oxigonium: in qua tres anguli sunt acuti. Figurarū autē quadrilaterarū. Alia est q̄dratum quod est equilaterū atq3 rectangulū. Alia est tetragonꝰ longꝰ: q̄ est figura rectangula: sed equilatera non est. Alia est helmuaym: que est equilatera: sed rectangula non est.

De principijs p se notis: 7 pmo de diffinitionibus earundem.

Plate 35: Euclid: *Elementa geometriae*, Venice, Erhart Ratdolt, 1482 (GW 9428), fol 2r. Göttingen State and University Library.

ἈΡΙΣΤΟΤΈΛΟΥΣ ΠΟΛΙΤΙΚΩ͂Ν. ΤῸ Η´.

Περὶ πολιτείας ἀρίστης τὸν μέλλοντα ποιήσασθαι τὴν προσήκουσαν ζήτησιν, ἀνάγκη διορίσασθαι πρῶτον, τίς αἱρετώτατος βίος. ἀδήλου γὰρ ὄντος τούτου, καὶ τὴν ἀρίστην ἀναγκαῖον ἄδηλον εἶναι πολιτείαν. ἄριστα γὰρ πράττειν προσήκει τοὺς ἄριστα πολιτευομένους ἐκ τῶν ὑπαρχόντων αὐτοῖς, ἐὰν μή τι γίνηται παράλογον. διὸ δεῖ πρῶτον ὁμολογεῖσθαι τίς ὁ πᾶσιν ὡς εἰπεῖν αἱρετώτατος βίος· μετὰ δὲ τοῦτο, πότερον κοινῇ καὶ χωρὶς ὁ αὐτὸς ἢ ἕτερος. νομίσαντας οὖν ἱκανῶς πολλὰ λέγεσθαι καὶ τῶν ἐν τοῖς ἐξωτερικοῖς λόγοις περὶ τῆς ἀρίστης ζωῆς, καὶ νῦν χρηστέον αὐτοῖς. ὡς ἀληθῶς γὰρ πρός γε μίαν διαίρεσιν οὐδεὶς ἀμφισβητήσειεν ἄν. ὡς οὐ τριῶν οὐσῶν μερίδων, τῶν τε ἐκτὸς καὶ τῶν ἐν τῷ σώματι, καὶ τῶν ἐν τῇ ψυχῇ, πάντα ταῦτα ὑπάρχειν τοῖς μακαρίοις δεῖ. οὐδεὶς γὰρ ἂν φαίη μακάριον τὸν μηθὲν μόριον ἔχοντα ἀνδρίας, μηδὲ σωφροσύνης, μηδὲ δικαιοσύνης, μηδὲ φρονήσεως. ἀλλὰ δεδιότα μὲν τὰς παραπετομένας μυίας, ἀπεχόμενον δὲ μηθενὸς ἂν ἐπιθυμήσῃ τοῦ φαγεῖν ἢ πιεῖν τῶν ἐσχάτων, ἕνεκα δὲ τεταρτημορίου διαφθείροντα τοὺς φιλτάτους φίλους. ὁμοίως δὲ καὶ τὰ περὶ τὴν διάνοιαν οὕτως ἄφρονα καὶ διεψευσμένον, ὥσπερ τι παιδίον ἢ μαινόμενον. ἀλλὰ ταῦτα μὲν λεγόμενα

υυυυ

Plate 36: Aristotle: Works (in Greek), Venice, Aldus Manutius, 1495-8 (GW 2334). Göttingen State and University Library.

Plate 37: Ptolemy: Geographia, Ulm, Lienhart Holl, 1482 (HC 15539), double-page map of Italy. Leipzig University Library.

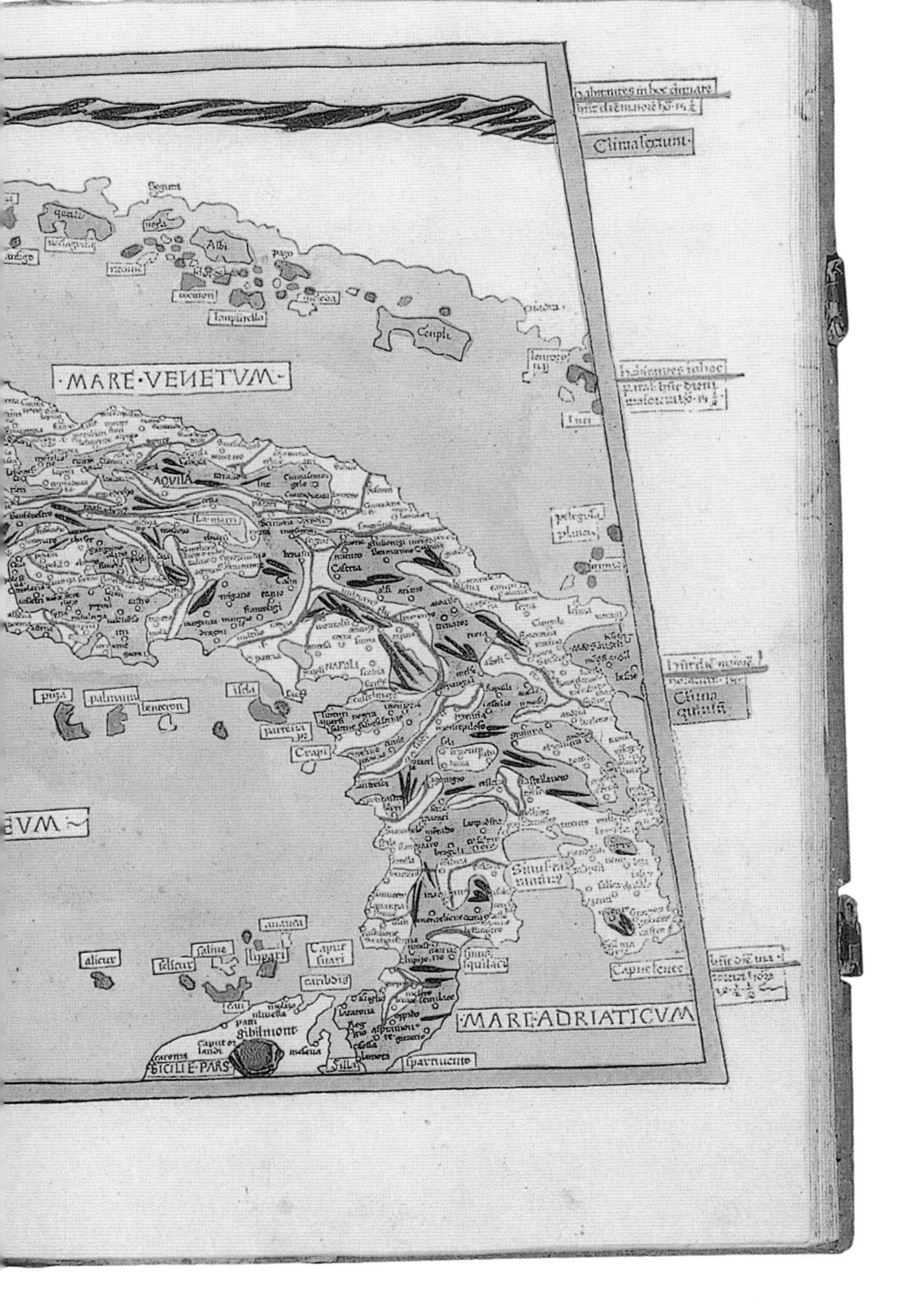

·MARE·VENETVM·
EVM
MARE·ADRIATICVM
SICILIE·PARS
AQUILA
NAPOLI
Caserta

viri nomen et dixit

Genitiuo האיש viri.Ruth.ij. ותאמר שם האיש

viro fiet ſic

Datiuo לאיש viro.Eſter.vi. ככה יעשה לאיש

dei virum

Accuſatõ איש את איש virũ.iiij.Regũ.vij. את איש האלהים

iniquo a uiro

Ablatiuo מאיש a uiro.p̃s.xviij. מאיש חמס

IN NVMERO PLVRALI

uiros viris uirorum uiri uiri

אישים vel אנשים האישים לאישים את אישים

viris a

ALIVD מאישים

verbo a uerbum uerbo uerbi uerbum

דבר הדבר לדבר את הדבר מהדבר

a uerbis uerba uerbis uerborum uerba

דברים הדברים לדברים את דברים מדברים

Vbi in quibuſdam duplicem articulum reperies.

Huius itaqꝫ declinationis primę cõmunis eſt regula.ut cuiuſcũqꝫ terminationis nomẽ maſculinũ numeri ſingularis tibi propoſitũ fuerit, ſimpliciter ei cata paragogẽ addas iod et mem q̃d p̱ hirek ſonabit im q̃d ſi regat poſt ſe caſum,aut ei cohęreat ,p̱nomẽ ſubiũctiuũ.q̃d dicitus affixum.deponit mem finale.exemplũ Deute.i. אלה הדברים Ideſt hęc ſunt uerba.iam hoc uocabulũ nihil regit. ſed pſalmo.xxxiij. בדברי יהוה ideſt uerbo dñi.hęc uox uerbũ,regit poſt ſe gtũ ſcilicet dñi ut infra de regimine ac cõſtructiõe dicemus.nũc q̃d ad hãc

Plate 38: Johann Reuchlin: De rudimentis Hebraicis, Pforzheim, Thomas Anshelm, 1506. From the reprint, Hildesheim.

bent. vnd als Pontus ſölichs vernam vnd er auch nit anderſt begerē was. antwurt daraff vnd ſprach. Er dancket dem künig vnnd ſeiner landſchafft faſt vnd wie der künig ſein erſter herr wär geweſen. vnd het jm vil eer vnd güts erbotten. vnnd vil mer dann er nymmer kund vnd mocht verdienen. vnd wen̄ er darzů würdig vnd geſchickt wäre das er die aller mächtigeſten frawen in aller dyſer welt möchte gehaben. ſo wolt er Sydoniam dar für nemen. vnd dancket aber faſt vnd vil dem künig. vnnd den herren vnnd freyen die do waren von ſeinem land vnd ſprach er wär gehorſam vnnd willig gefallen zů thůn. dann er hett ſy lieb für alle ander. dye wurden fro von ſeiner antwurt. vnnd giengen vnd ſageten die mär dem künig der ein groß wolgefallen dar ab het. vnd ſchicket von ſtundan nach dem biſchoff. vnnd lieſſen ſy gegen einander verſprechen.

VNd darnach am montag vermäheln. es iſt nit zů fragen ob Sydonia vnd Pontus groß freüd hetten. wann ſy hetten zů tauſent malen gröſſere freüd in jrem hertzen dan̄ ſy beyde außwendig erzeygten. vnd yederman klein vnd groß reych vnd auch arm erfreüten ſich an jrer hochzeyt. Pontus der was weyß vnd wolt auch nyemandts vnwill haben. vnd gieng zů dem burgunde vnnd zů des hertzogen brůder ymbert cholans. vnd zů dem grafen montbeliart die do kōmen waren. vnd beredt ſich gegen jn vnd ſprach. Die abenteüer die vngeuerlich geſchehen wär die wär jm faſt leyd von des herrē tod wegen. vnnd fürwar als er mit jm ſtäch das er nit weſt wer er wär.

i iij

Plate 39: *Pontus und Sidonia*, Augsburg, Johann Schönsperger, 1498 (H 13289). Göttingen State and University Library.

Ein lieplichs lesen vnd ein
warhafftige Hystori wie
einer (d da hieß Hug schäpler vñ wz metzgers gschlecht) ein gewaltiger küng
zů Franckrich ward durch sein grose ritterliche mänheit. vnd als die geschrifft sagt so ist er d nest gewessen nach Carolus magnus sun künig Ludwigē

Plate 40: *Hug Schapler*, Strasbourg, Johann Grüninger, 1500 (H 8970), title page. Göttingen State and University Library.

Von beheyligung des sibenden tags

ALs nu die werlt durch das gepew götlicher weißheit der sechs tag: volēdet vñ himel vñ erdē beschaffē geordnet gezieret vñ zu letst volbracht wordē sind. do hat der glori wirdig got sein werck erfüllet vñ am sybendē tag von den wercken seiner hendt geruet. nach dē er die gantzē werlt vnd alle ding die dar in sind beschaffen het do hat er auffgehört. nit als zewürcken muede. sunder zemachen ein newe creatur d' materi oder gleichnus nit vergangē wer dañ er hott nit auff zewürcken das werck der geperungen. vnd der herr hat den selbē tag gebenedeyet vñ geheiligt vnd inc geheyssē sabathū. das nach hebreyscher zūgē ein rūe bedeüttet darumb das er an dē selben tag ruet vō allem werck das er gemacht het. do vō auch die iuden an dem tag vō aigner arbait zefeiren erkant werdē. Dē selbē tag habē auch etlich haidenische völker vor dem gesetz fürlich gehaltē. vnd also sein wir zū end der götlichen werck komē. darumb so söllen wir dē in dem alle sichtliche vnd vnsichtliche ding sind förchten. liebhaben vnd eren. vnd von dem herren des himels. von dem herren aller gütter. dem gewalt gegebē ist in himel vnd erden. die gegenwürtigen güter. souer die gut sind. vnd auch die waren seligkait des ewigen lebēs suchen.

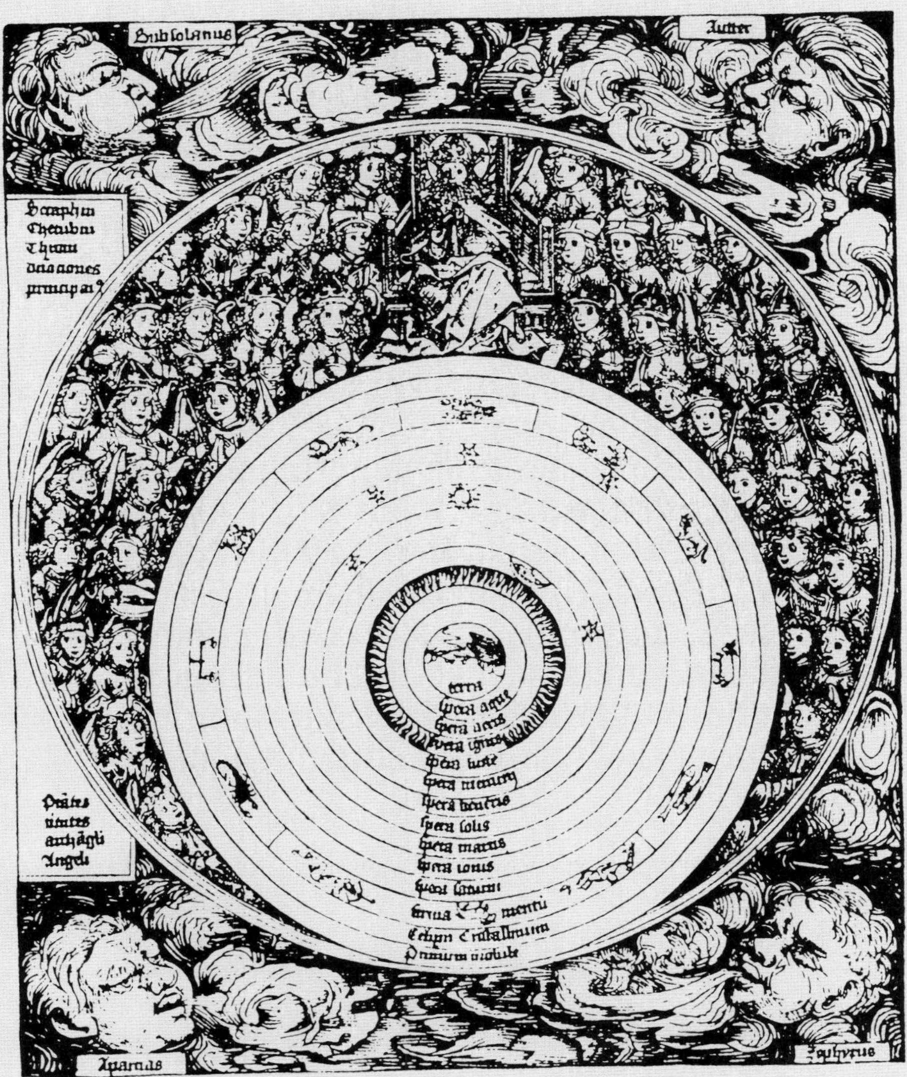

Plate 41: Hartmann Schedel: Weltchronik (The Nuremberg Chronicle), Nuremberg, Anton Koberger, 1493, fol 5v (the seventh day of Creation), woodcut by two different hands – the wind gods in the corners are attributed to the young Albrecht Dürer.

Eins mals ein affe kam gerāt· Do er vil guter
nusse vant· Der hette er gessē gerne· Im was
gesagt von dem kerne· Der wer gar lustiglich vnde gut· Beswert was sein thümer mut· Do er der
pitterkeit empfāt· Der schalē darnach zu hant· Be-
greiff er der schalē hertikeit· Von den nussen ist mir
geseit· Sprach er das ist mir worden kunt· Si haben mir verhonet meinen munt· Hyn warff er sie
zu der selben fart· Der kerne der nusse im nye wart·
Dem selben affen sein gleich· Beide jung arm unde
reich· Die durch kurze pitterkeit· Verschmehē lange susikeit· wenne mā das feuer enzuntē wil· So
wirt des rauches dick zu vil· Der thut einem in den
augen we· wen̄ man darzu bleset mee· Bis es en-

16. 1. Eth.

Plate 42: Ulrich Boner: Der Edelstein (The precious stone). Bamberg, Albrecht Pfister, 1461 (GW 4829), fable 1. Wolfenbüttel, Herzog August Library.

Vil leute das gros wūder nam·Wan̄ er mit eisen
bedecket wart·So verlos er auff der selben vart·
Sein schwere und alle sein krafft·Do sprach des
keisers meisterschafft·Der stein ist herē euch gleich
wan̄ uber alle kūgreich·Ist herre ewr gewalt·Al
des steīs manigfalt·Die weil ir mugt das lebē ge=
hā·So mag euch nymāt widerstā·So seit ir schwe
re als der stein·Alle dise werlt was euch clei·Aber
wan̄ ir gevallet nyder·So kumpt ewr krafft nit
wider·Als schnelle ewr haubt wirt bedacht·So
habt ir verlorn ewr macht·Darumb so rat ich·
Das ir seit bedechtiglich·wan̄ ir seit totlich·Das
sage ich euch sicherlich·Und sullet euch richtē auff

Plate 43: Ulrich Boner: Der Edelstein, Bamberg, Albrecht Pfister 1461, *fable* 72.

aper legē soltēt · do sprach die kacz· wie wol du vil vnd gnůgsam antwůrt hast· so bin ich doch nit in mainung / daz ich fasten welle· ¶ Dise fabel wyset dz die bösen von natur wā sie ettwaz böses in iere gemůt seczent / ob sie wol nit vrsach findent das glimpfflich ze volbringen· doch stand sie nit von ir angenomen boßhait·

¶ Fabula· v· de Vulpe et rubo·

Stultū est auxilium implorarē ab illis quibus a natura datum est obesse / potius q̄ alijs prodesse· de hoc audi fabulam· ¶ Vulpes cum sepem quandam ascenderet / vt periculum vitaret / quod sibi imminere videbat· rubu manibus oprehendit atq̧ volam sentibus profudit· et cū grauiter saucia foret / gemens inquit ad rubuz· vt me iuuares ad te confugi· et tu deterius me periclitasti· Cui rub9 Errasti vulpes ait· que pari dolo me capere putasti qua cetera capi consueuisti· ¶ Fabula significat / q̧ stulte implorat auxiliū ab illis qb9 natuale ē obeē

Plate 44: Heinrich Steinhöwel: *Aesop*, Ulm, Johann Zainer, 1476.

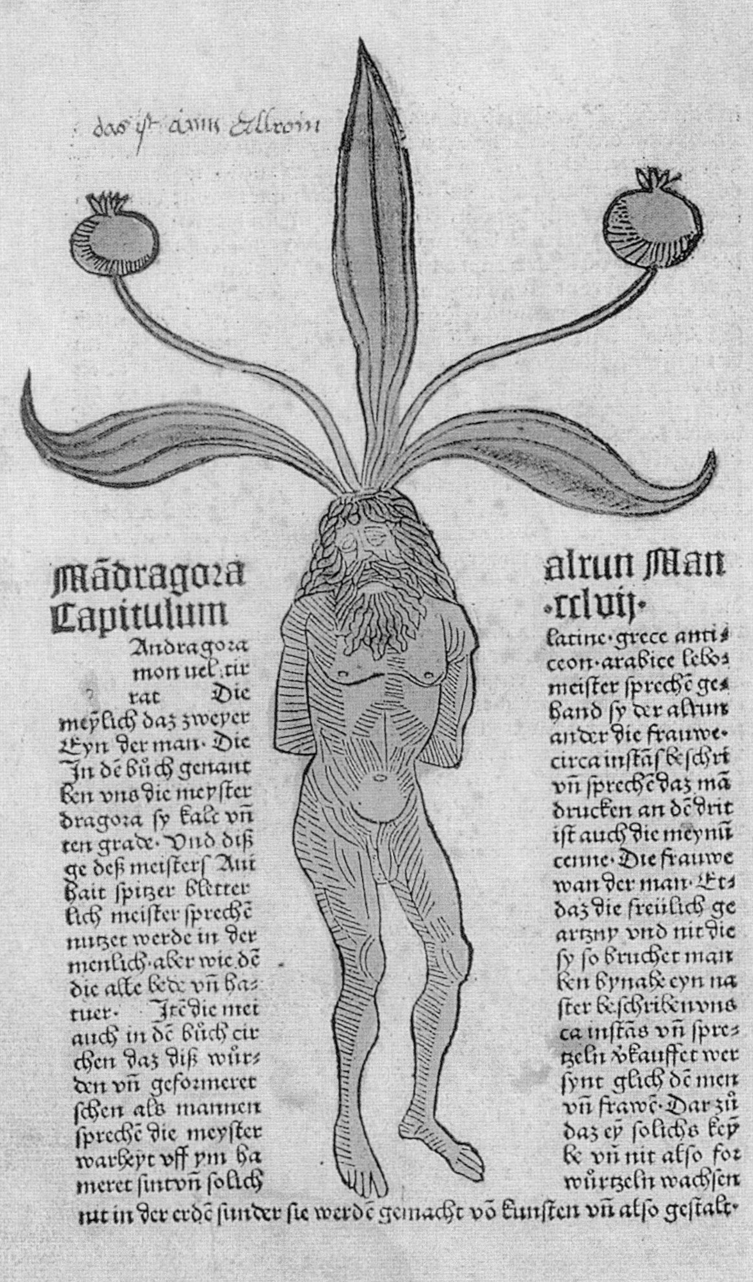

Mādragora Capitulum

Andragora
mon uel: cir
rat Die
meẏlich daz zweyer
Eyn der man· Die
In dē bůch genant
ben vnd die meyſter
dragora ſy kalt vñ
ten grade· Vnd diß
ge deß meiſters Am
bait ſpitzer bletter
lich meiſter ſprechē
nutzet werde in der
menlich· aber wie dē
die alte bede vñ ba:
tuer· Itē die mei
auch in dē bůch cir
chen daz diß wůr:
den vñ geformeret
ſchen als mannen
ſprechē die meyſter
warheyt vff ym ba
meret ſint vñ ſolich

alrun Man ·cclviij·

latine· grece anti-
ceon· arabice lebo-
meiſter ſprechē ge-
band ſy der alrun
ander die frauwe·
circa inſtās beſchri
vñ ſprechē daz mā
drucken an dē drit
iſt auch die meynū
cenne· Die frauwe
wan der man· Et-
daz die freülich ge
artzny vnd nit die
ſy ſo brucher man
ben bynabe eyn na
ſter beſchriben vns
ca inſtās vñ ſpre-
tzeln v'kauffet wer
ſynt glich dē men
vñ frawē· Dar zů
daz ey ſolichs key
be vñ nit alſo for
wůrtzeln wachſen

nit in der erdē ſunder ſie werdē gemacht vō kunſten vñ alſo geſtalt·

Plate 45: Gart der Gesundheit (Garden of health), Mainz, Peter Schoeffer, 1485 (H 8948). Leipzig University Library.

Rosegarten

¶ Item ob das kind geteilt lege oder vff seinem angesicht/ So soll die hebam̄ leichtlich ynlassē ir finger/vn̄ das kind in der sei/ten der müter vmbkerē Oder ob sie ein handt mag ynlassen /soll sie das kind ordnen vnd richten also/ Welche theil des leibs dem vßgāg aller nechst seind/diē sel/ben soll sie haltē vnd vßfüren. doch sol sie aller meist dz haupt süchen/halten vnd vßfüren.

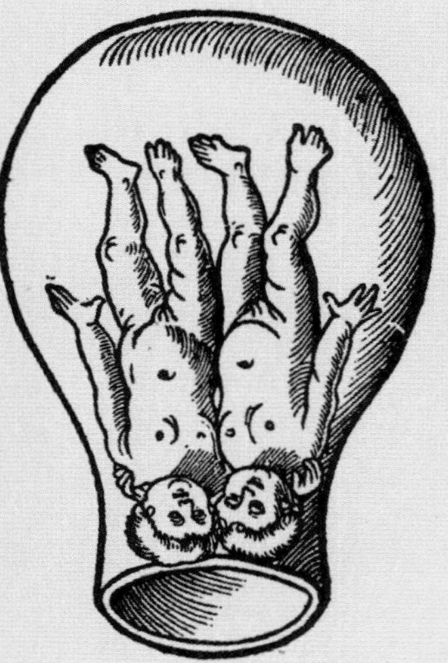

¶ Item ob der kinde mer dan̄ eins wer/als zwyling vnd sich gleich erzeugten mit den höuptern/So sol die hebam̄ eins nach dem andern vßfüren/besonder das erst empfahen /als ob stadt/vnd das ander nitt verlassen.

E.iij

Plate 46: Eucharius Rösslin: Der Schwangern Frauwen vnd Hebammen Rosegarten, (The pregnant woman's and midwife's rosarium), Strasbourg, Martin Flach, 1513. From the facsimile, Dietikon-Zürich, Stocker 1976.

(1532–34), and Michelangelo, among others, encountered them in this form in Italy; a French translation appeared in 1557, an Italian in 1591, and a Dutch one in 1622.

The humanistic recourse to the classical texts of antiquity and a new opening-up of the empirical method brought about a creative climate for fruitful research and development at university level. Lay admission to the universities and the new political power of the civic elite formed the background for vernacular texts to flourish. Printing brought the means to satisfy these educational needs with (relatively) large editions at reasonable prices. This gradual increase in the share of literature in the vernacular was a prelude to its furious growth-rate during the century of reformation.

Broadsides and the "latest news"

Communication changed radically in the fifteenth century. After centuries of restriction to oral discourse, the sermon and the manuscript, new possibilities for the multiplication of religious and secular knowledge were now opening up because of the woodcut and the manufacture of paper in Central Europe. Religious instruction had an age-old tradition, that ran in parallel with preaching, based on the pictorial exposition of spiritual and theological content through its iconographical transfer to church windows or bronze church doors and instructional columns. We think of such magnificent pictorial cycles as those contained in the stained glass of Canterbury and Bourges cathedrals. The chancellor of the University of Paris, Johann Gerson (1363–1420), who worked tirelessly for the reform of religious life in France, recommended at the beginning of the fifteenth century that: "instructional panels should be hung in churches in order to remedy the religious ignorance of the people". Nicholas of Cues renewed this suggestion three decades later in Germany. He must have discovered on his visitations to the German dioceses in 1451 and 1452 that even the basic prayers of the faith were all too frequently unfamiliar, thus he had so-called "Lord's prayer tablets" set up in several churches. One such wooden notice board has been preserved in Hildesheim. It opens with these words: "When the German cardinal Nicholas of Cues was sent to Germany during the pontificate of Nicholas V and in the year following upon the golden year (1451), he reproached the common lay people above all because they could not speak the 'our father' and the creed properly. Therefore he instructed that these should be written out and prominently displayed in the churches. This has been done, and so here follows the Lord's prayer . . .".

Nicholas of Cues might equally well have made use of another method of spreading religious imagery or prayer texts – and one which had been known about for at least fifty years – the single-sided woodblock print transferred to paper by burnishing. A celebrated early example, known as the Buxheim St Christopher, has survived from 1423 (see Plate 47). This popular image with its accompanying Latin couplet followed by that specific date was cut in wood and an impression taken by rubbing.

The picture contains further details from the legendary life and miracles of this saint which would have called for explanation by an instructor. Even the text would have needed to be translated, for it contains the crucial words which reveal the reason for the special position occupied by Christopher in popular devotion: "on the day that you look upon the image of the holy Christopher, you will not die a sudden death". Fear of the *mors repentina* or *mala* – that sudden or evil death which leaves no time for repentence, atonement or conversion – was a horror of which hell-fire preachers made much. This explains the wide distribution of images of St Christopher on church windows, frescoes or stelae, especially in southern Germany.

This saint's image reproduced on paper attests to new and exciting possibilities: in theory, every household could now hang its own St Christopher in a devotional nook, thereby transferring its uplifting powers out of the public arena of the church and into a private and domestic setting. That is why devotional pictures became favourite subjects for the new woodcutting technique. First the illustration and its text would be drawn in reverse on the woodblock by an artist, and then a craftsman would cut away the non-printing areas of the image, the printing surface would be inked, and a dampened sheet of paper placed over it and rubbed down with a burnisher. This relief printing process would yield 200–400 impressions, and possibly more, according to the type of wood used. The cracks which developed in some of the lines show what heavy demands were made of these woodblocks.

As well as St Christopher, we find prints of other patron saints and devotionalia, such as St George, St Barbara, St Catherine, St Michael and St Francis, and of course Madonnas and Crucifixion scenes. By the middle of the century, metal as well as wood had come into use as a surface for cutting.

When several of these woodcut-printed sheets are bound together, then we speak of a "blockbook". Where this happens, the close relationship between visual and textual information called for careful planning, since all the text had to be laboriously cut into the woodblocks. Surviving examples all happen to postdate Gutenberg's invention, but the two techniques developed in parallel to each other. Shorter texts were chosen for blockbooks, such as the *Ten Commandments*, the *Song of Songs*, popular guides to dying of the *Ars moriendi* kind in Latin or

German, and of course the *Biblia pauperum* or "poor man's *Bible*". Here, the message of a sermon was delivered in a clear educational framework, in which connections between Old and New Testaments were highlighted and presented with verbal and visual economy. The example from a *Biblia pauperum* in German (Nuremberg, 1471, see Plate 48) shows the annunciation by an angel to the Virgin Mary flanked by two Old Testament prefigurations: on the left, Eve, who as Mary's anti-type was led astray by the serpent in paradise; and on the right, as a sign of God's power to intervene in the course of nature, the story of Gideon's conversion. Gideon asked God for a sign, and on the second morning found that the fleece layed out before the tent was dry whilst the ground all around it was wet with dew (Judges 6:36–40). The text below tells us to regard this as a sign of godly omnipotence, likewise that Mary: "ohnzerstörung irs leibs unnd der jungfrawschafft durch den heiligen geist geschwengert ward" (without ravage to her body and virginity is made pregnant through the holy spirit). Further quotations from four prophets reinforce the links between the two testaments.

But worldly subject-matter also found its way into blockbooks as well: calendars and primers, for example, or Johann Hartlieb's *Chiromantia*, individual fables, and that most widely circulated of short Latin grammars – the *Donatus* – which we have already encountered.

Typographic broadsides can be traced back to Gutenberg, who printed an *Aderlass- und Laxierkalendar* (bloodletting and laxatives calendar) and a *Cisianus* or guide to the months of the year. Calendars became a reliable mass-production line from the earliest days of printing. As single-sided prints, they could be hung up in the parlour and inspected daily, and for that reason alone very few copies have survived. Some calendars show no more than the dates, and symbols – perhaps to highlight Sundays or the most propitious dates for bloodletting – for those less able to read. Additional text might be printed alongside in German or Latin to provide a calendar of events. A broadside belonging to the University of Göttingen, and unknown until quite recently, was printed for the year 1478 (see Plate 49). In the upper margin there is a "speech balloon" with the New Year's greeting "*Ain gut sälig iar*" which is decoratively supported by the newly born Christ-child, symbol of a new beginning. This same image is repeated within the coloured initial "D". In the six long lines which follow, the most important reference dates for 1478 are given: the initial for Sundays, followed by the golden number, and then the moveable feasts. The left-hand column gives a summary of the seasons, concentrating on the familiar festivals: "March begins the next day after Candlemas", "The month of August starts on the Wednesday after St James." The information in the right-hand column concerns the best days for bloodletting with regard to different generations and parts of the body: "On Monday after Mary's nativity good (for the) elderly (but) excepting the skin." Calendars of this kind ran into large editions of several thousand copies and were printed with undiminished success until well into the eighteenth century.

NEWS-SHEETS

Broadsides with sensational news, such as the latest information concerning theatres of war, freak births or glittering occasions of state, commanded a wide circulation. These were generally called "Newe Zeytung" after their main heading, and gradually the Middle High German term "Zeitung" (at first signifying just "news" or "tidings") gave its name to a new genre or medium. From the outset, this word was often qualified by an adjective such as "alarming", "happy" or "new". In contrast to the periodical press which first surfaced in the seventeenth century, these news-sheets were confined to a single topic and were aimed in each case towards a specific public. Most "current news-sheets" consisted of one news item – usually containing a woodcut, and not always one intended for the purpose – and a rhyming text in two or three columns purporting to be an eye-witness narrative. Without this widespread and popular medium, we would be at best ill-informed about many fifteenth- and sixteenth-century events, including certain natural catastrophies, legal proceedings, the campaigns against the Turks or the early history of the Thirty Years War. Many of the ruling houses exploited this new medium and commissioned writers to feature popular entertainments such as royal weddings and also to report on plans for the call to arms and the conduct of war. Emperor Maximilian I, whilst still regent, began to deploy this means of influencing public opinion. Quite a few publicists loyally disposed towards the empire supported his measures through the journalistic manipulation of natural occurrences.

As an instance of this, a meteorite impact in the neighbourhood of Ensisheim in Alsace was used by Sebastian Brant in order to support Maximilian's policies. On 7 November 1492 a meteorite fell to earth near Ensisheim. It weighed approximately 260 pounds. To this day a fragment of some 100 pounds is kept in Ensisheim town hall. It is the oldest existing meteorite fall for which there are sources and eye-witness reports, and many fragments are housed in the world's leading natural history museums. Sebastian Brant's broadside appeared in that same year from the Basle printer and publisher Johann Bergmann von Olpe, who identifies himself on the page through the initials J. B. and his motto: "Nüt on vrsach" (nothing without a cause; see Plate 50). An expressly prepared woodcut reproduces the exact trajectory of the meteorite, approaching from the west and striking the ground before the city gates of Ensisheim. The text is bilingual, Latin and German, and directed through its language and classical allusions towards a reasonably well-informed public. In building to a climax, Sebastian Brant talks of numerous strange phenomena in recent years which have culminated in this "thunder stone". The Latin text ends with the rather general wish that the misfortune to be expected as a result of this "fall of thunder" may strike evil enemies, whereas the German text speaks unequivocally of an evil omen for the French and Burgundians. The author then addresses a 22-line poem in German directly to Maximilian. He rouses him in theatrical language to advance against the French with the support of Austria and Germany, since fate is on his side. When this pamphlet came out, Maximilian was already on his way to Burgundy in order to exact revenge for a double personal insult: namely that Charles VIII of France had reputiated his marriage contract with Maximilian's daughter Margaret, and married Anne of Brittany, to whom Maximilian had been betrothed. In 1493 Maximilian regained a large part of Burgundy and part of his daughter Margaret's dowry.

This interesting broadsheet reports the meteorite impact in detail, and in its Latin text makes observations about meteorites from antiquity onwards. Sebastian Brant's vernacular text is less concerned to supply information, but comments on the significance of this portent and the support it gives to Maximilian's politics. This combination of an illustrative woodcut with text in two languages must have reached people from broad walks of life. We know of 25 surviving broadsheets in all in which Sebastian Brant comments on natural disasters and gives them a political slant.

The new medium of the broadside was not only available to report sensations, but also to warn against fraud, and counterfeit money in particular. Plate 52 shows a broadside "warning against false gulden" that was probably printed in 1482 by Johann Zainer in Augsburg. A counterfeiter was executed in Göttingen in 1481, after some four tons of forged coin had been confiscated. In order to warn against the circulation of such coinage, 11 identical pamphlets appeared in Augsburg, Basle, Magdeburg, Munich, Nuremberg, Reutlingen and Ulm, closely describing the forged coins and illustrating the obverse and reverse of each. This broadside offered factual information whilst gratifying morbid curiosity about criminal activities, thereby contributing to the prehistory of the popular press.

A BROADSIDE VIEW OF THE NEW WORLD

The news of Columbus's discovery of America, so momentous to us today, did not at the time generate quite the interest that we would have imagined. With hindsight, we know that it represented a decisive breakthrough into a "new world", whereas contemporaries had long grown used to hearing of the discovery of "new islands" in the western oceans by the Portuguese and Spaniards: the Canary Islands were found in the fourteenth century, and several times over in the course of the fifteenth century they learned of new, hitherto unknown peoples along the coasts of Africa, in the Cape Verde Islands and in Guinea. "New peoples" and "new islands" were constantly making news in those days, so when Christopher Columbus's letter appeared in print in 1497 under his title *Von jüngst gefundenen Inseln* . . . (Concerning the islands recently discovered in the Indian Sea) then – however spectacular this publication may seem to us today – it simply joined a long sequence of reported discoveries. His text had appeared in Spanish back in 1493, the same year as the Latin version was published in Rome, Basle, Paris and Antwerp, but it took until 1497 for a German version to reach Strasbourg. Sebastian Brant picked upon this intelligence in his *Narrenschiff* of 1494, and reported on the cultural differences and strangeness of a new people whom he likened to images from the "golden lands" woven into myth:

> Indeed we've since worked out a far way
> To lands beyond both Thule and Norway
> Such as Iceland and Lapland too
> Which in earlier times we never knew
> And lands by Portugal discovered
> And golden isles which Spain uncovered
> Inhabited by naked folk
> Of which the ancients rarely spoke.

The earliest illustrated news-sheets reported these discoveries too, and jumbled up imaginary figures of globetrotters from antiquity such as Herodotus with the narratives of the Portuguese mariners.

The letters of the Florentine scholar Amerigo Vespucci were accorded a very different reception after 1503. Vespucci made it clear that he was dealing with fundamentally new phenomena that were quite unknown to the ancients. He reported in a vivid and down-to-earth manner, giving precise geographical information and a wealth of cultural detail. His Paris publication of 1503 was followed by printings at Venice, Augsburg and Rome in 1504 and no fewer than 25 further editions over the next couple of years, 18 of them from German-speaking regions. The scholarly cosmographers Martin Waldseemüller and Mathias Ringmann based their *Cosmographiae introductio* (1507) on this weighty report, and in it they named the new continent "America" after its author. The single-sided news-sheet *Das sind die new gefunden menschen. . .* (These are the new-found people or race, in form and appearance as they stand here, through the Christian king of Portugal most wondrously discovered) has survived in this unique copy from 1505 (see Plate 51). It shows the landing of three ships of conquest in the New World, with aborigines who are gigantic in relation to the landscape. The woodcut, which takes up about half the page, is faithfully cut according to Vespucci's text: even the colouring follows the information given there. People are depicted from the viewpoint of a European whose attention has been caught primarily by their nakedness and the variety and unaccustomed form of their bodily decoration. Nudity is not interpreted as a positive way of being different, but as a sign of moral degeneracy, just as their (apparent) lack of any economical or political system earns the reproach that: "they live according to nature". The exaggeration of this immorality gave rise to accusations of cannibalism, which are increasingly vented in later pamphlets. A report that syphilis had been introduced to Europe by sailors returning from America also gained ground, together with dark rumours concerning aphrodisiacs. The plunder and "Christianisation" of this continent was justified by the blanket judgement that: "they uphold no regime, have no temples, and obey no laws".

EMPEROR MAXIMILIAN I

Maximilian I (1459–1519) was the first monarch to introduce all the benefits of printing for the furtherance of his rule in a systematic way. He had been chosen king of the Romans at the diet in Frankfurt in 1485, and crowned in Aachen. The death of his father Frederick III in 1493 left him sole ruler of Germany, and he strove at once for a crusade against the infidels and a campaign to be crowned as emperor in Rome – both lifelong aims which he pursued in vain. After many setbacks in campaigns in Northern Italy, he assumed the title of Roman Emperor Elect in the cathedral of Trentino. Decisions of great consequence for the centuries that lay ahead had to be taken under his rule, which affected, among other matters, the reform of the empire, the new regulation of armies and authorities (at the diet of Worms, 1495), and the extension of Habsburg marriage politics to Burgundy, Hungary and Poland (laying the foundations for the Austro-Hungarian monarchy in 1515). His reign was marked by constant menace from the Turks, and Luther's first appearance before the diet of Augsburg in 1518, at which the succession of Maximilian's grandson Karl V was settled with help from the Fugger family of bankers.

The arts and sciences experienced a marked upturn during Maximilian's reign, which the humanists celebrated as the beginning of a "golden age". He opened the University of Vienna to humanistic studies, and encouraged Latin poetry through specific commissions and the crowning of poets, giving attention to national literature in the vernacular (the *Ambraser Heldenbuch*) whilst at the same time endeavouring to imitate the Renaissance culture of the Italian princely courts (with the sequences of woodcuts for the *Triumphzug* and *Ehrenpforte*). Printing offered him a means of emulating the cultivation of these Italian princes with his "paper triumphs". He was open-minded towards any kind of technical, scientific or artistic innovation, and took the same interest in printing as he did in gun-making.

His interest in printing developed at two levels: on the one hand through the publication of pamphlets to influence public opinion in the direction of active political engagement, and on the other hand to manipulate his posthumous fame by compiling voluminous epics.

The pamphlets of Maximilian I

Whilst as a rule it was still customary during the reign of Frederick III for all official publications to be sent out under seal to a chosen circle of recipients (*litterae clausae*), Maximilian issued the majority of his announcements to the diet, proscriptions, mandates and patents as open letters (*litterae patentes*). Public dissemination through notice boards in town halls or announcements from the pulpit must have accounted for a significant part of a large edition of some three to four hundred copies at a time. In this way, the pulpit became an indispensible organ for communication and helped with the enforcement of the legal system: war and peace were announced from there, as were the imperial tax regulations. This fusion of spiritual and political interests is apparent to an exceptional degree in the appeal to engage in a crusade against the Turks, as can be seen from an advertisement recruiting entrants to the order of St George in 1494. The far-reaching audience this was intended to reach is listed comprehensively: "We send each and every of our and the holy empire's electors, spiritual and worldly, prelates, counts, freemen, gentlemen, knights, servants, captains, magistrates, guardians, administrators, officials, village mayors, lord mayors, judges, councillors, citizens and parishioners, and otherwise all others of our and the empire's subjects and followers of whatever dignity, rank and occupation, who come forward or are shown this our royal letter or copy thereof to see or to read, our every grace and every good."

A theoretically unlimited public throughout the empire, who read these writings or heard them read out, would be provided with full commentary on current political happenings: convocations of the diet contained detailed war reports, tidings of victory were broadcast in the form of royal mandates. Apart from the Turkish question, recurrent themes included wars against changing alliances in northern Italy, the campaign for Rome and imperial coronation plans, as well as such signal diplomatic successes as the Austro-Hungarian double betrothal of 1515. "Feldmären", or tales from the front, also reached wider circles as printed folk-ballads, the most popular news medium of the age; a few ballads mostly by unknown authors betray their direct dependence on, or are themselves versifications of, official bulletins.

However, Maximilian did not confine the use of printed pamphlets as a means of influencing the formation of political opinion to within the empire, he was the creator of a special form of psychological warfare as well. During his long drawn-out struggle against Venice he made three attempts (in 1509, 1510 and 1511) to incite the Venetians against the Signoria by means of propaganda leaflets printed in Italian. He let favourable winds waft balloons carrying this early agit-prop behind enemy lines before his archers shot them down. In well-formulated language, these leaflets spoke of freedom and equality, and incited the populace to arise and overthrow the "tyrants".

Maximilian's concern for a memorial

Maximilian certainly used new means of communication to influence his contemporaries politically, but in addition he saw in them a way to plan his own immortality. He put it thus in his autobiography, *Weißkunig*: "He who makes no memorial in his lifetime has no remembrance after his death, and that same man will be forgotten with the tolling of the bell, and therefore the money that I expend on this memorial will not be lost."

The recording of historical events for posterity – caring for what he calls the memorial ("Gedechtnus") – became the real foundation for his literary and artistic endeavours. He wanted to preserve traditions and at the same time to offer a model for his successors. Not actions alone but their *archiving* became in his eyes a vital task for every ruler. In his autobiography in Latin and its German translation as the *Weißkunig*, he attempted to assemble the materials for future historians. It is true that the *Weißkunig* remains skeletal, for at every turn he lacked sufficient space for narrative, and events were often inaccurately recounted. Complex historical situations were reduced to tournaments and battles between parties identified only by their heraldic colours, and the political background and diplomatic exchanges went unmentioned. We are left with 236 historically faithful woodcuts which were produced between 1514 and 1516 by Hans Burgkmair, Leonhard Beck, Hans Schäufelein and Hans Springinklee, among others. The *Weißkunig* encountered no contemporary reaction for it was not printed until 1775.

Maximilian did, however, have the Augsburg court printer Johann Schönsperger the elder print about forty copies on vellum and three hundred on paper of his verse epic *Theuerdank* in 1517. This epic poem, consciously modelled on medieval heroic literature, relates 80 of Maximilian's adventures on his journey to marry Mary of Burgundy (their identities are concealed behind the allegorical presentation). The individual adventures are loosely related to the courtship, and their outcome – carrying off the noble bride – is revealed, contrary to standard practice, in the opening chapter. A storyteller called Ehrenhold leads the hero through the 80 adventures that three malicious opponents with the expressive names "Fürwittig", "Unfallo" and "Niedelhart" have in store for him. Sir Theuerdank overcomes all perils, even natural catastrophes and diseases, through presence of mind, wisdom and courage. The marriage is postponed until after the capture of the Holy Land and the blessing of God which will follow from that achievement.

The fraktur typeface was specially designed by Vincenz Rockner, likewise the calligraphic flourishes which recall the manuals of the writing masters (see Plate 53). In order to keep up this imitation of handwriting, a few of the lower-case characters and most of the capitals have alternative versions: "D", "E", "J" and "M" had no fewer than eight variants cut and typecast for each. The large initials and flourishes to the ascenders and descenders were set and printed from a separate forme, and not from metal type but from woodcuts, so that a richer black resulted from the wood taking up and transferring the ink more effectively. Tell-tale cracks to some of the flourishes demonstrate that wood was used. The woodcutter Jost de Negker, who had come to Augsburg from Antwerp shortly beforehand, may have cut these, and he was also responsible for most of the 118 woodcut illustrations. Maximilian chose to have the *Theuerdank* printed, not because this was a quick and simple means of reproduction, but because he wanted to imitate a manuscript in print, and so increase its exclusiveness.

Printing and the Reformation

"Dr Martin Luther said: Printing is *summum et postremum donum*, that through which God drives the objectives of the evangelists forward. It is the last flame before the extinction of the world." With this enthusiastic encomium on printing, Johann Aurifaber closes his *Table-talk* (*Tischreden oder Colloquia Doctor Martin Luthers*) of 1566, in which he passes on the ideas of the Reformation in popular form through lively quotations. Aurifaber (1519–75) discerns in Luther's graphic dictum the central role of printing in the spread of Reformational doctrines, and above all of the *Bible* itself. The quotation also reminds us indirectly of the bilinguality of literature in the fifteenth and sixteenth centuries; works in Latin predominated, although nearly three times as much vernacular literature appeared between 1518 and 1526 as did between 1501 and 1517.

GERMAN BIBLES BEFORE LUTHER

The history of printing is inextricably bound up with the spread of the *Bible*: in the early 1450s it was the *Vulgate* – St Jerome's translation, which had been the standard one since late antiquity – that Gutenberg chose to be the first printed book of any substance and which he produced magnicently in a stately textura typeface. During the remainder of the fifteenth century, 94 editions of the complete Vulgate appeared in all, of which 22 were closely modelled on the *Gutenberg Bible*. The first book to be printed in Strasbourg was also a 49-line *Vulgata* (GW 4203) of about 1460, a copy of which in the university library at Freiburg is known to have been rubricated in 1460 and 1461. It was produced by Johann Mentelin, Strasbourg's first printer. Mentelin came from present-day Sélestat, where he is on record as a "Goldschreiber" (lit. "writer in gold") and notary. He was awarded Strasbourg citizenship in 1447, probably began to print there from about 1458, and went on to produce in 1466 the earliest complete *Bible* in German, based on a lost translation of more than a century earlier. This followed the Latin model so doggedly that its German text can only be grasped by someone who knows

Latin grammar as well. Furthermore, an example (Genesis 1:3–4) shows that its choice of words was already old-fashioned:

dixitque Deus	*fiat lux*	*et facta lux*
Vnd got der sprach.	liecht werde gemacht	Vnd das liecht ward gemacht.
And God said.	Let there be light	and there was light.

et vidit Deus lucem	*quod esset bona.*
vnd got der sache daz liecht	das es ward gut.
And God saw the light	that it was good.

Mentelin set the text to a column depth of 61 lines in a very small point size of a still clumsy-looking Gothic-roman typeface, so that the overall extent could be brought down to 812 pages. The order of the books is broadly conventional for the Vulgate, except that he places the Acts of the Apostles after Hebrews rather than after the Gospel according to St John.

The text area is generously laid out with wide column separation and de luxe margins, and the interlinear spacing is correctly judged for the typesize, so that excellent reading conditions are created despite the small typeface. Here, as in his other books, Mentelin makes no use of initials or woodcuts, but leaves spaces for a rubricator to insert the initials. Our specimen page (see Plate 54) shows the opening of the first book of Maccabees: the rubricator added the running headline and the opening of the *Prologos* by hand, as well as the seven-line initial for the prologue and the eight-line initial to the first book.

Despite its antiquated language, this version of the *Bible* went through 13 further printings, 9 of them in Augsburg alone. Individual words which had totally fallen out of use were replaced in the second printing by Heinrich Eggestein in Strasbourg (1470) and the third by Jodokus Pflanzmann in Augsburg (1475), but a thorough text revision with the help of the Vulgate was not undertaken until it came to the fourth edition, printed by Günther Zainer in Augsburg in 1476. In his publisher's announcement of 1476 – and one of the first printed book trade advertisements of all – Zainer described it as follows:

> The book of the German *Bible* with pictures, corrected with great industry and made faithful. Thus all words incomprehensible or

> foreign to German, such as there were in the first little *bibles* to be printed, have all been taken out, and it has been set and made after the Latin.

Besides improving and modernising the text, Zainer added illustrations to a German *Bible* for the first time. There were 73 pictorial initials for the openings of each biblical book, and these illustrated 45 biblical scenes, or showed portraits of the authors or the presentation of apostolic letters. (See Plate 55 which shows the presentation of the apostle Paul's letter to the Ephesians.) It so happened that these initials occupied a disproportionate two-thirds of the column width. The prologues themselves open with square initials decorated with lilies of the valley (the initial "P" appearing twice on this page) which are printed alongside the running headlines in black and the chapter headings in red. Zainer's accomplished Gothic-roman creates a restful and well-balanced page, to which the generous whites between columns and between sections contribute. The evenly spaced lines and the quality of the typeface are more apparent from our second example, with its expressive initial for the opening of Isaiah, showing the tree of Jesus coming forth out of the stem of Jesse (Isaiah 11:1–9, see Plate 56). Günther Zainer used this woodblock again in a second edition of 1477, and after his death it is to be found once more in an edition printed by Anton Sorg in Augsburg in 1480.

We are led from this style of illustrative book decoration towards the narrative woodcut – which does not merely edify Christians, but actively encourages reading and facilitates understanding of the *Bible* – through two *Bibles*, in Low German and the Lower Rhenish dialect respectively, which made their appearance in Cologne in 1478 and were probably printed by Bartholomäus von Unkel to the order of a publishing consortium formed by Messrs Johann Helmann and Arnold Salmonster from Cologne and Anton Koberger of Nuremberg. The Low German edition (GW 4307, see Plate 57) has 113 illustrations, whereas the other version (GW 4308) has 123. The woodcuts were evidently influenced by the "author portraits" (evangelists, prophets and apostles) of Zainer's edition, but they are also related to miniatures in manuscript *Bibles* and story *Bibles* from the Cologne-Netherlandish region. The plainly narrative character of these illustrations and a detailed introduction that exhorted every Christian to read the *Bible* are evidence of a drive on the part of the *devotio moderna* to bring the word of God within the reach of the laity as well. The publishers were probably Brethren of the Common Life and Carthusians from Cologne, who referred in their introduction to those pictorial representations handed down in churches and monasteries which served in the same way for the instruction of the faithful. The translation from Latin into these two dialects, which were spoken in the diocese of Cologne, shows these current initiatives being put into effect. Dominant, two-column woodcuts stamp their image on these *Bibles*, which are decorated with further ingenious marginal borders. Plate 58 shows the creation story from Genesis, with the creation of Eve from Adam's rib. This pictorial subject, taken over from manuscript illumination, became highly popular as a woodcut and was widely circulated in countless *Bibles*, and appeared in encyclopaedias as well. The creation picture shows God the Father in a circle of archangels contemplating the created firmament, with waters, winds, and animals and plants in a hilly landscape. The four blocks which make up the border were re-used a number of times, at the start of the volume, for example, and for the opening page of Revelation.

These woodcuts enjoyed further circulation through the great Nuremberg publisher Anton Koberger, who had been a partner in the Cologne *Bible* enterprise. He had acquired the woodblocks in Cologne, and had 109 of them printed and at least partly coloured in his own workshops for his *Bible* of 1483. The text relied on Zainer's edition, improved once again with reference to the Vulgate. In the colophon (fol. 586v) Koberger hints at rather more: "prepared against the Latin text . . . and with splendid pictures". Koberger had at his disposal a far-reaching network of European business contacts, and had obviously printed a very large edition. He used a distinctive bastarda typeface for the text, which still has resemblances to an Upper Rhenish book hand, but already constitutes a clear early form of the fraktur which was taking shape in Nuremberg at the time. Such a typeface gives a page of German setting an entirely different look and texture from a contemporary page of Latin set in roman. Whilst the running headlines and chapter headings are printed with the text, spaces are left free for the large initials, which, in the Göttingen University Library copy, have been richly painted in a variety of techniques (see Plate 59). The woodcut of the creation story taken over from the Cologne *Bibles* has a ground of gold leaf and has been painted over in transparent colours in which blue, green and yellow tones prevail. The second pictorial example (Plate 60) shows the opening of Luke's gospel: the evangelist is depicted with his symbolic calf, and there are allusions to the special significance of the childhood of Jesus for Luke in the scenes of the birth at Bethlehem, the three kings and the presentation in the temple.

These editions were as handsomely decorated by hand as if they had been manuscripts, and accordingly sold for a high price which made their aquisition by the "common man" out of the question. Simpler "utility *Bibles*" were printed by Johann and Silvan Otmar in Augsburg between 1507 and 1518, in which woodblocks from Johann Schönsperger's edition of 1487 were recycled.

The total of 18 German-language *Bibles* before Luther is a remarkable one, and if their impact was restricted, then this was largely due to high prices, outmoded language, and a word-for-word approach to translation that adhered too closely to the Latin model, blurring comprehension and garbling sense. These German versions were only really accessible to those who could have read the Latin text in any case. Added to this – as the Church pressed its claim to be the sole interpreter of the scriptures – the necessary incentive to purchase these editions was lacking.

The fundamentally new significance that Luther conferred on the *Bible* for theological thinking and religious practice – the principle of the primacy of the Holy Scriptures in questions of faith (*sola scriptura*) and the empowerment of the laity to read the *Bible* for themselves and to decide between revealed truth and the fraudulent practices of the "old Church" – in addition to the creative power of the language in which his new German version had been hewn from the Latin original, secured for Luther's *Bible* translation an unprecedented resonance: from 1522 until Luther's death (1546), more than three hundred High German *Bible* editions appeared in an estimated total of more than half a million copies. One third of all German book production in the first half of the sixteenth century is accounted for by Luther's writings.

"I am a peasant's son, my greatgrandfather, grandfather and father were true-born peasants. I had as a matter of fact, as Philipp Melanchthon says, a supervisor, a local mayor and the sort you would expect to find in a village where someone has to be chief labourer over the rest. That was after my father moved to Mansfeld and became a smelter. I am from there." Luther's autobiographical sketch in his *Table-talk* (no. 6250) describes conditions in a struggling Thuringian copper-mining district and the social transformation of his family. A year after his birth on 10 November 1483 in Eisleben, his parents Hans and Margarethe Luder settled in Mansfeld, where his father had found work in the mining industry. With this occupational change came a rise in the economical and social fortunes of the family; his father became a master smelter in 1491, and as owner of a copper smelting furnace, became one of the four members of the Mansfeld village council elected to defend the rights of citizens against the local authorities.

Their son Martin at first attended the Latin school in Mansfeld, then went on to the cathedral school in Magdeburg in 1496, and after 1498 to St George's school at Eisenach. In the summer semester of 1501 he signed the matriculation book of the arts faculty at the university of Erfurt, by 29 September 1502 he had graduated as *Baccalaureus artium*, and he obtained his master's degree in January 1505. In the first semester of his ensuing legal studies at Erfurt he changed direction radically and entered the Erfurt convent of the Augustinian Eremites. He commenced theological studies at the university of Erfurt on their instruction after he had taken orders on 3 April 1507, and thus renewed his confidence in Aristotelian philosophy and the nominalist scholastic philosophy and theology of William of Ockham (*c.*1285–1349) and the Tübingen philosopher Gabriel Biel (*c.*1410–95), and his opposition to those doctrines based on revelation – with their sharp separation of reason and faith – against which he was later to take a hard line.

In October 1508 the vicar-general of the order of Augustinian Eremites, Johann von Staupitz (*c.*1469–1524), moved Luther to their Wittenberg convent and immediately entrusted him with a lectureship in philosophy at the university in that town. He travelled to Rome in 1510/11 with a brother of the order on a mission on behalf of dissenting convents, in order to settle differences concerning the organisation of the order. His observations of the condition of the Catholic Church there under Julius II, which he was later to style his "Roman experience" (where, amongst other matters, a plenary indulgence had been issued in 1506 for the building of St Peter's, against which many countries, led by the German rulers, had spoken out), laid the foundation-stone for his critique of the venal power of the papacy.

In October 1512, under the presidency of Andreas Bodenstein of Karlstadt a doctorate in theology was conferred upon Luther and he took over the chair of biblical exegesis (*lectura in biblia*) from his religious mentor Johann Staupitz. Staupitz had moulded Luther in the spirit of Augustine and the *devotio moderna* of the late Middle Ages. As professor of biblical exposition, Luther concentrated in the years which followed on the interpretation of the Psalms (1513–15) and the epistles to the Romans (1515–16). The Pauline doctrine of sin and forgiveness stood at the heart of his strict inquiry, which was strongly aligned to the actual text of the *Bible*. He had both texts freshly printed for his lectures, with extra space between lines and generous margins so that his listeners could note down the elucidations; Luther's own copy of the *Psalter* with his handwritten notes is today kept at the Herzog August Library in Wolfenbüttel.

THE MAIN TEXTS OF THE REFORMERS

Luther's new theological approach is particularly apparent in his appraisal of the justice of God and his theory of the justification of man. He taught that God's justice is not a judgmental but rather a forgiving justice which can be received by the faithful alone, and in this he set himself not only against scholastic theology but also against the practice of piety at the time. His first writing in the vernacular dealt logically with the seven penitential psalms (*Sieben Bußpsalmen*, 1517), in which he drew the seriousness of penitence and judgment into the foreground and preformulated the attack on the "justification through works" of scholastic theology. These arguments culminated in his *Disputatio contra scholasticam theologiam* of September 1517, in which he turned against the easy remission of sins typical of his age and the thesis that every "common" man could find God through his own resources. He spoke instead of man's fundamental sinfulness, and the necessity of grace for salvation. From this position it was but a small step to condemning the Church's system of indulgences out of hand. In the well-known 95 *theses* – which Luther addressed on 31 October 1517 to Archbishop Albrecht of Mainz (who was responsible for farming the sale of indulgences from the pulpit), and which mark the beginning of the Reformation – he laments the false and deadly security which indulgences produce through deception (*Theses* 31, 49, 52); works of love and prayer are to be more highly valued than indulgences (*Theses* 41 and 74). In the letter to Archbishop Albrecht, he uses the surname "Luther" that is familar today, whereas up until then he had used the family name Luder. The fact that between 1517 and 1519 he made use of the Latinized Greek name "Eleutherius" (the free one) in parallel to this shows that it was a conscious and programmatic decision to be known as "Luther". He made an etymological connection with "Eleutherius", and incorporated the idea of Christian freedom into his own persona. This may be verified through a further letter which he wrote on 11 November 1517 to his Erfurt friend Johann Lang, which he signed "Fr[ater] Martinus Eleutherius, imo dulos et captivus nimis, Augustinianus Wittenbergensis", which translates as "Brother Martin, the [through God] free one, or much more servant and prisoner [of God], Augustinian in Wittenberg", thus anticipating the fundamental idea of his tract on freedom of 1520, *Von der Freiheit eines Christenmenschen*: "A Christian man is a free ruler over all things and subject to nobody. A Christian man is a willing servant to all things and subject to everyman." This apparent contradiction, based on St Paul (I Corinthians, 9:19), resolves itself through reflection on the dual nature of each person. The "inner man" has no need of worldly, external things: "The gospel alone, the word of God", "Only the faith makes devout, free and holy." The concept of freedom which Luther acknowledged through his change of name as early as 1517 signals that he was conscious of new beginnings in his own theological argumentation.

Counter to Luther's original intentions, the 95 *theses* (couched in Latin) had spread rapidly; in order to formulate these more understandably for wider circles, he brought out his sermon on indulgences and grace (*Sermon von Ablaß und Gnade*) in March 1518, which created such interest that it had to be reprinted 25 times in the space of two years. True Christians, who felt repentant for their sins, would perform the "works of satisfaction" as a matter of course; in contrast to which, indulgences only created "lazy and imperfect Christians", Luther explained in plain language. Those who would rebuke him as a heretic because of these theses were: "dark minds, who had never even smelt the *Bible*, had never read Christian teaching and had never understood their own teachers, but were well nigh rotting with their gaping and threadbare scholastic opinions . . .".

Only two months after that, proceedings against Luther commenced in Rome; on the instructions of Pope Leo X (*reigned* 1513–21) he was examined by Cardinal Cajetan (1469–1534) on the fringes of the diet at Augsburg, but he refused to recant; in December Luther's sovereign, the elector Frederick of Saxony, rejected Cajetan's application either to hand him over to Rome or to banish him from his territories. The furious exchange of discussions, lectures and sermons reached its climax in the 1519 "Leipzig disputation" which took place between the Ingolstadt professor of theology Johann Eck, Andreas Karlstadt and Luther. Luther treated the justification doctrine so broadly that he threw out every authority of the Church other than the *Bible*, reduced the office of the Church to a purely functional significance, and concluded that even Councils could err. Pope Leo X demanded of him that he retract all his *theses* within sixty days in a bull which threatened excommunication, *Exurge Domine* of 15 June 1520, whilst Luther published his most important Reformational works: *An Address to the Christian Nobility of the German Nation*, *On the Babylonian Captivity of the Church of God*, and *On the Liberty of a Christian Man*. Of these tracts alone, 36 editions appeared in barely two years in the German, Dutch, English, Spanish, Czech and Latin languages. The papal nuncio Giralamo Aleandro (1480–1542) caused these and others of his writings to be burnt in Cologne and Mainz; Luther, on the other hand, burnt the excommunication bull and a copy of canon law in Wittenberg on 10 December. On 3 January 1521 Pope Leo X pronounced the anathema against Luther in the bull *Decet Romanum pontificem*. In April 1521 Luther was summoned to appear before Emperor Charles V (1500–58) and the diet of Worms. His journey through many places on the way became a triumphal procession; but for all that, imperial outlawry was pronounced against Luther in the edict of Worms, and the printing and distribution of his writings was forbidden. Luther was able to hide away as "Junker Jörg" at the castle on the Wartburg under the protection of elector Frederick from May 1521 until March 1522; numerous sermons and writings emerged from there, among them the *Magnificat verdeutscht und ausgelegt*, and, in the space of only eleven weeks from December 1521 to February 1522, his translation of the *New Testament* from the Greek.

PAMPHLETS

It was not only Luther's own writings that were printed as leaflets of four, eight or sixteen pages, but also those of his fellow combatants and supporters. The pamphlets of Ulrich von Hutten (1488–1523) or Hans Sachs (1494–1576) call for special mention. The dialogue form adopted from Latin literature proved to be particularly suited to broadcasting the new ideas of the Reformation because of its instructional nature. Fundamental questions of theology could be grasped by the man in the street when presented as a game of question and answer. Hans Sachs has a canon and a shoemaker in earnest disputation (Nuremberg, 1524); through their dialogue, the canon is exposed as a shallow and unreflective pedant, whilst the cobbler "Hans" is shown as a believer who holds to his *Bible*. They explore three problematical fields which Luther had already identified in his appeal *An den Christlichen Adel teutscher Nation* (Address to the Christian Nobility of the German Nation): the exclusive right of the Pope to interpret the *Bible* and to call a Council, and the supremacy of spiritual over temporal power.

Representatives of both confessional sides make their respective appearances in these prose dialogues and leave a record of their words and actions. Abstract theological questions do not always take centre-stage, and the effects of religious attitudes on daily life also feature in dialogues about usury, false fasts, or the oppression and exploitation of the peasantry. It follows that these leaflets have a fundamental importance for the study of the intellectual background to the Peasant's War of 1524–25. The leaflet containing the *Zwölf Artikeln aller Bauernschaft* was distributed through a massive first printing and numerous reprints. It originally set out to be a discussion document between the peasants and the towns and noble landowners in particular. In it, the peasants rebel against tithes, against serfdom and against labouring for their landlords, and argue for the natural produce of field, wood and river to be freely available to them.

In the first thirty years of the sixteenth century more than 9000 pamphlets appeared, and with the Reformation, this rose to represent a 17 per cent share of total production by title after 1517. Within a year the peasant's "twelve articles" had appeared in over 24 editions from 18 printers in 15 different towns. This had the effect of a seven-fold increase in its share of the market for vernacular texts between 1519 and 1522, from which the mounting circulation of its contents may be inferred. Even assuming that editions of only 500 copies were the norm, the public they reached would have been disproportionately greater, for leaflets were read out and discussed in many places within each community. We know that Luther's Reformational hymns were first circulated in editions of 400 copies, which were then announced before public services so that the faithful could have access to them. There is a Reformational flyer of 1524 demonstrating just how flexible this practice was, which opens with the paradoxical sentence: "Dear reader, if you can't read, then find a young man who can read this text to you." The spread of Reformational ideas was achieved through printing, but their impact was relayed to wider audiences with the spread of these texts from the pulpit and through song.

Broadsides, moreover – mostly large-format sheets printed on one side only, and furnished with a lively woodcut and a text (usually in verse) – took on a new quality. Our example (see Plate 61) shows the persuasive impact of a woodcut with a text which clarifies it and at the same time takes the instructive form of a dialogue: *Ein neuer Spruch, wie die Geistlichkeit und etlich Handwerker über den Luther klagen* (a new poem: how the clergy and certain craftsmen complain about Luther). At first, its author Hans Sachs lends rhetorical support to the complaining workers who had brought home good money during the previous century as contractors to the Church: the bell-founder, the cutter of vestments, etc. Whilst these classes now complain that the Reformation is leading to cut-backs in this outward show, Sachs succeeds in drawing attention to the true inner value of the faith, and in putting Luther forward in both text and woodcut as the go-between for the "common man", who is seen to be praised by God the Father for discharging that role. The verse form suggests once again that this text would have been recited and discussed by the congregation. Schooled by such broadsheets and pamphlets and introduced to Lutheran theology with its wealth of ideas, believers were motivated to become more familiar with the *Bible*. As the translation of the New Testament was issued in serial parts from the outset, the text could be acquired at affordable prices and in manageable sections, and could thus be disseminated more rapidly than would have been possible with the sale of a complete *Bible*. The secret of its bestselling status, however, rests surely with Luther's matchless achievement as a translator.

LUTHER'S TRANSLATION PRINCIPLES

Even if the immediate occasions for the translation were the enforced exile on the Wartburg and – according to Luther's own account – an urgent request from Philipp Melanchthon, the motivations nevertheless lay deeper. Luther's public and clear avowal of the *Bible* as the highest authority in questions of faith and his steadfast reasoning from the *Bible* had awakened a great need for an accessible translation. At the heart of his *Bible* translation stands a humanistic turning back to original sources, the Greek and Hebrew texts, in contrast to the translations which had gone before which relied on the *Vulgata* alone. He freed himself from the slavish imitation of Latinistic style, in that he conveyed "not word for word, but sense for sense", as Heinrich Steinhöwel (1412–c.1478) had already postulated for his own prose translations in the fifteenth century. In a circular letter on translation (*Sendbrief von Dolmetzschen*, 1530), Luther took on the "literalists":

> For one must not ask the letters of the Latin tongue / how German should be spoken / as these asses do / but instead / ask the mother in the home, the children in the alleys / the common man in the market about it and watch what comes out of their mouths / how they utter things / and interpret that, then will

> they understand / and take note / that one is speaking with them in German.

For example, he does not translate *Ex abundantia cordis os loquitur* in a literal way as "Aus dem Überfluß der hertzen redet der mund" (out of the abundance of the heart the mouth speaketh, Matt. 12:34 KJV), but almost proverbially as "Wes das hertz voll ist, des gehet der munt über" (what the heart is full of, trips off the tongue). *Ut quid perditio ista ungenti facta est* comes out not as "Warum ist dise verlierung der salben geschehen?" (why was this waste of the ointment made? Mark 14:4 KJV), but as "Es ist schade um die Salbe" (it is a pity about the ointment). Freedom of wording finds its limits where the danger of falsifying the sense arises, as Luther explains:

> Again we have to linger / immediately after the words have been translated / over whether we could possibly have given other and clearer ones / for the reason / that something more is lying in the same words. (*Summarien über die Psalmen und Ursachen des Dolmetschens*, 1533)

If the literal sense of a sample can not be reproduced by a free translation (that is, if "something more is lying", or a richer, more subtle shade of meaning is encapsulated in the wording of the sample) then he brings this out through word-for-word translation. The supreme guiding principle for him was to convey the uncorrupted "meaning" of the text conscientiously: "auff mein bestes vermügen vnd auff mein gewissen" (to the best of my means and of my belief), as he puts it in the *Sendbrief*. It follows from this that writing is its own best interpreter (*scriptura sui ipsius interpres*), and therefore where translation problems occur, comparable places in the text have to be looked at together. He weighed up the individual line against the evidence of the *Bible* as a whole – the understanding of which he owed to his study of hermeneutics – and approached the analysis of questions of detail each time from the individual to the whole, from the letter to the spirit. The central example for the interdependence of linguistic and theological reasoning is his translation of Romans 3:28: "So we now hold / that a man is justified / without the deeds of the law / through faith alone." Luther defended himself vigorously against the objection that the word “alone” is not to be found in either the Greek or Latin texts, on the grounds that only by introducing “only” or “alone” could an “article of faith of Christian teaching” be clearly worded, namely the central message of St Paul that God is not to be influenced by good works in the distribution of his mercy.

The introduction of modal particles such as “alone”, “though”, “even”, “only”, “now”, “yet” etc., is typical of Luther’s style where it closely follows the spoken language. Along with sentence-rhythm, repetition, assonance and other means, they give his translations their sermon-like character. He was at pains “das Evangelium sprechen zu lassen” (to let the gospel speak). He specially favoured alliterations (“Der Herr ist mein Hirte”, “Dein Stecken und Stab”, Ps. 23; “Lasset euer Licht leuchten vor den Leuten”, Matt. 5:16) and words linked through rhyme (“Rat und Tat”, Prov. 8:14; “singen und klingen”, Ecclus. 39,20). The quest for the right choice of words was lifelong, and he revised his translations several times: at first he had the phrase “und er fing zu erzittern und zu engsten” in St Mark’s passion story, which changes in 1530 to “zu zittern und zu zagen” (to shiver and to shake, Mark 14:33). Similarly, he avoided the wooden nominative style of 1520, “und sie werden euer etliche zum Tod helfen” (and some of you shall they cause to be put to death, Luke. 21, 16 KJV) by changing in 1530 to “und sie werden euer etliche töten” (and they will kill some of you). Luther’s wrestlings for the right word still bear fruit in everyday speech: words he invented, such as “Denkzettel” (memo or reminder note), “Feuereifer” (burning enthusiasm), “Herzenslust” (heart’s content), “Morgenland” (the East) are still current, as are his turns of phrase “ein Buch mit sieben Siegeln” (a book with seven seals, Rev. 5:1), “seine Hände in Unschuld waschen” (to wash one’s hands in innocence, Ps. 26:6), “der Dorn im Auge” (a thorn in the eye, Num. 33:55), or “im Dunkeln tappen” (grope in the dark, Deut. 28:29).

BIBLE TRANSLATIONS FROM 1522 TO 1546

Luther’s *Bible* translations began with the New Testament, which he produced from the Wartburg. His source was a copy of the second edition of the original Greek text with Latin translation and *annotationes* by

Erasmus of Rotterdam which came out at Basle in 1519, and alongside which he used the familiar text of the *Vulgata*. There is no evidence that he referred systematically to any of the earlier German translations, although in rare cases he does incorporate a useful phrase which had passed into general currency. The accomplishment of the new version lay not merely in its language, but in Luther's interpretative additions by way of prefaces and marginal notes. In these prefaces he emphasises the separation of the New Testament from the Old Testament, the latter being "teaching and law", whereas the former on the contrary consisted of "gute Botschaft / gute Mehre / gute newe Zeytung" (gospel / good parables / glad tidings) which are revealed to the faithful through narrative sermons. The marginal notes contain definitions of terms, factual explanations and allegorical interpretations that concentrate on conveying the full meaning of the biblical words. With the parable of the kingdom of heaven, which is likened to a treasure hidden in a field or a merchant seeking goodly pearls (Matt. 13:44–46), Luther comments on the significance of the *Bible*: "The hidden treasure is the Gospel / that gives us mercy and justice on our merits / therefore it makes us joyful if we find it / that is / a good cheerful conscience / which we can not obtain through works alone." But direct confrontations with his opponents can also spill over into these notes, as when, for instance, he reprimands those who teach the commandments but do not follow them (Matt. 5:19) as a "herd of papists".

The book of Revelation has hardly any commentary, instead its metaphorical language was matched to 21 illustrations from Lucas Cranach's workshop. These were closely modelled on Albrecht Dürer's 14 woodcuts for the "Apocalypse" (1498 and 1511), but altered in a number of iconographical details and in order to correspond more strongly to the letter of the text. They exhibit a marked anti-Roman bias, which finds its climax in the identification of the whore of Babylon (i.e. the antichrist) with the pope.

In March 1522 Luther left the Wartburg and revised the translation as soon as he got back to Wittenberg with the help of the professor of Hebrew and Greek there, Philipp Melanchthon (1497–1560). After five months' printing time in the workshops of Melchior Lotter the younger, *Das Neue Testament Deutzsch* was published in folio format and in an edition of about 3000 copies by Lucas Cranach and Christian Döring in good time for the Leipzig autumn fair (29 September to 6 October 1522). The price of the so-called *September Testament* was about a gulden (although this would have varied according to condition, whether bound or otherwise), which would have represented about two months' wages for a schoolmaster, or the price of a calf. Nevertheless, the publishers were able to start printing a second edition immediately after the first had appeared, and this was ready on 19 December 1522 (the so-called *December Testament*); it contained several hundred improvements to word-selection and syntax, and the marginal notes were supplemented by more material of the kinds already noted. The work enjoyed no privileged protection, and in the following year 12 complete reprintings took place in Augsburg, Basle, Grimma and Leipzig: in 1523/4 no fewer than 14 authorised editions and 66 "piracies" appeared.

Whilst the printing of the *September Testament* was taking place, Luther began his translation of the Old Testament which was based once again on the original text and that of the *Vulgata*. This work was to extend over twelve years, which is partly explained by its considerably greater length and by the difficulty of making a new translation, this time from the Hebrew. But economic considerations also played a part, as editions of individual books from the Old Testament – which began to come onto the market from 1523 onwards – could be thought better value for money than the first complete *Bible*, which came out in 1534 from Hans Lufft in Wittenberg. The Hebrew language with its richness of imagery struck Luther as particularly suitable for translation into German. Nevertheless, problems of every kind arose in the process of "interpreting purely and clearly"; he often struggled for weeks to find the right expression in consultation with his colleagues, Melanchthon in particular, and some months he was only able to finish a few lines. However the reader confronts a problem-free and fluently readable text, unaware of those "Wackersteine und Klötze" (broken stones and stumps) that would have lain in his or her path: "Es is gut pflügen, wenn der Acker bereinigt ist" (ploughing is easy when the field is cleaned up). Just as he took pains over his translator's premise "sense for sense", so Luther was equally concerned to have the stylistic individuality of the examples in hand come across clearly, as when he re-phrased the Psalms, without any knowledge of Hebrew metrics, but in correspondingly free rhythms and with ingenious tone colours.

The notion of the biblical texts as a unified whole was increasingly emphasised in the prefaces: prophesies which are made in the Old Testament regarding Christ and salvation find their fulfilment in the New Testament; people and events were designated as prefigurations of the New Testament, following the example given by St Paul in which Adam is made a figure of the Christ that is to come (Rom. 5:14). Luther points this out movingly in his preface to the Pentateuch: "Here will you find the swaddling-clothes and the crib / in which Christ lay / there also the angel who guided the shepherds / scanty and poor are these swaddling-clothes / but dear is the beloved Christ / who lay therein."

The first part of the Old Testament, the five books of Moses, which appeared in 1523 from Melchior and Michael Lotter in Wittenberg, was once again furnished with woodcut illustrations from the workshop of Lucas Cranach which serve the text down to the letter and show such things as Noah's ark, the Ark of the Covenant or a seven-branched menorah. The historical books (Joshua to Esther), the poetic books (Job, Proverbs, Ecclesiastes, Song of Solomon) and the Psalter followed in 1524.

All these translated parts were brought together, revised, and finally published in 1534 as the first complete *Bible*, the *Biblia / das ist / die gantze Heilige Schrifft / Deudsch*, which included the translation of the apocryphal books (Judith, Tobit, Baruch, Maccabees, Esther) which had been newly undertaken for the most part by Melanchthon and Justus Jonas (1493–1555). There are altogether 118 woodblocks by the monogrammist MS from the Wittenberg workshop of Lucas Cranach, in this typographically ambitious volume from the printing house of Hans Lufft which enjoyed the protection of an electoral privilege against unauthorised reprinting. New editions with only minor improvements appeared in 1535, 1536, 1539 and 1540; a fundamental revision carried out from 1539 to 1541 resulted in the Wittenberg edition of autumn 1541 (known as the "Medium *Bible*" because of its large paper size); the illustrations were mostly undertaken by the MS monogrammist. This re-working was advertised on the title page: "Auffs new zugericht" (made as new), and much store was set on careful and faultless printing. Luther also introduced a "warning" in which he makes a powerful complaint against unlicensed and therefore unreliable reprinters: "As you solely seek [to gratify] your greed / ask yourself a little afterwards / how right or wrong it is to reprint something / as it has often happened to me / that I have read pirated reprints

/ and found them to be falsified / so that I have in many places failed / to recognise my own work."

The definitive text is the *Biblia / das ist / Die gantze Heilige Schrifft: / Deudsch Auff Newzugericht. D. Mart. Luth.*, which Hans Lufft published in Wittenberg in 1545. As it was the final version to appear during Luther's lifetime, it assumed almost canonical status and – contrary to Luther's own intentions – it has barely changed over the centuries. A few of Luther's own corrections were, however, incorporated into the edition of 1546, which appeared posthumously and was seen through the press by his close colleague and proof-reader Georg Rörer (1492–1557, see Plate 62).

Between 1522 and 1546 it is possible to identify 430 part or complete editions, so that there must have been some half a million Luther *Bibles* in circulation by the middle of the century. Besides that, there were attempts by the "old" Church to stem the flow of Lutheran doctrines by issuing its own translations. On the instigation of Duke George of Saxony (1471–1539), who had already prohibited the Luther *Bible* for his own subjects in 1552, Hieronymus Emser (1477–1527) published with Wolfgang Stöckel in Dresden a New Testament that he had compiled from Luther's *September Testament*, earlier *German Bibles*, and by reference to the original sources. This was illustrated by re-using the woodblocks from the *December Testament* which Cranach had sold to him. In an afterword, Emser did his best to dissuade people from reading the *Bible*, which was not intended for the laity and belonged in the safe hands of the clergy, and to this end he fell back on the old arguments of the previous century: "That is why those lay persons (who will follow my advice) should now concern themselves more with a pious and godly life / than with the *Bible* / which is recommended only to the learned."

The *Biblia / beider Allt vnnd Newen Testamenten* of the Dominican Johann Dietenberger (c. 1475–1537) met with greater success. It appeared in Mainz and Cologne – with the backing of an imperial privilege – in 1534, and in fact before Luther's complete edition. This Mainz professor of theology also made use of Luther's translation, directly and indirectly (through Emser's extensive borrowings). As well as earlier German versions, but he provided additional summaries of content for the books, and marginal notes – for variant translations and other explanations – where he also noted "falsifications" in Luther's interpretation. Dietenberger's *Bible* survived until 1776 in a total of 46 editions.

Plate 47: The Buxheim St Christopher, woodcut broadsheet dated 1423.
From a facsimile after the unique copy in the John Rylands Library, Manchester.

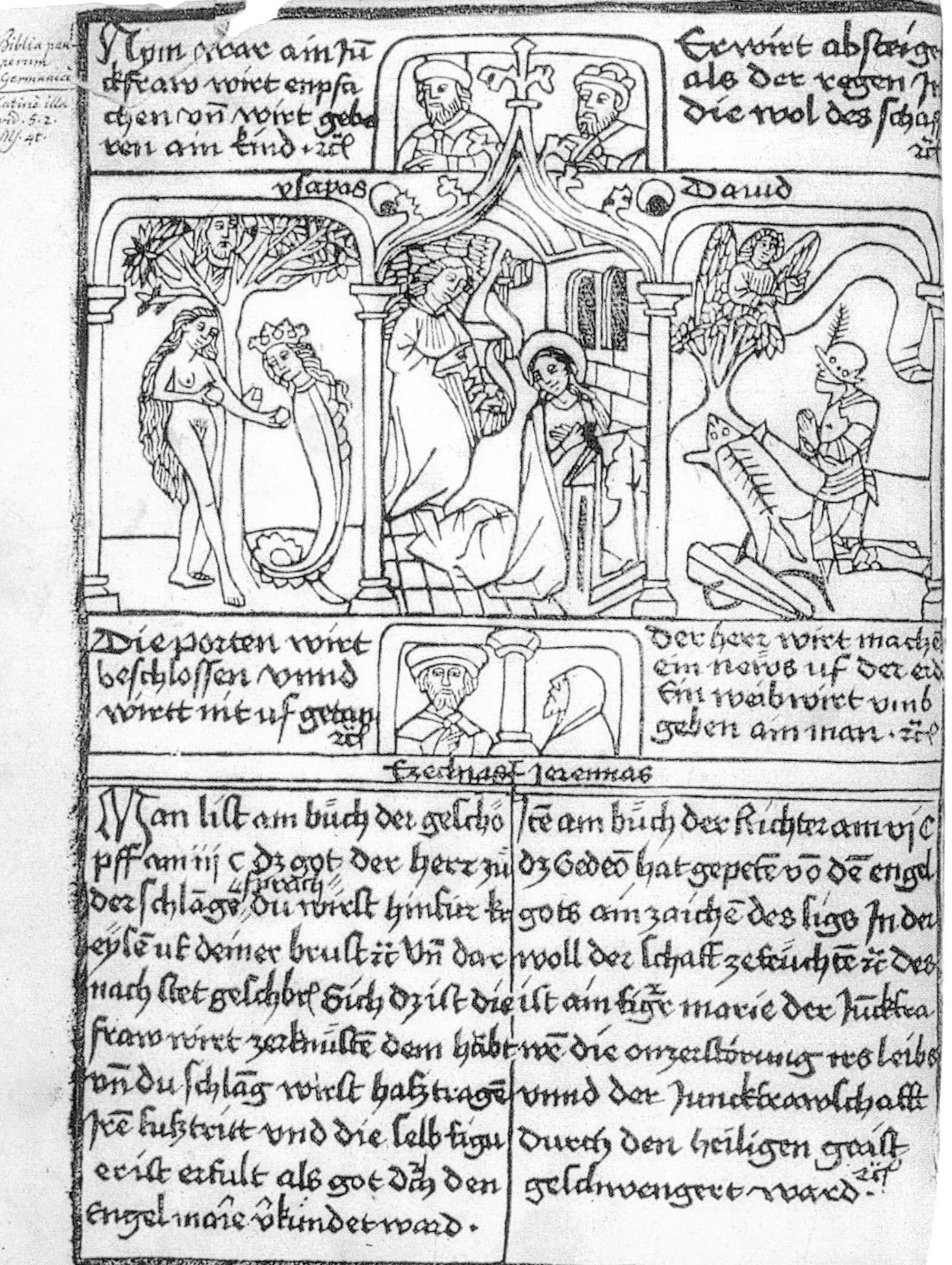
Biblia pauperum Germanica
Latine illa vid. 5.2.
Ms. 4t.

Nym war ain iu
ckfraw wirt enpfa
chen vn wirt gebe
ren ain kind · zc

Er wirt absteig
als der regen in
die wol des schaf
zc

ysayas
Dauid

Die porten wirt
beschlossen vnnd
wirtt nit uf getan
zc

Der herr wirt mache
ein newes uf der erd
Ein waib wirt vmb
geben ain man · zc

Ezechiel
Jeremias

Man list am buch der gescho
pff am iij c Dz got der herr zu
der schläge (sprach) du wirst hinfür k
eysẽ uf deiner brust zc Vñ dar
nach stet geschbn Sich dz ist die
fraw wirt zerknüste dem häbt
vñ du schläg wirst hasz tragẽ
jrẽ fuszstritt vnd die selb figu
er ist erfult als got dz den
engel marie v̈kindet ward ·

jrẽ am buch der Richter am vj c
Dz Gedeõ hat gepete võ dẽ engel
gots ain zaichẽ des sigs jn der
woll der schaff ze feuchtẽ zc Der
ist ain figur marie der junckfra
wẽ die on zerstörung irs leibs
vnnd der junckfrawschafft
durch den heiligen gaist
geschwengert ward · zc

Plate 48: Biblia Pauperum, *block-book*, Nuremberg, *Hans Sporer*, 1471. Wolfenbüttel, *Herzog August Library*.

Des iars als man zalt nach Christi geburdt·M·cccc·lxxviij·iar. So ist d.s.T. der suntäglich buchstab· ¶ Vnd xvj·die guldinezal ¶ Vñ von dē Christag biß auff der herren vaßnacht v· wochen vnd dreÿ tag. ¶ Die lxx·täg vahent an an sant Anthonÿ tag· Der herrn vaßnacht ist am nächsten tag vor liechtmeß. Der osttertag ist d nächst sontag vor Marie verkündung Die kreüczwoch an sontag nach sant Marx tag. Der pfingstag ist der achtent tag nach des heÿligen kreücz tag. Das aduent vahet an An sant Andreas abent·

¶ Hornüg wirt new am achtendē d vnschuldigē kindlin morgē wenn es·ix·schlecht·lij·minut ¶ Der pruch am nächstē tag nach Anthonÿ nach mittag·v·stund·lviij·mi·

¶ Mercz wirt new am nächstē tag nach Liechtmeß morgens frü so es·iij·schlecht·xxxix·mi· ¶ Der pruch am erichtag nach Valentini morgē so es·v·schlecht·xxviij·minut·

¶ Appill wirt new an mitwochē vor Perpetue Felicitatis nach mittag·vj·stund·xlviij·mi· ¶ Der pruch an mitwochē nach Gerdrudis v·stund nach mittag·liiij·minut

¶ Maÿ wirt new an sant Ambrosius abēt vor mittag so es·vj·schlecht·lv·minut· ¶ Der pruch am freitag vor Thiburcÿ morgen so es·vij·schlecht·xv·minut·

¶ Prachmon wirt new an des heÿligen kreücz abent· iiij· stund nach mittag·xxiij·minut ¶ Der pruch am sampßtag nach Seruacÿ·ix·stund nach mittag·xiij·minut·

¶ Der andprachmō Embolismalis wirt new am sontag nach Vrbani·xj stūd nach mittag·liij·minu· ¶ Der pruch an sant Veits tag wenn es xj·schlecht·xlij·minut·

¶ Häemō wirt new am nächstē tag nach Petri vñ pauli morgen weñ es vj·schlecht·xxxiiij·minut ¶ Der pruch am mitwochen nach Margarethe am morgens frü wenn es ij·schlecht·xxxviij·minut·

¶ Augstmon wirt new an mitwochē nach Jacobi nach mittag wenn es·j·schlecht xxxvij·mi· ¶ Hie wirt Eclipsis solis das ist ein finsterin Also der mon wirt drew teÿl der sunnē verdeckē ¶ Der pruch am donerstag nach Laurēti nach mittag·v·stund·xlij·minut·

¶ Säemō wirt new am donerstag nach Bartholomei·x stund nach mittag·v·mi· ¶ Der pruch am säpßtag nach vnserfrawē gepurd vor mittag so es vij·schlecht xxxvj·mi·

¶ Der erst Herbst wirt new an sampßtag nach sät Matheus tag morgens so es viij·schlecht·lij·mi· ¶ Der pruch am sontag vor sät gallen tag x·stund nach mittag xlv·mi·

¶ Der and Herbst wirt new an sontag vor Simonis vñ Jude nach mittag·x·stund·xxv·min· ¶ Der pruch an sant Martins abent so es·xj·schlecht xliij·minut·

¶ Der wintermō wirt new an dē nächstē tag vor Katrine nach mittag so es·ij·schlecht·lv·mi· ¶ Der pruch am mitwochē nach Nicolai xj·stund nach mittag xxj·minut

¶ Jenner wirt new an dem heÿligen Christ abent morgē vor mittag wenn es·ix·schlecht·xxiiij·minut·

¶ Nun volgent die Aderlässin·

¶ Hornung· ¶ Am pfincztag nach dē obrostē mittellässig dē jungen on die füß An freitag vnd sampßtag nach dem obrost güt den jūgen on das haubt. An der mitwochē vñ donerstag vor sant Pauls ker mittel dē altē an sant pauls ker güt den alten· An möntag nach sant pauls ker tag mittel den alten. An der mitwochen nach sant Pauls tag güt lassen den alten·nicht die diech· ¶ Mercz·

¶ An freÿtag nach sant Agathē tag güt dē jungē on das haubt An sant Valentins abēt mittel dē jungē on dz hertz An freÿtag vor sant Matheis tag güt dē alten· An d mitwochē nach Mathie güt dē altē on die diech ¶ Appill

¶ An sant Gregorii tag vñ den nächstē darnach mittel dē jūgen on das hertz· Am montag vnd erichtag vor vnser frawen kündūg güt den altē nit die diech. Am sampßtag nach vnser frawen tag güt lassen den alten· ¶ Maÿ

¶ Am donerstag nach Ambrosÿ mittel den jūgen on die prust. Am montag vor Thiburcÿ mittel den jungen· Am montag vor sandt Jörgen tag güt den alten on die diech An sampßtag nach sant Jörgen tag güt den altē An mōtag nach sant Jörgen tag mittel den alten on die füß Güt erczneÿ nemen· ¶ Prachmon

¶ An der mitwochen nach des heÿligen kreücz tag mittel den jungen on das hertz. Am freÿtag vnd sampßtag vor Vrbani güt den alten· An sant Vrbans tag mittel dē altē Am erichtag vñ mitwochen nach Vrbani güt den jungē nit das haubt. ¶ Embolismalis ander Prachmon

¶ Am afftermōntag nach Bonifacÿ güt den jungē· Am donerstag vor Viti mittel den jungen Am donerstag vnd freÿtag nach Viti güt den alten. An sant Johanns abent güt den alten on das haubt· ¶ Häemon

¶ Am montag vnd erichtag nach sant Vlrichs tag güt den jungen. An sampßtag nach Felicitatis güt den jungē on die diech An sampßtag vor marie Magdalene mittel den altē on die füß. An montag vñ erichtag vor Magdalene güt den alten on das haubt. ¶ Augstmon

¶ An montag vor sant Sixt tag güt den jūgen. Am säpßtag nach Sixti güt den jungen on die diech. Am montag Marie schidūg güt dē altē on dz haubt. ¶ Säemon

¶ An donerstag vnd freÿtag nach Egidÿ güt den jūgen on die diech An vnser frawen gepurd vnd den nächsten darnach güt den jungen. Am mōtag nach Marie gepurd güt den alten on das haubt· ¶ Herbstmon

¶ An dem mitwoch vnd donerstag nach Michaelis güt den jungen on die diech· An montag vnnd erichtag vor Dionisÿ güt den jungen· Am donerstag vor dionisÿ mittel den jungē on die füß Am sampßtag nach Galli mittel den alten·on die hertz oder prust· ¶ Ander Herbst

¶ An sant Narcissen tag güt den jungē on die diech· Am nächsten tag nach aller heÿligen tag güt den jungē· Am freÿtag sampßtag nach aller heÿligen tag güt den jungen on das haubt. Am freÿtag sampßtag nach Martini mittel den altē on die prust. Am freitag nach Elizabeth güt den alten. ¶ Wintermon

¶ An sant Andreas abent güt dē jungē Am freÿtag vnd sampßtag vor Nicolai güt den jungē on das haubt· Am donerstag nach Lucie güt den alten. Am sampßtag vor Thome mittel den alten. An sant Thomas tag Güt den alten. An sant Silvesters tag güt den jungē on dz haubt

D[illegible] tag vor vñ nach dē newen vñ pruch ist nit güt aderlassen· Darumb seind die selben wochen hie nit beschriben

Plate 49: Calendar for the year 1478, with new year's greeting scroll "Ain gut sälig iar" in head margin, broadside, Augsburg, Anton Sorg, 1477.
Göttingen State and University Library.

Von dem donnerstein gefallē im xcij. iar: vor Ensißhein.

De fulgetra anni xcij. Sebastianus Brant.

Perlegat antiquis miracula facta sub annis
Qui volet: et nostros comparet inde dies.
Visa licet fuerint portēta / horrēdaq3 mōstra
Lucere e celo: flamma / corona / trabes /
Astra diurna / faces / tremor et telluris hyatus
Et bolides / Typhon / sanguineus q3 polus
Circulus: et lumē nocturno tpe visum /
Ardentes clypei et / nubigeneq3 fere.
Montibus et visi quondā concurrere montes
Armorū et crepitus / et tuba terribilis.
Lac pluere e celo visum est / fruges q3 calybsq3
Ferrū etiam / et lateres / & caro / lana / cruor
Et sexcenta alijs / ostenta ascripta / libellis:
Prodigijs ausim vix similare novis.
Visio dira quidē Friderici tempore primi:
Et tremor in terris / luna q3 / sol q3 triplex.
Hinc cruce signatus Friderico rege secundo
Excidit inscript⁹ gramate / ab hymbre lapis.
Austria quē genuit senior Frideric⁹ / in agros
Terci⁹ hunc pprios. et cadere arua videt.
Nempe q̄dringētos / p⁹ mille pegerat annos
Sol nouies q3 decem signifer / atq3 duos.
Septē pterea dat idus / metuenda nouēbris:
Ad mediū cursum tenderat illa dies.
Cum tonat horrēdū: crepuitq3 per aera fulmē
Multisonū: hic ingens concidit atq3 lapis.
Cui spēs delte est / aciesq3 triangula: obustus
Est color / et terre forma metalligere.
Missus ab obliquo fertur: visusq3 sub auris
Saturni qualem mittere sydus habet.
Sēserat hūc Ensheī. Sūtgaudia sēsit: i agros
Illic insiluit / depopulatus humum.
Qui licet in partes fuerit distractus vbiq3:
Pond⁹ adhuc tamē hoc ptinet / ecce vides.
Qui mir est potuisse hyemis cecidisse dieb⁹:
Aut fieri in tanto frigore pgeries?
Et nisi anaxagore referant monimēta: molarē
Casurū lapidē. credere et ista negem.
Hic tū auditus fragor vndiq3 littore Rheni:
Audijt hunc Vri prim⁹ alpicola:
Norica vallis cū / Suevi / Rhetiq3 stupebāt:
Allobroges timeant: Francia certe tremit.
Quicqd id ē / magnū portēdit (crede / futur
Omen: at id veniat hostib⁹ oro malis.

Anno Dni 1492:

Sy ett wūndert mancher fremder gschicht.
Der merck vnd leß ouch diß bericht.
Es sint geschehen wunder vil
Im lufft / comet vnd füren pfil.
Brinnend fackel / flammē vnd kron.
Wild kreiß vn d zirckel vmb den mon
Am hymel blůt / vnd füren schilt /
Regen noch form der thier gebildt.
Stoß bruch des hymels vnd der erd /
Vnd ander vil seltzen geberd
Tratzlich zerstiessen sich zwen berg /
Grüßlich trümett / vnd harnesch werck /
Isen / milch / regen stahel korn
Ziegel / fleisch / woll / von hymels zorn
Als ouch ander der wunder glich
Dann by dem ersten Friderich
Noch ert bydem vnd finsterniß
Sach man drij sünn vnd mon gewiß
Vnd vnder keyser Friderich
Dem andern / fiel ein stein grüßlich
Sin form was groß / ein crütz dar inn
Vnd ander geschrifft vnd heimlich syn
By wil des dritten Friderich
Geboren herr von Osterich
Legt har in diß sin eigen landt /
Der stein der hie ligt an der wandt.
Als man zalt viertzehenhundert Jar,
Vff sant Florentzen tag ist war
Nüntzig vnd zwei vmb mittentag
Geschach ein grüsam donnerschlag /
Drij zentner schwer fiel diser stein
Hie in dem feld vor Ensißhein /
Drij eck hat der verschwertzet gar
Wie ertz gestalt vnd erdes var
Ouch ist gesehen in dem lufft
Slymbes fiel er in erdes klufft
Clein stück sint komen hin vnd har
Vnd wit zerfüert sust sichst in gar
Tünow / Necker / Arh / Ill / vnd Rin
Switz / Vri / hort den klapff der In /
Ouch doent er den Burgundern ver
Jn forchten die Franzosen ser
Rechtlich sprich ich das es bedüt
Ein bsunder plag der selben lut

Von Maximiliano. Romischem kuning:

Ich fur dich recht o Adler milt.
Erlich sint wapen in dim schilt
Brüch dich noch eren gen dim findt.
An dem all truw vnd ere ist blindt
Schlag redlich vnd mit froüden dran
Trib vmb das radt Maximilian.
In dim geuell das glück setzt stat
Ach sum dich nit / kum nit zů spat
Mit sorg den vnfal vff diß Jar
Mit vorcht din findt als vmb ein har
Sig / feld / vnd heyl von Osterich

Nüt on v sach
J. B.

Burgundsch hertz von dir nit wich
Romisch ere vnd tütscher nacion
An dir o höchster künig stan
Nym war der stein ist dir gesant
Dich mant gott in dim eigen lant
Das dü dich stellen solt zů wer
O küning milt für vß din her
Ring harnesch vnd der büchsen werck
Trümit herschöl / franzősisch berck
Ouch mach den grossen hochmůt zam
Rett schirm din ere vnd gůtten nam.

Plate 50: Sebastian Brant: *Der Donnerstein von Ensisheim (The Ensisheim meteorite)*, broadsheet, 1492.

Das sind die new gefundẽ menschẽ oð volcker Jn form vñ gestalt Als sie hie stend durch dẽ Cristenlichen Künig von Portigall/gar wunderbarlich erfunden.

¶ Albericus vespucius Laurentio petri Francisci vil grues mit glücklicher fart/am vierzehenden tag des monatz may thausent funffhundert ein jar schieden wir
von Olisippo nach gebot des obgenantẽ künigs mit dreyẽ schyffen zuersuchẽ Newe landt vñ Insell gegẽmittag/vñ sind also hin vñ her geschifft mit grosser vn-
gestümigkeyt des meres biß auff den sibendẽ tag des monats Augusto/des obgemeltẽ jars gefundẽ ein grosses Landt vñ Reygiõ/vñ so grossẽ völcker/scharen vñ
leüt/dz die nyemant erzelẽ mocht als man list in Apocalpsis/Ein volck sach ich ein mildt gütig vñ hantweysig/vñ gend all nackent/beyde weyb vñ man/vnnd
gantz on bedeckung irer leibẽ an allẽ enden/wie sie auß muter leib kumẽ/also gend sie biß sie sterbẽ/dan sie sind groß vñ leib vierschrötig/wol geschickt guter schön
er gestalt vñ geferbt etlicher maß gegẽ roten/das ich mein dise võ ð vrsach kumẽ das sie nackẽt gond vñ von der sunẽ bescheinẽ/also geferbt werdẽ sie haben weit
vñ groß harlockẽ vñ schwartz sie sind in irẽ gang vñ mit spil trebẽ thetig vñ gering/vñ gütiger vñ schöner antlitzẽ die sie doch jnẽ selbs heslich machẽ vñ vngestalt
dan sie porẽ jnen selbs löcher in die packẽ/die mundleffzẽ vñ die nasen vñ die oren. Du solt auch nit gedenckẽ dz solche löcher klein sein/oð sie eins alein habẽ dan ich
etlich geschẽ hab die in irem antlytz alein sibẽ löcher/der yegliches so groß was das ein kriech oð haselnus wol in eins gen möcht. sie ðstossen inẽ selbs solche löcher
mit plabẽ steinen/Cristallẽ/Marmor vñ Alabaster gar hübsch vñ schön/vnnd mit weyssen gebein/vñ mit andern dingẽ/so nit künstẽ gemacht werdẽ/nach jrer
gewonheit/Vnd ob du also schest ein so fremd vngewont ding/so mit grossem seltzamẽ ðwundungẽ/Nemlich einen menschẽ der do het in dẽ backẽ/allain vñ in
den leffzen/siben stein ð etlicher in der leng einer halbẽ span/du würdest nit on grosse ðwundung sein. Dan ich hab dick wargenumẽ vñ ober schetzt/dz sibẽ solch
er stein am gewicht habẽ .xvj. lot vber/vñ on das sie in dẽ oren/die mit dreyen löchern durch stochẽ sind/sie noch ander stein tragẽ/die in ringen hangẽ vñ dise weiß
vñ sittẽ ist allain der manẽ/dan die frawen zerstechẽ jnen selbs ir antlytz nit also mit löcherung/dan allain ir oren. Ein ander sitt vñ weiß/ist auch vnd vñ bey inẽ ge
nueg abweysig/vñ wider alle menschliche glaubung. Das ir frawẽ die eben gelüstig vñ gayl sind/vñ irn manẽ machen das jnen ire mendliche glit geschwellen in
solicher vber dick das sie vngestalt vñ schmelich erscheinẽ/vñ das thon sie mit etlichẽ giftigẽ thierlein/vnd võ solcher sach geschicht dz inen vil ir gemacht ðderben
die in von mangels wegẽ der artzeney faulẽ/vnd belaiben on gemecht. Sie habẽ kein thuech noch deck/weder leines noch baumwolles/dan sie es nit bedürffen vñ
haben kein aygen gut. Sunder alle ding seind vnder jnen gemein/sie habẽ auch keinen künig oder regierer. Sunder ein yeder ist im selbs ein herr/souil weiber nemen
sie so vil sie wöllẽ/vñ der sun mit der mutter/vñ der bruder mit ð schwester/vñ der erst mit ð ersten/vñ der begegner mit der begegnerin. Vnd ðeinigen sich als dick
als sie wöllẽ/schaidẽ sie die ee vñ halltẽ gantz kein ordenung/darumb haben sie auch keinen tempel vñ haltẽ kein gesatz/vñ seind nit abgötter/Was soll ich mer sagẽ
sie leben nach der natur dz siewol Epicuri bauchfüller genant werdẽ mügen dan Senici. Bey jnen seind kein kaufleüt noch kauffmans guet. Die scharẽ des volcks
haben auch krieg vñ an kunst vñ ordnung/jre eltern mit jren rethen vñ geboten vnder biegen die jungẽ zuthon was sie wöllẽ/vñ rüsten sich zustreytẽ/Jn solchem
sie einanð grausamlich zu tod schlahen/vñ welche sie also im krieg vñ strait fahen die füren sie hin/domit sie die bey lebẽ lassen/vñ sie behaltẽ das sie dar võ mestig
en vñ sie essen dan einer den andern der do obligt/vñ vnder anderm fleysch ist yr menschẽ fleysch ein speyß/So hat der vater sein sun vñ sein weyb gessen ich hab
einẽ gesehen von dem sagt man er het wol von dreyhundert menschẽ leyben gessen/ich bin gewesen an einem end da hab ich gesehen gesaltzen menschẽ fleysch vñ
auff gehenckt zu derren/wie hie bey vns das schweinẽ fleysch/sie verwunðn sich warumb wir vnser veint fleysch nit auch essen in vnser speyß/dan sie meinẽ dz es
das aller beste fleysch sey/ir waffen seind pogẽ vñ pfeyl vñ wen sie straiten/so bedeckẽ sie sich nit/Wir rieten in von solcher böser weyß zulassen/vñ sie ðhiessen vns
dar von zulassen/vñ ob die frawẽ schön ploß vñ nacket gend/so haben sie doch ir leib hübsch vñ wol gestalt vñ sauber vñ seind nit so schentlich als einer gedenckẽ
möcht wan sie gemeg leibig seind/so wirt ir scham minder gesehen vnd nan wind das vnder inen keine gesehen ward die do lampend prüst het oder die gekündet
heten dz der selben bauch anderst gestalt werdẽ dan ð junckfrwẽ vñ die nye gekindet/vñ on andern glidern vñ enden des leybs der geleichẽ ðmerckt ward/das ich
alles von ersamkeit weyter vngeendert laß/dan wan sie sich möchten zu den Cristen menschẽ gefiegen als sie auß der massen gayl sind/so legtẽ sie alle scham võ in
zu volbringẽ böse werck. Sie leben hundert vñ funffzig jar vñ werden seltẽ kranck/vñ ob sie etwan kranck werdẽ so heylen sie sich selber mit wurtzlen/vñ mit gutẽ
kreütern vñ so vil ich von in ðsteen vñ erkenen mocht/so ist in jrem land nymer kein pestilentz oder einicherley siechtagẽ/die võ bösem lufft kumend/vñ wo sie nitt
mit fraiel on einander tode schlüeg so möchten sie lange zeyt leben/ich mein das in dem land alle zeyt die mittegigẽ wind wehen vñ vorab allermaist/den wir nenẽ
etwen der inen also ist wie vns der mitnechtig wind genant Aquilo sie seind kunstreych mit Fischfahen/dan auch das selbig meer Fysch reych ist/vñ wen ich wolt
alle vñ yegliche ding erzellen/die in disem land seind/von seltzamẽ fogeln vñ thieren von edlem gestain/das wer ein ding gar zulang vñ on maß/vnd ich glaub das
vnser Plinius dem thausent theyl nit zu kunnen sey. Des volckes der sickustẽ/vñ der andern vogel vñ thieren in disem land mit so mancherley vnderscheyd der antlytz von frawen/das der volkunnestẽ leüt maller kunst berienbt maister Pollicletus die ab zemalen erligẽ müsten/vñ on zweyffel halt ich ob das irdisch paradeis
auff erdtrich das dz nit verr von diser lantschafft sey. So ist künlich vñ offenbar dz wir den vierdẽ theyl der welt durch schyfft haben. Vnd dise Epistel auß Ita
lischer sprach in Latein/vñ yetz gedeütsch. Der hübsch tholmetsch gezogẽ hat. Vmb das alle lateiner vñ deütschẽ ðstanden/wie vil grosser vñ wunderlicher dingẽ
von tag zu tag gefunden/vñ offenbar werden. Vñ diß missiue in deütsch gezogẽ/Auß dem exemplar das von Pariß kam ym Mayen monat. Nach Cristi geburt
Fünffzehenhundert vñ funff Jare.

Plate 51: Amerigo Vespucci: *Das sind die new gefunden menschen . . . (These are the new-found people or race . . .)*, Leipzig, 1505. Wolfenbüttel, Herzog August Library.

Hie seind ze mercken die zeichen der falschen guldin ym nyderland gemacht vñ seind Etliche mintzer zu Göttin gen yn sachssen/vnd yn andern stetten verbrant vnd auf vier thunnen von yn geminczet·

Item die guldin auff der vier herren schleg mit einem zwifal tigen·w·Das stat oben an dem menczer rad·Ist falsch·

Item die guldin mit einē apfel vnd sant Johanns auff der an= dern seiten Ein schilt mit einem leo·Etlich seind falsch·

Item die guldin mit einē apfel vnd die ander seiten sant Peter mit einē steren an der brust·solt stan sant Johañs auf den heim burger schlag·seind falsch·

Item die guldin mit dē bischoff mit einē grossen schilt auff den kölnischen schlag/vñ die ander seitten bey dem haubt ein b·mit einem tittel·Ettlich wöllent es sey ein v·mit einem tittel seind fasch·

Item die guldin mit einē apfel vnd die ander seitten zwischent den füssen ein kreucz mit einē stern auff den franckfurter sch= lag·Ettlich wöllendt es sey ein kron mit einē stern·oder ein gekrönter künig·sein falsch·

Item der vorgenanten guldin ·Ist einer nitt besser / dann fünff weisspfenning·vnd ist der raiff vmher guldin eins halben halms dick Vnd das corpus ist gantz kupfferin/ vnd über gült·Vñ das kupffer ist so hart geminczet vñ gesotten dz es wol klingt·Hierumb mag sy nyemant er kennen an dem klang·noch an dem striche· Vlm

Plate 52: "The signs of false gulden", *broadsheet, Ulm, Johann Zainer, c.* 1482. *Reproduced from* Carl Wehmer: Deutsche Buchdrucker des 15. Jahrhunderts, *Wiesbaden,* 1971, *plate* 54.

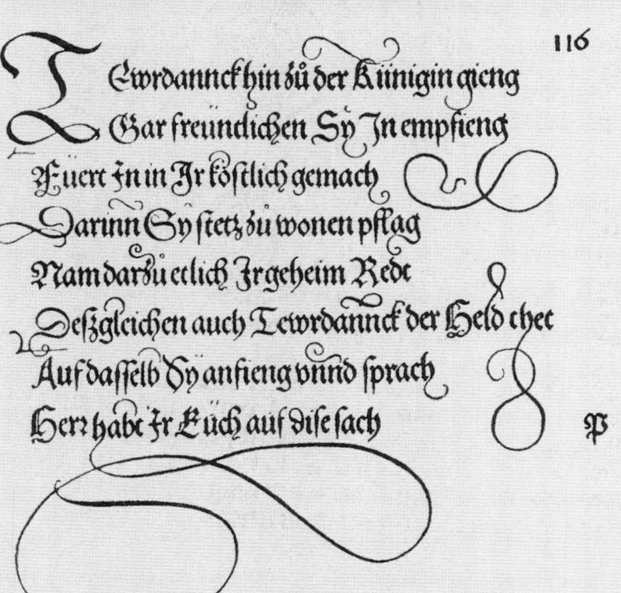

116

Tewrdannck hin zů der Künigin gieng
Gar freündlichen Sy Jn empfieng
Füert Jn in Jr köstlich gemach
Darinn Sy stetz zů wonen pflag
Nam darzů etlich Jr geheim Rede
Deßgleichen auch Tewrdannck der Held thet
Auf dasselb Sy anfieng vnnd sprach
Herr habt Jr Eüch auf dise sach

P

Plate 53: Maximilian I: Theuerdank, Augsburg, Johann Schönsperger, 1517.
Woodcut by Leonhard Beck (showing contraction of marriage to Mary of Burgundy).
From the facsimile by Simon Laschitzer in the Jahrbuch der Kunsthistorischen Sammlungen der Allerhöchsten Kaiserhauses, vol 8, Vienna, 1888.

Je zwei bůcher machabeorū das
ist der streiter die do beruren vns
die streite·die do seint geschehen
vnder den leitern oder fůrern der
hebreyschen vnd vnder den heiden
der von persis:iedoch ist zů wissē
das dz ander bůch der streiter·ist
ein sendbrief den gesendet hat judas machabe⁹ vnd
die eltsten der iuden mit im zů jerl'm·dē andern iudē
die do vmb vnd vm̄ zů streit waren in den landē ge
gen der sunē aufgang·vnd die selben bůcher sprech
en aus den streit der iuden der geschehen ist am sa:
both·vnd auch der edeln hertzogen oder leitern vnd
furern die do heisen machabeus:vnd besunder iude
machabey wie der vber wunden hat aus dem nam:
en dise bůcher iren namen haben. Vnd disse hysto
ria beschleuset in ir die erlichen wercke der brůder
machabeoꝝ:vnder dem kunig anthiocha vn̄ die hei
ligen gesetze haben gelitē. Bittre marter vnd die
selbe hat nit beweint die milde ir můter do man sy
nötigt mit der marter:sunder sy hat sy vil mer vet
mant frölichen zů der eren vnd wirdikeit der marē

S ist geschehen darnach als
alexander philipi el kunig in
macedo der des ersten reichse
in kriechen das der ausginge
von der erden ezetim das der
schlug darium den kunig per
sarum vnd medoꝝ·er hůb vil
streite:vnd behielt die feste:
nung sr aller:vnd döret die kunige der erdē. Vnd
nam die raube der menig der heiden:vnd die erde
schweig in seiner angesichte. Vnd er samelte die
kraft vnd ein her als starck:vnd sein hertz wart er
höhet vnd erhaben:vnd er beheilte die kunigreiche
der heiden vnd der wůtriche vnd sy wurden im zins
haftig. Vnd darnach nider viel er in daz bet:er be
kant das er wurd sterben. Er berieff die edelen sein
kinder die mit im von iungen tagen erneret wur:
den:vn̄ er deilt in sein reich do er dennoch lebt. Alex
ander reysches xij iar:vnd starbe. Vnd sein ge:
sellen behilten das reich ein ietzlicher in seiner stat:
vnd sy ale satztē in auf kunigliche krone nach sein:
em dot vnd ir sůne nach in vil iare vnd die vbel
wurden gemanigualtigt in der erdē. Vnd aus in
aus ging die wurtzel der sunden·der edel anthioch
us ein sun des kunigs anthiochi der zů rome was
geweßen ein pfant oder ein geisel:vnd der herschet
in dem C vnd xxxvij des kriechischē reichs. In den
tagen aus gingen aus isrl' die vngerechten sůne:
vnd die gabē rat vil sprechen. Gee wir vnd bestellē
wir einen punt des frides mit den heiden die neben
vns sein:wan̄ darnach als wir von in sein gegāg
en haben vns funden vil vbel. Vnd dise rede was
gesehen gůt in iren augen. Vnd ir etlich vō dem
volck ordentē daz vestiglich vnd ab gingen zů dem
kunig:vnd er gab in den gewalt:dz sy deten die ge

rechtikeit der heiden. Vnd sy pauwtē ein gemeine
schůle in ierl'm nach dem gesetze der heiden:vnd sy
liesen sich nit beschneiden:vnd gingent von dem
heiligen testament·vnd sy haben sich zů gefugt den
heiden:vnd gaben sich gantz dar zů das sy detten daz
vbel:vnd das reich ware bereit in dem angesichte
anthiochi:vnd er hub an zů reichsen in der erden
egipti:also das er reichset vber zwei reich. Vnd er
ein ging in egipten in schwerē menig in den wegē
vnd elephanten vnd die reitenden:vnd in grosser
menig der schife. Vnd er bestellet den streit wider
den ptolomeum kunig egipti:vnd ptolome⁹ vorchte
sich vnd floch vor seinem antlitz:vnd es vielen vil
verwunter. Vnd er begreif die gemurten stete der
erden egipti:vnd er nam die raub der erden egipti.
Darnach als anthiochus hette geschlagen egiptum
er wider kert in dem hundersten vnd xliij iare vnd
auf steige in isrl':vnd auf ging in ierl'm in seiner
menige:vn̄ in hoffart ein ging er in die heiligkeit:
vnd nam den guldin altar vnd den leuchtē des liech:
tes vnd allē sein gefesse vnd den tisch der brot furle
gung vnd die vasz der fuchten opffer vnd die schal
en der salben vnd die guldin morster vnd den fur:
hanck vnd die kronen vnd die guldin zprunge die
do was in dem angesichte des tempels:vn̄ der tzer:
mischet dise alle. Er nam silber vnd gold vnd die
begirlichen vasz:vnd nam die verborgen schetze die
er vant:dise alle furt er hindan vnd ging in seine
erden. Vnd machet ein grosze schlagung der mēsch
en:vnd er redt in groszer hofart. Vnd es wart ein
groses clagen in isrl':vnd in einer ietzlichen stat.
Vnd die fursten erseufftzten vnd die eltschten:die
iungen vnd die iungfrawen wurden kranck:vnd
schön gestalt der weiber wurden verwandelt. Ein
ietzlich man nam ein clagen:vnd die do sassen an
dem elichen bet die wainten. Vnd die erde wart be:
wegt vber die dar in wonten:vnd nach disem ein
ietzlich haus iacobs aus zoch daz bedrůptnis. Vnd
nach tagen zwei iar sendet der kunig einen fursten
der zinsz in die stete iuda:vn̄ der kam in ierl'm mit
grosser schar. Vnd er redt zů in fridsame wort in
falschheit:vnd sy glaubten im. Vnd also bald viel
er auf die stat:vnd schlug sy mit groser pflag:vn̄
verlosz vil volckes aus isrl'. Vnd nam die raub der
stat vnd er anzundet die mit fewer. Vnd zerstört
ir heuser vnd ir mauren in dem vmb kreisz:vnd sy
fůrten geuangen die frauwen vnd die kinder:vnd
sy besassen das vich. Vnd sy pauten die stat dauí:
des mit einer groszen starcken muren vnd mit stark
en türnē:vnd die ware in zů einer vestikeit. Vnd
do hin setzten sy das sundliche vnd heidnische volck
die vngerechten man:vnd sy wurden al zů starcke.
Dorumb sy legten dar in harnasch vnd speise:vnd
samenten den raub ierl'm vnd legten die do selbst:
vnd wurden in zů einem grossen stricke. Vnd das
geschach zů einer lagunge der heiligen stat vnd in
einem bösen schmertzen oder dollong teuffel in isrl'
Vnd sy vergussen das vnschuldig blůt durch den
vmkreis der heiligen stat:vnd vermeiligten die heil
igkeit. Vnd die woner in ierl'm fluhē durch ir wil
len:vnd sy wart zů einer wonung der auslendischē

Plate 54: The first German Bible, Johann Mentelin, Strasbourg, 1466 (GW 4295), fol 301r. Göttingen State and University Library.

czů den Laodiciern. LXvij.

creütz vnsers herrē Jhesu christi durch den mir die welt ist gekreüczigt · vnd ich der welt. Wañ in christo ihesu ist nit etwas nütz die beschneydung noch auch die überwachsung · aber die new creatur · vnd alle die da nachuolgent diser regel. Frid vnd erbermd seye über sy vnd über israhel gots Füro hin brůder keyner seye mir leydig · Wann ich trag das zeychen des herren ihesu in meim leyb. Brůder die genad vnsers herren ihesu christi sey mit euwerem geyst Amen.

¶ Die epistel ad galathas hatt ein ende. Vnnd hebt an die Epistel zů den Laodicern.
Das erst capitel.

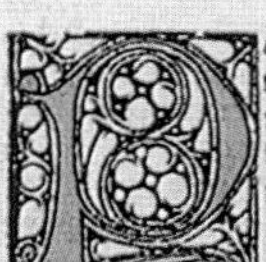

PAulus bot nicht von den menschen noch durch den menschen · aber durch ihesum christum . Den brůdern die da seind zů Laodici . Die genad sey mit euch · vnd der frid vō got vnserm vatter vnnd von dem herren ihesu christo. Ich wirck gnad meim got durch alles mein gebett. Darumb das ir seyt beleybent in im vnnd czů volenden in gůtten wercken. Beytent der verheyssung an dem tag des vrteyls verwůstendt euch nit mit etlicher üppiger red das die eroffendt das euch abkeret von der warheit des ewangeliums das da wirt gepredigt von mir. Vnd nun got der macht die dinge die da seind von mir · dienent zů dem nutz der warheit des ewangely · vnd thůnd die güttigkeyt der wercke die da seind der behaltsam des ewigen lebens. Vnd nun meine band die seind offen · die ich erleyde in cristo vnn die ich mich freüwe · vnd frew mich vnd ditz ist mir zů der ewigen behaltsam · Dasselb ist gethan euch zehelffen in euwern gebetten · vnd von der dienung des heyligen geysts. Es sey durch das leben · oder durch den todt · wann mir zeleben · ist eyn leben in christo · vnd sterben ein gewin. Vnd derselb thů sein erbermbd in euch · das ir habt dieselben lieb vnd seyt einhellig. Darumb aller liebsten als ir habt gehört die vorwissenheit des herren · also behabt sy vnd thůt sy in der vorcht gots · vnnd euch wirt das leben ewigklich · wañ got ist d' da wirckt in euch. Vnd wölch ding ir thůt die thůt on hinderred oder on sünd. Vnd aller liebstē es ist das beste · freüwet euch im herren

Vnd hůt euch vor aller vnreyner gewinnung. All euwer eyschung seind offenbar bey got · vnd seyt vest in dem synn christi. Vnd die ding die da seind ganncz vnd gewer vnd keüsch vnd zymlich · vnnd recht vnd lieblich · die thůt. Vnnd die ding die ir habt gehört vnd empfangē · die behabt im herczen. Vnd der frid gots der wirt mit euch. Euch grůssendt all heyligen. Die genad vnsers herren ihesu christi die sey mit euwerm geyst · vnd macht die epistel zelesen den colosensern zů euch Amen.

¶ Ein ende hatt die Epistel czů den Laodicern Vnnd hebt an die vorred über die epistel zů den ephesiern

EPhesi seid asiani · dise da Sy ēpfiengen das wort d' warheit da bestůnden sy vest in dem gelauben · dise lobt der Apostel · vnnd schreybt in vō Rom auß dē kercker bey dē ewāgelier thyticū

¶ Die vorred hatt ein ende. Vnnd hebt an die epistel zů den ephesiern ·

¶ Das erst Capitel.

PAulus ein apostel Jhesu christi · durch den willen gots allē den heiligen die da seind ephesi · vnnd den gelaubigen in ihesu christo. Genad sey mit euch · vnd fride vō got vnserm vatter · vnnd von dem herren ihesu christo. Got der seye gesegent vnn der vater vnsers herrē ihesu christi · der vns hat gesegent in allem geystlichen segen in den himelischen dingen in christo · als er vns hatt erwöllt in im selber vor der saczüg der welt · dz wir seyen heylig vnn vnuermeyligt in seinem

Plate 55: German Bible, Augsburg, Günther Zainer, 1475-76, (GW 4298).
Göttingen State and University Library.

Die vorreden habent ein ende. Vnd hebet an der prophet ysaias.

Das erst capitel.

Je gesicht ysaias des sun Amos die er sach úb' iudam vñ úb' iherusalem in den tagen ozie ioathan Achas vñ ezechie der künig iuda. Jr himel hörent vñ du erde empfach mit den oren. wann der herre hatt geredt. Jch hab erzogē sün. vñ hab sy er höhet. ab' sy haben mich verschmäht. Der ochs erkant seinen besitzer. vnd der esel die krüpp seines herren. Aber jsrahel der erkant mich nit. vnd mein volck das vernam mich nit Wee dem sündigen volcke. dem schwären volck vor missetat. dem schalckhafftigen samen. dē úbeltättigen sünen. Sy habent verlaussen den herren. Sy habent gelösteret den heyligen israel. sy seind abkeret hinder sich. Warczü schlach ich eüch fürohin. die ir zülegent die übergeung. ein yegklichs siechs haubt. vnnd ein yegkliches traurigs hertz.

Plate 56: German Bible, Augsburg, Günther Zainer, 1475-76, (initial showing stem of Jesse).

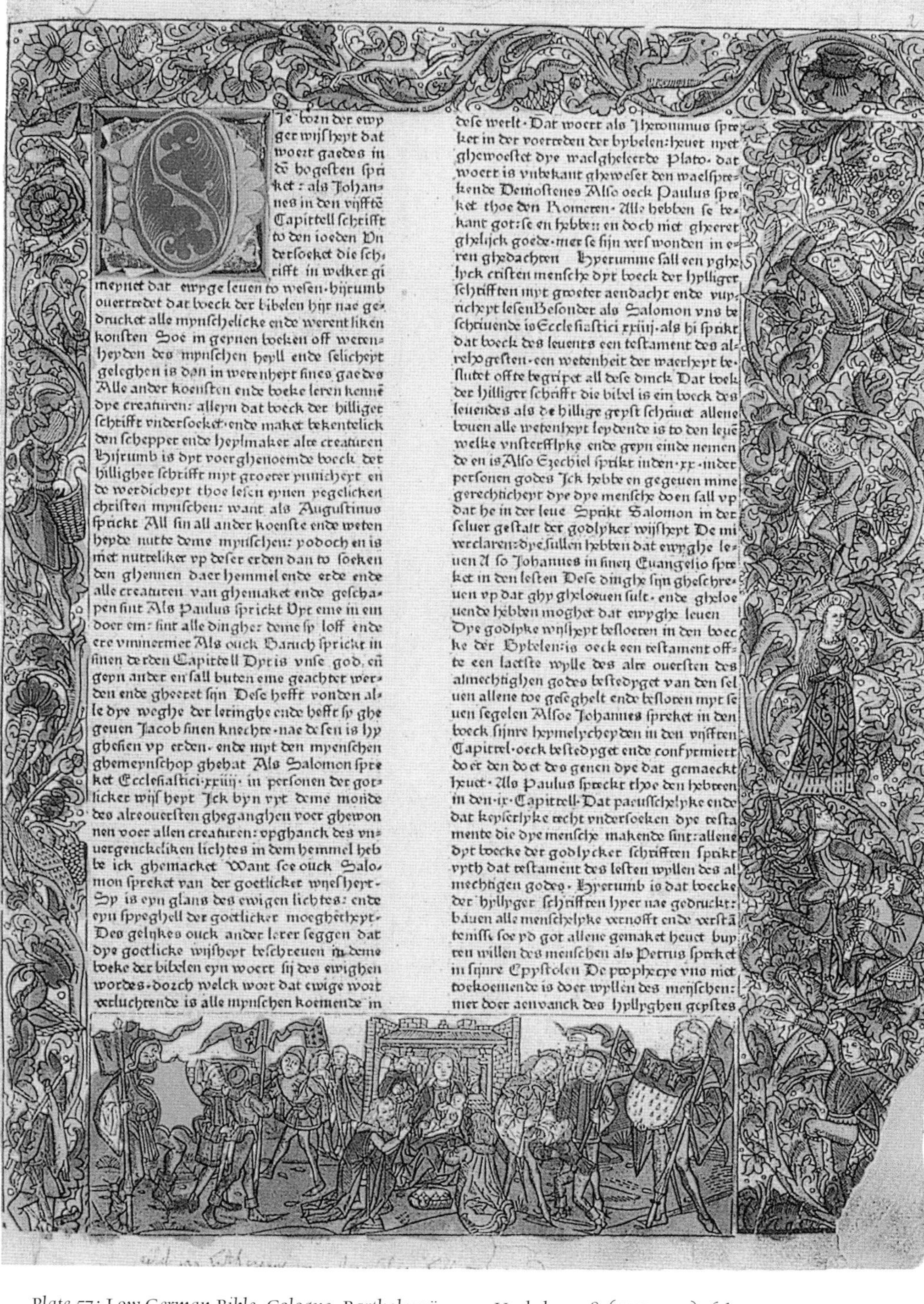

DJe born der ewy
ger wijsheyt dat
woert gaedes in
dē hogesten spr
ket : als Johan-
nes in den vijfftē
Capittell schrifft
to den ioeden Vn
dersoeket die sch-
rifft in welker gi
meynet dat ewyge leuen to wesen· hijrumb
ouertredet dat boeck der bibelen hijr nae ge-
drucket alle mynschelicke ende werentliken
konsten Soe in geynen boeken off weten-
heyden des mynschen heyll ende selicheyt
geleghen is dan in wetenheyt sines gaedes
Alle ander koensten ende boeke leren kennē
dye creaturen: alleyn dat boeck der hilliger
schrifft vndersoeket· ende maket bekentelick
den schepper ende heylmaker alre creaturen
Hijrumb is dyt voerghenoemde boeck der
hillighet schrifft myt groeter ynnicheyt en
de werdicheyt thoe lesen eynen yegelicken
christen mynschen: want als Augustinus
spricket All sin all ander koenste ende weten
heyde nutte deme mynschen: yodoch en is
niet nutteliker vp deser erden dan to soeken
den ghennen daer hemmel ende erde ende
alle creaturen van ghemaket ende gescha-
pen sint Als Paulus spricket Vyt eme in em
doer em: sint alle dingher deme sy loff ende
ere vmmermer Als ouck Baruch spricket in
sinen derden Capittell Dyt is vnse god, eñ
geyn ander en sall buten eme geachtet werden ende gheeret syn Dese hefft vonden alle dye weghe der leringhe ende hefft sy ghe
geuen Jacob sinen knechte· nae desen is hy
ghesien vp erden· ende myt den mynschen
ghemeynschop ghehat Als Salomon spre
ket Ecclesiastici·xxiiij· in personen der got-
licker wijs heyt Jck byn vyt deme monde
des alreouersten ghegangen voer ghewon
nen voer allen creaturen: opghanck des vn-
uergenckeliken lichtes in dem hemmel heb
be ick ghemacket Want see ouck Salomon spreket van der goetlicker wyes heyt·
Sy is eyn glans des ewigen lichtes: ende
eyn spyeghell der goetlicker moeghetheyt·
Des gelykes ouck ander lerer seggen dat
dye goetlicke wijsheyt beschreuen in deme
boeke der bibelen eyn woert sij des ewighen
wordes· dorch welck wort dat ewige wort
verluchtende is alle mynschen koemende in
dese werlt· Dat woert als Jheronimus spre
ket in der voerreden der bybelen: heuet nyet
ghewoestet dye waelgheleerde Plato· dat
woert is vnbekant ghewesen den waelspre-
kende Demostenes Alsoe oeck Paulus spre
ket thoe den Romeren· Alle hebben se be-
kant got: se en hebben en doch niet gheeret
ghelijck goede· mer se sijn vers wonden in e-
ren ghedachten Hyerumme sall een yghe
lyck cristen mensche dyt boeck der hylliger
schrifften myt groeter aendacht ende vyn-
richeyt lesen Besonder als Salomon vns be
schriuende is Ecclesiastici xxiiij· als hi sprikt
dat boeck des leuents een testament des al-
rehogesten· een wetenheit der waerheyt be-
slutet offte begripet all dese dinck Dat boek
der hilliger schrifft die bibel is ein boeck des
leuendes als de hillige geyst schriuet allene
bouen alle wetenheyt leydende is to den leuē
welke vnsterfflyke ende geyn einde nemen
de en is Alsoe Ezechiel sprikt inden·xx·inder
personen godes Jck hebbe en gegeuen mine
gerechticheyt dye dye mensche doen sall vp
dat he in der leue Sprikt Salomon in der
seluer gestalt der godlyker wijsheyt De mi
verclaren: dye sullen hebben dat ewyghe leuen Also Johannes in sinen Euangelio spre
ket in den lesten Dese dinghe syn ghescre-
uen vp dat ghy ghelouen sult· ende ghelo
uende hebben moghet dat ewyghe leuen
Dye godlyke wijsheyt besloeten in den boec
ke der Bybelen: is oeck een testament offte een laetste wylle des alre ouersten des
almechtighen godes bestedyget van den sel
uen allene toe geseghelt ende besloten myt se
uen segelen Alsoe Johannes spreket in den
boeck sijnre heymelycheyden in den vijfften
Capittel· oeck bestedyget ende confyrmiert
doer den doet des genen dye dat gemaeckt
heuet· Als Paulus spreckt thoe den hebreen
in den·ix·Capittell· Dat pauwschelyke ende
dat keyserlyke recht vndersoeken dye testa
mente die dye mensche makende sint: allene
dyt boecke der godlycker schrifften sprikt
vyth dat testament des lesten wyllen des al
mechtigen godes· Hyerumb is dat boecke
der hyllyger schrifften hyer nae gedruckt:
bauen alle menschelyke vernofft ende verstā
tenisse soe yd got allene gemaket heuet buy
ten willen des menschen als Petrus spreket
in sijnre Epystolen De prophecye vns niet
toekoemende is doer wyllen des menschen:
mer doer aenvanck des hyllyghen geystes

Plate 57: Low German Bible, Cologne, Bartholomäus von Unckel, 1478 (GW 4307), fol 2r. Göttingen State and University Library.

Hijr beghynt Genesis dat erste boeck der
vijff boecken Moysi. Dat erste capittel ys
van der geschyppenis der werlt vnde aller creaturen vnde de wercke der sees daghe

In dem anbegynne schoep
god hemmel vnde erden.
Mer de erde was leddych
vñ de dusternisse weren vp
deme antlate des affgron-
des. dat ys vp deme ange
sichte der elementen do vn
uerscheiden. vnde der geist
godes wart gevoert bouen
de watere. Vñ god de sprak
dat licht werde: vñ dat licht ward: vñ got de
sach dat licht dat dat gud was. vnde he delde
dat licht vā der dusternisse. vñ dat licht nom

de he den dach. vñ de dusternisse de nacht. vñ
der auent vnde morgen wart een dach. Vnde
got de sprak: dat firmamēt werde i dem midde
le der watē vñ he schedde de watē vā dē wate
ren Vñ god makede dat firmamēt: vñ delde de
watere de dar werē vnder dem firmament vā
dē de dar werē bauē dem firmament vñ dat ge
schach also. Vñ got nomde dat firmament dē
hēmel vñ dat wart der auent vñ de morghen
de ander dach Vñ god sprack euer De watere
de vnder dem hemele sint werden vergaddert
an eene stede. vñ erschyne de dorricheit. vnde
dat geschach also. vñ god hete de dorricheyt
dat ertrijke. vñ de vergaderinge der watere he
te he dat meer. vñ got sach dat dat gud was
Vnde he sprack. De erde groye groyende krut
vñ dat saet make. vñ holt dat appel drage nae
syme kunne. des saet sij in eme sulues vpp der

Plate 58: Low German Bible, Cologne, 1478, fol 5r.

Der Geſchopf .V.

Hie hebt ſich an. Geneſis das erſt buch der
funff bucher moyſi. Das erſt Capitel iſt võ
der ſchöppfung der werlt vnd aller creaturen.
vnd von den wercken der ſechs tag.

N dem anfang
hat got beſchaf
fen hymel vnd
erden. aber dye erde was
eytel vnd lere. vnd die vin/
ſternus warn auff dẽ ant/
litz des abgrunds. vnd der
geiſt gots ſwebet oder ward getragen auff dẽ
waſern. Vñ got der ſprach. Es werde dz liecht
Vñ das liecht iſt worden. vñ got ſahe dz liecht
das es gutt was. vnd er teylet das liecht võ der
vinſternus. vnd das liecht hyeß er den tag. vnd
die vinſternus die nacht. Vñ es ward abent vñ
morgen eyn tag. Vnd got der ſprach. Es wer/
de das firmament in dem mittel der waſſer. vñ
tayle die waſſer võ dẽ waſſern. Vñ got machet
das firmament. vnd teylet die waſſer. dy do wa
ren vnder dem firmament. von dẽ dy do waren
ob dem firmament. vnd es iſt alſo geſchehen
vnd got hieß das firmament den hymel vnd es
iſt der abent vñ der morgẽ der ander tag wordẽ
vñ got ſprach aber. Es ſullẽ geſamelt werdẽ dy
waſſer. die vnder dem hymel ſeynd. an eyn ſtatt.
vñ erſcheyne die durre. vnd es iſt alſo geſchehẽ
Vñ got hieß die durre dz ertreich. Vñ dy ſam
nungen der waſſer. hieß er die mere. vnd got ſa
he das es was gut. vnd ſprach. Die erde gepere
grunendt krawt. das do bringe den ſamen. vnd
dy öpfelbawm. dz holtz. dz do bringe dy frucht
nach ſeym geſchlecht. des ſame ſey in ym ſelbs
auff der erde. vnd es iſt alſo geſchehen. vnd die
erd bracht grunend kraut. vnd bringenden ſa/

Plate 59: *The ninth German Bible, Nuremberg, Anton Koberger, 1483 (GW 4303), fol 5r. Göttingen State and University Library.*

alſo das alle dinng wurden volbracht die lucas ſchreybt.in dem buch actus apoſtolorum. darnach zu dē letſten gab paulus ein beſchlieſſūg vnd ein vollendung mit ſeiner predig deſſelben buchs. Wañ den ſelbē der herr erweelt hat. Darnach als er lang het geſtrytten.wider die anfehtung des leybs. Vñ wiewol das iſt. dz es nütz wer den.die do gern leſen.vñ die gott den herrē ſuchen.dz wir dē ſelben hetē beſünderlich mer vñ mer beſchriben. Jedoch ſo wayß ich dz der ackerman der do arbeyt des erſten ſoll eſſen vō ſeinen früchten.vñ darumb habē wir vermiden öffenlich fürwitzigkeit dz wir nit erſehen würden.zeerzaigen den dy got wöllen.auch dē wöllen got offenbarn.die in verſchmehen.

Ein ander vorrede

WAnn vil habē ſich geflyſſen zeordē die rede der ding.die do ſind erfült an vns Als vns die gegeben habē. Dy auch ſy haben geſehen.vñ ſind geweſen diener der predig. Iſt auch mir geſehen wordē. der ich fleyſſigklichē von anfang alle ding begriffen hab ordenlich zeſchreyben.dir du allerliebſter Theophile.daz du erkenneſt die warheit.der wort.von den du biſt gelert.

Hie hebt an das buch luce des euangeliſten.

Das erſt Capitel.wy der engel zacharie erſchine.Zacharias dē engel nit gelaubet.vñ darūb erſtūmet. Wy maria vō dē engel gegrüſt ward. vñ auß vermanūg des engels elizabeth heiſucht.vñ grüſſet. vñ wy elizabeth gepare.vñ zacharie ſei mūd eröffent ward

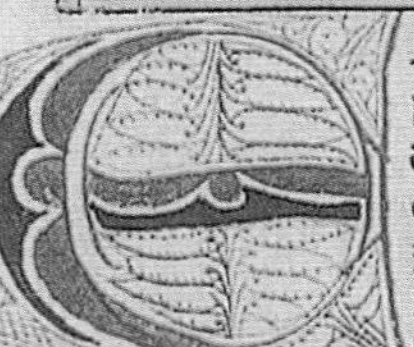

ES was i dē tagen herodis des künigs iudee ein prieſter mit namē zacharias. Von dem geſchlecht abia.vñ ſei eeweyb von den töchtern aaron.vñ ir nam was elizabeth. Wañ beyd warn ſie gerecht vor got ſie giegen in allen gerechtigkeyten.vñ in den geboten des herren on klag.vñ ſie hetten keinen ſun.darumb dz elizabeth was vnberhaftig.vñ beyde warn ſie vbergangen in iren tagen. Vñ es geſchah als brauchet zacharias die prieſterſchaft in d' ordnung ſeins ampts vor got.er gieng auß nach dē lohe das er legt das brinnend opfer.vñ gieng.in dē tempel des herrē.vñ alle menig des volcks wz außwendig bettend zu der ſtund des brinnenden opfers. Vnd der engel des herren erſchyn im.ſteend zu der gerechten des altars des wey⸗

Plate 60: The ninth German Bible, Nuremberg, Koberger, 1483.
The gospel according to St Luke.

Ein newer Spruch/ Wie die Geystlicheit vnd etlich Handtwercker vber den Luther clagen.

Der geitzig clagt auß falschem műt/
Seit im abget an Eer vnd Gűt.
Er zürnet/ Dobet/ vnde Wűt/
In dürstet nach des grechten plűt.

Die warheit ist Got vnd sein wort/
Das pleibt ewiglich vnzerstort.
Wie ser der Gotloß auch rumort/
Gott bschützt sein diener hie vnd dort.

Der Grecht sagt die Gotlich warheit/
Wie hart man in veruolgt/ verleit.
Hofft er in Gott doch alle zeit/
Pleibt bstendig in der grechtigkeit.

H. B. 26

Die clag der Gotlossen.

Hör vnser clag du strenger Richter/
Vnd sey vnser zwitracht ein schlichter.
Eh wir die hend selb legen an/
Martin Luther den schedlich man.
Der hatt geschriben vnd gelert/
Vnd schir das gātz Teütsch land verkert.
Mit schmehen/ lestern/ nach vnd weit/
Die Erwirdige Gaistlichait.
Von iren Pfründen/ Rent vnd Zinst/
Vnd verwürfft auch iren Gotzdinst.
Der Våtter gepot/ vnd auffsetz/
Hayßt er vnnütz/ vnd menschen gschwetz
Helt nichts von Aplaß vnd Fegfewr/
Die Meß kum̃ auch kainr Sel zu stewr.
All Kirchen Pew/ Zir/ vnd geschmuck/
Veracht er gar/ er ist nie cluck.
Des clagen die Prelaten ser/
Pfaffen/ Münch/ Stationirer.
Glockengiesser vnd Organisten/
Goltschlager vnd Illuministen.
Hādtmaler/ Goltschmit vñ bildschnitzer
Ratschmit/ Glaßmaler/ seydenstitzer.
Stainmetzen/ Zim̃erleüt Schreiner/
Paternoster/ Kertzen macher.
Die Permenter/ Singer vnd Schreyber/
Fischer/ Zopffnun vnd Pfaffen Weyber.
Den allen ist Luther ein bschwert/
Von dir wirt ein Vrteil begert.
Sunst werdt wir weiter Appelliern/
Vnd dem Luther die Prend recht schirn/
Műß Prinnen/ oder Reuociru.

Antwort .D. Martini.

Actuum.1. O du erkenner aller hertzen/
Hör mein antwort des ist kein schertzen.
Die schreyen fast ich thűn mich irren/
Vnd wöllen doch nit Disputirn.
Sonder mich mit worten schrecken/
In thut we das ich thu auffdeckn.
Ir grossen geytz vnd Simoney/
Ir falsch Gotzdinst vnd Gleissnerey.
Ir Bannen/ Auffsetz vnd gepot/
Vor aller welt zu schand vnd spott.
Mit deinem wort/ das ich denn ler/
Nun in abgeet an gut vnd Eer.
So kunden sy dein wort nit leiden/
Thunt mich schelten/ hassen vnd neiden.
Wenn ich hett gschriben vnd gelert/
Das sich ir Reicht umb het gemert.
So wer kein besser auff gestandn/
In langer zeit in Teutschen Landn.
Dis ist auch die vrsach ich sag/
Das gegen mir auch stent in clag.
Der Hantwercks leüt ein grosse zal/
Den auch abgeet in disem val.
Seyt diß Apgötterey entnimpt/
Also seynd vber mich ergrimt.
3.Regū.18. Von erst des Baals Tempel knecht/
Den ir iarmarck thut nimmer recht.
Actuū.19. Vnd Demetrius der werckman/
Dem sein handtwerck zu ruck wil gan.
Her durch dein wort das ich thű schreibn/
Ir droen soll mich nitt abtreibn/
Bey deinem vrteil will ich pleiben.

Das Vrteil Christi.

Joānis.5. Das mein gericht das ist gerecht/
Nű merck vermaints gaistlichs geslecht.
Was ich euch selb beuolhen han/
Das ir in die gantz welt solt gan.
Mar. vltio. Predigen aller Creatur/
Das Euangeli rain vnd pur.
Dasselbig hant ir gar veracht/
Vnd vil newer Götzdinst auff pracht.
Mathei.15. Der ich doch kein geheissen hab/
Vnd verkaufft sie vmb gelt vnd gab.
Mit Vigil/ Jartåg vnd Selmessen/
Math.23. Den witwen ir die hewser fressen.
Vnd verspert auch das Himelreich/
Ir seyt den Doten grebern gleich.
Vñ schlacht zu dot auch mein Prophetn/
Der gleich die Phariseer thetten.
Also veruolgt ir die warhait/
Die euch teglichen wirt geseit.
Luce.13. Vnd so ir euch nit pessern wert/
Ir vmkum̃en. Darumb so kert.
Von ewerm falschen widerstreit/
Dergleichen ir handtwercks leyt.
Die ir mein wort veracht mit trutz/
Von wegen ewerß aygen nutz.
Vnd hört doch in den worten mein/
Mathei.6. Das ir nit solt sorgfeltig sein.
Vmb zeitlich gűt/ geleich den Haydn/
Sőder sucht das Reich gots mit freudn.
Das zeitlich wirt euch wol zufalln/
Sunst wert ir in der hellen qualln/
Das ist mein vrteil zu euch alln.

Hans Sachs Schuster.

Plate 61: Hans Sachs: *Ein neuer Spruch, wie die Geistlichkeit und etlich Handwerker über den Luther klagen* (A new poem: how the clergy and certain craftsmen complain about Luther). Broadsheet, Nuremberg, Hieronymus Höltzel, 1524, woodcut by Sebald Beham. Nuremberg, German National Museum.

Biblia: das ist:
Die gantze Heilige
Schrifft: Deudsch
Auffs New zugericht.
D. Mart. Luth.
Begnadet mit Kür-
fürstlicher zu Sachsen Freiheit.
Gedrückt zu Wittem-
berg / Durch Hans Lufft.
M. D. XLI.

59. 4. Th.

Plate 62: Martin Luther: Biblia, das ist: Die gantze Heilige Schrifft: Deudsch. Auffs New zugericht, Wittenberg, Hans Lufft, 1541. Wolfenbüttel, Herzog August Library.

Countless legends have arisen concerning the language of the Luther *Bible*, which the research into linguistic history of recent years makes it simpler to evaluate. It is important to keep in mind that the wide distribution of Luther's pamphlets and *Bible* translations, the pains he took to avoid regional dialect expressions, and his use of the printed language of south-east Germany all contributed positively to that levelling-out of language within the German empire which had already begun, and to the development of a common German printed language. Luther's own hope that the language of the Saxon chancellery would become universally understood ("*Ideo ist communissima lingua Germaniae*", *Table-talk*, 1040 and 2758) hopelessly overestimated the rôle of official language. In the southern towns his translations required a supplementary glossary of Middle German/South German words, whereas northern Germany was quickly provided with its own Low German renderings. But in tandem with this conscious striving towards standardisation, he exercised a formative stylistic influence through the new words he coined, his phraseology and his metaphorical language. Recent research has underplayed his apparently direct and "popular" address, and suggests that he was striving for a "sacral" language that was impregnated with classical rhetoric and closely matched stylistic qualities in the original text.

The influence of Luther's language and style does not go back just to the widely circulated *Bible* itself, but also to his theological tracts, the later writings of his pupils of which the *Table-talk* is an example, and eventually to the church hymns and Protestant sermons of the centuries which followed. Many authors quoted from the Luther *Bible* in their fictional texts, from Hans Sachs to the *Historia von D. Johann Fausten* (1587). The devotional literature and biblical drama of the sixteenth and seventeenth centuries used "Luther-German". Writers of the enlightenment and classical period from Hamann to Klopstock and Goethe in the eighteenth century engaged anew amongst themselves with the language of the Reformer, which resonated through Nietzsche, Thomas Mann and Brecht far into the twentieth century. The Reformation and printing are consequently first-hand participants in the emergence of a High German literary language.

Gutenberg goes electronic

THE ON-GOING MEDIA REVOLUTION

Gutenberg had grasped that what was practical in the fourth decade of the fifteenth century – such procedures as impressing stamps into clay or tooling bookbindings or printing fabrics, the engraving skills of goldsmithery and the casting techniques used in bell-founding, and harnessing the power of the wine- or paper-making press to print or impress – could lead to an epoch-making new process, whereby he could cast virtually unlimited numbers of identical letters in lead, from which he could then print at will, and so create a means of multiplying information such as no earlier age had enjoyed.

This invention survived virtually unchanged down the centuries: only some four hundred years later did the development of the cylinder press give rise to new working practices, but even then there was no real departure from his principles for letterpress printing. Similarly, few fundamental changes were brought about by the Monotype or Linotype systems of mechanical composition, the introduction of reel-fed paper, or the replacement of wood-engraving for pictorial reproduction. Offset printing was the first innovative printing process that relied neither on the relief principle nor on the intaglio principle represented by copperplate-engraving, but instead used a planographic or flat printing surface. But the most significant step – the introduction of photo-typesetting – which would allow offset to supplant letterpress, still lay some decades ahead. For over five hundred years, lead had ruled supreme, and now its place was to be taken by film. Typefaces would no longer be cut and cast in metal, but their designs exposed onto film masters for photo-composition. The beginning of the end for Gutenberg's invention – quite unremarked by the press – might be dated from 1971, when the Association of German Typefounders voted to dissolve itself. The current digital revolution is superseding not only metal types and photographic film, it may even bring about an electronic alternative to paper itself. At the moment we are experiencing the digitisation of the printing process and the spread of information in electronic form at a variety of levels and in a number of emergent technologies.

Digital printing has the following characteristics:

- text and images held exclusively as digital data;
- printing directly from the author's files;
- no use of films or sensitized papers;
- creating the image by transferring it dot by dot onto the printing surface.

The digitised data is directly transferred from software onto an erasable printing cylinder, and thence, without using any carrier, onto the printing surface. The procedure of preparing the data and illustrating and scanning the work is entirely carried out on the computer. At the time of writing, electro-photography is the most successful of the various printing systems available. Its technique, which is also that applied in laser printers and photocopiers, is centred on a photo-semiconductor that immediately loses its conductivity when in the dark. A cylinder that is covered with a semiconductor of that kind is statically charged through corona radiation to the effect that it obtains an even electric charge. This charge is fully retained as long as the cylinder is kept in the dark. But as soon as it is touched by a laser beam, which is used to transfer the image to be printed from the software onto the cylinder, it will release its charge. This results in a latent image of charge on the cylinder that is then coloured with an electromagnetic toner that only adheres to the charged areas. Finally, this image is either fixed on the cylinder and then printed onto the printing surface (direct process) or first printed onto the printing surface and then fixed through pressure or heat (indirect process). In either process, the cylinder needs to be cleaned and discharged again before printing the next image.

What appears to be a work-intensive process at first sight, proves to be very advanced particularly for small and sophisticated orders, for it needs to be remembered that this process requires none of the intermediate operations of the earlier printing processes – no typesetting or photocomposition is involved, and neither do stereos or films need to be made for transfer to the printing cylinder. Hence, electrophotography facilitates interrupting the print run to introduce changes to the text or layout of individual pages.

Electro-photography has an advantage over offset printing in radically simplifying the pre-press stages. Since data is utilised just as it is received from the customer, the risk of introducing mistakes into the final printed work with each further operation is eliminated. Production costs are significantly reduced since no films or printing plates are required, thus making the process ideal for very short print runs, in contrast to offset printing which generally becomes economical only with runs of over 1000 copies. As a result, smaller editions need less storage space, and the publisher does not have to risk too high an initial edition as further tiny runs can be printed as called for. The files can easily be archived for later use, and corrected or updated at will. As touched upon before, electrophotography makes it possible to interrupt a run to insert changes or to customise pages for different users. Last but not least, the process gives publishers the chance to split a job and allocate it to different printers. This procedure is already in practice amongst larger publishing houses, where it is quicker and cheaper to mail data than printed editions.

Digital printing still fails to match the standards and output of offset printing, but for the moment it comes into its own for runs of less than 1000 copies. Since editions, particularly of technical, scientific and academic works, are progressively decreasing in size worldwide (in the USA, for example, half of all books appear in runs of fewer than 1000 copies), the market for digital printing will continue to develop and ensure that such books and journals can continue to appear in printed form.

PRINT ON DEMAND

So-called "print on demand" has recently gained an increasing importance, particularly for books, journals, dissertations, and out-of-print material of specialised interest. Whereas such publications were formerly printed in an edition and then distributed, they may now just be publicised, and printed subsequently to individual order.

As users increasingly prefer direct access to electronic data rather than receiving it in print form, librarians find themselves confronted with completely new jobs. Libraries worldwide have mounted their catalogues on the internet so that ultimately, time-consuming book searches will become history. Large libraries, such as the British Library and the Bibliothèque Nationale are even one step ahead for they have already started to make complete works available on screen. Likewise, "Project Gutenberg" in Germany aims to achieve an electronic database that will eventually contain all the most important works of world literature.

MANUSCRIPTS ON SCREEN

Although the internet is inevitably thought of as the source of the most recently updated information on any topic, it also lends itself to providing scholars with access to valuable manuscripts and early printed books. The internet has brought about a new approach to the concept of facsimile editions, thus contributing to the conservation of old and fragile originals. For example, some sixty of the most important manuscripts of our cultural heritage held by the Biblioteca Apostolica Vaticana can be read on screen: thus manuscripts such as Virgil's, which date from the fourth century, or Euclid's from the twelfth century may be studied in screen-resolutions and with high quality printouts that easily satisfy the demands for scientific research work. Accordingly, researchers are no longer under pressure to travel, say, to the Jagiellonian University in Kraków to study the most important astrological work of early modern times, the *De Revolutionibus* by Nicholas Copernicus, for they can easily find it on the University's website. Likewise, researchers or, in fact, everyone interested can find the complete facsimile edition of the *Gutenberg Bible* belonging to the Göttingen State and University Library on the internet (*www.gutenbergdigital.de*). Users are offered the chance to study all 1286 richly illuminated pages – to compare them with other copies through the Keio University of Tokyo project (*www.humi.keio.ac.jp/treasures/incunabula/B42-web*) or the British Library (*www.bl.uk/treasures/gutenberg/homepage.html*) – or simply to look at them for their beauty. Moreover, as the internet makes it possible to compare the Latin *Vulgata* text side by side with a German or English translation, or to compare passages in the illuminations with their sources in the contemporary *Göttingen Pattern Book*, this electronic facsimile edition has become a standard research tool for philologists, theologists and book historians. It is beyond doubt that the precious old book and the new medium have thus formed an impressive and invaluable symbiosis.

This new development of electronic media takes place in parallel to a stable market for book market in the western world. Production by title continues to rise, reaching new heights with, for example, some 70,000 titles annually in the German-speaking area or 300,000 titles worldwide. The Frankfurt Book Fair – the world's most important book fair – held each October, provides an important market place for hundreds of thousands of academic, non-fiction and fiction titles. The national libraries, whether in Budapest, Frankfurt or London, are moving over to the storage of electronic media as well. Whereas books, in theory, are produced to survive for centuries, the question of how best to store electronic information has long remained unsettled.

ELECTRONIC INK

Recent developments at the Massachusetts Institute of Technology of "electronic ink" or "digital paper" promise to synthesize the advantages of the traditional book with those of the internet. The team working under Joseph Jacobson in the nanotechnology department has developed a digital paper which takes Gutenberg's invention forward: whereas the latter had made it possible to print the identical text many thousands of times onto sheets of paper, the advent of digital paper makes it possible to print many thousands of constantly changing pages of information onto the same sheet of paper. The technique may be described as follows: a carrier is printed with tiny micro-encapsulated pellets (10,000/cm^2) filled with black electronic ink containing particles of positively charged white pigment. When the pellets are loaded with a negative charge they appear white but when they are loaded with a positive charge they immediately turn black. Similar to the pixels in newspaper printing, the digital paper can be filled with textual or graphical information of any nature.

Indicative of its ultimate goal, Joseph Jacobson calls his project "The last book". It is his vision that in the not-too-distant future every child will be given his or her "last book", which, because it has some 240 pages of digital paper, can be refilled infinitely with any desired text and so will make further books superfluous. Even the problem of receiving information on the internet will be solved in the next couple of years by means of broadband transmissions over cellular phone systems. As, in all likelihood, Joseph Jacobson's invention will give rise to a new form of communication, he and his team were awarded the Gutenberg Prize of the International Gutenberg Society in Mainz in 2000. But whatever the future will bring we may legitimately say in the twenty-first century that Gutenberg has gone electronic.

Bibliography

ABBREVIATIONS

GJ: *Gutenberg-Jahrbuch*. Founded by Aloys Ruppel (1926), edited on behalf of the Gutenberg-Gesellschaft by Stephan Füssel, Mainz.

GW: *Gesamtkatalog der Wiegendrucke*. Published by the Kommission für den Gesamtkatalog der Wiegendrucke: vols. 1–8,1 Leipzig 1925–40; second revised impression, vols 1–7 Stuttgart: Hiersemann 1968; vols 8ff Stuttgart: Hiersemann 1978 ff.

H: Hain, Ludwig: *Repertorium bibliographicum, in quo libri omnes ab arte typographica inventa usque ad annum MD typis expressi . . . recensentur.* Stuttgartiae et Lutetiae Parisorum 1826–38. Reprint, Milano: Görlich 1966.

1. BIBLIOGRAPHIES / RESEARCH REPORTS

Corsten, Severin and Reinmar Fuchs assisted by Kurt Hans Staub: *Der Buchdruck im 15. Jahrhundert: Eine bibliographie*. 2 vols. Stuttgart: Hiersemann 1988/93.

Füssel, Stephan: "Gutenberg-Forschung Neunzehnhundert-Zweitausend" In: GJ 2000, pp. 9–26.

2. GUTENBERG: LIFE AND WORK

Bechtel, Guy: *Gutenberg et l'invention de l'imprimerie: Une enquête*. Paris: Fayard 1992.

Davies, Martin: *The Gutenberg Bible*. London, The British Library 1996.

Davies, Martin: "Juan de Carvajal and Early Printing." In: *The Library* 18/3 (1996), pp. 193–215.

Dolgodrova, Tatiana: "Die Miniaturen der Leipziger Pergament-Ausgabe der Gutenberg-Bibel: zur Zeit in der russischen Staatsbibliothek, Moskau." In: GJ 1997, pp. 64–75

Füssel, Stephan: "Gutenberg and the advent of printing in Western culture." In: *Hyphen* vol. 2. Athens 1998, pp. 70ff.

Füssel, Stephan: *Johannes Gutenberg in Selbstzeugnissen und Bilddokumenten*. Reinbeck: Rowohlt 1999. (=rororo Monographie 134).

Geldner, Ferdinand: *Der Türkenkalender*. Facsimile und commentary. Wiesbaden: Reichert 1975.

Hellinga, Lotte: "Das Mainzer Catholicon und Gutenbergs Nachlaß: Neudatierung und Auswirkungen." In: *Archiv für Geschichte des Buchwesens* 40 (1993), pp. 395–416.

Hoffmann, Leonhard: "Die Gutenbergbibel: Eine Kosten-und Gewinnschätzung des ersten Bibeldrucks auf der Grundlage zeitgenössischer Quellen." In: *Archiv für Geschichte des Buchwesens* 39 (1993), pp. 255–319.

Ing, Janet: *Johann Gutenberg and his Bible*. New York: The Typophiles, London: The British Library, 2nd printing 1990.

International Symposium on Printing History in East and West, edited by the Korean National Commission for Unesco. Seoul 1997.

Johannes Gutenberg: Die 42-zeilige Bibel. Commentary to the facsimile of the Burgos copy. Valencia: Vincent Garcia Editores 1997.

Johannes Gutenberg: Regionale Aspekte des frühen Buchdrucks. Papers of the international conference on the 550th anniversary of printing 1990 in Berlin. Berlin 1993 (= Beiträge aus der Staatsbibliothek zu Berlin 1).

Johannes Gutenbergs 42-zeilige Bibel. Commentary volume to the facsimile, by Paul Schwenke. Leipzig: Insel-Verlag 1923.

Johannes Gutenbergs zweiundvierzigzeilige Bibel. Facsimile of the example in the Staatsbibliothek Preußischer Kulturbesitz Berlin. Commentary volume edited by Wieland Schmidt und Friedrich Adolf Schmidt-Künsemüller. Munich: Idion-Verlag 1979.

Kapr, Albert: *Johannes Gutenberg: Persönlichkeit und Leistung*. Leipzig: Urania 1986. 2nd edn. Munich: C. H. Beck 1988.

Kapr, Albert: *Johann Gutenberg: The Man and his Invention*. Translated from the German by Douglas Martin. Aldershot: Scolar Press, Burlington Vt: Ashgate 1996.

Köhler, Johann David: *Hochverdiente und aus bewährten Urkunden wohlbeglaubte Ehren-Rettung Johann Gutenbergs* (...). Leipzig: Fritsch 1741.

Köster, Kurt: "Gutenbergs Straßburger Aachenspiegel-Unternehmen von 1438/40." In: GJ 1983, pp 24–44.

Lehmann-Haupt, Hellmut: *The Göttingen Model Book*. Columbia: Univ. of Montana Press 1972.

Lehmann-Haupt, Hellmut: *Gutenberg and the Master of the Playing Cards*. New Haven and London: Yale Univ. Press 1966.

Lehmann-Haupt, Hellmut: *Peter Schoeffer of Gernsheim and Mainz*. Rochester, N.Y.: Leo Hart 1950.

Man, John: *The Gutenberg Revolution: The story of a technical genius and an invention that changed the world*. London, Hodder Headline, 2000.

Mazal, Otto: **Der Mainz Psalter von 1457**. Facsimile and commentary volume. Dietikon-Zürich: Stocker 1968.

McMurtrie, Douglas C.: *The Gutenberg Documents: With translations of the texts into English*. New York: Oxford Univ. Press, 1941.

Miner, Dorothy: *The Giant Bible of Mainz*. Washington D.C.: Library of Congress 1952.

Morrison, Blake: *The Justification of Johann Gutenberg: A Novel*. London: Chatto & Windus 2000.

Needham, Paul: "The Paper Supply of the Gutenberg Bible." In: *The Papers of the Bibliographical Society of America* 79 (1985), pp. 303–74 (with census).

Painter, George D.: "The untrue portraits of Johann Gutenberg." In GJ 1967, pp. 54–60.

Painter, George D.: "Gutenberg and the B36-group: A Reconsideration." In: *Essays in Honour of Victor Scholderer*. Mainz: Karl Pressler 1970, pp. 292–322.
Powitz, Gerhardt: *Die Frankfurter Gutenberg-Bibel: Ein Beitrag zum Buchwesen des 15. Jahrhunderts*. Frankfurt am Main: Klostermann 1990 (= Frankfurter Bibliotheksschriften 3).
Ruppel, Aloys: *Johannes Gutenberg: Sein Leben und Werk*. Berlin: Gebr. Mann 1939, 2nd edn. Berlin 1947, reprint Nieuwkoop: de Graaf 1967.
Ruppel, Aloys: *Gutenbergs Tod und Begräbnis*. Mainz 1968 (= Kleiner Druck der Gutenberg-Gesellschaft No 81).
Schneider, Cornelia: *Peter Schöffer: Bücher für Europa*. Mainz: Gutenberg-Museum 2003
Schneider, Heinrich. *Der Text der Gutenberg-Bibel zu ihrem 500. Jubiläum untersucht*. Bonn: Hanstein 1954 (= Bonner biblische Beiträge 7).
Schorbach, Karl: "Die urkundlichen Nachrichten über Johannes Gutenberg." In: *Festschrift zum fünfhundertjährigen Geburtstage von Johann Gutenberg*. Edited by Otto Hartwig. Mainz 1900, pp.133–256.
Schorbach, Karl: "Neue Straßburger Gutenberg-Funde." *Gutenberg-Festschrift*. Mainz 1925, pp.130–43.
Sproule, Anna and Pollard, Michael: *Johann Gutenberg: Master of Modern Printing*. Farmington Hills MI: Blackbirch Press 1999.
Stüben, Jochen: "Das Rendsburger Fragment der Gutenberg-Bibel." In: GJ 1998, pp. 56–79.
Thorpe, James E.: *The Gutenberg Bible: Landmark in Learning*. 2nd edn. San Marino: The Huntingdon Library 1999.
Widmann, Hans: *Der gegenwärtige Stand der Gutenberg-Forschung*. Stuttgart: Hiersemann 1972.
Zedler, Gottfried: *Die Mainzer Ablaßbriefe der Jahre 1454 und 1455*. Mainz 1913.

3. THE BOOK AND SOCIETY IN THE FIFTEENTH CENTURY AND LATER

Birkerts, Sven: *The Gutenberg Elegies: The fate of reading in an electronic age*. New York and London: Faber and Faber 1994.
Blockbücher der Mittelalters: Bilderfolgen als Lektüre. Exhibition monograph ed. by the Gutenberg Society and the Gutenberg Museum. Mainz 1991.
Borgman, Christine L.: *From Gutenberg to the global information infrastructure*. Cambridge MA: M.I.T. Press 2000.
Brandis, Tilo: "Die Handschrift zwischen Mittelalter und Neuzeit: Versuch einer Typologie." In GJ 1997, pp. 25–57.
Bühler, Curt F.: *The Fifteenth-Century Book: The Scribes, The Printers, the Decorators*. Philadelphia: Pennsylvania Univ. Press 1960.
Burger, Konrad: *Buchhändleranzeigen des 15. Jahrhunderts*. Leipzig 1907.
Burke, Peter: *A Social History of Knowledge: From Gutenberg to Diderot*. London: Blackwell 2000.

Clair, Colin: *A History of European Printing*. London, New York: Academic Press 1976.

De Hamel, Christopher: *A History of Illuminated Manuscripts*. 2nd edn. London: Phaidon 1994.

De Hamel, Christopher: *The Book: A History of the Bible*. London: Phaidon 2001.

Eisenstein, Elizabeth L.: *The printing press as an agent of change*. 2 vols. Cambridge and New York: Cambridge University Press, 1979.

Febvre, Lucien and Martin, Henri-Jean: *L'apparition du livre*. Paris 1958 (= L'évolution de l'humanité 49).

Febvre, Lucien and Martin, Henri-Jean: *The Coming of the Book*. London and New York: Verso 1976.

Flasch, Kurt: *Nikolaus von Kues: Geschichte einer Entwicklung*. Frankfurt am Main: Klostermann 1998.

Fleischmann, Isa: *Metallschnitt und Teigdruck: Technik und Entstehung zur Zeit des frühen Buchdrucks*. Mainz: von Zabern 1998.

Füssel, Stephan (commentary): *The Luther Bible of 1534*, complete facsimile edition. Cologne, London, Las Vegas, Tokyo: Taschen 2002.

Füssel, Stephan (commentary): Emperor Maximilian I: *The adventures of the knight Theuerdank*, complete facsimile of the 1517 edition. Cologne, London, Las Vegas, Tokyo: Taschen 2003.

Füssel, Stephan (commentary): Schedel, Hartmann: *Chronicle of the World: The complete and annotated Nuremberg Chronicle of 1493*. Cologne, London, Las Vegas, Tokyo: Taschen 2001.

Füssel, Stephan (ed.): *Deutsche Dichter der frühen Neuzeit: ihr Leben und Werk*. Berlin: Erich Schmidt 1993.

Füssel, Stephan (ed.): *500 Jahre Schedelsche Weltchronik*. Nuremberg: Hans Carl 1994 (= Pirckheimer-Jahrbuch 1994).

Füssel, Stephan: "'Dem Drucker aber sage er Dank . . .' Zur wechselseitigen Bereicherung von Buchdruckerkunst und Humanismus." In: *Artibus. Festschrift für Dieter Wuttke zum 65. Geburtstag*. Wiesbaden: Harrassowitz 1995, pp. 167–78.

Füssel, Stephan: *Die Welt im Buch: Buchkünstlerischer und humanistischer Kontext der Schedelschen Weltchronik von 1493*. Mainz: Gutenberg-Gesellschaft 1996 (= Kleiner Druck der Gutenberg-Gesellschaft 111).

Füssel, Stephan and Honemann, Volker (eds.): *Humanismus und früher Buchdruck*. Nuremberg: Hans Carl 1997 (= *Pirckheimer Jahrbuch 1996*).

Geldner, *Ferdinand*: *Inkunabelkunde: Eine Einführung in die Welt des frühesten Buchdrucks*. Wiesbaden: Reichert 1978 (= Elemente des Buch- und Bibliothekswesens 5).

Gier, Helmut and Janota, Johannes: *Augsburger Buchdruck und Verlagswesen*. Wiesbaden: Harrassowitz 1997.

Giesecke, Michael: *Der Buchdruck der frühen Neuzeit: eine historische Fallstudie über die Durchsetzung neuer Informations- und Kommunikationstechnologien*. Frankfurt am Main: Suhrkamp 1991.

Grenzmann, Ludger and Stackmann, Karl (eds.): *Literatur und Laienbildung im Spätmittelalter und in der Reformationszeit*. Stuttgart: Metzler 1984

Grimm, Heinrich: "Die Buchführer des deutschen Kulturbereiches und ihre Niederlassungen in der Zeitspanne von 1450 bis um 1550." In: *Archiv für Geschichte des Buchwesens* 7 (1967), cols. 1153–1772.

Gumbrecht, Hans Ulrich and Pfeiffer, K. Ludwig (eds.): *Materialität der Kommunikation*. Frankfurt am Main: Suhrkamp 1988.

Gutenberg: 550 Jahre Buchdruck in Europa. Exhibition catalogue of the Herzog August Library, edited by Paul Raabe. Wolfenbüttel 1990.

Hirsch, Rudolf: *Printing, Selling and Reading* 1450–1550. *Wiesbaden*: *Harrassowitz*, 2nd edn. 1974.

Inkunabel- und Einbandkunde: Beiträge des Symposions zu Ehren von Max Joseph Husung 1995 in Helmstedt. Wiesbaden: Harrassowitz 1996

Kind, Helmut and Rohlfing, Helmut: *Gutenberg und der europäische Frühdruck: Zur Erwerbungsgeschichte der Göttinger Inkunabelsammlung*. Göttingen: Wallstein 1993.

Kock, Thomas and Schlusemann, Rita: *Laienlektüre und Buchmarkt im späten Mittelalter*. Frankfurt am Main and Berlin 1997.

Köhler, Hans-Joachim (ed.): *Flugschriften als Massenmedien der Reformationszeit*. Stuttgart: 1981 (= Spätmittelalter und frühe Neuzeit 13).

Kleinschmidt, Erich: *Stadt und Literatur in der Frühen Neuzeit*. Cologne and Vienna: Böhlau 1982.

Krafft, Fritz and Dieter Wuttke (eds.): *Das Verhältnis der Humanisten zum Buch*. Boppard: Boldt 1977 (= Kommission für Humanismusforschung, Mitteilung IV).

Kunze, Horst: *Geschichte der Buchillustration in Deutschland: Das* 15. *Jahrhundert*. 2 vols. Leipzig: Insel-Verlag 1973.

Lowry, Martin: *Nicholas Jenson and the rise of Venetian publishing in Renaissance Europe*. Oxford: Basil Blackwell 1991.

Lowry, Martin: *The World of Aldus Manutius: Business and Scholarship in Renaissance Venice*. Oxford Univ. Press and Cornell Univ. Press 1979.

Ludwig, Walther: "Der Humanist und das Buch: Heinrich Rantzaus Liebeserklärung an seine Bücher." In: *Illinois Classical Studies* 19 (1994), pp. 265–81.

Park, Seon Re: "Six perspectives in the history of printing." In: GJ 1998, pp. 42–7.

Schmidt-Künsemüller, Friedrich Adolf: *Die Erfindung des Buchdrucks als technisches Phänomen*. Mainz: Gutenberg-Gesellschaft 1931 (= Kleiner Druck 48).

Scapecchi, Piero: "Subiaco 1465 oppure Bondeno 1463?: Analisi del frammento Parsons-Scheide." In *La Bibliofilia* Anno CIII, Disp. I., pp. 1–24.

Schedel, Hartmann: *Chronicle of the World: The complete and annotated Nuremberg Chronicle of* 1493, introduction and appendix by Stephan Füssel. London and New York: Taschen 2001.

Smith, Margaret M.: *The Title-Page: Its Early Development* 1460–1510. London: The British Library 2000.

Teichl, Robert: "Der Wiegendruck im Kartenbild." In: Bibliothek und Wissenschaft 1 (1964), pp. 201–65 with 1 map.

Tiemann, Barbara (ed.): *Die Buchkultur im* 15. *und* 16. *Jahrhundert*. 2 vols. Hamburg: Maximilian-Gesellschaft 1995/1999.

Widmann, Hans: *Der deutsche Buchhandel in Urkunden und Quellen*. Hamburg: Hauswedell 1965.

Widmann, Hans: *Vom Nutzen und Nachteil der Erfindung des Buchdrucks: aus der Sicht der Zeitgenossen des Erfinders*. Mainz: Gutenberg-Gesellschaft 1973 (= Kleiner Druck 92).

Widmann, Hans: "Die Wirkung des Buchdrucks auf die humanistischen Zeitgenossen des Erfinders." In: Krafft and Wuttke: *Das Verhältnis der Humanisten zum Buch*. Boppard: Boldt 1977, pp. 63–88.

Wuttke, Dieter: "Sebastian Brant und Maximilian I: Eine Studie zu Brants Donnerstein-Flugblatt des Jahres 1492." In: *Die Humanisten in ihrer politischen und sozialen Umwelt*. Ed. by Otto Herding and Robert Stupperich. Boppard: Boldt 1976, pp. 141–76.

Wuttke, Dieter: *Humanismus als integrative Kraft: Die Philosophia des deutschen "Erzhumanisten" Conrad Celtis*. Nuremberg: Hans Carl 1985.

4. THE BOOK IN BRITAIN

Davies, Martin: "Incunabula." *In Studies in Fifteenth-Century Printed Books presented to Lotte Hellinga*. London: The British Library 1999.

De la Mere, A. C. and Hellinga, Lotte: "The First Book Printed in Oxford: The Exposition Symboli of Rufinus." In *Transactions of the Cambridge Bibliographical Society* 7 (1977–80), pp. 184–244.

Early English Printing: A Series of Facsimiles of all the Types used in England during the XVth Century. With an Introduction by Edward Gordon Duff. London: 1896. Reprint Hildesheim and New York: Georg Olms Verlag 1974.

Feather, John: *A History of British Publishing*. London and New York: Croom Helm 1988.

Hellinga, Lotte: *Caxton in Focus: The Beginning of Printing in England*. London: The British Library 1982.

Hellinga, Lotte and Trapp, J. B. (eds): *The Cambridge History of the Book in Britain*. Vol III: 1400–1557. Cambridge University Press 1999.

Hellinga, Lotte and Härtel, Helmar: "Book and Text in the Fifteenth Century." Proceedings of a conference held in the Herzog August Library Wolfenbüttel. Hamburg: Hauswedell 1981.

Painter, George D.: William Caxton: *A Quincentenary Biography of England's First Printer*. London: Chatto & Windus 1976.

William Caxton: An Exhibition to Commemorate the Quincentenary of the Introduction of Printing into England. The British Library 1976.

PICTURE CREDITS

The author and publisher would like to thank the following libraries for their permission to reproduce works in their collections. Most of the illustrations were kindly provided by the Staats- und Universitäts Bibliothek Göttingen, plates 6–11, 15, 17, 18, 22–30, 32–36, 39, 40, 49, 54–60. The Biblioteca Pública in Burgos supplied plate 5; the Universitätsbibliothek in Leipzig, plates 19, 20, 37, 45; the Gutenberg-Museum in Mainz, plates 1, 13, 16; the Germanische Nationalmuseum in Nuremberg, plate 61; the Universitätsbibliothek in Tübingen, plate 50; the Library of Congress in Washington, plate 4; and the Herzog August Bibliothek in Wolfenbüttel, plates 14, 31, 42, 43, 48, 51, 62. The other plates are taken from facsimile sources with acknowledgement as appropriate.

Index

WITHDRAWN
Undergraduate Lending Library

THE
PAUL HAMLYN
LIBRARY

DONATED BY
THE PAUL HAMLYN
FOUNDATION
TO THE
BRITISH MUSEUM

opened December 2000

WITHDRAWN

Managing Historic Sites and Buildings

The *Issues in Heritage Management* series is a joint venture between Routledge and English Heritage. It provides accessible, thought-provoking books on issues central to heritage management. Each book within the series is designed to provide a topical introduction to a key issue on heritage management for students in higher education and for heritage professionals.

Preservation and presentation are arguably the means and ends in the conservation of the historic environment. In an accessible format, this volume examines the choices and tensions involved in the conservation and interpretation of the historic built heritage.

This volume:

- Provides economic, social, cultural and educational perspectives on the tensions between conservation practice and public access to the heritage.
- Discusses the issues arising from these tensions through an examination of real problems faced by those who manage historic sites and buildings.
- Presents introductory and illustrative case histories for students of today's debates and controversial questions.

This volume is essential reading for students and professionals concerned with heritage management, archaeology and planning.

Gill Chitty and **David Baker** are consultants in historic environment conservation.

ISSUES IN HERITAGE MANAGEMENT SERIES
Published by Routledge in association with English Heritage

Series editor: Peter Stone, University of Newcastle

Managing the Historic Rural Landscape
(ed.) Jane Grenville

Managing Historic Sites and Buildings
Reconciling Presentation and Preservation
(eds) Gill Chitty and David Baker

Managing Historic Sites and Buildings

Reconciling Presentation and Preservation

Edited by
Gill Chitty and David Baker

363.69 CHI
WITHDRAWN

First published 1999
by Routledge
11 New Fetter Lane, London EC4P 4EE

Simultaneously published in the USA
and Canada by Routledge
29 West 35th Street, New York,
NY 10001

Routledge is an imprint of the Taylor & Francis Group

© 1999 Selection and editorial matter,
Gill Chitty and David Baker; individual
chapters, the contributors

Typeset in Bell Gothic and Perpetua by
The Florencetype Group, Stoodleigh, Devon

Printed and bound in Great Britain by
Biddles Ltd, Guildford and King's Lynn

All rights reserved. No part of this book may be reprinted or reproduced or utilized in any form or by any electronic, mechanical, or other means, now known or hereafter invented, including photocopying and recording, or in any information storage or retrieval system, without permission in writing from the publishers.

British Library Cataloguing in Publication Data

A catalogue record for this book is available from the British Library

Library of Congress Cataloging in Publication Data
Managing historic sites and buildings: balancing presentation and preservation / edited by Gill Chitty and David Baker.
p. cm. — (Issues in heritage management)
Includes bibliographical references and index.
ISBN 0–415–20814–9 (hardbound). —
ISBN 0–415–20815–7 (pbk.)
1. Historic sites—Management. 2. Historic buildings—Management.
I. Chitty, Gill. II. Baker, David, 1941–. III. Series.
NA105.M26 1999
363.6′9—dc21 98–54678
CIP

ISBN 0–415–20814–9 HB
0–415–20815–7 PB

Contents

CONTENTS

List of Figures

LIST OF FIGURES

LIST OF TABLES

LIST OF CONTRIBUTORS

Martin Allfrey joined English Heritage in 1985, as a curator of archaeological collections. He has recently been appointed as Head of Collections Team for the North of England where he is responsible for the conservation and display of collections from properties managed by English Heritage. He is currently working with The Bowes Museum, County Durham, on the preparation of a Conservation Plan.

David Baker is a consultant. He managed an integrated historical conservation service for Bedfordshire County Planning Department until both were disbanded by cuts in 1997. His *Living with the Past* (1983) explored a holistic approach to historic aspects of the environment. He has been a member of English Heritage's Churches and Cathedrals Advisory Committee and is a member of St Albans Diocesan Advisory Committee.

Marion Blockley is Director of the Ironbridge Institute, a centre for postgraduate studies in Heritage Management and Industrial Heritage. She is a member of the strategy group preparing the management plan for the Ironbridge Gorge World Heritage site and sits on the ICOMOC UK World Heritage Site Committee. She edited the magazine '*Interpretation*' for the Society for the Interpretation of Britain's Heritage and has published widely on interpretation and archaeological heritage management.

Krystyna Campbell trained and worked as an archaeologist and then as a landscape architect. With experience in local government, private practice and then nearly ten years with English Heritage she is now working as a freelance landscape consultant specialising in the repair, restoration and management of historic landscapes.

Gill Chitty has worked as an independent consultant since 1992. She was Principal Archaeologist for the Greater London Council before joining English Heritage as an Inspector in 1986. Her current consultancy projects include national reviews for industrial heritage, archaeological training and historic environment information resources. She has published a number of articles on conservation history and practice.

Glyn Coppack is a senior Inspector of Ancient Monuments at English Heritage. Better known for his work on medieval monastic sites, he has specialised for the last 15 years in the conservation of major ruins. His publications include *Abbeys and Priories* (1990), *Fountains Abbey* (1993) and *The White Monks* (1998).

Catherine Croft is Architectural Officer for the Theatre's Trust and Vice-Chair of the Twentieth Century Society. She worked for several years with English Heritage as an Inspector of Historic Buildings in the East Midlands and in London. She has published numerous articles on post-war architecture, most recently the Introduction to '*On the Road. The Art of Engineering in the Car Age*' (1999).

Chris Gingell is the National Trust's Property Manager for the Avebury Estate and nearby properites. Before joining the National Trust in 1988 he directed archaeological projects in Wiltshire for 15 years, based at Devizes Museum and later with Wessex Archaeology. He has published articles in a wide range of journals, together with a monograph '*The Marlborough Downs*' (1992).

Elain Harwood is English Heritage's Inspector responsible for the post-war research and listing programme. She has written (with Andrew Saint) *Exploring England's Heritage, London*, and (with Alan Powers), *Tayler and Green Architects*. She is now writing a book on post-war architecture in England for Yale University Press.

John Schofield is an Inspector of Ancient Monuments in English Heritage with responsibility for several thematic reviews in the Monuments Protection Programme and for its implementation in southern England. He is managing English Heritage's survey of recent fortifications and edited their recent publication *Monuments of War* (1998).

David Start is Director of the Heritage Trust for Lincolnshire, which combines archaeological work with building preservation and interpretational projects. He is a past Chair of the Institute of Field Archaeologists. Currently, he is a Treasurer of the Standing Conference of Archaeological Unit Managers and Vice-Chair of the Society for Lincolnshire History and Archaeology.

Margaret Warhurst has spent most of her working life in museums in the North West of England. She joined the Norton Priory Museum Trust in 1987 and has enjoyed the opportunity to review the site and its potential, to plan how to realise it and begin to make it happen.

Christopher Young was English Heritage's Regional Director for the North. Since 1995, he has been responsible for the completion and implementation of the Management Plan for the Hadrian's Wall World Heritage Site. He is also English Heritage World Heritage Policy Advisor, and has worked for UNESCO on developing site management in Laos.

FOREWORD

Foreword

This book is the second volume in the new series *Issues in Heritage Management*. The series, a joint initiative between the English Heritage Education Service (EHES) and Routledge, is based on discussions at professional seminars, organised and facilitated by the EHES, where those involved in particular aspects of the heritage were able to meet and exchange views, ideas and approaches. It is important to note that the seminars were conceived as educational, rather than policy-forming, events. They were intended to provide a 'snap-shot' of current policy and current practice and actively encouraged debate and positive criticism of the *issue* under discussion: they certainly were not intended to put forward a particular English Heritage view or policy (although, as would be expected given the subject matter, English Heritage experts contributed to all of the seminars).

Most of the chapters in this volume are based on papers presented at the seminar, although some additional contributions, identified at the seminar as being of major importance to the discussion, were especially commissioned.

The seminar, *Presentation and Preservation: Conflict or Collaboration?*, was held at the Society of Antiquaries, London, in October 1997 and was organised by Gill Chitty and David Baker. I should like to put on record my thanks to Gill and David for all their hard work and diligence in planning and running the seminar. Without them the seminar would not have taken place and you would not be holding this volume. I should also like to thank David Morgan Evans, Secretary of the Society of Antiquaries, for hosting the seminar, Liz Hollinshead, who is the EHES Education Officer responsible for the series, for all her support and Michelle Mulvihill, also of the EHES, for dealing with the administration of the seminar.

Peter G. Stone
Department of Archaeology, University of Newcastle, August 1998

The other conferences held were *The Management of the Rural Landscape* and *Traffic and the Historic Environment*. They will shortly be published within this series.

Introduction

CONTEXTS FOR COLLABORATION AND CONFLICT

David Baker

Introduction

What You See is What You Get, says information technology in the age of the consumer; but many things were once not what they now appear to be. The differences carry meanings about the significance of the past, for itself and for us in the present. Visitors to prehistoric Avebury may be disappointed by the part-survival of spectacular embankments and wide-spaced stone circles, but how do they react when told that much of what they see is largely a drastic and controversial reconstruction of the 1930s? Do they feel that their experience is devalued or do they want the National Trust to finish the job? Such ambiguities, conveniently shrouded in the mists of prehistory, become more starkly visible as the landscapes of post-war industrial recession become part of history and industrial archaeology (Figure 1). The population with first-hand memories, often bad ones, of former working lives in factories and mines, is gone or fast reducing, and new generations want to know about things that are now largely outside their experience. Throughout the history of industry, buildings and sites have been abandoned after becoming obsolete for reasons that may be technological, economic or political. Their surviving remains, usually complex and often extensive, provide 'heritage managers' with major problems of selection and even greater difficulties of interpretation, especially when original machinery, markets and social context have been lost.

Difficulties about perception and explanation are, therefore, not confined to prehistoric times; there is plenty of scope for misunderstanding the historic survivals of the millennium now ending. As change accelerates and history laps at the feet of the living, the moving border between personal memory and history or legend has even less time to sweep across the remains of recent industrialisation and world warfare.

Figure 1 Washington 'F' Pit, Tyne and Wear, was closed by the National Coal Board in 1968; in 1964/5 it had employed a workforce of 1500

Source: Gill Chitty

The opportunities for first-hand communication bring with them risks that the inevitable baggage of personal experience will hinder attempts to provide broader perspectives. By contrast, conserved buildings and ruins of the pre-industrial age acquire different complexities with their own sequences of adaptation and change over time, patinas of use and ecologically shrouded decay. These can be sources of confusion and, at the same time, valuable elements in a holistic view of the historic environment. What is now becoming understood as a truly 'sustainable' approach seeks to retain a full range of options for choice in the future, and not to diminish long-term historic assets for the short-term purpose of making them instantly and easily intelligible.

These are just some examples of complexities surrounding the relationship between preservation and presentation. They are central activities, arguably means and ends, in the conservation of the historic environment. Are they self-reinforcing or do they work against each other? More usually they are considered separately, and each tends to look in different directions. Preservation of what has been inherited from the past is a matter for ethical frameworks, technical procedures and managing threats from economic development or natural decay; presentation focuses upon communication, education, marketing and visitor management.

If you start from the position that the fundamental purpose of the whole process is to communicate understanding about the human past, however, it becomes much more important to know how far the ideologies, strategies, tactics and techniques of the two activities are mutually supportive. The ways in which we preserve sites and buildings inescapably emphasise particular attributes; but do we consciously either restrict potential meanings, or impose identities, or keep presentational possibilities open, or perhaps not restrict them sufficiently? Do certain approaches to presentation imperil future preservation, because of what is done to the fabric of the survival, or because of the impact of the attention and interest it generates? Alternatively, do they threaten it in another way, with ascribed meanings misleadingly altering priorities for resources that could ensure it gets passed on to future generations?

Questions such as these were raised in a stimulating seminar held at the Society of Antiquaries of London in October 1997, as the basis for this collection of essays which was finalised by mid-1998. We have tried to respect the live and developing nature of our topic, keeping synthesis tentative and putting down markers for unfinished business, though we have also gone further than merely collecting together case studies in the hope that general lessons will emerge of their own accord. The mixture of essays is designed to display a range of issues and approaches: some chapters deal with a specific site or building but explicitly raise wider matters; other chapters are general studies of broader issues raised by particular topics or classes of historic survivals. Between them, they cover many of the different circumstances that arise from various combinations of period, location, type, function, accessibility and popularity. Some readers may prefer to obtain a feel for the subject by sampling some of these chapters before returning to the broader and more generalised discussion that is the intention of this introduction.

The three main purposes of this introduction are interrelated, but not necessarily interdependent. First, a few comments on the post-war history of the conservation movement provide some context. After all, what makes this study possible and necessary is the expanding scope of historical recognition, in parallel with changing approaches to the philosophy, management and practice of conservation. There are interesting tensions in a *fin de siècle* world inhabited by residual certainties of antiquarianism and hopeful uncertainties of sustainability. Second, it looks at some aspects of a methodological or theoretical framework for considering tensions between preservation and presentation – whether constructive or destructive. In the sequence of activities that together constitute historical conservation, can we view preservation and presentation as a naturally collaborative partnership, to the extent that even conflicts can take the process forward? There is the range of issues that arise in attempting to present this increasingly complex and diverse historic environment: assessing intelligibility and recognisability; devising compensatory strategies; drawing upon the right media for well-chosen messages; and, perhaps leading everything, identifying the human needs to which interpretation and presentation must respond. Finally, and not least, it introduces the chapters themselves, relating common themes to the wider framework for historical conservation, with brief comments on the major issues each covers, and a coda on some unfinished business.

Developing approaches and expanding philosophies

One of the best pieces of evidence for claims of maturity in the conservation movement is its acquisition of a past. Some appreciation of what happened in that past is essential as background for our topic. Fortunately, it has been chronicled and analysed in a growing number of studies (such as Carman 1996; Hunter 1996), so that little more than the main headlines are needed here, dealing with the growth of understanding about significance, context, process and connections.

Widening scope

Interest has expanded to encompass a widening range of elements in the historic environment, moving out from specific sites and buildings to their interrelated contexts of urban and rural settlement, and natural and semi-natural habitats, together with the visual aspects of townscape and landscape. Care of the inherited past became engaged with a much wider range of contemporary concerns through topics such as the archaeological evolution of landscape, the attribution of historic value to buildings erected within living memory, and, once money became available, the best ways of devising financially affordable priorities for preservation.

Some over-arching themes have emerged to lend coherence to diverse elements and to integrate them with other environmental and economic interests. In the 1970s, the 'cultural resource' drew on intellectual influences from America and Europe; in the 1980s, the 'historic' environment emphasised human interaction with the 'natural' world; in the 1990s, 'sustainability' is a concept of custodianship suitable for the leap between millennia.

Developing controls

In parallel, mechanisms of control have been devised that now range from detailed prescriptive statutory requirements to voluntary partnerships. A growing awareness of past losses tightened controls over potentially damaging works. Statutory provisions moved from mere notification of intention to a formal procedure that ensures that permission is obtained in advance. The change came for listed buildings in 1968, Conservation Areas (partially) in 1974, and scheduled ancient monuments in 1981; in due course it may sweep over the most recently introduced 'material considerations' in the land-use planning process, parks and gardens, battlefields and ancient hedgerows. These latter topics also illustrate how controls have tended to become less restrictive, the greater the quantity of land or buildings affected, reflecting the economic implications of increased constraint, and the need for collaborative rather than imposed solutions.

Social integration

The conservation movement grew in the last third of the twentieth century partly through the expanding cultural horizons already mentioned, and partly as a function of greatly increased rates of destruction affecting what was recognised as a finite heritage. The basic impacts of visitors upon visited places – worn pathways across ancient earthworks, coaches crammed into the centres of historic cities, and queues snaking through roped-off rooms in the stately homes of England – were recognised over a generation ago (Figure 2). The advent of public policy for conservation and grants in the post-war period amplified rather than created tensions between reconstruction and repair already familiar to doughty Victorian architects and their SPAB opponents. Those seminal pressure groups, SAVE Britain's Heritage and RESCUE, the Trust for British Archaeology, found tourism and restoration already in place when they assembled their demonology of threats to relics of the past.

There has been a progression from reactive and anecdotal litanies of juxtaposed threat and historic survival towards a more established and proactive position. Though there will always be good old-fashioned pitched battles with destruction, progress and profit, the outlook of the conservation movement has broadened out and is now achieving new levels of social integration. Sharing in wider social and economic objectives, it is expected to contribute to their achievement, through generating income and increasing environmental appreciation. With this has come a greater obligation to examine preconceptions, purposes and processes, looking at systems and organisations to ensure that its judgements are properly informed, academically, culturally and socially. 'Conservationists' also have to watch their backs: social acceptance does not automatically equate with political support. Having arrived, you need to fight to hold your position, as the new Labour

Figure 2 Visitors queuing outside Westminster Abbey

Source: David Baker

government's apparent lack of understanding about the historic environment shows (DCMS 1998; Morris 1998).

Divergence and convergence at the century's end

Historical conservation continues to be divided between two legal codes. One operates primarily at local level through the land-use planning system, dealing with listed buildings, townscape and archaeological sites unprotected by statutory scheduling. At national level, a separate legal code controls scheduled ancient monuments; there are additionally reserve or appeal procedures for especially significant issues that arise locally. (See Ross 1996, Hunter and Ralston 1993, for an introduction to statutory protection and public policy for the built environment and archaeology; *Planning Policy Guidance Note [PPG] 15: Planning and the Historic Environment* [DoE 1994] and *PPG16: Archaeology and Planning* [DoE 1990b] are the principal sources of government guidance on heritage policy.) This division can seem anomalous in an inclusive view of the historic environment, or when trying to relate historical and other aspects of conservation. It does, however, reflect some important assumptions about the roles assigned to different categories and classes of survival. Those handled by the local planning system are the subject of balances struck between the competing claims of economic development and environmental conservation: usefulness that embodies other social and environmental values as well as intrinsic worth can weigh heavily here, especially if it helps bridge the gap. The 'best' items, 10 per cent or less of all that have been identified, sit firmly at the conservative end of the spectrum of permitted change, and are managed at the national level with a strong presumption in favour of preservation or minimal alteration.

The traditionally separate approaches to the archaeological and architectural heritage perpetuated in current legislation have encouraged compartmentalised attitudes. On the archaeological side, 'preservation' has led to the 'monumentalisation' of earthworks, standing stones, ruins and unoccupied buildings. Isolated in a constantly changing social and economic context, they are sustained by a presumption against development or physical change that would adversely affect them. The 'conservation' of historic buildings and places involves a more dynamic relationship with their context, and a presumption that broadly favours change in order to ensure viable economic or social use, providing that it is within design parameters that take account of 'special interest'. Some would say that the distinction between preservation and conservation has become artificially over-defined in the interests of adversarial planning and political arguments.

All is not division and divergence, however. Integrated strategies are being developed for managing and interpreting the historic environment in its totality, in partnership with a range of other conservation interests. The most fundamental change has come with the reception of ideas about the sustainability of the global environment, as they have cascaded down from the Bruntland Commission (WCED 1987), to United Kingdom government policy (DoE 1989), and evolved via the agendas of the Earth Summits in Rio in 1992 (UN 1992) and Kyoto in 1997. These offer the potential for building bridges between environmental specialisms through the concepts associated with working for sustainable change, and they are being promoted for action at the local level (Local Agenda 21) as well as globally (see Chapter 3, p. 58). Although this approach originated in a concern for the survival of the 'natural' world, it is also fundamentally involved with historical process. It is no coincidence that the Bruntland Report's *Our Common Future* (WCED 1987) underwent a characteristically British renaming at the hands of Whitehall policy makers to appear as *This Common Inheritance* (DoE 1990a).

Sustainable working represents a benign form of top-down management, usefully challenging because a prerequisite is a proper understanding of what is being managed. Its starting point, that our actions must not needlessly prejudice the right of future generations to enjoy the environmental benefits that we ourselves inherited, when applied to cultural survivals, successfully removes them from the questions about the worthiness of conservation that were being seriously asked a generation ago.

Initially, a formal articulation of historical survivals, or assets, was proposed within two broad categories: *critical* (to be conserved at all costs) and *constant* (subject to limited change provided that the overall character of the resource is maintained); as the concepts developed, so a third was added: *tradeable* (suitable for exchange in return for other benefits). This hierarchy of value judgements aimed to embrace the widening range of recognised survivals and control mechanisms, as described above. The helpfulness of these categories for discussion of presentation and interpretation is that they offer a single system of values which, by focusing on intrinsic merit, tends to bridge rather than perpetuate the division between the useful and the useless.

More recent work on environmental values has recognised that the rigid categorisation of particular features or assets – almost reverting to the traditional habits of grading for statutory protection – may 'block change rather than encourage the kinds of changes that are consistent with sustainability' (Cole *et al.* 1998; CAGE *et al.* 1997). What has evolved is the concept of 'affordances' – the benefits or services that are offered by an attribute, or group of attributes, in the environment. An evaluation of the services afforded by the historic attributes of a particular feature or area will vary according to the scale at which it is assessed, whether within the local community, the neighbourhood, the district, or in a regional or national perspective. This is well expressed in the recognition that the heritage 'owes its present value and significance to people's perceptions and opinions . . . to their personal beliefs and values', and can give people 'a sense of belonging, defining their identities at national and local scale, and providing depth and character for their working and living environment' (English Heritage 1997, 2).

Preservation and presentation in the conservation process

Activities, connections and systems

Neither preservation nor presentation occurs within a vacuum; nor does one follow blindly on from the other. They are stages within a set of activities that together manage the conservation of the historic environment, in a process that is dynamic, sequential, and relies upon in-built mechanisms for feedback. Figure 3 shows how, properly managed, the relationship between preservation and presentation can be naturally collaborative. Three sets of points are particularly worth stressing for present purposes.

First, the various activities are causally and sequentially connected in a continuous process. Things work best, and produce the best results, when done in the right order; bad outcomes can be caused as easily by good intentions badly sequenced as by explicitly destructive decisions. It is essential to understand the identity, nature and significance of a historic feature as far as possible before deciding what to do with it. Failure to clarify properly the historical characteristics of a whole class of survivals can lead to uncertainty as to whether individual ones belong to it or another category; in turn, that can lead to inappropriate conservation strategies and misunderstandings about interpretation and presentation. Preservation, properly achieved, facilitates presentation of what has been preserved; proper presentation supports continuing preservation. Both are

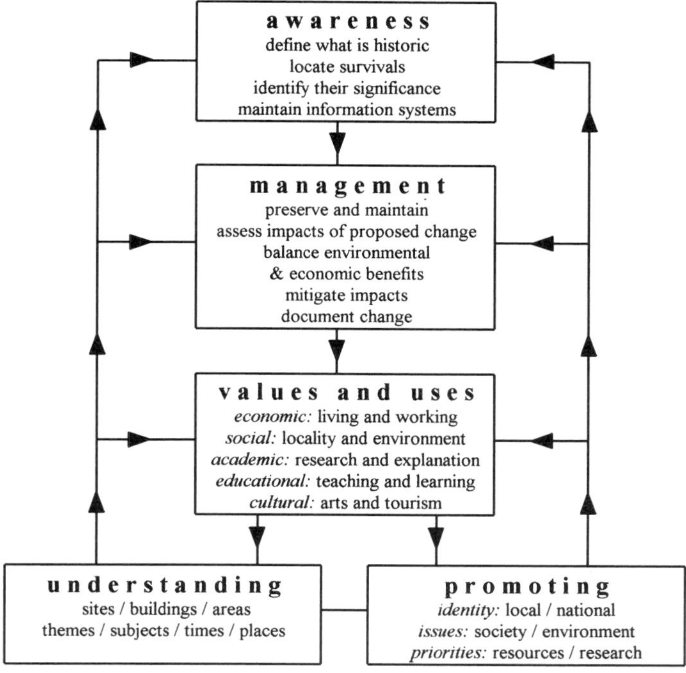

Figure 3 Conserving the historic environment

equally dependent for their effectiveness upon acquiring data, analysing it so that it becomes information about the subject in hand, and then using it appropriately. In this approach, much of the feature-specific data needed for interpretative and presentational purposes will be assembled while carrying through a programme of preservation work. Moreover, it is the approach adopted by the device of the Conservation Plan with its fundamental tool, assessment of significance (Heritage Lottery Fund 1998).

The model of historical conservation processes recognises not only multiple potential outputs – economic, social, academic, educational and cultural – but also potential feedback under the twin headings of understanding and promotion. Perhaps these are the purpose of the whole process anyway. Thus it is important to view the relationship of preservation and presentation not just analytically from the viewpoint of the resource manager, but through the minds of customers, the direct consumers of 'heritage', and also from the perspectives of the politicians and administrators who need to respond to their reactions and needs. It is easy for the heritage professionals to take a purist and slightly idealised approach, though this has distinct value as a statement of first principles and as a necessary defence against the degrading aspects of commercial heritage. It does, however, tend not to embrace some real-life situations, such as the difficulties of under-subsidised private owners who have to sell the attraction of their properties by whatever means are available in order to provide an adequate income for maintenance or shareholders.

Second, the model has internal and external systems. Conservation management *per se* is a micro-cycle: repairs initially require information inputs and subsequently create information outputs that can be fed back; these are as potentially useful for explaining and presenting as for the next round of works. Conservation activities also relate to the wider social and economic processes of which they are a part; similarly, presentation is informed by values and serves uses, both of which are wider than the immediate purpose and processes of preservation. Thus, values and uses interact, leading to review and feedback, and driving the whole cycle.

Third, diagrams like this can test how realistic theory is in practice. One can envisage, for example, a sequence of stages between the making of a heritage discovery and the perceiving of a presentation about it: *investigation* > *recording* > *interpretation* > *preservation* > *presentation* > *perception*. That does, however, raise several questions, some familiar and most problematical. Can you record without interpreting and vice versa? At what stage does data (stored in records systems) become information (fit for purpose), and how can you tell the difference, especially if one user's data is another's information? There is also the danger of treating the words interpretation and presentation as interchangeable, when interpretation ought to be a prelude to both preservation and presentation. Perhaps presentation involves at least three stages – *interpretation*, which decides what the available information signifies, *selection*, which chooses what aspects of significance are to be presented, and *presentation*, which applies the appropriate techniques to communicate what has been selected. There are also tactical side-issues and dilemmas – how far, and in what way, should presentational strategies and techniques seek to counter pre-existing misperceptions if this risks reducing the level of support for preservation?

Sources of conflict and collaboration

Focusing more directly on tensions between preservation and presentation, several strands can be drawn out for examination in practical situations such as those described in the following chapters, confirming or modifying aspects of the model of process just outlined. Historic survivals derive presentable meaning from recorded past uses and perceived present ones, which do not always coincide, creating a major problem with some industrial survivals (see Chapter 10). Preservation and conservation create those present uses, guided by suites of ethical principles, legal controls and practical techniques, which have their own capabilities for presentation and misrepresentation.

One recurring issue is the difference in treatment for presentation of sites and monuments that have lost original uses, and buildings and places with continuing uses. Are these differences inevitable, or are they exacerbated by inherited sets of legislative procedures and interpretative practices? Do they unhelpfully divorce things that were once in simultaneous use, like the ruined castle in the middle of a surviving historic town street pattern, or does that kind of contrast, properly explained, make helpful points about change, altered uses and the passage of time? In one sense, preservation as 'monumentalisation' inevitably detaches the survival from its social and economic context, which then continues to evolve; in another sense, however, the monument has a new role in that context as a relic that helps define the present, and how it views the past. Such matters are starkly and poignantly illustrated by the case of recent military remains (see Chapter 12 and Figure 4).

When a site or building becomes obsolete or wears out, there is usually one of four outcomes: it is abandoned as useless and allowed to decay; destroyed, perhaps to be replaced; given a new alternative use; or preserved as a monument to its former use which may be partially reintroduced artificially. Larger areas with many historic components have a more complex, multi-directional mutation, as do large monuments occupying several different environments, like Hadrian's Wall, which faces a wide range of pressures and opportunities for presentation, controlled through a consistently articulated core conservation policy (see Chapter 2).

Figure 4 Dismantled sections of the Berlin Wall (1995) stored for use in future conservation and presentation projects

Source: Gill Chitty

Presentation can be destructive – rather than preservative – for several sets of overlapping reasons, mostly generalised here to avoid legal action and to allow readers to supply their own examples. Some strategies can be directly and deliberately damaging physically: they may wish to serve a particular version of intelligibility by removing things that obscure the period or message chosen for display, such as the traditional approach to the presentation of great houses, intentionally not taken at Brodsworth Hall (see Chapter 8). More subtly but no less destructively, presentation may be manipulated to emphasise a particular aspect for reasons of popularity or sensationalism, at the expense of the physical neglect and devaluation of other, equally important aspects: such was the fate of many monastic outer courts and home farms in earlier days when heritage was the ruins of the core buildings rather than the remains of the whole economic unit. Some are indirectly damaging because, for lack of forethought or alternatives, they create vulnerabilities to wear by millions of feet, theft or vandalism: this is one of the problems facing churches and cathedrals (see Chapter 7). Linked with this are economically driven strategies to make the heritage 'wash its face', to subsidise something else, or to support the local economy, something handled beneficially and constructively at Norton Priory (see Chapter 5). This raises the idea of sacrificial sites, akin to the sacrificial layers capping the walls of ruined monuments: the heritage consumable that is 'tradeable' capital because there are plenty of them (even though the chosen victim may be special to a particular place); this is at least an implicit problem in relating the results of rescue archaeology to the communities in which it occurs (see Chapter 3). Another set of motives, loosely characterised as politically driven, covers the use of the past to make points about the perceived worthwhileness of those who look after a place, as well as the place itself. This can be difficult territory: on the one hand, the development of local environmental awareness deserves every encouragement; on the other, there can be serious distortion in the hands of the ill-informed and self-important, more concerned with the agendas of their day and a small piece of personal immortality than with what has made their place significant. The wish of mayors to inscribe their names and titles on plaques attached to historic structures whose presentation their councils have grant-aided is a recurring problem.

Things go wrong when interpretations of use are imposed upon inadequately understood survivals. There may be pressures to over-interpret or over-present, out of a sense of local pride, 'ownership' by the interpreter, or even as a way of boosting status to improve chances of preservation. The battered remains of Bedford Castle, its motte reduced in height and increased in width by thirteenth-century slighting, have so far escaped being pressed into service as a symbol for the regeneration of a run-down county town, despite distortive and destructive proposals for 'reconstruction' emerging at regular intervals from complex and factional local politics. Things can go doubly wrong when the imported generalisations are themselves misunderstood, and this is how much so-called historical re-enactment shades imperceptibly but often riotously into modern entertainment. Further twists can be added to an increasingly complex sequence of distortion when presentation gets caught up in historiography, and gives itself a pseudo-legitimacy by re-enacting, for example, the essentially Victorian view of Merrie Englande.

English Heritage's announcement of recent discoveries at Tintagel in Cornwall provides a richly complex concluding illustration. This site combines spectacular coastline with extensive multi-period archaeological deposits and a firm place in myth as the place of King Arthur's conception. The great find, a small piece of slate inscribed with the name 'Artognov' in sixth-century script, was presented to the public on the main evening television news in August 1998. English Heritage, doubtless mindful of its duty to promote public enjoyment of the heritage, was seen to describe it as the 'find of a lifetime' and an 'inescapable' link with a historical Arthur, a beleaguered war-lord glimpsed dimly behind the legendary figure. The more cautious professor responsible for the excavation appeared not to find an easy connection. It was necessary to read the detailed press release in order to get beyond adversarial journalistic probing and to appreciate that both were talking harmoniously about different aspects of the same rather complex and subtle historical problem. Other issues and agendas climbed aboard this iconic piece of slate. Both interviewees appeared to favour the idea of further (inevitably destructive) excavations on this otherwise unthreatened and incompletely published site in pursuit of the strengthened possibility that it held a Dark Age royal palace. This would be grist to the mill of the good folk in the nearby village of Tintagel and their Arthurian presentations, driven by an almost total economic reliance upon tourism.

Presenting a complex and diverse historic environment

The last quarter-century has seen a steady increase in the range of perceptions about the complexity of the historic environment, the diversity of survivals within it and the range of social and economic uses that it can serve. Presentation has to serve two masters at once: the integrity of what is being presented, and the desire of customers for an intelligible product. The path from data to presentation is rarely smooth: many of the potholes represent original deficits or imbalances whose creative plugging is essential for a coherent result. One way of looking at the process is as a sequence of four stages: explaining what survives; reconstructing the larger physical whole of which it was a part; reconstructing its use at the place where it is; and providing a wider context in terms of period, subject and national history or prehistory. This may not fit every case, and does not have to show in the finished result, but going through the sequence can keep a check on the balance between material that is original, real and specific to the site or building, and material that is imported or merely analogous.

Intelligibility factors

It may be useful to consider various types of historic survival and different historic environments in terms of their 'intelligibility', while recognising the innate subjectivity of the concept. It depends upon a combination of survival/preservation together with interpretation plus presentation, and manifests itself at various levels from the impressionistic to an in-depth articulation capable of supporting wider ranges of meaning. What is a viable minimum for each level must vary between categories of survival and strategies for presentation, and how the two interrelate. Some things are so small, simple or incomplete that little can be said about them or nothing definite is known about their original form because no remains have survived. 'Intelligibility factors' include *scope* and *scale*, *completeness* and *potential for reconstruction*, and *recognisability*. Applying them explicitly in particular cases might help to identify strengths and compensate for weaknesses, such as information *deficits* to be made up by further work on ordering or collecting basic data, or information *surpluses* to be stripped away by selecting for interpretation and presentation.

Scope and scale

These two factors draw attention to the all-embracing nature of the historic environment. At the broadest end – settlements and landscapes – the historic survivals are likely to be large, complex, multi-period and more difficult to identify coherently amidst the constructions and land-uses of today, unless those uses happen to favour conservation, a point well illustrated by the case of parks and gardens (see Chapter 9). Thus, in the upland National Parks, the overwhelming presumption is in favour of preserving and explaining an outstanding natural and historic resource, and factors tend to work together, despite some conflicts between agriculture, access and archaeology. In the prime historic towns, the economic imperatives of tourism strongly favour the preservation of historic characteristics that contribute to a sense of place: street plans, ancient buildings and street furniture. The landscapes and townscapes of distinctive but not obviously outstanding historic character are, however, more difficult to present. Techniques such as Conservation Area Character Analysis, compiled with proper community involvement, can fill some of the gap. Contemporary approaches to historic landscape assessment are also evolving ways to redress the balance in favour of 'white land' (the 'rest' of the historic environment to which no special historic character or environmental value has hitherto been assigned) and recognition of local and neighbourhood value. Whilst primarily a tool for land-use planning, the process of identifying and characterising local distinctiveness and its vulnerability to change offers valuable material for interpretative and presentation purposes (see Fairclough *et al.* forthcoming, for the background to English Heritage's Historic Landscape project and other work on integrated policies for the historic environment).

Completeness and potential for reconstruction

These factors are concerned with information deficits, and how far they have to be made up to a desired level of understanding before the probability of accuracy reduces to an unacceptable level. This readability of a site or building varies according to age, type and the extent to which it has altered or been changed over time through reuse. The chapters that follow present a wide range of cases. At one extreme, major prehistoric earthwork monuments like Avebury require some conjecture about both upstanding structures and the activities they supported before any coherent 'sense' can be made of them (see Chapter 1). At the other extreme, the display of Brodsworth Hall (see Chapter 8) requires no such reconstruction because it is present as its last owner left it, rather than in the condition of its heyday for which the detailed evidence survives much less completely. In the middle sit more subtly difficult cases, with an all-purpose life-in-an-English-monastery easily but rather anonymously planted on to the foundations of Norton Priory (see Chapter 5), the difficulty of getting beyond token reconstruction of life at the heart of the Industrial Revolution (see chapter 10), and the deceptive impression of medievalism given by the interior of many ancient parish churches whose present-day arrangements are the product of up to three liturgical reorderings (see Chapter 7).

There is an obvious divergence between sites or monuments where the primary intention is to preserve what is there as unchanged as possible, and buildings or places where continuing uses repair, renew and add new elements, thereby opening up wider possibilities. Extreme difficulties are presented by earthwork sites (if the ultimately mysterious crop-mark sites are excluded), usually in evidence as grassy blurs in the landscape, echoes of superstructures and activities mostly predating the creation or survival of useful documentary evidence. Ruins provide more answers and beg more questions: the last surviving carefully repointed stump of wall core has high symbolic value for preservation, but as a conveyer of meaning it will hardly stretch to an understanding of the whole building and all its uses (Figure 5). Shells of buildings surviving to wall-plate height allow an inquiring eye to reconstruct by noticing suspended fireplaces, staircases half-way up walls and slots for axial beams and floor joists. The visitor to a fully roofed and floored country house has an easier task, especially if the furnishings are still there, and can mentally remove the roped-off tourist corridor, repopulating rooms with those whose

Figure 5 The consolidated ruins of Bury St Edmunds Abbey: 'high symbolic value for preservation, but as a conveyor of meaning it will hardly stretch to an understanding of the whole building'

Source: Gill Chitty

portraits often hang on the walls. Matters get more complicated in that most complex of historic artefacts, the conserved historic town centre, where elements accumulated over the centuries are all self-conscious to a degree, either having to respond to pre-existing plan, form or functional areas, or choosing to respect or imitate past forms and styles. It is often difficult to differentiate amongst the survivals from many periods to interpret a reconstruction of any one of them.

Recognisability

This problem with differentiation connects with the search for recognisability, which may require the removal of information surpluses, a frequent source of controversy in preservation and conservation policy. There are tensions between stripping back to a certain stage to tell a story, classically controversial with the removal of Georgian structures at Bury St Edmunds Abbey, and telling the story largely 'conserved as found', with the archaeologically exact but rather confusing display at Denny Abbey (Baker 1983, 156–7). In the former case, is it adequate compensation to make a record of what you then remove? How should the holes made when the modern intrusion is removed be presented? Should the damage thus caused be shown accepted as part of cumulating history, or is it logically consistent to hide the holes with a small amount of calculated reconstruction? The same kind of problem was raised on a much larger scale in terms of historic townscape and archaeology at Chester during the 1980s, with the controversial proposal to demolish listed Georgian housing in Chester so that the Roman amphitheatre could be excavated and displayed in its totality.

Presentation strategies for human needs

Presenting or interpreting the historic environment, and perceiving what seems to be there, is a two-way process with some risk of ships passing each other in the night. The spectrum of presentational possibilities ranges between anecdote and analysis, and from spectacle to interactive experience; both general tastes and particular requirements deserve to be satisfied. Most people encounter heritage as specific sites or buildings; only a minority have an interest sufficiently developed to pursue particular periods and subjects. Even amongst those who are professionally involved with it, there are three different strands of attitude, often temperamental inclinations: to let the past 'speak for itself', to be explicit about the theoretical and methodological assumptions behind any work, or to relate academic or research-based perceptions with social issues. Interpretative theory suggests that – for the 'non-captive audience' (most of us who are not there for professional or educational reasons) – it is an emotional response to the physical experience of a place that is the principal means of engaging the mind and interest of the viewer (see Chapter 10, p. 151 for discussion of theoretical work on interpretation and cultural values). An engaged relationship, even better a physical relationship, with a historic place is reckoned to result in a much more valuable experience for the individual, and will in its turn promote a more responsive and engaged attitude towards conservation of the historic environment in general. Several recent studies explore and theorise about the diversity of different pasts to which people respond, and the associative and symbolic values that connect them together; in surveying the evolution of the 'heritage' phenomenon and extending into the terrain of sociology, cultural values and psychology, they go beyond the scope of this collection of studies (Fowler 1992; Hewison 1987; Lowenthal 1985, 1996; Lipe 1984). It is, however, true to say that, on the whole, the business of conservation has so far failed to achieve a successful integration of these dimensions of human response within its overall mission.

It might further encourage that essential integration if the development of projects of preservation and interpretation were informed by a check-list of broad categories. These include matters that are *feature-specific* – a site/building, topic, period; *process-related* – investigation, recording, preserving, interpreting, presenting; and *relational* – the links of individuals with their localities and roots, townscape with landscape, humanity and environment, nature and history, past to present to future, and local to regional to national to European to international. Of course, selections would be made to suit subjects and circumstances, but at least the questions would have been asked, the alternatives considered, and explicit choices made. Such a framework might also help the intelligent and accessible mixing of themes or categories, helping to accommodate both minority and majority tastes. Also, it might convey, at least subliminally, the vital holistic message that these categories are not mutually exclusive: process-related and relational matters cannot be explained without illustrations and references to matters that are feature-specific.

In explaining the core concept of conservation, we tend to talk about its value for research, planning, education, tourism and general interest, which are structured justifications in the terminology of social and environmental accountability. We also need a different list, or at least different priorities, including curiosity, entertainment, metaphor and roots; these are needs that presentation can satisfy, but perhaps need to be expressed more in terms of audience or customer outlook. A practical example is provided by Stokesay Castle (see Chapter 6), which clarifies the distinction between expert specialist interpretation and opportunities for the individual to have a personal non-expert experience of the unique qualities of a historic place. Engaging minds creatively, if only to generate the short leap of an informed emotional response, can be a long step along the road towards social and environmental responsibility.

It is the failure to work the agendas in both directions towards each other that has led to some of the excesses of the heritage industry. This has hungrily expanded to fill the gap, encouraged by needs to make the past pay for itself, to promote local and national attractions, and to use the past for resonances with present situations. The scope for confusion increases: entertainment, pastiche and virtual reality can contradict what is known about the past uses of sites and buildings, making 'real' explanation more difficult and less exciting by comparison.

Topics, themes and issues

The twelve chapters that follow can be generally categorised as six based on specific sites – Avebury, Hadrian's Wall, Wigmore Castle, Norton Priory, Stokesay Castle and Brodsworth Hall – and six dealing with general topics, either generally – community archaeology, churches and cathedrals, parks and gardens, and recent military remains – or using a group of examples – industrial archaeology at Ironbridge Gorge and twentieth-century architecture. Temporal coverage is comprehensive, loosely reflecting the incidence of surviving displayable heritage, with one study for each of the prehistoric and Roman periods, two medieval, two medieval and post-medieval, three post-medieval, two modern and one multi-period.

As far as the elements of the historic environment are concerned, the collection is inevitably strongest on *individual sites and buildings*, though in all cases with more than a nod towards historic setting and modern environment. *Portable artefacts*, together with museum displays and interpretation of material detached from its primary context, are not covered explicitly here. *Landscape and townscape*, perhaps the most difficult and complex aspects for relating together the activities of preservation and presentation, are treated in other volumes in this series of *Issues in Heritage Management*; here, elements of designed or planned examples are raised in Chapters 9 and 11, but systematic treatment at greater length is not attempted. Another topic not covered is maritime archaeology, despite its basket of distinctive problems, perhaps excusably given the challenges posed by its intrinsic inaccessibility *in situ*.

The chapters

Chris Gingell's discussion of visiting Avebury in Chapter 1 deals in paradoxes and tensions. Massive reconstruction of this prehistoric site has brought a level of intelligibility that nonetheless still relies upon an informality of access and views around the landscape. That kind of visiting experience is possible only within a limited 'carrying capacity', yet (entirely merited) designation as a World Heritage Site is likely to generate greater pressures, conflicting with the management regimes whose devising has been one of the first positive outcomes from attaining its new status. This offers a much more challenging context, using the attraction of Avebury to focus the need for wider 'management' by distributing interested visitors around other major Neolithic sites whose care and interpretation can benefit from the lessons learned in Wiltshire.

In Chapter 2, the discussion of Hadrian's Wall raises similar and distinctively different issues. As Christopher Young describes, it too is a World Heritage Site, managed by another of Britain's major heritage players; a management plan has recently been published. The Wall's extreme linearity means that it appears in different forms and conditions in different places, is set in a multiplicity of modern working environments, some of them with high levels of urban or rural unemployment, and has many things expected of it by a wide range of visitors. The challenge here is how to balance unity and diversity, matching vulnerabilities and controls, spreading the impact in a way that is still attractive to the visitor, and involving the interests of local communities.

That holistic approaches are needed at all levels is the message David Start imparts with justifiable passion in 'Community Archaeology' (Chapter 3), which deals with some of the problems that arise when the interrelated processes within historical conservation become semi-detached from each other. Getting archaeology properly preserved or recorded through the planning prescriptions of PPG16 pitchforked an academic discipline firmly into a commercial sphere, fundamentally uninterested in its basic purpose, which is research as a means of presenting the past to a wide range of social audiences. The fault lies not with PPG16, a welcome symbol of archaeology's social maturity, but with the view of it as panacea, which further hinders the creation of compensatory mechanisms for feedback in already adverse financial and political conditions. What we ought to be achieving on the ground is well shown in an uplifting vignette about the Roman town of Ancaster.

Wigmore Castle (Chapter 4) is one of three classic medieval monuments that provide food for wider thoughts. Glyn Coppack had a rare privilege for the current generation of Inspectors of Ancient Monuments, starting from scratch with a major castle site rather than inheriting a product of early and mid-twentieth-century preservation policies. A thoughtful approach did not flinch from incorporating conservation perspectives that have emerged over the last few decades, and trying to make them work together. A strategy for nature conservation forms part of a plan to retain the sense of place in a romantic, unspoiled ruin whose trajectory down the path of decay is nonetheless brought under realistic control. Destructive investigation is limited to essential works associated with preservation and creating frameworks for future management, research and presentation.

In contrast, Margaret Warhurst's exposition of Norton Priory in Chapter 5 takes a monastic site that has been both substantially excavated and fully displayed in the traditional way with capped footings and mown grassy areas. There is a triple challenge here: making the site speak for itself in a language that is intelligible to the majority of visitors; retaining its special atmosphere while keeping an evolving visitor experience well under review through surveys of responses; and giving what was historically a closed and exclusive institution a special role in the modern local community. This is an important economic factor in sustaining a site that is well off the beaten tourist track, and also an opportunity to develop artistic and creative activities which, by being so firmly associated with a real place, can be a useful antidote to the tinsel excesses of the heritage industry.

Elements from both these two very different situations figure in Gill Chitty's study of Stokesay Castle (Chapter 6), the third traditional medieval monument. These are roofed buildings, not romantic ruins or stone plans, with their own unique qualities of setting, grouping, atmosphere and patina. There are many stories to be told about the buildings and the people who lived there down the centuries, but the more explicitly this is done on site, the more those qualities might be affected. In taking a carefully calculated and sensitive but light-handed approach to interpretation, many visitors are helped on personal explorations of the place and its individuality, without being pressured to understand certain things in certain ways – surely the way many visitors take their pleasure in ruins.

In Chapter 7 – the first of several chapters dealing with whole classes of historic buildings or sites – I look at the case of churches and cathedrals. These embody a clash between two agendas for presentation, two significances, of the 'living church' religious, and of the historic building cultural. It is this theme that runs through a great range of scale, from small rural parishes benefiting from the Open Churches Trust to great cathedrals captive at the heart of historic city tourist venues. Places like

Westminster Abbey and York Minster embody some of the most direct examples of a potentially unsustainable vicious circle. The sheer weight of visitor through-put and the facilities needed to care for their needs all generate impacts, yet can also boost incomes to repair some of the damage they have caused.

Perhaps the secular equivalent of the cathedral, in terms of potential pressures and interpretative problems, is the great country house. In the first of five chapters dealing with aspects of the post-medieval historic environment, Martin Allfrey recounts the fascinating tale of how conservation strategy for Brodsworth Hall was devised and implemented (Chapter 8). In a break with traditional approaches that used to force difficult and selectively destructive choices about the period to which the house should be 'restored', it was decided to accept all past change and to tell the story of all the years from the 1860s as it appeared in the 1990s. The whole process began with a detailed, often archaeological record of the building and its contents as found, an ensemble of largely individually unexceptional features and artefacts, taking an explicit view about the significance of everything there. The intention is to engage the visitor, not only in the story of the house together with its social and cultural meanings, but also by making visible the process by which conservation professionals have created a contemporary representation of the past.

At Brodsworth, the gardens had so grown out that they could not be treated in the same way as the house. This wider topic of parks and gardens is discussed by Krystyna Campbell in 'Time to "Leap the Fence"' (Chapter 9), focusing on the importance of the unifying context for designed landscapes and their buildings, in planning, aesthetic intention, and in social and economic terms. A holistic approach must be taken to their investigation, restoration and management, and to presentation strategies. Full initial survey, in the field and the written sources, is needed to establish significance and the complexity of development so that the landscape can be treated as more than merely the setting of the building, and the value of the two as interdependent elements can be properly recognised. Too easily attention principally focuses upon the house itself, and perhaps the immediate garden or parkland setting. This ignores outlying areas of tremendous importance to the understanding of the whole, often overlaid by complex use changes and divided by modern land-holding interests.

Preservation, restoration and presentation of the industrial heritage, discussed in Chapter 10 by Marion Blockley with special reference to Ironbridge Gorge, raises a tangled web of difficult issues. Until relatively recently, industrial archaeology was conserved on a largely *ad hoc* basis, uninformed by research agenda, and without any clear view of how much conservation could be supported by local economies. There was also an emphasis on the preservation of monuments rather than the study of industrial processes and social context, reflected in the lack of statutory protection for machinery. The use of the open-air museum as a device for saving important buildings in difficult primary locations led to some confusions at Blist's Hill in Ironbridge Gorge, as the immigrants mellowed or rusted alongside what had always been there. The over-supply of potential attractions for the domestic tourist market and the difficulties of achieving adequate visitor circulation around small factories may lead to difficult choices. Limited resources might have to be directed towards comprehensive 'preservation by record' in advance of demolition, rather than preservation and presentation whose enforced selectivity makes very poor historical communication.

If the industrial heritage is a challenge, the conservation of twentieth-century buildings (Chapter 11) is doubly so. Not only is much of what is now regarded as historically important architecture intrinsically unpopular (and its architects possibly still alive), but it is also likely to be still in use, militating against keeping original detail and facilitating access for the casually curious, let alone the serious student. This is not to deny the validity of bringing such recent items within the sphere of the conservation movement, but it does require rather more explaining than is needed for more traditional categories of heritage as well as possibly a customised analytical framework. Catherine Croft and Elain Harwood trace the genesis of protection for twentieth-century buildings and the evolution and application of listing for its buildings, and give some useful case studies of examples where accommodations have been reached between continuing use and display. That these are mostly small, architecturally important private houses rather than the large repetitive structures so characteristic of modernity, such as factories, housing estates and offices, indicates the scope of the problem in being able to deliver a representative selection for presentation.

In 'Conserving recent military remains' (Chapter 12), John Schofield provides a fitting final contribution to this book and the immediately pre-millennial year in which it is published. The twentieth century is already self-consciously history, and one of its defining characteristics has been human conflict and bloodshed on an unprecedented scale, with harnessed technology magnifying the mayhem and making everyone more aware of it. Despite not having been invaded in recent centuries, Britain is not short of its military remains, and those from the last great conflict are now moving steadily into that hinterland of recollection by a shrinking minority of the population, many with painful personal memories, while an inevitably increasing majority associates them primarily with what they see on television or read in books. War is the most destructive agent of change in the historical process: those of its relics not destroyed in acts of disassociation soon after the event are easily pressed into the service of a partisan view about a conflict or all warfare itself.

Themes and issues

Various chapters engage different stages in the processes of historical conservation as sketched out in Figure 3 above. In the cases of Norton Priory, Stokesay Castle and Brodsworth Hall, relatively easily controllable and self-contained site entities, the *identification or survey phase* that underpins conservation and presentation has been completed, and the chapters describe the rationale behind what was planned and executed. Avebury and Hadrian's Wall are in the same general category, but, due to their nature, environments and visitor pressures, are less controllable and far less self-contained respectively. The need to acquire adequate information and create *records systems* as the basis for making decisions about what is to be preserved and how it is to be presented comes through strongly in discussion of the developing scheme at Wigmore Castle and the approach to ensuring that parks and gardens are recognised in their historic totality and landscape context before restoration programmes are devised.

Management arises at several scales. The starkest choices, about which examples should be preserved as the most practicable and affordable way of presenting a particular period or topic, are faced, particularly in the discussion of industrial heritage at Ironbridge and recent military remains. They confront us with a variant on a familiar phrase, by raising the prospect of 'presentation by record', a response to the impossibility of widespread preservation and the desirability of giving each community memories of its roots; ensuring adequately made records presented through appropriate media would be the vehicle for communication to present and future generations.

Threats to heritage, as obstacles to effective presentation, arise in several cases. How to slow or halt *decay*, and the associated problems of conserving 'as found', practically and ethically, appear in classic form at Wigmore Castle and Brodsworth Hall. *Visitor pressures* are prominent issues at Hadrian's Wall, Avebury, in cathedrals, and at Brodsworth, perhaps in ascending order of controllability. *Potential clashes of uses,* requiring the site or building to present or achieve something other than what it represents historically, arise in the case of Norton Priory – benignly in terms of community involvement through arts programmes – and with greater difficulty for churches – where there can be conflicts between changing architectural expressions of liturgy and worship. The chapter on twentieth-century buildings too raises the difficulties of taking an alternative or continuing use, other than display and interpretation, whether or not 'monumentalised', and the effect this can have upon presentability; custodians of such buildings face the difficulty of striking a balance between continuing viability in the housing stock and an accurate display of the innovations that they originally introduced. *Obsolescence* has already struck most other categories of survival discussed in this book. There are various approaches to handling it sensibly and achieving some kind of financial viability; these are best exemplified at Hadrian's Wall, where long-term planning is reflected in a variety of multiple management methods, with active uses on adjacent land partnerships along its length. World Heritage Sites and other places in the guardianship of English Heritage or inalienably in the care of the National Trust are generally enfolded within larger organisations specifically set up to provide the necessary overall financial support, though the stresses reported at Ironbridge sound a clear warning. The problems of dealing with recent military remains show that obsolescence bites more deeply where national ownership is not so well defined, in the public consciousness and the remit of current landlords, and where the physical survivals do not fit easily into an income-generating tourism trail.

Aspects particularly close to people and everyday life are covered in three chapters. 'Community archaeology' is directly concerned with the process of involving local people in the identification, preservation and presentation of what is historic and interesting in their surroundings. 'Twentieth-century buildings' deals with attitudes to a built environment whose aesthetic and historic value is slowly and sometimes controversially emerging as people continue to live in and use the buildings. 'Recent military remains' considers the relics of the defence of Britain in this century, primarily from the Second World War and the subsequent Cold War. These are emblems of major world events within the direct experience and sometimes faltering memories of a large proportion of the existing population; they raise tensions between rejection of the surviving symbols of the unpleasant and acceptance that they are becoming tangible survivals from a period of history that is safely past.

Continuing business

The relationship between preservation and presentation is still developing and ought always to be dynamic. A great facilitating stimulus will continue to be the opening up of new possibilities through essentially technical and methodological developments which, whilst strictly means to ends, do also widen horizons and bring into range possibilities hitherto regarded as unthinkable or at least impracticable. Examples are the groundbreaking projects of research into the conservation of materials sponsored by English Heritage and others, the potential of rapidly evolving information technology for reconstruction and creating virtual realities, and the power of relatively simple methods like the Conservation Plan for cutting through accumulated procedural tangles in managing historic sites and properties.

Stepping back from the mass of issues raised by our topics, and looking at the broad trends of the larger picture, there does seem to be a good case for encouraging what might be termed 'holistic diversity', a concept whose internal tensions provide it with a usefully self-renewing dynamic. Much has been made of the need to bridge gaps, between above- and below-ground heritage, history and nature, economics and environment, management and ideology. This does not mean that everything has to handled in the same way, but rather that the interests and processes relating to each segment of the historic resource, or each part of the conservation process, need to be aware of each other and show that awareness in the ways they go about their work. The best way of achieving this is through shared understanding of wider systems and purposes. Perhaps the most challenging area of activity, and one directly relevant to present concerns, will be working out the logic of having a sustainable local heritage, with all its implications for how people understand their day-to-day surroundings, and how their feelings about them can be translated into economic and political action.

A critical area around which debate, policy-making and training could focus is the number of tensions between preservation-led presentation – giving the people what the professionals have identified as worthwhile for them to see – and perception-led demand – what people want from the heritage – which may only partly overlap with what is on offer, and may also include other different agendas. There is a real gap here between the tangible processes of conservation and, to a lesser extent, interpretative professionals working within carefully devised technical and ethical guidelines, and the more wayward and less controllable ways in which people perceive and understand what is placed in front of them. So-called 'edutainment', hailed by tourism practitioners as the best product to fill expanding leisure time, may be the right kind of information to put a charge across the essential connections between experience and curiosity, as long as, in the spirit of holistic diversity, it remains possible to be clear about what assistance has been given to the possibly impossible task of reconstructing the past.

■ ■ ■

Acknowledgement

The debts that this introduction owes to the following chapters will be evident: they helped to develop ideas tentatively advanced at the original seminar and provided further stimulus. Of greatest value was the initial brief from Gill Chitty and discussions of the chosen themes, which avoided preserving greater densities of expression and helped to clarify their presentation. Any residual problems are entirely my own responsibility.

References

Baker, D. (1983) *Living with the Past: The Historic Environment*, Bletsoe, Bedford: Baker.

CAGE and Land Use Consultants (1997) 'What Matters and Why, Environmental Capital: A New Approach', a report to Countryside Commission, English Heritage, English Nature, Environment Agency (unpublished).

Carman, J. (1996) *Valuing Ancient Things, Archaeology and Law*, London: Leicester University Press.

Cole, L., Fairclough, G. and Coupe, M. (1998) 'What matters and why', *English Heritage Conservation Bulletin*, 33, 8–10.

DCMS (1998) 'The Comprehensive Spending Review: a new approach to investment in culture – the Built Heritage', Department of Culture, Media and Sport home page (unpublished).

DoE (1989) *Sustaining Our Common Future: A Progress Report by the United Kingdom on Implementing Sustainable Government*, London: HMSO.

DoE (1990a) *This Common Inheritance: A Summary of the White Paper on the Environment*, London: HMSO.

DoE (1990b) *Planning Policy Guidance Note 16: Archaeology and Planning*, London: HMSO.

DoE (1994) *Planning Policy Guidance Note 15: Planning and the Historic Environment*, London: HMSO.

English Heritage (1997) *Sustaining the Historic Environment: New Perspectives on the Future – a Discussion Document*, London: English Heritage.

Fairclough, G., Lambrick, G. and McNab, A. (eds) (forthcoming) *Yesterday's Landscape. Tomorrow's world: The English Heritage Historic Landscape Project*, London: English Heritage.

Fowler, P. (1992) *The Past in Contemporary Society: Then, Now*, London: Routledge.

Heritage Lottery Fund (1998) *Conservation Plans for Historic Places*, London: Heritage Lottery Fund.

Hewison, R. (1987) *The Heritage Industry: Britain in a Climate of Decline*, London: Methuen

Hunter, J. and Ralston, I. (eds) (1993) *Archaeological Resource Management in the UK*, Stroud: Alan Sutton Publishing.

Hunter, M. (ed) (1996) *Preserving the Past, the Rise of Heritage in Modern Britain*, Stroud: Alan Sutton Publishing.

Lipe, W.D. (1984) 'Value and meaning in Cultural Resources', in H. Cleere (ed.) *Approaches to the Archaeological Heritage*, Cambridge: Cambridge University Press, pp. 1–11.

Lowenthal, D. (1985) *The Past is a Foreign Country*, Cambridge: Cambridge University Press.

Lowenthal, D. (1996) *The Heritage Crusade and the Spoils of History*, London: Viking.

Morris, R. (1998) 'Riding down the road to regional chaos', *British Archaeology* 37, September 1998, p. 15.

Ross, M. (1996) *Planning and the Heritage: Policy and Procedures*, London: Spon.

UN (1992) *Earth Summit '92*, United Nations Conference on Environment and Development, Rio de Janeiro 1992, London: Regency.

WCED (1987) *Our Common Future*, World Commission on Environment and Development, Oxford: Oxford University Press.

Chapter 1

VISITING AVEBURY

Chris Gingell

> It's circular, 1,400 feet across and is the best place to celebrate the new millennium. What is it?
>
> Jonathan Glancey 'On the Greenwich Dome's greatest rival', *Guardian,* 20 July 1998

Perhaps more than any other prehistoric site in Britain, Avebury presents an extraordinary range of faces to the scholar and inquiring visitor alike. To Wiltshire residents, it is an icon of their county: the postcard image of Neolithic stone circles, quaint estate cottages and quintessential English church amidst the ancient lime trees of the Manor grounds. To more eclectic tastes, the old highway passing through the eastern henge entrance by a watering pool for the flocks of the downland landscape – now grassed over – together with the thorns, ashes and old gardens, all enlivened the views taken by William Stukeley 275 years ago. From higher ground above the henge can be seen, in a typically bowl-like setting, almost a full assemblage of the well-known forms of Late Neolithic monument clustered about the headwaters of the River Kennet (and more that are invisible in a sprawling complex beneath the valley floor), each appearing as an informal, almost natural component of the landscape.

With new sites revealed or excavated – like the palisaded Neolithic enclosures between Silbury Hill and the Sanctuary (Whittle 1997), an enclosure or possible Middle Neolithic barrow ditch within the Avebury henge (Bewley *et al.* 1996) and a Romano-British settlement near Silbury Hill (Corney 1997) – and as medieval settlements, vernacular buildings and even museum archives are re-examined, it becomes ever clearer just how much more Avebury is than merely chalk countryside punctuated with standing stones. Just as new sites are unveiled to the specialist, so for the exploring visitor there also is a strong sense of discovery. Earthworks and barrows, often disguised by clumps of trees or as boundaries to meadows ancient in themselves, and lichen-encrusted stones can all appear almost to be stumbled upon in the landscape. This informality has been the joy of Avebury for generations of visitors, as has the freedom of access.

We must not forget, however, that Avebury is also a place distinguished by the presence of some of the most didactically restored prehistoric monuments in Britain. Whether the bold restoration and display of standing stone and earthwork by Alexander Keiller at Windmill Hill from 1925 and at Avebury from 1934, or the opening by Atkinson and Piggott of a blocked and collapsed chambered long barrow in the 1950s, these are sites whose very condition sets them apart from the surrounding countryside. As such, they exert a dominating influence on the perceptions of visitors.

In these paradoxes lie many of the contradictions to be reconciled in the management of Avebury. The sheer accessibility of the sites, together with what have become almost traditions of use, much of it recreational, conspires to present its managers with a level of expectations that may far exceed what in the long run can be realised. A little background may better explain the contradictions that have developed.

Out of the chrysalis

The Avebury of John Aubrey's celebrated hunting visit of 1649, of Stukeley's meticulous but increasingly speculative record, of Philip Crocker's plans and reconstructions for Colt Hoare, and of Sir Henry Meux's excavations of 1894 was a place of private and enclosed land. Of the henge itself, arcadian views survive of cottage, orchard and chicken run. This was the Avebury recorded by H. St. George Gray (1935) from his fieldwork of 1908–22 (Figure 1.1), just as the manor and village were the scene so lightly disguised by Vita Sackville-West as Kings Avon in *Greywether*. Whilst the whole ensemble enjoyed some celebrity, and was much visited, the monuments themselves were private and the curious do not seem to have wandered far. The Cove features in many photographs, as do landmarks like Silbury Hill, and a maypole setting was used in the Southern Inner Circle (Smith 1965, 191): a fact not lost on some of today's pagan interests. Otherwise, only a footpath across a small part of the henge afforded any right of access, although worn paths near the southern henge entrance and on Silbury Hill suggest some customary use.

When Alexander Keiller embarked, using his capital and income from the family confectionery and preserves business, on projects of extensive excavation ('very marmaladish', Reginald Smith told Stuart Piggott, who was employing Keiller's area excavation techniques in Sussex) and on restoration at Windmill Hill and later at Avebury, it was apparently the enterprise, rather than any immediate ambitions for public access, that seems to have driven him (Figure 1.2). Both surviving notice

Figure 1.1 Avebury: the eastern henge entrance as seen by Gray before the First World War. Along this lane Aubrey passed, entering Avebury for the first time in 1649

Source: Alexander Keiller Museum

Figure 1.2 Avebury Manor: Alexander Keiller (right) and Stuart Piggott working at reports in about 1937. The suitably technical nesting set of garden furniture by Lister suited Keiller's precise mind

Source: Alexander Keiller Museum

boards and a contemporary cartoon view of the 1939 season (Alexander Keiller Museum archive) testify to firmness of control of visitors, and other cartoons in the same archive lampoon the perceived populism of Wheeler's concurrent campaigns at Maiden Castle. Nevertheless, this dour seriousness about the technical exercise itself concealed clear intentions about public benefit. The 35mm film made at Windmill Hill, popular guides from the Morven Institute of Archaeological Research – 'just another name for Keiller and Co' (Piggott, pers. comm.) – and of course the opening in 1938 of the site museum in the former stables of Avebury Manor, all demonstrate the aim of informing an interested public.

Keiller intended that eventually the monuments on which he had worked would pass into the care of the nation. In 1943, after protracted discussions with both the National Trust and the Office of Works, he sold the henge, avenue and Windmill Hill to the Trust, together with the Avebury Museum and most of his land. The Trust linked this with purchases of farmland and other property, 370 hectares in all, and emphasised in its contemporary papers that it was seeking to protect both monuments and their landscape settings.

As was its custom as a small, largely London-based charity with a rapidly growing portfolio of estates and countryside, the National Trust placed the principal monuments into the Guardianship of the Office of Works. In this new responsibility, the

Figure 1.3 West Kennet stone avenue: Alexander Keiller scrutinising the reassembly of a standing stone in 1934. The background download scarp was still grassland; the hedged enclosed fields were recorded by Stukeley

Source: Alexander Keiller Museum

Office of Works was extending its existing role at Avebury, since it had taken on a gift to the nation of the Sanctuary, presented by the Wiltshire Archaeological and Natural History Society following the excavation by the Society's curator, Maud Cunnington, in 1930. There, as at Woodhenge, Mrs Cunnington had instigated a singular form of partial reconstruction using cast concrete markers.

Old plans in new bottles

For exactly 50 years, the Office of Works and its successors maintained and managed the main monuments. Keiller's express wish, accepted by both the National Trust and the Office of Works, was that he should return after the Second World War to clearance, excavation and further re-erecting of stones.

In the event, health and possibly diminishing finances prevented him. The spirit of the enterprise persisted, however, in the partnership between the Ministry of Works, the National Trust, the Rural District and County Councils in clearing cottages, barns and even a chapel in the period before 1960. This and other aspects of this period deserve to be fully related elsewhere.

Characteristic of the Avebury henge for much of that period was the way in which visitors were constrained to using a definable route. Parking in the High Street at a car park formed on the site of the Strict Baptist church, visitors entered the western half of the site, where Keiller's re-erected stones beckoned, and walked a fenced corridor (Figure 1.4) around the Outer Stone Circle, often maintained with lawnmowers, whilst the centre of the henge itself was fenced off. Only in the 1980s were the tenanted farm fields within these areas opened up. Nevertheless, the relative freedom of Avebury contrasted with the increasingly close management of access necessary at Stonehenge, and as the former became less cluttered, increasingly claustrophobic conditions developed at the latter.

The only consistent record of visitor numbers to Avebury during this period comes from paying visitors to the Alexander Keiller Museum (for example 1969/70 – 50,000, 1973 – 64,000 and 1977 – 78,000). It is reasonable to extrapolate from these that by the second half of the 1960s, some 150,000 were visiting the site annually. The popularity of Avebury increased markedly with the BBC *Chronicle* television documentaries on R.J.C. Atkinson's tunnel and other excavations at Silbury Hill.

In the mid-1970s, the National Trust was increasingly conscious of the congestion within the henge, especially at weekends, and of the effect on the lives of the village community. Aware also of the need to find new uses for the Manor Farmyard buildings north of the church, it commissioned architects (Manning Clamp Partners) to look at the infrastructure and also to prepare what would now be called a conservation plan. This was circulated in 1976 (Avebury Study 1976), recommending the relocation of some facilities outside the henge and freeing properties in the High Street, for example, to re-establish a Post Office. Conceptually linked to a new car

Figure 1.4 Avebury: the north-west quadrant after the restoration of 1937, looking towards the Manor Farm buildings. Only the outer circuit was an unfenced route for visitors

Source: Alexander Keiller Museum

park to the north of the henge, this might have led to the establishment of a conventional Visitors' Centre. By this time, however, a number of authorities were becoming engaged in the management of the Avebury sites.

In 1975–6, independent of the National Trust's plans for a northern car park (eventually turned down on highway access grounds), Wiltshire County Council was negotiating the lease from the Diocese of Sarum of the Glebe Field to the south-west of the village and henge to open a new, main car park. This was prompted by the closure of the temporary car park that had served the greater visitor numbers during the BBC-sponsored excavation at Silbury Hill. The location of the new car park had a strong influence on subsequent visitor movements. Now arriving to the south of the village, visitors encountered the henge itself on the route in, before reaching any facilities.

Shortly afterwards, the Department of the Environment opened an information point and bookshop in the High Street, from which the National Trust was removing its own shop and information point. Thus one possible advantage that might have flowed from the Avebury Study was already being eroded. Further influenced by the opening of a Rural Life Museum in the Barn at the Manor farmyard and of a privately operated gift-shop and gallery in the High Street, visitor use of the site moved steadily away from concentration on the henge circuit and the site museum. A small sign in the High Street still pointed, as it had for a generation, 'to the Museum behind the Church', but in 1981 only 33,000 visitors made the journey.

One of the most distinctive yet under-recognised aspects of Avebury is the presence of nationally important collections of artefacts and excavation archives curated and displayed amongst the monuments from which they derived, rather than residing in some provincial or national museum. The changes of the 1970s, in spite of the concept behind the Avebury Study, were diminishing the impact of this relationship on the experiences of visitors to the site. Other aspects, however, were greatly adding to the attractions of the site for many visitors.

The progressive extension of areas of open space access within the henge itself has already been described. Now served by a more substantial free car park (enlarged in 1985) with attendant ice cream van, and from 1985 by a successful restaurant in the Manor farmyard, visitors to the site have greater freedom and more reasons to prolong their visit. Yet remarkably this changing environment, with the first facilities added to the place in half a century (excluding those plumbed-in during the 1950s for the visitors' comfort), was brought about without any loss to the essentially informal character of the place. This quality, which must contribute to the high level of repeat visits identified in surveys, has been treasured, consciously or unconsciously, by successive generations of visitors and students. The absence of reception points, tickets, signs and recommended routes and, above all, of interpretation may confuse but can also be seductive.

Living with success

The contrasting Avebury elements of impressive monuments that appear to represent the natural fixed points in the landscape itself and the didactic, the restored and the recreated artefacts of twentieth-century archaeology have been described. Both aspects contribute to enjoyment and appreciation, and equally to strain the fragile fabric. It is obvious that re-erecting an imposing arc of standing stones beside the turf-covered crest and slopes of a surrounding earthwork that affords most of the best views places greater strains of use upon the latter. Equally obvious is the impact of devising a route behind the forecourt facade of the West Kennet Long Barrow into a restoration of the very burial chambers that the great blocking sarsen stones were erected to seal. Management plans for the site (see below) are rightly concerned with the question of the carrying capacity of the sites, but not only the easy accessibility from convenient roads and the free use both of facilities and the sites, but the very fact that such modern public works have been undertaken, suggests that compromise may now be an inevitable recourse of management.

Previous attempts to identify the numbers of visitors using the Avebury monuments have varied widely. A new survey by the National Trust using automatic people counters and linked to a major questionnaire survey conducted for the Trust by Bournemouth University suggests that a little over 300,000 visitors visited the henge and village during the period April 1997–March 1998. (This figure had previously been proposed by Michael Pitts [1996, 121]). The impact of attempts to introduce further commercial attractions (Pitts 1990) may have had little long-term effect, despite wide publicity, but other pressures have welled up to ensure that Avebury is never long out of the headlines. The growing range of pagan and spiritual interests have been described (Gingell 1996; Pitts 1996, 123–127; and a wide-ranging debate in Bender 1998). Other stories from straying peacocks from the Manor Gardens to graffiti vandalism (Chippendale 1996, 501) are eagerly seized upon by national and even international media. Cuttings files in the National Trust's estate office make quite alarming reading for those who would wish to restrain the external promotion of the site.

The growing interest amongst producers of documentaries and of educational material is consistent with the purpose of conserving such places, and other producers of travel and tourism material can and do often co-operate in focusing on alternative locations suggested to them. When a public house agrees to location filming for a major feature film, however, we realise how limited our influence can be, and are restricted to working closely with location managers to limit the impact.

Of course it is by no means only those who are concerned with the management of places like this on whom fall the pressures of accommodating visitors. At the heart of the Avebury site is a present-day community, with dependent hamlets around. We may expect that many who themselves came first as visitors and then settled, as with similar populations from Cornwall's fishing villages to Lake District valleys and beyond, will be tolerant of those who come in their wake as visitors, yet every community has a right to a certain dignity in its day-to-day existence. Congestion at peak times is just one way in which this can be impaired.

Pitts (1996, 119–20) has entertainingly related some of the entrenched attitudes that have developed in the Avebury area, often amongst long-standing residents. Such perceptions probably have their roots in a more paternal age; re-reading of estate files from the 1940s and 1950s reveals a wealth of correspondence and discussion between National Trust agents, Ministry civil servants and local government housing and public health offices, as the fate of dwellings was determined in pursuance of a philosophy dating back to Keiller and to the Avebury Preservation Fund (1937, 492–3), whose patrons included Stanley (then Lord) Baldwin. Little of this appears to have involved wide consultation, and if, in a more democratic age, one price is the regular exposure of a National Trust manager to Parish Council meetings, it is a small one to pay.

Plans and lists

The history of planning policy and management aims applied to the Avebury sites has been in part related elsewhere (Pitts 1990); current philosophy and future initiatives may now be of more interest.

During the 1980s, the resources available to English Heritage in the maintenance of Guardianship property at Avebury diminished. Both the direct labour ground staff and Curator of the Alexander Keiller Museum became roles filled on a part-time basis by peripatetic staff. In April 1994, the National Trust took on the day-to-day management both of the Guardianship areas and the Museum under a Local Management Agreement with English Heritage.

In 1997, the National Trust released its Management Plan (National Trust 1997) after a period of consultation, as its own guide to the day-to-day responsibilities of management which observes a process from defined long-term objectives, through policies to action plans. The broad objectives of the Trust's plan, developed from the themes of a Management Statement prepared during the early 1990s in a Working Party chaired by English Heritage, address both the wide conservation purposes of the Trust itself and the specific character of the sites. Targets in the fields of nature conservation and the presentation of historic buildings balance the attention paid to the improvement of the landscape settings of monuments. Crucial to the subject of this chapter is the recognition that visitor numbers have long ago passed an optimum level at which the sites 'heal' themselves and that sensitive but active conservation measures are now inevitable.

The World Heritage Site Management Plan in preparation, funded by English Heritage (Pomeroy 1998), is necessarily more ambitious. Avebury with Stonehenge, one joint site in two parts, was included on the World Heritage list in 1987 with arbitrary boundaries that embraced an area three times the size of the present National Trust estate. Not only does the World Heritage Site Management Plan rightly set out to identify broadly agreed management improvements for this additional privately owned land, but it sets in some respects more exacting standards to be met in the management of visitors.

Drawing largely on the work of consultants engaged to report on landscape assessment and visitor and traffic management, the Plan seeks to apply two particularly demanding criteria for the successful management of the sites and environment of the World Heritage Site. The first is to apply conventional tests to the sustainability of current activity within the site. With the methodology adopted, ASH Consulting Group (1997, appendix C) concluded that current levels of visitor activity were not sustainable when measured by visitor numbers, traffic levels, wear and tear to sites, incidence of inappropriate development and conflicts with the local community. The second exercise will apply the Limits of Acceptable Change model to future management initiatives and development.

Readers familiar with the Avebury landscape, with its widely spaced and often roadside monuments, its busy roads serving both the communities within the site and the needs of commuter and other traffic linking places like Swindon, Bath and Newbury, and its intensive arable farming economy, will easily imagine the obstacles confronting attempts to bring about substantial change in both the activities of visitors and the facilities and services provided to them.

In considering the questions of carrying capacity and sustainability of the restored or partially restored monuments, as opposed to the rather different questions that arise in open countryside, it is worth bearing in mind that much of the visitor pressure is borne by areas in which the most substantial restoration was carried out precisely to prepare the site for visitors. How clearly both Alexander Keiller and Eardley Knollys of the National Trust envisaged this can be judged from correspondence in 1945 and 1946 relating to their urgent search for a car park site (with lavatories) at Avebury:

> A very large number of visitors to Avebury must be expected. The number in 1939 is estimated at over 50,000; 12,000 paid for admission to the museum. It is essential to provide a car park and the best site is now being considered.
> (Committee paper by Eardley Knollys, 1945, Avebury Estate Archive)

Careful study of the turf of the stone circles and the crest of the henge bank will reveal large areas of almost pure rye grass from earlier repairs, distinguished from the herb-rich communities on unworn areas.

If managing monuments sometimes involves accepting a regime of mitigating the inevitable effects of public access, equally visitors may have to accept the limits that must be applied before the primary duty of conserving the resource. At Avebury this may increasingly involve the temporary resting of parts of the site. (When this has been necessary recently, prominent notices inviting comment have elicited no response.) Less obvious measures may also need consideration.

A few years ago, substantial damage was caused by campfires to the blocking stones in the entrance of West Kennet Long Barrow (this in fact was the incident to which Hutton refers in Bender 1998) . Although misuse has recently diminished, it may be necessary to consider the removal of the 1950s concrete capping to the main chamber and to parts of the passage in order to reduce its suitability as a 'shrine' or bothy. At the other extreme, if present efforts to secure access to the quarry ditch and meadow around Silbury Hill are successful, practical measures to provide safe and legitimate access to the hill may need to be devised.

Turning to the Limits of Acceptable Change model, one caution can be urged. Sixty years ago, and even forty years ago, the 'insanitary' and inconvenient cottages of the Avebury street were being condemned and removed – 'all which is truly hideous shall ultimately disappear' (Avebury Preservation Fund 1937, 493) – although a later generation would see them as worthwhile examples of vernacular architecture, or at least as fit to adorn an estate agent's window. Consequently, the frontages are unnaturally gap-toothed, yet as has been clear during consultation whenever modern practical improvements to gates or paths are proposed, these very gaps afford 'cones of vision' out onto the monuments that are now almost sacrosanct to residents.

The sentiment of the Preservation Fund that 'Avebury itself will remain in its country peace' (Avebury Preservation Fund 1937, 492) is one that millions who have met or known the place would wish to echo. As a device to secure consensus for the future sensitive management of the place, World Heritage Site listing may well prove its worth. We have to ask, however, whether in the longer run it does not represent a crude expression of the 'honeypot' approach to presenting the prehistoric past, which is scarcely consistent with any principles of sustainable tourism.

It seems a truism to say that what is important is Avebury, not any designations it may receive, yet there is an undeniable clamour to highlight the status of World Heritage Site listing, as much away from the site as within it. Much of this stems from the needs of international organisations themselves, and managers of the sites have no control over the use of any resulting promotional material. Policies are undoubtedly influenced by the needs of many, perhaps a majority of sites, for income from increased tourism. Does Avebury need promotion by airline shorts? Those in doubt should re-read the quotation with which this chapter started.

In as much as any works of humankind are ever unique, there are undoubtedly sites on the World Heritage List for which it is hard to find parallels; yet many more, whether English cathedrals or small towns in Bohemia and Moravia, are but splendidly representative of the cultural context that created them.

Avebury, whether or not its arbitrary boundaries – here a map gridline, there a parish boundary – are marked with 'gateway' signing, celebrates cultures whose stunning works can be found throughout the British Isles. Is it naive to expect that in a more enlightened age the public's attention will be drawn to other great sites, then more in need of conservation, and that the accolade and buying power of international status will be applied where they are most needed to secure improved standards of management? Then surely those who love Avebury would wish the acronym army well as it marches on.

■ ■ ■

References

ASH Consulting Group (1997) *Avebury World Heritage Site. Visitor and Traffic Management Study.* Report to Avebury World Heritage Site Working Party.

Avebury Preservation Fund (1937) 'The plan for Avebury. An appeal to the nation', *Antiquity* 11, 490–3.

Avebury Study (1976) *Avebury Study*, Manning Clamp & Partners, Richmond, Surrey.

Bender, B. (1998) *Stonehenge. Making Space*, Oxford: Berg.

Bewley, R., Cole, M., David, A., Featherstone, R., Payne, A. and Small, F. (1996) 'New features within the henge at Avebury, Wiltshire: aerial and geophysical evidence', *Antiquity* 70 (269), 639–46.

Chippendale, C. (1996) 'The future of Avebury again', *Antiquity* 70 (269), 501.

Corney, M. (1997) 'New evidence for the Romano-British settlement by Silbury Hill', *Wiltshire Archaeol. Mag.* 90, 139–41.

Gingell, C.J. (1996) 'Avebury: striking a balance', *Antiquity* 70 (269), 507–11.

Gray, H.St.G. (1935) 'The Avebury excavations, 1908–1922', *Archaeologia* 84, 99–162.

National Trust (1997) *Avebury Management Plan.*

Pitts, M. (1990) 'What future for Avebury?', *Antiquity* 64, 259–74.

Pitts, M. (1996) 'The vicar's dewpond, the National Trust shop and the rise of Paganism', in D.M. Evans, P. Salway and D. Thackray (eds) *The Remains of Distant Times. Archaeology and the National Trust*, London: Society of Antiquaries, pp. 116–31.

Pomeroy, M. (1998) *Avebury World Heritage Site Management Plan*, London: English Heritage.

Smith, I.F. (1965) *Windmill Hill and Avebury. Excavations by Alexander Keiller 1925–1939*, Oxford: Clarendon Press.

Whittle, A.W.R. (1997) *Sacred Mound, Holy Rings. Silbury Hill and the West Kennet Palisaded Enclosure: A Later Neolithic Complex in North Wiltshire*, Oxford: Oxbow.

Chapter 2

HADRIAN'S WALL

Christopher Young

Young

Introduction

This chapter discusses sustainable access to the Hadrian's Wall World Heritage Site, which has sometimes been depicted as a major clash between preservation and presentation. This is one of the important aspects of the management of the Site, but it is one aspect only. The work described below is just one part of an integrated approach to the overall management of the World Heritage Site, guided by the Management Plan published in 1996 (English Heritage 1996).

Archaeological and historical background

Hadrian's Wall and its associated sites form the best preserved and most elaborate of all the frontiers of the Roman Empire (Johnson 1989). As such, it was inscribed by UNESCO as a World Heritage Site in 1987. The World Heritage Site is tightly defined around its known archaeological elements, but around it there is a broad Setting that acts as a buffer zone (Figure 2.1).

The Wall marked the north-west frontier of the Empire, save for a few intervals, for nearly three centuries. The original concept was of an elaborate linear barrier, 80 Roman miles in length, across north Britain, studded with watch towers and small fortlets, and supported by larger garrisons based either on or near the Wall. This barrier was itself just one element of an overall defensive system involving roads and communications, storage depots, outpost forts to the north and a network of forts stretching back to the south and anchored on the legionary fortresses of York and

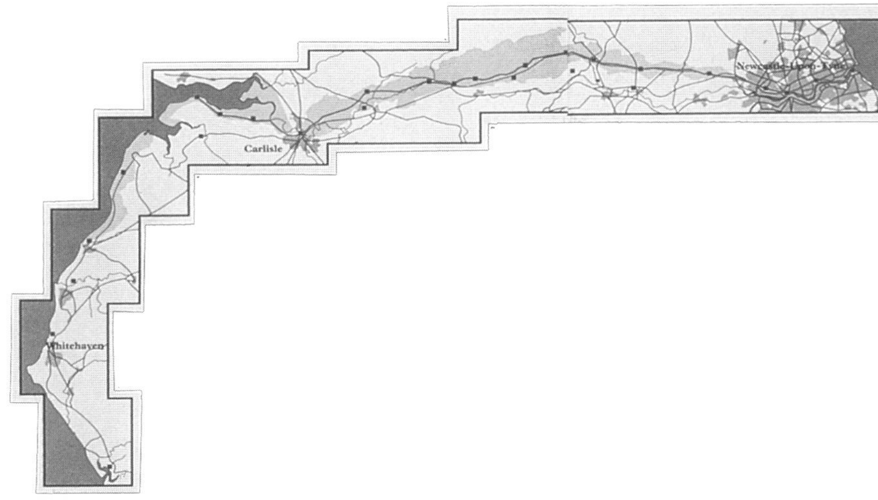

Figure 2.1 Map of the Hadrian's Wall World Heritage Site and its Setting

Source: English Heritage

Chester. Whilst the Wall itself ended at Bowness-on-Solway, its concept was continued by coastal defences down the Cumbrian coast, probably as far as Ravenglass. Alongside the defensive zone, attracted by the market of the garrisons, there developed towns of lesser civilian settlements. The whole was overlaid on an existing pattern of settlement and land-use that was part disrupted and part stimulated by the military presence.

Elements of the frontier system and its related features survive in a variety of conditions and in a very wide range of landscapes. Around 10 per cent of the Wall underlies the modern conurbations of Tyneside and urban Carlisle. Much of the rest of the eastern part of the Wall and its associated features is under arable cultivation. To the west in Cumbria, outside Carlisle itself, the land-use is predominantly pasture with some arable. In between, along the prominent basalt intrusion of Whin Sill in the centre of the isthmus formed between the mouths of the rivers Tyne and Solway, the land-use is predominantly hill farming with well-preserved earthwork and masonry remains of the frontier system.

The survival of the Wall and its associated features is correspondingly varied, reflecting the different land-uses over the sixteen centuries since its abandonment. Except where excavated, the Wall in the urban areas is buried below ground, though it often survives well as an archaeological feature. In predominantly arable areas, features sometimes survive as earthworks, though often there is no surface trace despite well-preserved buried remains. A particular characteristic in east Northumberland is that the Wall itself is buried beneath the eighteenth-century

Military Road, with its associated features visible to north and south as earthworks. In the central sector, as already noted, the World Heritage Site survives well and visibly as earthworks. In other pastoral areas, there is often a reasonable survival of earthworks both of the Wall itself and of features such as the Vallum and the Wall ditch.

Visible masonry remains of the Wall, its forts and their associated civil settlements (*vici*) can be found at various places in its eastern two-thirds. The stone used for the western third does not survive well when exposed. Some of the visible masonry has survived exposed since the Roman period, but mostly its visibility reflects archaeological intervention to expose and display the remains. Much of the visible Wall itself in the central sector is actually a nineteenth-century restoration, known as the Clayton Wall after its excavator, though towards the western end of the Whin Sill and around Birdoswald and Gilsland there are long stretches of original Roman masonry. Substantial excavated remains of forts are visible at Birdoswald, Vindolanda, Housesteads, Chesters, Wallsend and South Shields (see Johnson 1989). The last two sites demonstrate the degree of survival that can be expected even in developed urban areas.

Also significant for an appreciation of its character is the landscape setting of the World Heritage Site. This varies very much across the Site from the urban industrial setting of Wallsend and the streets of central Newcastle (Figure 2.2) through the open uplands of the Whin Sill to the mud-flats of the Solway Estuary. In places the landscape is important for an understanding of the nature of the Roman frontier, whose siting and design were conditioned by the basic form of the isthmus. Elsewhere the landscape and setting arouse strong emotional and aesthetic responses. The landscape and surrounding countryside also have other strong values that are not necessarily cultural associations with the World Heritage Site. These include landscape and natural beauty, and nature conservation as well as important economic values, particularly as farmland. There are also other associated cultural values that have been acquired over the years. Many of these are predictable; others, such as the association of the Wall remains in Sycamore Gap with the film star Kevin Costner and the film *Robin Hood, Prince of Thieves*, are not, but are still important factors influencing the behaviour of visitors. All these values need to be taken into account in managing the World Heritage Site which has to be approached holistically.

Current access to the world heritage site

Hadrian's Wall has been a focus for antiquarian visitors since the sixteenth century. From the mid-nineteenth century, visitor numbers have increased, as have their range of interests, to include not just the archaeology and history of the Roman frontier but also the landscape, nature conservation and simple recreation. Broadly, there are three types of access to the World Heritage Site.

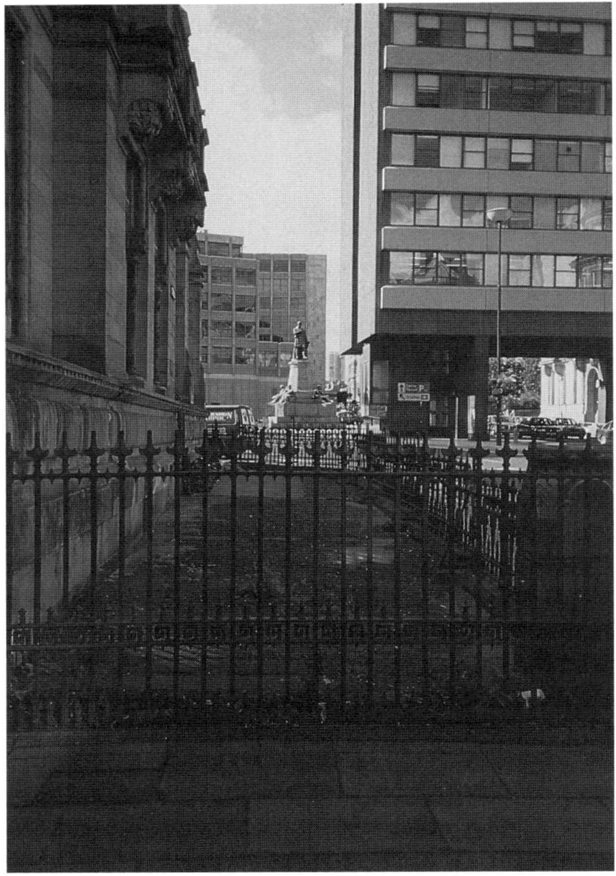

Figure 2.2 Line of Hadrian's Wall, Westgate Road, Newcastle

Source: C.J. Young

First are a number of sites that are staffed and managed for public access. Typically, these levy a charge for admission, have parking and other basic facilities, and provide some interpretation. Most provide services such as catering and shops. Sites in this group are mostly excavated or part-excavated forts, such as South Shields, Housesteads or Vindolanda, but also include the Roman town at Corbridge, and museums, for example the Roman Army Museum at Carvoran.

Second are free sites that have been excavated, conserved and made available for public access. Nearly all of these are stretches of the Wall itself, with or without the remains of turrets or milecastles, but there are also temples at Benwell and Carrawburgh and other ancillary features. Most of the sites in this group are in the care of English Heritage, though some may have local managers. They have basic interpretation on site and are maintained as ancient monuments managed for access.

The legal agreements by which they came into public care include provision for access from the nearest public highway. Some are within urban Tyneside, but the vast majority are in open countryside and the agreed access routes cross agricultural land.

The third type of access is by use of the public rights-of-way network which, in the central sector in particular, provides access along the line of the Wall for many miles as part of a well-established and well-used network of paths. The lengths of Wall that can be reached in this way include many of the free access sites mentioned in the previous paragraph but also long stretches of unexcavated Wall and related sites in private ownership. A substantial part of the central sector is in the ownership of the National Trust, whilst virtually all of it lies within the Northumberland National Park, which includes around 25 km (15 miles) of the Wall. Much of the Wall in the ownership of the National Trust is the so-called Clayton Wall, the nineteenth-century dry-stone reconstruction that is vulnerable to pressure of use. By definition, all access in this third category is across agricultural land. Mostly it is used for rough grazing but there are also areas of improved grassland used for grazing and fields that are cropped for hay or silage. This type of access will be greatly increased in the next few years by the Hadrian's Wall National Trail. This is being developed by the Countryside Commission and will provide for the first time a safe walking route alongside the whole length of Hadrian's Wall (see also Countryside Commission 1993).

Because so much of the access to the World Heritage Site is informal, there is comparatively little exact data about numbers of visitors to it. Accurate numbers are collected for the major sites managed for public access (Table 2.1) and the last All Parks Visitor Survey carried out for the national parks estimates the number of visitors in 1994 to the Hadrian's Wall corridor within the Northumberland

Table 2.1 Hadrian's Wall World Heritage Site

Visitor figures to major sites, staffed and managed for public access, 1996 (rounded to nearest 1,000)		
A.	**Within the Northumberland National Park**	
	Housesteads Roman Fort	122,000
	Vindolanda Roman Fort	72,000
	Roman Army Museum	55,000
	Total visitors to major sites within Northumberland National Park:	249,000
B.	**Outside Northumberland National Park**	
	Birdoswald Roman Fort	40,000
	Chesters Roman Fort	75,000
	Corbridge Roman Site	23,000
	South Shields Roman Fort	80,000
	Total visitors to major sites outside Northumberland National Park:	218,000
Total visitors, categories A and B :		**467,000**

Table 2.2 Hadrian's Wall World Heritage Site

Estimated visitor numbers to the World Heritage Site, 1996			
	Major sites	*Free access*	*Total*
WITHIN Northumberland National Park	249,000	751,000	1,000,000
OUTSIDE Northumberland National Park	218,000	32,000	250,000

National Park at one million. Of these, about a quarter were visiting managed sites and the remainder were walking within the open countryside. Given that there are a number of free sites outside the National Park, and the fact that there are over 200,000 visitors to managed sites outside the Park, the best estimate of the total number of visitors to the World Heritage Site is around 1.25 million (Table 2.2).

Outside the National Park visitors are concentrated primarily on sites of the first two categories apart from the 5,000 people estimated to walk the full length of the Wall each year. Inside the Park, the position is reversed with most access being informal and across farmland.

The opportunities and problems of access

The World Heritage Site faces a number of pressures from development proposals, from agriculture, and in connection with access (see Young forthcoming for a general survey). Access raises both opportunities and problems. At its most basic, access provides the opportunity for education, enjoyment and recreation of the visitor. It also brings a large number of benefits both to the World Heritage Site itself and to the region. Improved understanding and appreciation of the World Heritage Site itself, and of its significance, is in itself a major benefit to its long-term conservation, since the existence of an increasing constituency of those who value the Wall will in itself create support for it. The income earned from visitors also contributes directly to the conservation of the World Heritage Site. Whilst some site managers, such as English Heritage and the National Trust, can to a greater or lesser extent draw on other resources to support their work, others, for example the Vindolanda Trust, are wholly dependent on visitor income for their support.

More widely, visitors to the area can stimulate the local economy and, particularly if staying locally, help to create new businesses and employment. Tourist income can also be of major importance in supporting existing local businesses, such as village shops, which are of benefit to the economy as a whole but which might otherwise go out of business. As other major industries of the region decline or disappear, tourism becomes more and more significant as a generator of employment and wealth. Geoff Broom Associates estimated for the Countryside Commission that in 1994 the total visitor spend in the Hadrian's Wall area (defined as extending 16 km/10 miles on either side of the Wall) was of the order of £184 million; this was forecast to rise to £235 million by 2006 (Broom 1996, tables 2.1 and 3.3). Whilst only a small part of this is directly associated with visits to the Wall, the figures do demonstrate the contribution that tourism from outside the region, as well as day visits within it, can make to the local economy.

Tourism does, however, bring problems in its wake as well as benefits. A number of adverse effects of visitor pressure can be seen within the World Heritage Site. By and large, these do not occur at the major staffed sites. Because they are staffed, it is possible to manage visitors and also to maintain the sites so that damage does not occur. This is also true, largely, of the second group of sites which, despite being free and unstaffed, are checked and maintained on a regular basis. The major difficulties occur where there is uncontrolled access by the public rights-of-way network. This happens mainly within the Northumberland National Park where visitor numbers are at their greatest. The greatest problems currently occur in the area between Housesteads and Steel Rigg. These two places are about 5 km (3 miles) apart and this area receives by far the greatest number of visitors.

The problems can be divided into those that have a direct effect on archaeological features, those that affect the local community, and those that impact on the Setting of the World Heritage Site. The first category covers damage to the Wall itself, and erosion of areas close to the Wall that are, or are likely to be, of archaeological significance. There have been a number of collapses of the Clayton Wall that appear to be the result of excessive numbers walking along its top. In the past there has been direct damage to Roman masonry, but this has been dealt with since 1980 by a programme of work by the National Trust with support from English Heritage. Erosion on footpaths has occurred for a number of years to the west of Housesteads, and in some places has caused damage to archaeological deposits (Figure 2.3).

The local community is affected in a number of ways. The number of people working directly in tourism businesses is a small proportion of the local population, whilst the number working in non-tourism-related business is distinctly higher. The major local industry in the most visited areas of the World Heritage Site is still agriculture. Anecdotal evidence suggests that farmers suffer from damage to hay or silage crops, and disturbance of stock. The latter can occur through uncontrolled dogs, through leaving gates open or even walking through stock at crucial times of year such as tupping or lambing. It is, however, very difficult to quantify this evidence. There are also some concerns among farmers about the risk to visitors with inadequate understanding of animal behaviour, for example from cows with young calves. The other perceived impacts on the local community relate to traffic. Concerns here include congestion, the use of unsuitable roads by coaches, and parking in inappropriate places. They relate both to inconvenience and also to genuine fears over road safety.

Figure 2.3 Foothpath erosion west of Housesteads (Autumn 1995)

Source: C.J. Young

The final area of concern relates to the provision of facilities for visitors. These need to be relatively close to the things that people are visiting, which means that often they will be close to the World Heritage Site itself and almost certainly within its Setting. This means that a very high standard of design is required if an adverse impact is to be avoided.

The World Heritage Site Management Plan

Access and tourism are only two of a number of factors affecting the long-term well-being of the World Heritage Site. Others include development pressures, conservation needs and agriculture pressures. It is difficult to treat any of these in isolation, and successful management of the World Heritage Site will be achieved only by a holistic and integrated approach. This approach has also to be one of partnership, since so many different bodies and individuals are involved in the management of the Wall. English Heritage therefore took the lead in 1993 in the development of a Management Plan for the World Heritage Site, completed after extensive consultation in 1996. The Management Plan (English Heritage 1996) is essentially a consensus document, produced by a partnership of local authorities, government bodies and representatives of landowners and farmers.

It aims to achieve an appropriate balance between conservation, access, the interests of the local community, and economic benefit to the region. Essentially, because of the size of the World Heritage Site, the Plan lays down a series of strategic principles that then need to be worked up into detailed policies and work programmes by appropriate partnerships of the involved bodies. English Heritage have established a small Hadrian's Wall Co-ordination Unit to implement the Plan through such partnerships.

Tourism and access were two of the issues that stimulated the move to develop a Management Plan and are a major part of the Plan. Particular attention was focused on this issue because of the proposals for the Hadrian's Wall National Trail, then under consideration and arousing concern because of the potential impact on both archaeology and agriculture. Development of the Plan benefited from the fact that the main tourism providers (the managers of the sites staffed for public access), including English Heritage, and the main tourism promoters (the local authorities and Tourist Boards) joined together in 1994 under the leadership of the Northumbria Tourist Board to form the Hadrian's Wall Tourism Partnership. From the outset, the Partnership has been committed to the sustainable development of tourism in accordance with the Rio Declaration and United Kingdom government guidance (see Chapter 1, p. 5). The Partnership appointed a Project Manager in 1995 and works closely with the Co-ordination Unit to implement the tourism component of the Management Plan. Also closely involved with the implementation of the Plan is the Countryside Commission, who have in post a Trail Officer charged with the creation of the National Trail.

Implementation of the Management Plan policies for tourism and access

The tourism-related policies set out in the Management Plan (English Heritage 1996, 29–37) are intended to achieve a sustainable balance between the conservation of the World Heritage Site and its Setting, the interests of the local community and the needs of tourism and the visitor to the World Heritage Site. There are a number of prerequisites to achieving this. Much more needs to be known about visitors, their motivation and their behaviour. Any policies have to be sustainable, both environmentally and economically, and implementation needs to be based on partnerships. It is worth looking briefly at these in turn.

The paucity of hard information on visitor numbers and behaviour has been mentioned above. Away from the staffed sites, even our information on numbers is less than satisfactory. For effective management, there is a need to know much more precisely how many people are visiting the World Heritage Site, which parts of it they are going to, and how far they walk when they get there. A start has been made on this within the Northumberland National Park, particularly through the use of stile counters at significant points. These have already produced significant information on the extent of activity away from car parks and have confirmed the previous view that the bulk of usage by visitors is over the 5-km (3-mile) stretch between Housesteads and Steel Rigg. The counters are now to be extended so that it is possible to measure more precisely how far from the main car parks visitors actually go. It is important that this measurement is extended outside the National Park, particularly as the National Trail extends access.

There is also a need to know much more about the motivation of visitors. Understanding of this is obviously a major contribution to management of visitors' behaviour. Work on focus groups in 1995 (Arden 1995) has shown that motivation is far from simple. This demonstrated a wide range of reasons for awareness of the Wall, including its role in the film *Robin Hood: Prince of Thieves*, and the consequent and abiding popularity of Kevin Costner's tree at Sycamore Gap (Figure 2.4), and an equally wide range of reasons for visiting the World Heritage Site itself, including its archaeological significance, the nature and remoteness of the countryside, and its convenience and accessibility compared to some other areas.

Much more research, both quantitative and qualitative, is needed into visitor behaviour and motivation and also into the physical effects that they have on the World Heritage Site. It is possible in some instances to make use of the research projects of other bodies and individuals. The Countryside Commission, the Tourism Partnership and the Co-ordination Unit are planning a research contract with the University of Northumbria to work on tourism-related aspects of the Plan to build on what is known.

Figure 2.4 'Kevin Costner's' tree at Sycamore Gap

Source: Hadrian's Wall Tourism Partnership/P. Nixon

The second prerequisite of any successful implementation of the Plan is sustainability. Sustainable use of resources is government policy and is particularly important with regard to archaeological sites since they are non-renewable. It is essential therefore that any exploitation of them for access is done in such a way that no damage is caused or is likely to be caused to significant archaeological deposits. In the case of the Hadrian's Wall World Heritage Site, it is also important to ensure that its landscape setting is treated sustainably or enhanced because it is so significant to appreciation of the site. This means not that the landscape must not change but that it must change in a way that is sympathetic to its character. Also very important is the need for any tourism-related enterprise to be sustainable economically. Unless there is sufficient income either directly from visitors or from some other source to maintain and service a development, it will fail.

The third prerequisite of successful implementation is partnership. Partnerships are becoming more and more central to success in most areas of work. They are crucial in the case of the World Heritage Site because of the large number of bodies involved and because of the very varied nature of their responsibilities, with no one organisation having lead responsibility for all aspects of the Plan. By working together it is possible to achieve much more than otherwise, not only by pooling funding but also by gaining synergy. The benefit of partnerships spreads beyond individual projects, since working together develops habits of co-operation and mutual understanding that can be applied to other issues connected with the World Heritage Site and its management.

Current examples of successful partnership are the work of the Management Plan Committee, which oversees the Hadrian's Wall Co-ordination Unit and the implementation of the Plan, and the Hadrian's Wall Tourism Partnership. Other more specific groupings that are improving communications and developing specific projects are the Museums Advisory Committee, the regular meetings of the managers of the staffed sites, and the Marketing and Media Groups that are helping to develop a coherent identity for the World Heritage Site under the auspices of the Tourism Partnership. Some of these build on groupings that were already established, such as the partnership that has developed the Hadrian's Wall Bus for over twenty years (a public transport alternative for the main visited sites on the Wall); others are the direct result of the Plan.

Six of the Plan's nineteen specific five-year objectives relate directly to the sustainable management of access (English Heritage 1996, 17). They aim to:

1 Monitor the impact of tourists and visitors to the Wall, and encourage them away from areas at risk of erosion by defining and applying the concept of 'limits of acceptable change'.
2 Minimise conflict with existing land-uses and safeguard sensitive locations by management of visitor behaviour.
3 Encourage steps towards the introduction of an integrated, sustainable transport strategy to improve visitor access to the World Heritage Site and its Setting.

4 Explain the importance of the World Heritage Site designation and its implications to residents and visitors, and to decision makers.
5 Develop a co-ordinated approach to interpretation including non-archaeological aspects such as wildlife and geology at Roman and other sites throughout the World Heritage Site and its Setting, and to their marketing to achieve other objectives of the Plan.
6 Maximise the local benefits of sustainable tourism through the promotion of stronger links with local services and businesses and through appropriate marketing and tourism developments in the wider area.

The Plan also recommended the preparation of a more detailed Interpretation Strategy for the World Heritage Site. This was completed in 1997 (English Heritage/Hadrian's Wall Tourism Partnership 1997). This, in its turn, has been followed by Local Interpretation Plans which provide detailed proposals for local areas within the overall prescriptions of the Strategy. The sizes of these areas reflect a range of environments, from a village and its hinterland (e.g. Gisland) to quite large stretches, such as that within the National Park or urban Tyneside. Work has also now begun on the development of a Transportation Strategy.

These various plans and strategies provide the framework for implementation on the ground of the Management Plan policies. A number of initiatives have been developed within this framework. The Tourism Partnership have taken steps to spread visitors more widely through the World Heritage Site and to disperse them from the most heavily visited free sites. Measures include the *Hadrian's Wall Visitors Guide*, now the primary leaflet promoting the World Heritage Site, the use of press briefing trips to make journalists aware of the less popular parts of the Wall, and the promotion of photographs other than of the most visited sector. The Partnership have also begun to install Orientation Points at strategic entry points to the area. The first one was opened at Southwaite Services on the M6 in 1997. The second will shortly be opened at the Tyne ferry terminal. The purpose of these is to make visitors fully aware of all the parts of the World Heritage Site available to be visited and encourage them to move away from the most sensitive parts.

Coupled with this are a number of physical measures. These include major capital developments at Wallsend to provide a focus for visitors to the Wall at its eastern end, and the development of the Hadrian's Wall Path, a trail that will help to spread visitors along the line of the Wall. It is clear that for many walkers the major attraction is the countryside; part of the Trail project, therefore, is the development of linking and circular routes that aim to lessen the pressure on the paths that are close to the line of the Wall itself.

A major study is underway to integrate the management of the Housesteads area to improve both the visitors' experience and the conservation of the site and its setting. Coupled closely to this is the plan to redevelop the nearby National Park Information Centre at Once Brewed as an orientation centre for the central part of the Wall. These linked plans will need to look not just at the sites themselves, but also at their wider surroundings and at the management of visitors and traffic before they reach the site. There are opportunities to do this through such measures as improved public transport and the use of car park charges (recently introduced by the Northumberland National Park) to influence people's choice of transport.

There are a large number of other recommendations coming forward through the various Local Interpretation Plans that will help managers within the World Heritage Site and its Setting to achieve the balance that is the objective of the Management Plan. Those outlined above merely indicate some of the action that is being developed.

Conclusion

There are clearly parts of Hadrian's Wall where the potential for conflict between preservation and presentation is high and where such a conflict has in fact occurred to some extent already. It is clear that, on the whole, the large staffed sites can be managed to avoid such a conflict, even when they have high numbers of visitors. This is because the presence of staff enables managers to manage and maintain them proactively. The major risk of conflict occurs at points where access is unmanaged and it is not possible to ration it by price or by timing.

The development of the Management Plan has identified the problems here very clearly and it has been possible to develop ways of tackling the problems through partnership, mutual understanding, persuasion and marketing, and through investment in some places. It is clear that an approach that seeks just to restrict access will not work. It is possible to manage access to avoid damage, but it has to be done through partnership and persuasion. This chapter has outlined some of the ways in which this is being achieved on Hadrian's Wall. The results will not be quick or spectacular, but it will be possible to achieve the appropriate balance through the types of approach outlined above.

■ ■ ■

References

Arden, J. (1995) *Hadrian's Wall Area Management Plan Market Research Survey* (March 1995): Presentation of Results.

Broom, G. (1996) *Economic Impact of Hadrian's Wall Path: Study Prepared for the Countryside Commission*, Geoff Broom Associates.

Countryside Commission (1993) *The Hadrian's Wall Path: Submission to the Secretary of State for the Environment* (CCP 409), Cheltenham: Countryside Commission.

English Heritage (1996) *Hadrian's Wall World Heritage Site: Management Plan*, London: English Heritage.

Hadrian's Wall Tourism Partnership/English Heritage (1997) *Hadrian's Wall World Heritage Site Strategy*, Hexham: English Heritage.

Johnson, S. (1989) *Hadrian's Wall*, London: English Heritage.

Young, C.J. (forthcoming) 'The Hadrian's Wall World Heritage Site: the view from English Heritage', paper presented to Association of Independent Museums Annual Conference, May 1997.

Chapter 3

COMMUNITY ARCHAEOLOGY
Bringing it Back to Local Communities

David Start

Introduction

Most of the chapters in this volume are site specific, concerned primarily with the issues of conservation and presentation in set-piece visitor attractions. There is, however, another conflict between presentation and preservation which is operating at a far more mundane level. This conflict is systematically distancing ordinary people in their communities from their local archaeology, both in terms of opportunities for participation in archaeological activities and of archaeological presentation and promotion. The situation has arisen out of the major changes introduced following the publication in 1990 of *Planning Policy Guidance Note [PPG] 16: Archaeology and Planning* (DoE 1990). This chapter will highlight the changes in local archaeological organisations that have led to a conflict between the processes of archaeological management introduced by PPG16 and the presentation, promotion and interpretation of archaeology at the local level.

The changes wrought by PPG16 are steadily eroding the involvement of ordinary people in their local archaeological heritage. Their opportunity to participate in, enjoy and understand the archaeology and local history around them (what can be termed 'people's archaeology') has markedly decreased, although, it has to be said, there is much variation across the country. Post-1990 local archaeology faces a serious problem and a major challenge: we have taken archaeology away from the people, and we need to find a way to bring it back.

In Lincolnshire, a scheme known as 'community archaeology' has successfully weathered the changes of the past decade by combining the demands of current archaeological resource management processes with a recognition of the need to identify and respond to community needs. Lincolnshire's community archaeology operates at district council level and offers a fully integrated archaeological service to local councils and their communities.

A brief history of British archaeology

Early beginnings

Archaeology acquired respectability, if not widespread popularity, during the late nineteenth century. Local archaeology societies sprang up, and the well-to-do amused themselves by digging into barrows, forts and sundry field monuments. In the 1920s, Sir Leonard Woolley delighted and fascinated a great many ordinary people with his accounts of excavations at Ur, published in many popular books, notably the early Pelicans (e.g. Woolley 1937). In the 1950s, Sir Mortimer Wheeler popularised archaeology through his writing and broadcasting. His book *Archaeology from the Earth* (Wheeler 1954) inspired a generation of amateur archaeologists (and perhaps the handful of professionals then in existence) and the radio (and later television) programme *Animal, Vegetable or Mineral?* captivated a wide audience.

The 1950s were a time of fascination with archaeological discovery; in 1954, the excavation of the Walbrook Mithraeum in London drew thousands. On 27 September 1954, an article in the *Daily Mail* reported:

> All day they rolled up for a glimpse of history. Patiently they waited as the queue moved slowly on. Then came the reward – a look at the crumbling walls of London's Roman temple near the Mansion House. More than 35,000 people were there yesterday. Nearly 5,000 had to be turned away.

Perhaps, however, one could argue that archaeology was merely patronising the masses. At heart it remained an academic and aloof discipline, concerned about its scholarly integrity and fearful of being taken over by mere practitioners.

The heyday of the amateur

The late 1960s and early 1970s became the heyday of the local archaeology society. Archaeology was done by amateurs – a sort of community archaeology – although largely limited to middle-class archaeological society members. The publication of the *Collins Field Guide to Archaeology* (Wood 1963) led many (including this writer) to the recognition and appreciation of field monuments, and to many enjoyable site visits. Opportunities to participate in archaeology were readily available through seasonal and weekend excavations, the bulk of the work being carried out by enthusiasts and amateurs, with just a few professionals, usually based in museums or universities. Perhaps this was the golden age for people's archaeology.

The birth of the professional archaeologist

The explosion of property development and road building in the 1970s brought the birth of rescue archaeology and, with it, the professional archaeologist (Thomas 1974). Was this the beginning of the end for people's archaeology? Archaeological field units were set up, methodologies were developed and honed, techniques became ever more rigorous, and the local amateur, at first tolerated, was eventually scorned. The archaeological unit and the circuit digger took archaeology away from the people. They complicated it, theorised it, sterilised it, and reduced it to a series of numbers. Most importantly, they excluded ordinary people from their activities and even their publications; the excavation report of the day became a vast and prohibitively expensive tome written in impenetrable jargon.

The age of the Community Employment Programme – a return to the community?

A brief respite occurred in the 1980s with the development of the Manpower Services Commission (MSC) Community Employment Programme, a government-funded scheme intended to give work experience to the long-term unemployed. This put much-needed cash into the hands of archaeological units for non-rescue projects and gave an experience (and sometimes a lead into the profession) of archaeology to many people who might never otherwise have considered it. Some of them continue as practitioners in archaeology today (Keevil 1986; Tindall 1987). A fundamental aspect of the Community Programme was that in order to qualify, schemes had to have a community element – often this was interpreted as educational. The excavation of a large Roman site on the top of the Pennines (for the Greater Manchester Archaeological Unit) had, for two years, one member of staff permanently engaged in school/educational activities, at its peak dealing with eight to ten school or group visits per week. These Community Programme projects went further, grasping opportunities to fund interpretative projects that provided guides, information panels, leaflets, books, etc. for local heritage sites and monuments. For a few brief years, almost anything was possible.

The end of people's archaeology

The MSC employment schemes underwent a radical change in 1988 with the introduction of a new variant entitled Employment Training (Drake and Fahy 1988). This removed the community element from the schemes and, by virtue of its structure, effectively excluded most archaeological organisations from using the funding available. Archaeology and archaeologists underwent a brief and uneasy period of limbo that ended in 1990 when responsibility for archaeological investigations was passed to the property developers in a remarkable twist of Margaret Thatcher's 'polluter pays' policy. This was achieved by the introduction (and perhaps, more surprisingly, the application) of PPG16. Almost, but not quite, overnight, archaeology became a competitive, commercial enterprise. The profession split into planning (or curatorial) archaeologists who decided what had to be done (but didn't actually do it) and contracting (or commercial) archaeologists who actually carried out the fieldwork.

Where, then, in this brave new world, is the people's archaeology? The curatorial archaeologists are fully occupied with processing planning applications, writing briefs for archaeological work, assisting with Local Plans and policies and fending off irritated property developers who have no wish to contribute any part of their profit to archaeology. The very offices and officers who had previously devoted so much time to the promotion and presentation of archaeology for the public are now completely swamped by development control processes; there is no time for the people here.

The commercial archaeologists have their work cut out attracting clients in order to stay in business. Archaeological investigations must be carried out quickly and efficiently (no report, no money) and overheads must be kept to an absolute minimum in order to remain as competitive as possible and not be squeezed out of the market place. Health and safety considerations and insurance restrictions frequently preclude allowing the general public onto the archaeological sites, which anyway are usually only in progress for the shortest time possible in order to minimise costs. Even media publicity of sites and finds is curtailed. Press interest can be involved only with the agreement of the clients/property developers who, as they never wanted the archaeologists there in the first place, often do not permit it; there is definitely no spare capacity for the people here (Morris 1998).

Thus, arguably, people's archaeology is now in the worst state that it has ever been. Only the museums (and possibly some local societies and trusts) retain any form of capacity to bring ordinary people into contact with their local archaeological heritage. There could be a very interesting excavation going on just 200 m (220 yd) away from your house or place of work and the odds are you would never hear about it.

Community archaeology

So into this rather gloomy picture comes community archaeology; what it means depends upon where you are. Lincolnshire has no monopoly of the term, nor invented it. The first formalised use of the term probably came from Leicestershire, where Peter Liddle, then Archaeological Survey Officer with Leicestershire Museums Service, published a booklet entitled *Community Archaeology*, which is a handbook on field survey for local societies (Liddle 1985). His aim, in which he had some considerable success, was to encourage the formation of local archaeological societies, and steer them into field survey. The term is also used by others: Swindon have (or had) a community archaeologist, Brighton use the term in their Web page, and Hertfordshire have a community archaeology scheme.

The Leicestershire experience may have been the original model for community archaeology in Lincolnshire. In truth (and perhaps it is the usual mechanism for change in archaeology) the introduction of community archaeology in Lincolnshire was crisis led. It was one of several solutions to a funding crisis. In the late 1980s, as English Heritage funding for archaeological units declined and MSC employment schemes disappeared, the local archaeology unit (the Trust for Lincolnshire Archaeology – TLA) was facing an uncertain future. Following a review of archaeological provision in the county, Lincolnshire County Council decided to withdraw funding from the unit because it felt that the TLA was not giving the people of Lincolnshire a reasonable return for the cash. That is not to say that they were misusing funding; as unassigned core funding it was being used on the least visible parts of the organisation's work, such as backlog post-excavation work, archiving, etc. The County Council's case was that the TLA was not delivering a service to the community in return for their cash; they were not informing people of the county about their work, nor were they (overtly) promoting an appreciation of the county's heritage. This may or may not have been true, but that is how the County Council felt about it. In place of their funding to the TLA, they created a Heritage Trust of Lincolnshire. The response of the TLA to the loss of county council funding was to seek district council funding, not for core purposes, because that would have been most difficult to achieve, but for a specific set of services relating to the promotion of local history and archaeology in their districts. They called it 'community archaeology', and in 1988 three out of the seven Lincolnshire district councils were persuaded to participate. It was the vision and foresight of my predecessor, Brian Simmons, who, by virtue of his excellent relationships with elected members and chief officers, was able to set up these archaeological staff posts against all the odds. The scheme employs an identifiable archaeologist to work within each participating district on all aspects of archaeology, local history and heritage, the programme being led by the needs of specific council officers and the local community (Symonds 1989).

Initially the community archaeologists did minimal work connected with planning applications. In 1988, PPG16 was a mere gleam in the official eye. From the first, however, the community archaeologists did check planning applications, informing the relevant planning officer, who, usually, politely ignored them. Then, most of a community archaeologist's time was spent on interpretative projects for the benefit of local schools (Figure 3.1), tourism and the community, and that was, indeed, the main selling point of the scheme.

When PPG16 came into being in November 1990, these three districts suddenly found themselves with an ideal system to implement its recommendations. It took a little time, but the relevant planning policies and procedure were in place within two years, and, more importantly, the existing relationships with planning officers quickly led to a working development control system. Most importantly, however, the posts were structured in a way that did not let development control work preclude the community elements of the job. At least 50 per cent of the community archaeologist's work is still involved with people's archaeology.

Figure 3.1 Flint knapper John Lord demonstrates his art at an activity day in North Kesteven

Source: Heritage Trust of Lincolnshire

Why does it matter?

So why does this odd regional variant of the provision of archaeological services matter? What right has anyone got to preach community archaeology today, when there are actually more archaeologists doing more archaeology in England than ever before?

The problem has already been touched upon. The mainstay of local archaeology in England, the network of county, unitary and district archaeologists and their departments, have become swamped with development control work. They have, not unwillingly, made it their *raison d'être*. For many it is a lifeline to continued funding, since, whilst planning archaeology is not a statutory requirement, most planning authorities now recognise the need for specialist archaeological advice. This shift of local government archaeologists almost wholly into the curatorial role has been to the great detriment of their interpretative, promotional and presentational work – always a soft option for elimination. In addition, we have already seen that the new breed of commercial archaeologist is generally far too busy just staying alive to get involved in promotional work.

It is vital for all those concerned about this issue to lobby their local authorities to deliver a full archaeological service instead of the limited, partial service that has now evolved. By sheer accident or good luck, the community archaeology

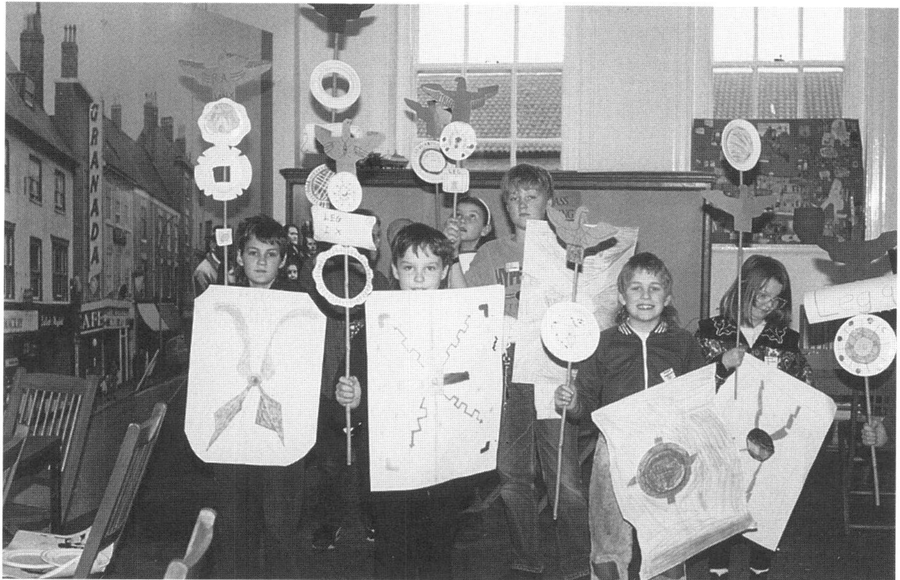

Figure 3.2 Schoolchildren display Roman shields and standards following a project day run by community archaeology in partnership with the local museum

Source: Heritage Trust of Lincolnshire

scheme developed in Lincolnshire meets those requirements. Most local authorities seem unaware of (or choose to ignore) the shortcomings that have developed in their provision of archaeological services. We should be making them aware of what we really need. We should be lobbying for a better service.

Whilst the processing of planning applications is a necessary and vital element in the nation's current strategy for cultural resource management, it is not the whole story. We have a primary and crucial responsibility to recognise and meet the needs of the community. If we do not inspire and foster enthusiasm, care and pride in the nation's heritage, we will ultimately lose public support for our activities and for the preservation and conservation of the material remains of our past (Figure 3.2).

Job description for community archaeology

What does community archaeology do? Probably everything you might expect from the title. The following is a summary of the job descriptions for community archaeologists currently working in Lincolnshire:

- Provision of archaeological development control facilities to the district council planners. Input into Local Plan and policies, Sites and Monuments

Record maintenance, hedgerow applications, Scheduled Ancient Monument issues. Production of archaeological briefs, monitoring archaeological contractors, pre-planning enquiries and liaison with applicants.

- Supporting and working with local societies to enable them to meet their needs and the needs of their local community. To stimulate the formation of new local groups and societies.
- Facilitating visits for schools and local societies to local evaluations and excavations.
- Providing a regular programme of walks and talks and the production of local trails, guides, leaflets and exhibitions.
- Working with district community or arts workers, integrating archaeology and local history into other activity programmes so that archaeology reaches out to people who would not normally be involved.
- Working with district tourism officers to develop the district's/county's heritage for tourism.
- Working with schools, colleges and community groups on educational and interpretative projects.
- Giving advice, information and encouragement to all those interested in local heritage.

A community archaeology case study – Ancaster Roman project

Ancaster is a large village straddling the Ermine Street in the South Kesteven district of Lincolnshire. As its name suggests, Ancaster has Roman connections, with a first-century fort that later developed into a small walled Roman town. In 1994, the local headteacher approached the South Kesteven community archaeologist (Jenny Stevens) with a view to developing a Roman trail with the help of school pupils. At the same time, though independently, members of the church fête committee had decided to adopt a Roman theme for 1995 and had also contacted the community archaeologist. During the course of the resultant meeting, it was decided that all the interested parties should pool their ideas, and a group was formed in early 1995, meeting monthly in the run-up to the June fête.

The community archaeologist prepared a set of temporary exhibition panels for the fête describing Ancaster's Roman heritage, and the school displayed the results of their own Roman project work. There was an enthusiastic response to the display from both villagers and visitors, which, combined with the realisation by the organisers that they were already well on the way to creating a village trail, led to the formation of the Ancaster Roman Project Group. A bank account was opened and fund-raising began. The aims were to have the trail marked out with attractive and durable information panels and to publish an accompanying trail booklet. All was to be finished and open to the public by autumn 1996 (Figure 3.3).

Applications were made to a number of local grant-making bodies, including the District Council, local businesses, banks, building societies and individuals.

Figure 3.3 Local scouts clear the creepers and undergrowth from Roman stone coffins in Ancaster churchyard in preparation for the opening of the Roman Trail

Source: Heritage Trust of Lincolnshire

Soon the first £1,000 had been collected. In September 1996, the village took part in 'Lincolnshire Heritage Open Days' weekend. Their event involved free guided walks along the proposed route of the trail and the sale of refreshments to the weary walkers afterwards. One of the group members, who worked at the local printers, produced a series of postcards from pen and ink drawings already prepared for use on the information panels. These were sold at the event, and the overall proceeds from the day raised a further £120 for the project.

Village contacts were vital to the success of the enterprise. The local printer produced the information panels and the trail booklet, *Ancaster – A Roman Town*, at reduced rates, paid for by a local coach company and garage business. Through another contact in the village, the metal work for mounting the panels, which included a two-dimensional Roman eagle, was made by students of De Montfort University, Caythorpe Campus, at minimal cost. A local agricultural trailer manufacturer then arranged the necessary welding free of charge.

The trail was officially opened on St Martin's day (the dedication of the local church) in November 1996. The trail consists of eight A3 information panels, all with their distinctive eagle emblem. The first is at the village hall and the remainder are at key points throughout the village where Roman remains are visible or have been found in the past. One of the panels, designed by some of the schoolchildren, is situated just inside the school grounds. The school hopes to become a village resource centre for local history, and has already hosted a number of schools from outside the area who have visited to walk the trail and use the resources.

The booklet (Stevens and Shotter 1996), which sells for £1.00, was launched on the same day as the trail was opened. Proceeds from sales of the booklet go to Ancaster parish council to help towards maintenance of the trail.

A few weeks after the trail was opened, the final feature was installed: a replica of the Roman *Deae Matres* (three mother goddesses) found at Ancaster in 1831 was mounted on the church wall, near its original find-spot. The figures were carved in Ancaster stone by a local artist and paid for by the Halifax Building Society.

At first sight this may all seem astoundingly trivial. The important aspect of this project, however, is not what was done, but how it was done. This was a project responding to local needs and harnessing the resources and enthusiasm of local people. Everyone felt part of the project – this was not something that the council or the heritage trust were doing, but something that *they* were doing. The project has stimulated local pride in heritage and interest in archaeology and has established Ancaster School as a local resource. The council and the heritage trust, through the community archaeology programme, have been of service to their local communities and have won their support and thanks in the process.

Local Agenda 21

There is another facet to community archaeology that has a global context. In 1992, a global environment strategy and action plan, Agenda 21, was produced as part of the Rio Earth Conference and has also been adopted as an objective by the UK government, as set out in the White Paper *This Common Inheritance*. Importantly, the Rio summit recognised that much of the action required to achieve global environmental objectives is at the local level, hence the development of Local Agenda 21 (LA21). Local authorities have been encouraged to draw up their own Agenda 21s to reshape the policies, laws and regulations of their districts. Chapter 28 of Agenda 21 states:

> as the level of government closest to the people, local authorities play a vital role in educating, mobilising and responding to the public to promote sustainable development. By 1996 most authorities in each country should have undertaken a consultative process with their populations and achieved consensus on 'Local Agenda 21' for the community'.
>
> (Agenda 21, 1993)

In Lincolnshire, the County Council and some district councils have produced 'State of the Environment Reports' or policy documents setting out their position in relation to LA21 (Lincolnshire County Council 1995).

For the participating local authorities, community archaeology gives a positive boost towards helping them meet their LA21 commitment in those aspects of environment linked to heritage. Many of the aspects of a community archaeologist's work are instrumental in developing the community-led vision, knowledge and action that are the building blocks of sustainable communities under LA21. Most important is the contact with communities and the development of knowledge and appreciation of local heritage that takes place through schools, local groups, individuals and organisations. Local groups are encouraged to undertake local appraisals and topic surveys as part of wider community action plans.

It has to be said, however, that for many local authorities Agenda 21 is a chore they believe they can do without. Enquiries to local councils concerning LA21 policies are quite likely to be met with blank incomprehension at best, or hostile suspicion ('what do you want to know for?') at worst. Heritage conservation comes at the very bottom of the list of the environmental issues involved. It is therefore up to us, all of us who care about local heritage and the involvement of the community in it, to challenge our local authorities to develop policies for the conservation of their local heritage.

■ ■ ■

References

Agenda 21 (1993) *Agenda 21: The United Nations Project of Action from Rio,* United Nations Dept of Public Information, New York, Chapter 28.1–28.2.

DoE (1990) *Planning Policy Guidance Note 16: Archaeology and Planning*, London: HMSO.

Drake, J. and Fahy, A. (1988) 'Employment training – can it replace the community programme?', *The Field Archaeologist* 9, 144–5.

Keevil, G.D. (1986) 'MSC, the circuit and beyond', *The Field Archaeologist* 5, 66.

Liddle, P. (1985) *Community Archaeology*, Leicestershire Museums Publication No. 61, Leicester: Leicestershire Museums, Art Galleries & Records Service.

Lincolnshire County Council (1995) *Lincolnshire State of the Environment Report*, Lincoln: Lincolnshire County Council.

Morris, R. (1998) 'Collapse of public interest archaeology', *British Archaeology* 31, 15.

Stevens, J. and Shotter, H. (1996) *Ancaster – A Roman Town*, West Willoughby, Lincs: Highfield Press.

Symonds, J. (1989) 'Archaeology at district level – a Lincolnshire response', *The Field Archaeologist* 10, 163.

Thomas, C. (1974) 'Archaeology in Britain 1973', in P.A. Rahtz (ed.) *Rescue Archaeology*, Harmondsworth: Penguin, pp. 3–15.

Tindall, A. (1987) 'Training and the Community Programme', *The Field Archaeologist* 7, 100–1.

Wheeler, R.E.M. (1954) *Archaeology from the Earth,* Oxford: Oxford University Press.

Wood, E.S. (1963) *Collins Field Guide to Archaeology*, London: Collins.

Woolley, L. (1937) *Digging up the Past*, London: Penguin Books.

Chapter 4

SETTING AND STRUCTURE
The Conservation of Wigmore Castle

Glyn Coppack

Wigmore Castle, one of the greatest castles of the Welsh March and the principal castle of the Mortimer dynasty, is one of the few major castles in Britain that has not been conserved since it was abandoned in the sixteenth century (Figure 4.1). Allowed to decay naturally for four centuries, it remains a substantial ruin within an area of historic woodland pasture, apparently little changed since it was recorded by the Buck brothers in the early 1730s. Natural decay has left a spectacular and romantic ruin, unchanged by human intervention, a remarkable archaeological resource with buildings buried by their own collapse to approximately first floor level. Although many parts of the site had stabilised quite naturally, others have remained unstable, and a section of the curtain wall fell as recently as 1988 (Shoesmith 1987, 3).

A Scheduled Ancient Monument, Wigmore had been identified as being at risk by English Heritage in a survey that placed it historically and archaeologically as the most significant unconserved castle of the Welsh March (Streeten 1993). The continuing threat of catastrophic collapse on a site that had long been accessible to visitors required major intervention, well beyond the resources of a private owner, and after lengthy and difficult negotiations, the present owner, John Gaunt, placed the site in the guardianship of the Secretary of State for National Heritage in November 1995. The challenge facing English Heritage was to find a method of repair that would both minimise intervention and preserve the current appearance of the site while ensuring stability and making the site safe for visitors.

Figure 4.1 Wigmore Castle from the south before the site was taken into state guardianship

Source: English Heritage

The condition of the site

There has been a castle at Wigmore since 1068, though the structures that are visible today date predominantly from the thirteenth and early fourteenth centuries, the period of the Mortimers' greatest power and the castle's greatest extent. The castle was built of a local mud-stone with dressings of a soft sandstone, originally plastered to protect it from weathering. Most of the plaster had gone and the masonry was generally eroded, though it still contained many archaeological features. Wall tops were protected by a dense mat of vegetation that contained a number of rare species of fern but also briars and small trees that were starting to destabilise the masonry (Figure 4.2), as well as dense ivy that had been cut at ground level and was now well rooted into the upper walls. The ground surface throughout the site was rough grass, though the lack of grazing in recent years had led to large areas being colonised by nettles, blackthorn and brambles. Some areas were eroding and others were covered by a scree of fallen masonry. In most areas, the earthworks of buried buildings were at least partially obscured and it was difficult to 'read' the site. In fact, Wigmore Castle was a proper ruin, undamaged by earlier intervention, and important in public perception as a romantic ruin with an unspoiled sense of place.

Figure 4.2 The north wall of the shell keep before repair

Source: Glyn Coppack

It was the lack of earlier conservation that made it possible to design a consistent scheme of repair for the site that not only took account of the surviving structure but also retained the natural mechanisms that had stabilised and preserved so much of the castle, as well as enhancing its setting. From the very start, English Heritage intended that after its repair the castle should not look greatly different from its appearance in 1995.

The philosophy of repair

Theory

Wigmore Castle was untouched, and therefore an ideal site for developing a philosophy of repair tailored to suit its needs and to reflect current developments in conservation practice. So often, repair is constrained by what has been done in the past, however well intentioned that work was. The policy of 'conserve as found', an expression that dates from the days of Sir Charles Peers and Sir Frank Baines in the first half of this century, has been taken to mean different things to each generation, to the extent that 'conservation' is often in fact no more than replication with some if not all of the original elements, and 'found' reflects the expectation of the time or the idiosyncrasies of the conservator. What it has never meant is the leaving of a monument as close to its state as originally found, which is also consistent with its long-term stabilisation and public access, yet this is what a site like Wigmore requires.

The benefit of starting with a completely undisturbed site is that it is possible to approach repair in a well-ordered if not leisurely fashion without having to worry about an earlier philosophy of repair. At Wigmore, the site itself provided the basis of the repair strategy, its state and component parts being the only factors that controlled the approach adopted. Immediately before the site was taken into guardianship, a full photographic survey was made of all of the surviving masonry, followed by a fully digitised photogrammetric and rectified photographic survey which has formed the basis of all subsequent work. A topographic survey was made of the whole of the site, including outworks not in guardianship, and a detailed ecological survey followed. It was apparent from the outset that the surviving elements of the castle were not as fragile as they looked, that they contained a vast amount of archaeological data, and that they supported an extensive and important ecosystem that was more fragile than the ruins. It was also obvious, and had been for some time, that there were serious structural problems that might require massive intervention, including extensive ground disturbance, unless a more sensitive approach could be developed. Wigmore presented an interesting challenge if its repair were not to damage significantly its 'soft' and natural appearance, the flora and fauna it supported, as well as the archaeological evidence it retained and the buried evidence it contained. The site, effectively, presented a unique opportunity to develop the least intrusive techniques of repair and presentation, based on the site itself and designed to enhance its qualities. For once, it was possible to 'conserve as found' with the minimum amount of reconstruction and intervention, to set the standard for the future repair of ruined structures, and to monitor the effectiveness of the approach adopted.

Practice

Repair was to be done by contract, which required the preparation of a full specification of works before the site could be properly examined. Most of the higher masonry was obscured by ivy which could not be removed without destabilising the ruins, and only limited access to examine the upper levels was possible. The only way in which work could be specified was to identify a series of appropriate treatments, which included perhaps more taking down and resetting than was actually going to be necessary, and applying these as it seemed appropriate to the photogrammetric survey drawings by examining what could be seen of the masonry from ground level. This approach requires a great deal of experience if it is to be at all meaningful and a close working relationship between curator, architect and civil engineer. It also requires constant attention to detail in the course of the conservation contract, and a willingness by both the contractor and curator to modify their approach as the true nature of the problem becomes apparent.

To ensure that the specification was realistic and to identify more precisely what problems would be encountered in the course of the works, a section of the east curtain wall was scaffolded, stripped of ivy, and used as a test-bed for different conservation techniques. The area chosen seemed fairly typical, with a fragile wall-head, exposed core, and a well-preserved outer face. Whatever work was done on this trial area, it would be reworked in the main contract. This allowed the opportunity to experiment with mortars and new stone, the use of additional corework to support and protect fragile areas, and the removal and replacement of the soft capping on the walls. All this work informed the main contract and was essential for understanding how the site worked.

Archaeology

The decision to preserve the castle's archaeology undisturbed was taken long before the site came into guardianship, and had been a central plank in English Heritage's protracted discussions with the owner. Some excavation was unavoidable, to inform the civil engineers about stability and levels, and to provide access for repair, but that was to be kept to an absolute minimum, consistent with good archaeological practice. It was, however, designed within an archaeological research strategy that maximised the capture of information whilst avoiding the reduction in ground levels that would expose unweathered masonry.

Unfortunately, the first trench to be dug, a section inside the south curtain of the outer bailey, revealed some 9 m (30 ft) of buried deposits, a timber kitchen of the twelfth century, and masonry of exceptional quality, leading to the suggestion that Wigmore was the ideal site to research castle development and decline. Perhaps it is, but preserving its archaeology intact for future research was the option followed, though a research design for future work has been prepared that firmly places the castle in its local and national context, and the current research was redesigned to fit within this. Only one further area will be excavated in the course of conservation, the east tower, a thirteenth-century corner tower that has become detached from the curtain wall and is slowly subsiding into the ditch. After reinforcement and repair, this tower will be backfilled and displayed at its current level. The two areas excavated, together with a detailed study of the surviving fabric, will provide a good framework for the longer-term research of the site.

The main thrust of the archaeological research will be the detailed recording and analysis of the surviving masonry, carried out immediately in advance of conservation and in the course of repair, to standards set by the Central Archaeological Service of English Heritage, using a methodology in part developed at Windsor Castle after the recent fire. Deciding on the level of recording required is always a tricky matter on a site where it is quite often difficult to decide where one stone stops and another starts, and where all the masonry is eroded. Here it was determined before the main contract began by carrying out an experimental area of recording on the east curtain wall to different levels and standards. The surviving structures are particularly rich in structural evidence, some of it fugitive and most of it difficult to identify. It will be the recording and interpretation of these data that will inform the final method and extent of repair chosen, as well as providing the interpretation of the buildings for future display and publication. The archaeologists who record the masonry 'as found' will also record it 'as repaired', so that a consistent record is made. The 'as repaired' drawings will provide the record against which the effectiveness of repair can be audited as well as making a positive record of all interventions.

The repair of masonry

Because the surviving ruins at Wigmore were the product of a continuing process of collapse, many parts of the site remain unsupported and unstable, and if not restrained will ultimately fall. Most of the serious damage resulted from two causes: Civil War slighting to make the castle indefensible, and trees growing on the walls. In the 1640s, sections of curtain wall were destroyed, either by mining or explosives, leaving stress fractures in the surviving structure that had widened with water penetration. More recently, tree roots have been the problem, though many of the trees were felled after the damage had been done. As their roots had rotted out, water was again able to penetrate the core. This was the cause of the collapse of a section of the south curtain in 1988 and of the instability of the east tower. Stone robbing has removed large areas of the inner face of the curtain wall, again exposing corework. Elsewhere there has been rather desultory robbing of quoins and dressings, leaving rubble walling exposed to weathering and slow collapse. Remarkably, the remaining structures were reasonably sound, the original mortar had survived well, and only the wall tops were friable, the result of root penetration. The ivy, though rooted into the walls, had in fact preserved more than it had destroyed.

Minimum intervention requires an acceptance that masonry will not be entirely repointed and capped to run off water. It also means that there will be a continuing need to monitor the site and carry out small-scale repairs as they are needed. The processes adopted were designed to slow further degradation, not stop it in its tracks. Central to all of the work was the requirement to minimise disturbance to historic fabric. Where support was needed for over-hanging masonry, it was provided by under-building with new stone in preference to building-in support into the existing fabric. The fallen face of the south curtain will be rebuilt to protect its surviving core and inner face, and where walls have cracked they will simply be stitched and grouted with mortar that is no harder than the original bedding mortar. It is only at the wall-head that a minimalist approach will not work. The experimental stripping of a part of the east curtain wall demonstrated that parts of the parapet and wall-walk had survived, well protected by the vegetation that had colonised the site from shortly after its abandonment. It could be preserved as it was found and made secure with the minimum of taking down, but it was too fragile to leave exposed. The natural soft capping had worked very effectively for 400 years, and its return to the wall-top would continue the process of preservation. It would mean, however, covering the wall-walk and parapet again, so important features of the site would not remain visible after repair. The alternative would have been to rebuild the whole of the wall-top, which would then be didactic but not historic. Consistency required that it be left as it was found, its grass and fern capping restored, and its form can now be seen only in the archaeological record.

Perhaps a typical area is the south tower, an early fourteenth-century residential tower on two storeys over a partially vaulted basement that houses a small bat colony (Figure 4.3). Generally, its rubble work was sound and required very little repointing. Where pointing mortar could not be scratched out with a wooden spatula, it was to be left alone, and only failed mortar and voids were to be repointed, using a lime putty mortar matched to the original. Where stone had failed, as it had in some areas, it was to be replaced with new matching stone quarried locally or recovered from the tons of rubble that littered the site, laid to matching courses. Unsupported rere-arches were to be supported with new ashlar quoins and voussoirs cut to the dimensions identified by their surviving bedding rather than packing up voids with slates or rubble. Below the grass capping on the walls, the wall-head survives for the most part, together with a part of the parapet.

Figure 4.3 The interior of the south tower in 1983

Source: Ron Shoesmith

Until this area is accessible, it is assumed that the top metre or so of the wall would require lifting and rebedding, but a decision on just how much repair might be needed can be taken only when the masonry is fully visible. Experience to date has shown that estimates of the extent of rebedding required are too generous, and can be substantially reduced to retain the maximum amount of historic fabric. The intention is to stabilise high-level masonry, and not necessarily to repair it to the extent that it is stronger than the undamaged masonry at a lower level. The wall-heads will be left very much as they are found, perpetuating the evidence they contain of roof structure, wall-walks and water spouts. As with the east curtain wall, however, these features will be largely invisible after repair.

The vaulted basement of the tower, often described as the most interesting feature of the site, was virtually intact. Access to it was restricted to the summer months as it was a recorded bat roost. It was entered down a flight of twelve steps between masonry retaining walls that were badly deformed by tree roots. Here, it was decided that the protection of the bat colony was more important than public access. On an open site, no grille would survive in the door for more than a few weeks, the steps were dangerous, and the repair of the flanking walls would have been archaeologically damaging. After the basement and the stair were recorded, the vault was supported on permanent scaffolding, the door blocked to within 15 cm (6 in) of its lintel, and the stair backfilled. This was, in fact, the first major intervention on the site dictated by public access. The only other modification to the site was to be the adding of additional core to the base of robbed ground-level window openings to raise their cills, openings that would otherwise require grilles to ensure the safety of visitors.

The soft landscape

Although it was the instability of the masonry that required urgent intervention at Wigmore, most of the site comprises buried buildings defined by their earthworks in a landscape that had been developed as rough pasture since at least the early eighteenth century but that had not been grazed or managed for a number of years. Although most of the mature trees had been felled before the site was taken into guardianship, many semi-mature trees and saplings remained within the castle, and outside the guardianship area the owner was developing an area of woodland that complemented commercially managed woodland on the ridge to the west. The setting of the castle (see Figure 4.1) is very emotive, and very fragile. Not all of the castle site is in care: a base court to the east with no standing masonry was omitted from guardianship because it required no positive intervention, though it remains a part of the overall Scheduled Ancient Monument (see general discussion in Chapter 9).

The treatment of the landscape was as difficult as the treatment of the masonry, for one complements the other in perceptions of the site as it had existed for the past four centuries. The soft landscape at Wigmore protects the buried elements of the site as well as providing substantial information on the planning of the castle. It also provides the only public access to the ruins. A balance between preservation as found and public access is essential on a site conserved at public expense and accessible to the public on a regular basis.

The castle occupied a central location in a substantial area of managed landscape, and the reintroduction of a management regime to the part in guardianship that was consistent with the areas surrounding it was the starting point for the development of the site and its setting. The existing tree-cover will be maintained, and managed effectively; some of the young saplings are being retained to strengthen the existing planting and provide for the future, which is the very same policy that the owner had adopted for his land surrounding the castle. The first requirement, on the advice of an ecologist, however, was to recover the coarse pasture land from the invading scrub, opening up the recently colonised parts of the outer and inner baileys for both sheep and public access. Blackthorn and nettles have an important part to play in controlling public access, and are far less intrusive than fencing in areas that would otherwise be unsafe. Paths around the site could be identified by differential cutting, dangerous holes filled, and the screes of loose masonry removed. An important element in the approach to public access was the decision that not all parts of the site would be easily accessible, though where access was allowed it would have to be safe. For most of the outer bailey, this was not a serious problem, though no parts of the site can be described as disability-friendly. For the inner bailey, on top of a steep motte, some steps built up on the surface in order to reduce gradients will be the only positive intervention in the landscape. As with the conservation of the structure, this goes against existing policies of maximising public access and information capture. At Wigmore, it was accepted that the setting of the castle and its ecosystem were no less important than public access; their protection was central to the display of the ruins.

The castle is, of course, only one element of a much larger whole, and must be treated as such. To the east, the village of Wigmore is a planned town with an important pre-Conquest church, whilst to the north are substantial remains of Wigmore Abbey, the Augustinian house established as the Mortimers' mausoleum. It is part of a much greater whole, the frontier with Wales and a base for the English colonisation of that country. Its conservation and display must be seen in that wider context and it must not be separated from that context by modern intervention. It is for this reason that access to the site will be by foot only from the village itself, with no intrusive car park or visitor facilities close to the castle, which must remain a central feature of a remarkable and important landscape, uncluttered and unspoiled.

Wigmore will be maintained very much as it was, a site that still has a real sense of discovery, little changed from its natural state, though stable and accessible, perhaps understated but preserved without serious damage for posterity.

■ ■ ■

References

Shoesmith, R. (1987) 'Neglect and decay: Wigmore Castle – home of the Mortimers', *Rescue News* 42, 3.

Streeten, A.D.F. (1993) 'Medieval castles in the Central Marches: an Archaeological Management Review', unpublished paper presented to the Ancient Monuments Advisory Committee, London: English Heritage.

Chapter 5

NORTON PRIORY
A Resource for the Community

Margaret Warhurst

Norton Priory is on the outskirts of Runcorn on the northern edge of Cheshire and close to the River Mersey. Historically, it was home to a community of Augustinian canons for 400 years from 1134, and subsequently home for the Brooke family who lived there for almost another 400 years, converting the priory buildings into a manor house, later replaced by a Georgian mansion around 1750. Since the Augustinian order was the most populous in England, evidence from the site has been much valued by specialists in a national context as representative of medium-sized English monasteries. The site was abandoned and partly demolished in the 1920s and Norton Priory then slipped out of public knowledge, except on a local scale. This 800 years of continuing history is the basis for how the site is interpreted today.

The site comprises 15 hectares (38 acres) of historic woodland, the core of the historic estate, which contains the excavated and standing remains of the medieval priory (a scheduled ancient monument, and a Grade I listed building), a collection of site-specific contemporary sculpture, a purpose-built site museum, and a 1 hectare (2.5 acre) Walled Garden. It has been open to the public since 1975, managed by the Norton Priory Museum Trust.

For almost thirty years, Norton Priory has had a great influence on our understanding of monastic sites and their interpretation, very much due to the work of its first director, Patrick Greene, who was responsible for the excavations, research and original displays for the Museum which opened in 1982 (Greene 1989). Considerable public money has been invested there, originally through the Runcorn Development Corporation which initiated the project, from 1984 through Cheshire County Council, and since April 1998 through Halton Borough Council.

The Trust has been fortunate in having funding partners who have shared its vision that Norton Priory should above all be developed in ways in keeping with the site, and that it should be a centre of quality, excellence and innovation, providing an outstanding level of visitor service whilst retaining fundamental museum values and priorities of caring for collections, site and visitors. The Trust has always seen its role as educational, and based on strong, innovative scholarship.

Inevitably, the inherent tensions between preserving a historic site and presenting it for visitors must be addressed and constantly revisited at Norton Priory, but this chapter concentrates on outlining the original aims of the project, looks at who forms the community referred to in the title, and examines how the Trust's vision translates into practice.

Location, setting and partners

Neither the geographical nor the physical setting can compare with the classic monastic sites like Fountains and Rievaulx. The geographical setting of Norton Priory is on flat land that slopes gently northwards to the River Mersey. The physical remains of the priory are slight, with only the foundations surviving, apart from the late twelfth-century storage range. This survived encapsulated within the eighteenth-century mansion which was demolished in 1928. The foundations of the main monastic buildings were exposed during extensive excavations, and the site is now subsumed within the Runcorn New Town area, with housing to the south and a modern business park immediately to the north.

Norton Priory does, however, have a strong and special sense of both time and place that continues to move many of the visitors; I hope that the essence of this will become apparent. The key has been to understand and work to strengthen and enhance the special quality of Norton Priory to which visitors respond, and to allow them to experience its essence through their senses and imaginations. In many ways we have followed and developed what Runcorn Development Corporation began.

After Runcorn was designated as a New Town in 1964, the master plan drawn up for its development included a large open area set aside for public recreation which became known as the Town Park. Sir Richard Brooke gave the site of Norton Priory, which adjoined the Town Park, in trust to the Development Corporation for public benefit. Work began in 1970 to rescue Norton Priory from the sycamores and rhododendrons that engulfed the site. The results from exploratory archaeological trenches led to twelve seasons of excavations. The Corporation's aims were that Norton Priory should provide both a focus for community activities and a sense of history for the new population. It is very much to the credit of the Development Corporation that they had the vision to invest in an extensive research excavation which revealed a site that has added tremendously to knowledge of the medieval period. Only a development corporation would have had both the freedom and the resources to carry out such a project at that time, because of the restrictions on local authorities, and it was made to happen in an exciting and innovative way. Indeed, Norton Priory may in the end prove to be the longest-lived and most successful expression of the Corporation's overall vision for Runcorn.

The Norton Priory Museum Trust, which was established in 1975 as a charitable trust to ensure that the project could have a future, has always depended heavily on another partner, initially the Development Corporation, later Cheshire County Council, for the bulk of the funding required to preserve the site and develop what it can offer for visitors. This is an appropriate time to reflect on what Norton Priory was in the past, what it is today, and what it might become in the future following the recent change in partnership in April 1998, when ownership of the site passed to Halton Borough Council on its becoming a unitary authority.

Original aims

One of the Development Corporation's initial aims was to 'recognise the contribution of the past; old places [are] to be cherished and affectionately woven into the fabric of the new surroundings' (Runcorn Development Corporation 1967). Other aims included social development and the provision of a pleasant living and working environment.

The scheme at Norton Priory met all of these. Many people living in established communities within Runcorn could, and do, see Norton Priory as part of their history, particularly because one or more family members had worked for the Brooke family. Those who were moved into Runcorn, however, did not identify readily with a medieval monastic site. Their roots lay elsewhere, mainly north Merseyside. For them, Norton Priory was not their heritage, although the Development Corporation strove to make it theirs as part of a strategy for establishing new communities.

There were other obstacles: first, Runcorn has one of the lowest car-owning populations in the country and yet the Development Corporation routed the bus lanes as far as 1 km (half a mile) away from Norton Priory. This created a lasting problem, since the surrounding area is not the safest to walk through at any time of day as it is well away from housing, isolated and wooded.

Second, the electoral ward in which Norton Priory lies is among the most economically disadvantaged in Cheshire, with over 80 per cent of households in receipt of some form of benefit. The general level of unemployment is 15 per cent, rising to 34 per cent of under 25 year olds. The area exhibits high levels of stress, deprivation, drug abuse, crime and significant educational under-achievement. Vandalism is a serious issue (Halton Borough Council 1997).

In the optimistic climate that then prevailed, the first director of Norton Priory wrote in 1975: 'It will act as a catalyst for a variety of cultural activities in Runcorn' (Greene 1975). Initial enthusiasm led to predictions of 100,000 visitors a year, which the site is far too fragile to withstand. The reality is that it is very hard work to get around 30,000 visitors a year, because North Cheshire is not an area for tourists and holidaymakers; instead the site is very much reliant on the day visitor market and a core of visitors from the immediate area. Norton Priory is tucked away with no possibility of passing trade and, as the annual visitor surveys consistently show, 99 per cent of visitors have previously heard of the site and made specific plans for their visit.

The Development Corporation's Community Development Department made active use of the site at Norton Priory in the 1970s and early 1980s for what now look like very lavish events at Bank Holidays. It was not unknown for £2,000 to be spent on a single event, whereas these days the year-round programme of events and exhibitions has to be run on less than that. Actually, there was not much competition twenty years ago, and an all-day beer tent was quite a lure in its own right. The audiences came for a specific event and had no interest in its location, however, with the result that there seems to have been no lasting benefit for Norton Priory.

In 1984, the Development Corporation handed over responsibility for funding to Cheshire County Council, which has provided substantial annual revenue funding for fourteen years. Unlike the Development Corporation, however, Cheshire County Council was unable to provide 100 per cent support. The grant aid covered general running costs but not events or capital development. The initiative for events passed more and more to the borough council, Halton, which made use of facilities that were more central and convenient for the specific communities at which they were aimed.

After 1984, then, sustaining public interest in Norton Priory very quickly became, and remains, a major concern. Volunteers, for example, were plentiful in the heady days of excavation, but interest waned. A small organisation like Norton Priory needs a band of dedicated volunteers if it is to realise its potential. Finding those volunteers in Runcorn, and keeping them, is a problem. There are currently thirty-eight active volunteers, of whom only sixteen live in Runcorn.

For me, museums are very much 'windows into the world' in the nineteenth-century tradition. Museums and sites like Norton Priory can provide a sense of both time and place. We are, therefore, as much interested in the present and future as we are in the past. One theme running through the past thirty years has been the identification and continuation of Norton Priory's strengths. This is evident in the permanent gallery in the Museum which tells the story of the site with extensive displays on the arts and crafts practised there, especially stone carving and tile making. In the medieval period, Norton Priory would have been a major patron of the arts, a centre of creative energy and artistic activity. We have sought to rekindle this by working with contemporary artists and crafts-people, a very different approach from that taken at many 'set piece' ancient monuments.

Community

Norton Priory can continue to change and develop, as it has done since the canons first arrived at the site. We do not want it to get stuck in 1134, nor in 1391 when it became an abbey, nor in 1536 when it was closed down, nor in 1545 when Sir Richard Brooke bought the estate, nor in 1928 when the Brookes' mansion was pulled down, nor at any particular date. The site has a continuing history – that is a real strength and a part of its special atmosphere and relevance. Both the site and the setting will remain relevant to the community it seeks to serve by evolving appropriately.

In this respect, Norton Priory is very different from archaeological sites that have been monumentalised. They are frozen in time and can become ever more isolated from their surroundings, which usually change and develop through continuing use. In one sense they exist in a vacuum and have no links with any community. Norton Priory, however, has been able to develop into a site that is visitor- and community-based.

We have embraced two different definitions of 'community' at Norton Priory: it can be 'a body of people having something in common', as well as 'a body of people living in the same locality'. The range of events we organise is specifically aimed at the local population, with whom it is essential that we have links. These include an annual Community Open Day run by the Community & Education Officer for representatives from local societies. On average about fifty people take advantage of this opportunity to visit free-of-charge. Each autumn half-term, the Community & Education Officer organises a Teachers' Day, when teachers can find out about the award-winning education programmes and discuss their requirements, while their families take part in various activities both indoors and outdoors. The 1997 day was extremely successful because of unexpectedly glorious October weather! Many of those who came along were regular users or had already booked a visit. There is a 50:50 success rate in converting teachers new to the site into users. We also offer twilight sessions for schools (the teaching staff come along as soon as the pupils have gone home for a session with the Community & Education Officer) and in-service training days both on and off site.

We work closely and regularly with a number of Halton primary schools. The Grange Junior School was the Trust's partner for the 1997 Cheshire Show's 'Education Out of School' marquee, which showcases six venues and schools each year. The school won a silver award for their display on their project about rehousing the unique 600-year-old, 3.5-metre (12-ft) high, sandstone statue of St Christopher at Norton Priory. For many years we have run Victorian Christmas parties. These can be used to deliver aspects of the National Curriculum, but above all they are great fun and a wonderful first introduction for children to museums and the past (Figure 5.1). The vaulted priory storage range, which was converted in 1868 to form the entrance to the Brookes' mansion, is decorated with greenery. Everyone is invited to come dressed up, bring traditional decorations for the trees and join

Figure 5.1 Victorian Christmas parties are held in the medieval storage range of the Priory

Source: Michael Hadfield

in Victorian games and activities. Staff and volunteers appear mainly as maids and gardeners plus the governess and the butler. Sponsorship enables us to offer these events at reduced rates for children with special needs.

For the past five years, Halton Borough Council's Arts Development Team has used Norton Priory as a venue for the annual performing arts festival held during June. The aim is to showcase local groups. The grounds of Norton Priory provide a lovely setting for performances of all kinds, although the weather can affect both performers and audiences. The performers are given tickets so that they can invite family and friends to what has proved to be a very happy and successful event for local people.

The Trust also participates in the National Archaeology Weekend/Heritage Open Days held in September. Thanks to the enthusiasm of the Merseyside Archaeological Society membership, an enormous range of activities is on offer and it is now established as a key annual event.

A number of local organisations, such as elderly persons' homes and the local branches of TocH and Scope, have a special relationship with Norton Priory. We particularly value our strong links with Astmoor Day Services, a training centre in Runcorn for adults with learning difficulties. We have benefited from the work they carry out at Norton Priory and it has been pleasing to see those involved gaining new work and social skills. A number of groups of clients currently work in the grounds. One group has helped for five years and it was because of them that we were able to take advantage of a grant under the Countryside Stewardship Scheme to restore a nineteenth-century pear orchard that had become an impenetrable jungle. This has become an asset that all our visitors, but especially those living nearby, can enjoy for informal recreation, and which attracts a range of wildlife. The group, now highly skilled, undertakes work for other organisations. Another group has more recently started to produce such items as bird boxes, signs and planters in our workshop for us and other organisations. Craft items made at Astmoor's base have proved popular with our visitors – we sell them on commission alongside the work of other local craftspeople.

These are examples of our successful attempts to attract local people, but to date we have been more successful in building a community of those who share our view that Norton Priory *is* a very special place. The Trust's band of volunteers is one example. There is also the season ticket scheme with 277 members in 1997, of whom only 72 were from Runcorn. We work with a number of secondary schools from the north-west but with only one from Halton on a regular basis.

Of our general visitors, over 40 per cent are repeat visitors and often regular repeaters. Over 70 per cent travel from within a 32-km (20-mile) radius (regarded as local) but, because of the site's location on the edge of the county and close to large metropolitan populations, it is perhaps not surprising that the general split is 40 per cent from Cheshire and 60 per cent from outside. That split holds true for schools too.

We also have to be realistic about balancing the budget. Each year we need to generate on-site income equivalent to over a third of our running costs. That inevitably means attracting sufficient visitors who are prepared to pay our very modest entrance charges and to spend money in the shop and on refreshments.

The Trust's vision in practice

Our core values of caring for the site and the collections are balanced with those of caring for our visitors. Collecting and conserving are essential activities, but it is the third 'c' activity, communicating, that brings everything to life. Without this we would become like the Sleeping Beauty's palace or a mausoleum, with which museums are all too readily identified in popular imagery! What is important, I believe, is that communication is very much a two-way process – we deliberately take a lot of time to listen to what our visitors say. One essential tool in listening is the annual visitor survey. Of course, it tests the effectiveness of our marketing and it shows what visitors think of our services, but crucially it allows us to find out what people feel about Norton Priory, what they would like to know about the site, and what additional facilities they would like us to provide. It has become an indispensable planning tool and it keeps our feet on the ground: 95 per cent of the sample claim only a general interest in history. It was visitors who reminded us that Norton Priory was not just a monastic site because they wanted to know more about the site's recent history. It was visitors who told us, who are always telling us, that they value the 'haven of tranquillity', 'the opportunity to relax in a beautiful, peaceful setting', 'a very special place', what they perceive as the non-commercial approach that the annual revenue grants have enabled us to take. Like most sites, we have an immense amount of information that we focus, direct and layer to suit *their* requirements.

We take an integrated approach to caring for all the aspects of the site we manage. Conservation of the gardens and grounds is as important as the conservation of the historic site. For example, we hold the National Collection of *cydonia oblonga* (tree quince) and this forms part of our strong 'living history' element – the historic varieties of fruit, vegetables and plants grown (and sold) at the Walled Garden. The Head Gardener takes an organic approach to encourage as wide a range of insects to the gardens as possible. In managing the historic woodland, we take into account the fact that the stands of invasive rhododendrons provide an important roost in the winter months for many species of birds, in bad weather often in considerable numbers (over ninety bird species have been recorded at Norton Priory in recent years). In this way we have encouraged a much wider understanding of what constitutes our heritage, and reached out to people who would normally consider themselves uninterested in history.

We have been fortunate in benefiting from an organisation called Business in the Arts North West; in particular, during 1992 we worked with a director from British Gas to produce a vision for Norton Priory, our long-term aims for the site. He made us take time out to think and express what we want Norton Priory to be. All staff at Norton Priory are recruited carefully to ensure that they are comfortable with these values, making Norton Priory a centre of excellence in every respect. The vision forms a planning tool, it gives the context for deciding and evaluating opportunities as they occur and for everything we do. It confirmed much of what we were already doing, but the real advantage has been that we are now confident about which new opportunities to take because they fit, and which quickly to let go by without expending resources because they are not right for Norton Priory.

Research needs to underpin everything to release the site's untapped potential for public benefit. This applies to the unexcavated site, the excavation archives, the collections, the documentation we hold, and to historical sources elsewhere. How we treat the priory remains influences how others value them, and so their conservation and presentation is important. All the interpretation is based on the research and the site's strengths. It seeks to make sense of the visible remains and the invisible history. Wherever possible, medieval images are used in the displays to provide a context. Access for all, whether physical or intellectual, is taken very seriously. We are gravelling the internal spaces to help people understand the layout of the priory, so that, when visitors look down on the excavated priory foundations from the first-floor viewing gallery, the former priory rooms stand out in a different colour from the surrounding grass. We choose to use simple terms to describe buildings rather than unfamiliar architectural vocabulary, for example, 'storage range' rather than 'undercroft'. We have developed a series of themed trail guides, which visitors may borrow on site, for topics identified through the visitor survey. People-centred events are used to bring everything alive. Some of the most successful and popular include Bank Holiday events for families, a Horticultural Show, an Apple Day festival and outdoor sculpture workshops (see Figure 5.2). These latter are a key component in the work we do with contemporary artists and craftspeople as part of the continuing history of Norton Priory. This contemporary work is very interesting in itself but it also brings a new audience, one that will travel further. It opens up new areas and ideas. We have built up a collection

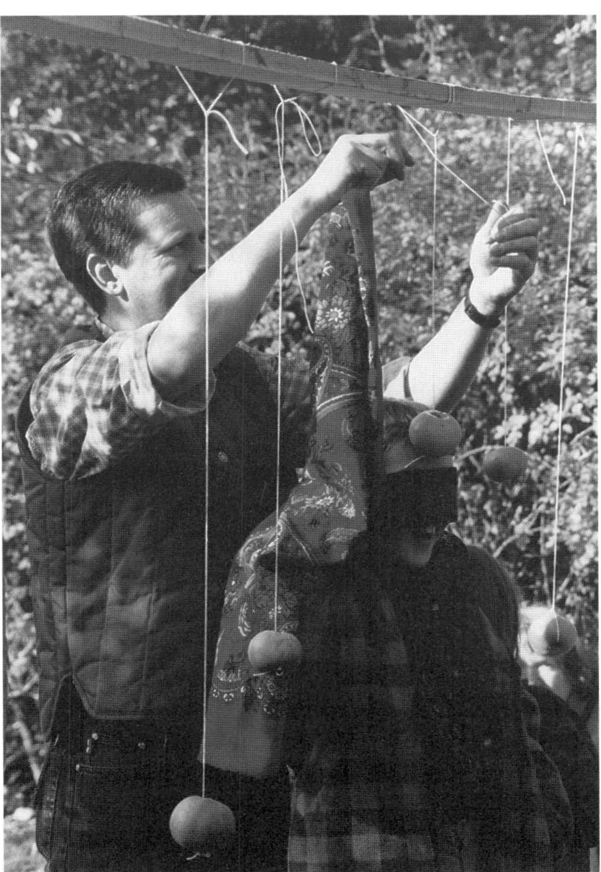

Figure 5.2 Apple Day celebrations take place at Norton Priory in October each year – fun and games and sampling produce in the Walled Garden

Source: Michael Hadfield

Figure 5.3 'The Pigs' by Phil Bews (1992) in the Walled Garden at Norton Priory: *the* favourite from the contemporary sculpture collection

Source: Cheshire Museums – Chris Johnson

of over twenty commissioned sculptures which are mainly sited in the grounds (Figure 5.3). These represent a major regional resource and one that shows how individual artists have chosen to respond to different aspects of the site. The 1997 commission developed the project further by, amongst other things, having a poet working with a sculptor.

I believe that sites should dare to be different, not for the sake of it but to bring out strengths and emphasise specificity rather than uniformity, to raise issues of conflicting information and what we can or cannot know. The key is to strengthen and enhance the strong sense of both time and place that exists at the site, allowing visitors to experience through their senses and imaginations the essence of Norton Priory. I believe that there is a role for some sites to let visitors become the active force and experience the story (a very different approach from how I see many 'living history' heritage sites, which seem to predetermine what experience their visitors are going to have). I am not advocating letting a site speak for itself: this is something I learnt the hard way. Norton Priory does speak for itself but usually in a language completely unintelligible to the majority of visitors. In order to make the site relevant and understandable to visitors, we have to be sure we are using the language used by them. Where appropriate, technology can be used to enhance the visitor experience, but we have had more success developing 'low tech' interactives that are in harmony with the site.

Norton Priory has had a real impact on what is known about monastic sites and how they are interpreted, and yet there is nothing remarkable about the site. Its strength is the continuum of history that is continuing; its special magic is being a peaceful haven within an urban landscape, allowing people time and space to experience for themselves a very specific place that has moved from a closed community through a place of privilege and is now open to all (see Chapter 6 for related discussion).

We have learnt to welcome changes that enhance the experience for our visitors and open up opportunities for tapping into the enormous resource that Norton Priory provides whilst preserving its integrity. The change in ownership in 1998 has potentially opened up many opportunities for the Trust, particularly in working in new ways with local people. For example, we believe we can contribute to Halton Borough Council's commitment to address educational under-achievement and raise basic literacy and numeracy skills in the borough. Encouraging social skills and offering opportunities for lifelong learning are other areas where we would like to develop further what we are already doing with other agencies in Halton. The borough has a panel of residents, Halton 2000, which it uses to gather local views and for market research. Since the Development Corporation's awareness research in the 1970s, we have not had the resources to do more than carry out surveys on site. We would be very interested to test current awareness of Norton Priory against the 1976 figures of 32 per cent throughout the borough and 18 per cent in the New Town area. Public transport is an issue for Halton and improvements in that area could help with access to Norton Priory (Halton Borough Council 1997).

The discussions that will lead to a new shared vision for the site – so that its history continues, its special atmosphere is retained, and it evolves appropriately whilst remaining relevant to the community it serves – need to take place. Norton Priory is dependent on public money for its existence, and those providing the funding have to continue to believe that the Trust's work is relevant, meets a need and is value for money.

As a small organisation, the Trust merely constitutes a vehicle to achieve an end: we could not carry out our work without many partners, both organisations and individuals. They ensure that the Trust can continue its stewardship of the site and that business skills are used to support this and not to seek commercial success. Nothing we do is particularly unusual or grand, but for such a small organisation we do undertake a great deal. Thanks to a team of dedicated staff, we remain ambitious and determined that colleagues and specialists will continue to need to see how Norton Priory does it!

Finally, a very exciting major opportunity arose in 1996 in relation to one of the great treasures of medieval Christendom – a 3.5-m (12-ft) high statue of St Christopher that belongs historically at Norton Priory. It is a fantastic piece of sculpture, of the highest quality and a sign of Norton Priory's wealth in the medieval period. It is unique in this country and has until recently been completely overlooked by scholars. It is, moreover, a very powerful object for local people. They believe it should be at Norton Priory. It belongs to the National Museums & Galleries on Merseyside (NM&GM) because it was given to Liverpool Museum in the 1960s by the Brooke family for safekeeping. It was lent to Norton Priory in 1981 but has been removed for a programme of research and conservation (Figure 5.4). The Trust is committed to providing a suitable building so that it can soon return, and staff from NM&GM have been very supportive. We are also delighted

Figure 5.4 The colossal medieval sculpture of St Christopher – here being removed for conservation in 1996 – will soon be returned to its home at Norton Priory

Source: Cheshire Museums – Chris Johnson

by the positive response from local people. They have given money, written letters, come in to see the display about the project, and spoken of their support to staff. The local press have given extensive coverage. St Christopher has become a symbol of the importance the local community places on Norton Priory and a wonderful opportunity to fulfil our mission 'to delight, educate and intrigue'.

■ ■ ■

References

Greene, J.P. (1975) 'Norton Priory: history for a New Town', *Museums Journal* 75 (2).

Greene, J.P. (1989) *Norton Priory: The Archaeology of a Medieval Religious House*, Cambridge: Cambridge University Press.

Halton Borough Council (1997) *Realising the Benefits: Towards a Regeneration Strategy for Halton*, Halton Borough Council.

Runcorn Development Corporation (1967) *Runcorn New Town*, Nottingham: Hawthorne.

Chapter 6

THE TRADITION OF HISTORICAL CONSCIOUSNESS
The Case of Stokesay Castle

Gill Chitty

> I have rarely had, for a couple of hours, the sensation of dropping back personally into the past so straight as while I lay on the grass beside the well in the little sunny court of this small castle and lazily appreciated the still definite details of mediæval life.
>
> (James 1905, 219)

Stokesay Castle in Shropshire has been described with some justification as the most perfectly preserved example of a thirteenth-century manor house in England. It lies at the heart of the Marches of the Welsh border, and in the Middle Ages it enjoyed a site of strength and security, lying on the west side of the River Onny as it breaks through the wooded escarpment of Wenlock Edge, above the road between the two strongholds of Shrewsbury to the north, and Ludlow to the south (Figure 6.1).

Castles in this turbulent part of the Welsh Marches were plentiful: 'Shropshire is replenished with castles standing thick on every side', wrote the Elizabethan antiquary, William Camden, 'by reason it was a frontier country' (Camden 1610, unpag.). Between the castles of Shrewsbury and Ludlow were at least half a dozen smaller ones, lying in an arc to the west and all within 16 km (10 miles) of Stokesay: Richards Castle, Wigmore, Brampton Bryan, Hopton, Clun, Bicton, Bishops Castle and so on northwards. Many of these were seriously defensible strongholds, built to the pattern of Marcher lordship and sited to signal their status as well as to enhance their defensive character. The buildings of Stokesay, by contrast, seated in the valley bottom, rise sedately into view from the roadside and have a different character. In fact to call Stokesay a castle

Figure 6.1 Stokesay Castle, looking south down the valley of the Onny towards Ludlow, to the east, across the river, are the wooded slopes of Wenlock Edge

Source: Gill Chitty

was something of a misnomer. 'This was rather a castellated mansion than a castle of strength', as the antiquarian, Francis Grose described it in 1787, and indeed it was not until the Tudor period that Stokesay became known as 'castle'. The deliberate archaism of this naming marks Stokesay as the site of a self-conscious historicism which, as this chapter will show, is an enduring theme in its story. One of the most characteristic attributes of Stokesay's life, as a residence and as an ancient monument, is the tradition of conservatism that has preserved it and which invokes for the modern visitor a particular historical consciousness. This chapter takes the case of Stokesay and its place in conservation history and reflects on some of the conflicts implicit in the contemporary gaze on heritage places (Urry 1990, 104–35).

The quotation at the beginning of this chapter is from an essay published in 1877, written by the American novelist Henry James on a visit to Shropshire. He fell in love with the landscape of the Welsh Marches and what he called 'that density of feature' which is the great characteristic of English scenery. 'There are no waste details; everything in the landscape is something particular – has a history, has played a part, has a value to the imagination', wrote James. 'Such a landscape seems charged and interfused', he continued, 'it has, has always had, human relations and is intimately conscious of them'(James 1905, 212). His recollections of Stokesay convey vividly the experience of his visit there:

> The place is a capital example of a small *gentilhommière* of the thirteenth century. It has a good deep moat, now filled with wild verdure, and a curious gatehouse of a much later period – the period when the defensive attitude had been well-nigh abandoned. . . . This is part of the charm of the place; human life there must have lost an earlier grimness; it was lived in by people who were beginning to believe in good intentions. They must have lived very much together; that is one of the most obvious reflections in the court of a mediæval dwelling. The court was not always grassy and empty, as it is now, . . . there were beasts tethered in it, and hustling men at arms, and the earth was trampled into puddles.
>
> (James 1905, 223)

The conjuring of this 'historic vision', as James called it, around the buildings of Stokesay is characteristic of the response that the place continues to evoke today in visitors to this small group of medieval buildings. It is a place that holds an enduring expression of antiquity and human history, invites imaginative contemplation, and even reckless romantic speculation. These are very particular qualities and Stokesay is a unique place. To say this, however, is not to suggest that it is exceptional, for every historic place is distinctively different and has its own special significance. Most can afford particular opportunities for personal imaginative investigation and enjoyment, even if apparently few give tongue as readily as Stokesay. Nevertheless, the notion of letting the monuments 'speak for themselves' has been discredited, or at least become unfashionable, in recent decades. This *laissez faire* approach to the presentation of ancient monuments – which was typical of the way in which many ruined sites in state guardianship were presented in the earlier part of this century – only ever worked well for a small, well-educated minority of people who understood what they were seeing, or for those who were content simply 'to take pleasure in ruins' (Macaulay 1953, Thompson 1981). The notion that a monument could ever simply be preserved or presented 'as found' was ill-conceived, and plainly untrue in many cases (see Chapter 4).

Much of what has developed, then, in contemporary heritage management orthodoxy about interpretation and presentation of historic places has been to redress this balance: to verbalise the unspoken and to visualise the unseen, to recreate what has gone, or is concealed, in the passage of time, and to make modern intervention explicit. Inevitably the tendency of such presentations is to provide information, and to aid specific understanding rather than provoke imaginative discovery. Arguably, we do need information to understand what we are seeing and experiencing; but the process of presenting that information can be over-whelming.

It can have the effect of distancing, distorting and over-simplifying the historical truth of the very thing that it is intended to enhance. In other words, rather than an enriching experience, it can become an imaginative straitjacket. To take pleasure in what we are seeing, and to make a personal discovery of a historical consciousness for oneself, of the kind that James conveys so vividly, we need to be free to explore imaginatively too. There are problematic consequences of contemporary interventions – in presentation and preservation – for the quality of personal experience of historic places.

Stokesay Castle lends itself as a case study for this chapter because it is one of that minority of historic places that has been claimed to 'speak for themselves', and legitimately so, since it is easy, in many respects, to understand its history. Its surviving buildings comprise a comparatively complete ensemble, the layout of inter-communicating buildings and stairways invite exploration, and the whole group is on a human scale. The visitor is encouraged to experience a sense of what it would have been like to live there in medieval times. Paradoxically, this apparent accessibility conceals many subtleties and complexities, as the outline of Stokesay's history that follows below, will illustrate. Through the multiple strands of its life as a medieval residence, a gentry house, a country retreat, a farm, an ancient monument, and most recently as a visitor attraction, there is woven the tradition of a consciousness of history and of preservation at Stokesay which forms a significant part of its distinctive character.

'The still definite details of medieval life'

One enters Stokesay Castle today, as one would have done in the thirteenth century, crossing over the moat and passing through a gatehouse. The present one is an early seventeenth-century, timber-framed building, constructed on the site of an earlier entrance whose form is unknown: it may have been another timber-framed structure or perhaps a more impressive masonry tower. Once through the gatehouse, the visitor crosses a grassy court with a cottage garden which adds to the homely atmosphere of the enclosure. Both the vernacular character of the gatehouse and court, and the absence of an enclosing curtain wall, lend the site a much more domestic feel than it would have had in medieval times. The principal building range is late thirteenth-century and lies opposite the entrance: a magnificent, airy open hall of four bays (its windows remain unglazed) with a first floor solar to the south, reached by an external stair. To the north and south, the hall range is connected to towers which provided private apartments for the family and commodious lodgings for visitors. The kitchen and service range, and other ancillary buildings for storage and stabling, would once have filled the courtyard but have long since been demolished (see Cordingley 1963 for a full description and analysis).

The early history of South Stoke manor appears to have been uneventful until, in the early 1280s, the tenancy of the manor was sold to a highly successful, local wool merchant, Lawrence of Ludlow, who was one of the wealthiest entrepreneurs of his day. The principal medieval buildings at Stokesay are generally agreed to be the product of a single period of remodelling and new building, attributable to the new tenant's wealth and ambition. Whilst we do not know what appearance Lawrence's manor presented to the busy Shrewsbury road – because his gatehouse has gone – the face that the west front of the castle presented to the Welsh side is less changed. Beyond the narrow moat at the foot of the tower was an impressive artificial mere, created by damming a small tributary of the Onny river (Figure 6.2). The building ensemble, whose impressive height was mirrored in the still waters of seemingly extensive water defences, presented the appearance of a polygonal twin-towered gatehouse in the manner of Welsh Edwardian castles, or another royal castle, Leeds in Kent, with which Lawrence may have been familiar (Taylor 1998, 5). The mere was linked to a series of ponds and other designed landscape features, possibly an orchard or formal gardens along the west side of the castle. These were deliberately sited to be viewed from the apartments of the south tower, and possibly from an elevated viewpoint on the hills to the west over which Lawrence had hunting rights.[1] It seems, then, that what Lawrence aspired to was not just a well-appointed country manor, but a tradition of Marcher lordship which lent status to his *arriviste* wealth and social position. Arguably this was consciously expressed in the way that the buildings of Stokesay manor were remodelled, and there is much about the design of the building that is perversely old-fashioned

Figure 6.2 Stokesay Castle, photographed *c.*1875, before the lake was partly drained

Source: Gill Chitty

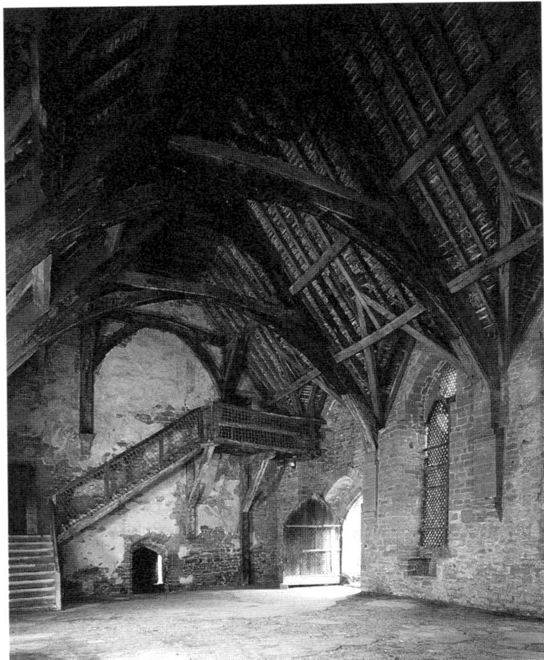

Figure 6.3 The great hall, Stokesay Castle, after conservation

Source: English Heritage Photographic Library

as well as much that is innovative. Stokesay's private apartments, with their fireplaces, separate stairs and garderobes, and the sophisticated landscape that was designed to be viewed from them, suggest the tastes one might expect to find displayed in the house of a wealthy merchant, well travelled in the capital and on the continent. The traditionally placed great hall, however, with its old-fashioned arrangements (Figure 6.3) – the heart of legal administration and hospitality for the manor – must have had a symbolic value for Lawrence, too, as one who aspired to the status of lordship within the established hierarchy of medieval society.

In a sense, then, the theme of conscious conservatism – which runs through Stokesay's history and has ensured its survival – has its origins as far back as the thirteenth century. With remarkable consistency, later owners of the manor made few changes to its buildings and seem to have been content to live with its archaic facilities and old-fashioned arrangements. A new gatehouse, kitchen and other timber-framed buildings were added in the seventeenth century, but even after the Civil War, when Stokesay was briefly sieged and slighted, the damage was repaired with faithful attention to historical detail, adopting an old-fashioned Jacobean style harking back to the beginning of the century in the fitting out and rehabilitation of the castle (Cordingley 1963, 104).

'Advancing to ruin'

Around the beginning of the eighteenth century, Stokesay Castle finally ceased to be occupied as a house and entered a period of relative neglect. The changes over the next century and a half were in many ways far more intrusive than all the years in which the building had been lived in and adapted as a home. Used as a barn, a cooper's workshop and a smithy, part of the building was gutted by a serious fire. The neglect of the roof in the great hall had the most serious results, however, and decay in the feet of the four great cruck trusses that supported the massive open-timbered roof brought the building to a state of near-collapse (Cordingley 1963, 102–6)

The first measures to stabilise the building took place as early as the 1830s, on behalf of the estate's owner, Lord Craven. From this time on the building was a subject of conscious conservation, and a very early example in the history of such acts of altruistic preservation (Cordingley 1963, 103). In 1869, Stokesay Castle was bought by J. D. Allcroft, who dedicated himself to preserving the castle as a historic monument, beginning a ten-year programme of careful repair and conservation that brought the building into an excellent state of repair. Photographs taken in 1875, a few years after he acquired the property, show that externally at least the buildings were in a sound state. Internally, Allcroft did much to restore the castle in a simple and unaffected way. A hundred years later it looks beguilingly like ancient work. From the 1870s, too, Stokesay became a favourite destination for Victorian tourists and a popular locality for sketching and meditation on the Shropshire countryside. On his visit at that time, Henry James found the castle in a state of pleasing decay but far from being a ruin. Indeed, throughout the literature of the eighteenth and nineteenth centuries, Stokesay is repeatedly depicted in the character of a fragile decay, yet, despite everything, it continued stubbornly to endure.

By the 1930s, however, the Stokesay Court estate, like so many others, was hit by financial difficulties. Clearly the days were numbered for the private patronage of a monument demanding careful and skilled conservation on a regular and costly basis; and so, after decades of negotiation about the possibility of public guardianship for the monument, an acceptable formula for the future was finally agreed between Lady Jewell and Sir Philip Magnus-Allcroft and the newly formed English Heritage in 1984. Stokesay passed into the public domain, but the challenge that remained was to sustain the special character and atmosphere of the place in the tradition of careful stewardship and historicism that had prevailed there (Tolley *et al.* 1991).

'To pursue the historic vision'

The tradition in which Stokesay has been handed down to us is one of conscious conservatism – from the deliberate architectural archaism and historicist taste of its earlier owners, to the conservation programmes of its nineteenth- and twentieth-century guardians. One of the outcomes of this tradition is the expression of their careful restraint in the fragility of worn, weathered and faded finishes that robustly persist despite the inexorable processes of ageing. Very little is concealed at Stokesay. There is scarcely any furnishing, no floor coverings or hangings, no interpretative panels, no labels. The few internal walls with plastered finishes are overlain by a patina of centuries of graffiti; only two rooms have glazing. This is how the interiors were found when the Magnus-Allcroft family handed over the buildings to English Heritage in 1984. Thoughtful decisions had to be made about the kind of repair and refurbishment that was possible or desirable for such a sensitive situation, and it was the character of Stokesay itself, its own particular qualities, that shaped the principles of the five-year conservation programme that followed. What is special about the place for most visitors is simply the quality of Stokesay's tranquil testimony to the passage of time, the outcome of a long tradition of careful conservation and sensitive repair of ancient work. There is also the particular opportunity that the place seems to offer for personal discovery of a sense of historical relationship and event. The right approach for the conservation programme was one that would respect these attributes, recognise and guard their vulnerability, and allow the visitor to discover his or her own pleasures in the qualities of Stokesay's ancient presence.

The use of traditional repair techniques and materials was fundamental to this approach and was carried out with great sensitivity and inventiveness by a local firm of craftsmen builders under the direction of a skilled conservation architect. Wherever possible, renewal was resisted. If the surface of stonework was badly decayed, but the masonry still performed its function, its surface was stabilised and it was left. Graffiti-covered lime plaster was gently washed and consolidated to leave the faded testimony of generations of visitors (additions are still being made). In some places the introduction of new stone or timber was an unavoidable necessity. Occasionally, the sheer physical disruption of these repairs using traditional techniques had to be weighed against the use of alternative modern interventions to strengthen, unseen, the failures resulting from past neglect. (A detailed account of the repair programme is published in Tolley *et al.* 1991.)

A whole series of choices about visitor presentation and interpretation were also available for consideration. Stokesay was a faded canvas on which any number of new images could have been projected. It could have been refurnished, with hangings and floor coverings introduced into some of the rooms; but what period would one have chosen as the moment at which to show it? Perhaps 1300, as the newly furnished country residence of Lawrence of Ludlow? Or 1500, as an old-fashioned, provincial Tudor manor house? Or 1650, as a quaint country home for a London lawyer, refurbished after the Civil War in a style deliberately harking back to its Stuart heyday? The curators could have searched the auction houses of Britain for authentic medieval and Tudor furniture (with all the problems of security, conservation and environmental control involved in the public display of such precious items) or, alternatively, might have commissioned a set of reproduction furnishings less vulnerable to the wear and tear of unattended and unheated rooms open to visitors and the elements.

Other alternatives could perhaps have presented themselves, too. The story of Stokesay's preservation as an archetypal site of conservation awareness could lend itself as a theme for a presentation about contemporary conservation thinking, practical craft technique demonstrations and workshops in the great hall. In other sensitive historic monuments, the living history approach has been adopted successfully as an alternative to the encumbrance of information boards and labels: costumed guides populate the rooms and talk to visitors about the life of the household and its people (see Chapter 10 for discussion of the effectiveness of 'active' interpretation). If not endless, the possibilities for presentation at Stokesay were, and remain, many and varied.

The approach that has been taken for the site's presentation is, as with the conservation work, one guided by the respect for the special qualities of the place. It interferes as little as possible in the relations between people and place, and allows visitors to explore Stokesay freely for themselves. There is a well-illustrated guidebook and an (optional) audio-guide is available to all visitors. Inevitably, though, some changes in the atmosphere of the place have occurred, if only to meet the expectations of the modern tourist for comfort and consumption. In the courtyard – where Henry James was able to lie on the grass and envision beasts tethered, hustling men at arms and the earth trampled into puddles – today there are tables and chairs, visitors taking tea and scones, and plants for sale. One of the strangest experiences at Stokesay now, however, is to encounter a room full of visitors gazing in eerie silence at the remnants of medieval life – and to realise that they are rapt, not in contemplation of what is before them, but in listening through their headphones to the voice of their audio-guide-from-history, Mrs Stackhouse Acton. It invites questions about how this might inhibit basic human responses of wonder and curiosity at what is being regarded. Or should one reflect that the audio-guide is probably no more alien or prescriptive than walking round a historic place, guidebook in hand, and pausing periodically to peer at an information board?

The problem, and the endless delight, of all old places that have been transmitted to us through generations of change is that they seldom offer straightforward linear narratives. Their richness is their plural existence. Attempts to impose overarching themes – at Stokesay, for example, it might have been, 'The story of a Manor of the Marches' – break down almost immediately because individual historic places are invariably atypical and incompletely understood. Moreover, it is rarely possible to present in a formal way more than one or two of the multiple narratives of history implicit in an ancient place; and it is impossible to do so without ignoring or suppressing several other equally important aspects of it. What begins as a well-intentioned aid to a better appreciation of history can end in a bland and artificially constructed 'heritage' that has tenuous links with the reality of experiencing the place itself.

In the same way, what begins as necessary repair and preservation work can irreversibly alter authentic surviving structures and result in a similarly artificial generalisation. Both preservation and presentation can convey a convincing physical and factually-based sense of historical reality that is apparently more authentic than the historic place itself. By providing unchallenging audio-visual presentations, reconstructions and 'closed' explanations, which eliminate the possibilities of critical engagement, the experience can become a predominantly passive one. We risk marginalising the value of authenticity or, worse, preventing people from actively seeing what is actually there.

Concerns about false historicism and authenticity are not new. They were exemplified in the anti-restoration movement of the later nineteenth century, in reaction to the work of Victorian restorers (Pevsner 1976; Denslagen 1994; Miele 1996). Those early debates were focused on the effect of physical interventions to repair and renew historic buildings, and, as a consequence, such works today are subject to well-codified rules of principle, documentation and good practice. By contrast, the much more subtle interventions of interpretation and presentation have not been as rigorously appraised. Such superficial interventions, it could be argued, are always reversible and will inevitably be subject to frequent change as technology moves on, resources fluctuate, and design fashion evolves. This is indisputable but, whilst the style of presentation for the visitor is reversible, the individual's experience of a place is not. Personal discovery of a sense of place and self-consciousness of historical process and change – that sense of 'dropping back personally into the past' in Henry James's historic vision – are becoming a rare privilege at an increasingly small number of historic places. There are exceptions – the National Trust's recent work at Chastleton exemplifies a conscious intention that 'nothing should come between the visitor and the spirit of this most romantic of manor houses' (Drury 1998, 3). Similarly, at Wigmore Castle, English Heritage's aim has been to give visitors safe access to a site 'that still has a real sense of discovery, little changed from its natural state' (Chapter 4, p. 69). At the majority of historic places, however, the trend in presentation generally continues to be towards adding layers of extraneous experience and information.

Returning to Stokesay's faded canvas, then, there has been no intention to project on to it anything new. It has, nevertheless, been changed by the continuing process of preservation and a fresh approach to its presentation, but in ways that respect its special significance and vulnerability. What was there remains accessible and with the progress of decay and weathering staved off for a time. It is true that if you visit without a guide and know nothing of medieval life, then the architectural history and the detailed story of the people who lived there will pass you by. More importantly, however, there is still the experience of the place itself which is all the richer, some would say, for being unencumbered by formal historical knowledge. In subtle ways, that are appreciable only when there are minimal distractions, awareness and imaginative enjoyment are heightened. The textures and contours of age are all in reach and offer a tactile experience – people remember the worn smoothness of the finger groove in the stair rail, as they cautiously ascend the steep timber staircase from the great hall. Up in the solar they get a glimpse, through the small shuttered hatch in the panelling, across the airy roof space of the great hall where the martins swoop in the summer. In their mind's eye, they people the room below with noise and smoky activity. Sitting in the stone window seats of the lodging tower, with the wooden shutters open to gusts of wet wind, they gaze across the valley to the tree-covered slopes of Wenlock Edge, wondering how people kept themselves warm.

The tradition of such personal experience and exploration of historical places has, itself, a long history and it is worth ending with a look back over that legacy. The roots of popular historical awareness lie in the Georgian period, as the conventions of picturesque tourism extended the tourist gaze from works of nature to the works of humankind in the landscape. The traditions of Romantic poetic discourse encouraged a deeply personal experience of landscape and of the human history inscribed in it. If, however, it was William Wordsworth who taught his readers to 'walk with nature', then it was Sir Walter Scott, above all, who taught them to walk with history. It was the historical novels of Scott – long before the flowering of the narrative historians of the Victorian period, Carlyle, Macaulay, Froude, Freeman – that revealed history as part of popular culture. Scott's stories, scarcely read now, had a huge nineteenth-century readership for whom he populated the historical landscape and revolutionised the experience of history by 'direct inspection and embodiment' (Carlyle 1838, 367). The human terms in which great historical trends become tangible had never before been represented in this way (see Lukacs 1962). It is no coincidence that Scott was the favourite author of two figures who were among the most influential in the formative period of nineteenth-century architectural conservation; John Ruskin and William Morris.

In this perspective, we recognise that the formal presentation of a site or building's history – whether written, verbal or visual – is by no means the most characteristic, or arguably important means by which people have traditionally gathered their experience of historic places. Today the sources of such experience are, if anything, more diverse and pluralistic than ever (see Lowenthal 1996; Arnold *et al.* 1998). If, however, ancient monuments cannot speak for themselves – and, as Margaret Warhurst has written elsewhere (Chapter 5, p. 81), if they could do so it would probably be in a language meaningless to most modern visitors – they are experienced by us in very specific ways. Preservation needs to have regard not just for important historic fabric but for the equally significant and diverse expressions of human history with which it is also invested. In the rare cases where we are fortunate enough to have inherited such a fragile legacy, it is important to recognise its significance and to strive to let nothing interfere with a keen awareness of those particular enduring qualities. They are the source of multiple, imaginative experiences that defy explicit prescription. Information will always be needed; but we can remind ourselves that ancient places are animated by other symbolic and allusory meanings, too, which can lead on to a value-rich and more meaningful apprehension of human history and its future. Such animation is a rich source for sustaining historical self-consciousness in the context of a lively modernity.

■ ■ ■

Acknowledgement

I wish express my thanks to all my former colleagues at English Heritage, particularly Jeff West, and to Robert Tolley (S T Walker & Partners) and Stephen Treasure (Treasure & Son), for helping these ideas to take shape during the time that we were privileged to work together at Stokesay.

Note

1 See Everson (1998), and Taylor (1998) on Stokesay as one of a group of 'water castles' associated with consciously designed and symbolic landscape settings; also Munby 1993, pp. 8–11. Campbell (Chapter 9) discusses the importance of designed landscape environs for historic buildings.

References

Arnold, J., Davies, K. and Ditchfield, S. (eds) (1998) *History and Heritage: Consuming the Past in Contemporary Culture*, Shaftesbury: Donhead.

Camden, W. (1610) *Britain, or a Chorographicall Description of the most flourishing Kingdomes, England, Scotland and Ireland*, trans. Philemon Holland, London: Bishop & Norton (first published in Latin in 1586).

Carlyle, T. (1838) unsigned review of Lockhart's *Life of Sir Walter Scott, Baronet, London and Westminster Review*, 28 (January 1838), 293–345; repr. in Hayden, John O. (ed.) (1970) *Scott: The Critical Heritage*, London: Routledge, pp. 345–73.

Cordingley, R.A. (1963) 'Stokesay Castle, Shropshire: The chronology of its buildings', *Art Bulletin* 45, 91–107.

Denslagen, W. (1994) *Architectural Restoration in Western Europe: Controversy and Continuity*, Amsterdam: Architectura & Natura.

Drury, M. (1998), 'Strength in diversity', *National Trust Magazine* 83, 3.

Everson, P. (1998) ' "Delightfully surrounded with woods and ponds": field evidence for medieval gardens in England', in P. Pattison (ed.) *There by Design: Field Archaeology in Parks and Gardens*, Swindon, Royal Commission on the Historical Monuments of England (also published as British Archaeological Reports, British Series, no. 267, pp. 32–38).

Grose, F. (1787) *The Antiquities of England and Wales*, VIII, Supplement, London, p.121.

James, H. (1905) 'Abbeys and Castles', in *English Hours*, London: Heinemann (first published as an essay in 1877).

Lowenthal, D. (1996), *The Heritage Crusade and the Spoils of History*, London: Viking.

Lukacs, G. (1962) *The Historical Novel*, Mitchell, H. and S. (trans), London: Merlin.

Macaulay, R. (1953) *The Pleasure of Ruins*, London: Weidenfeld & Nicolson.

Miele, C. (1996) 'The first conservation militants: William Morris and the Society for the Protection of Ancient Buildings', in M. Hunter (ed.) *Preserving the Past: The Rise of Heritage in Modern Britain*, Stroud: Sutton, pp. 17–37.

Munby, J. (1993) *Stokesay Castle. Shropshire*, London: English Heritage.

Pevsner, N. (1976) 'Scrape and anti-scrape', in J. Fawcett (ed.) *The Future of the Past: Attitudes to Conservation 1174–1974*, London: Thames & Hudson, pp. 35–54.

Taylor, C. (1998) 'From record to recognition', in P. Pattison (ed.) *There by Design: Field Archaeology in Parks and Gardens*, Swindon, Royal Commission on the Historical Monuments of England.

Thompson, M.W. (1981) *Ruins: Their Preservation and Display*, London: British Museum.

Tolley, R.J., Babington, C. and Chitty, G. (1991) 'Stokesay Castle: the repair of a major monument', *Transactions of the Association for Studies in the Conservation of Historic Buildings* 15 (1991), 3–24.

Urry, J. (1990) *The Tourist Gaze*, London: Sage.

Chapter 7

CHURCHES AND CATHEDRALS

David Baker

Introduction

Keynote statements often lack small print. On the one hand, received conservation wisdom identifies original uses as the best way to preserve historic buildings; on the other, evolving function and modernisation can sometimes be no less destructive than the impact of a new use. Tourism is 'a great occasion to welcome the public to the house of God and to display and explain some of the essential purposes of the building' (Archbishops' Commission on Cathedrals 1994, 12); yet, especially in smaller churches, what many visitors expect to see may have been altered in response to evolving doctrine and liturgy, or in the course of heroic efforts to stave off redundancy.

The central theme of this chapter is the tension between two agendas for presentation, one communicating the contemporary religious significance of the 'living church', and the other the wider cultural significance of historically evolved buildings. More familiar issues – repair techniques, alternative uses, alterations and extensions – are incidental. These are not the clear-cut clashes triggered by loss of original uses and conversion to monument or exhibit, and indications of complexity are not hard to find. The churches accept ownership of both agendas, recognising the need to accommodate and inform visitors, but many visitors and conservators do not find the practice of religion indispensable for historical and architectural appreciation. Visitors themselves can be encouraged as potential contributors to the costs of repair and maintenance, or restricted in order to minimise damaging impacts. State aid for conservation reflects both the inadequacy of church resources and the wider social ownership of 'heritage': if the church resources increased should the state aid decrease notwithstanding social interest staying at least constant?

The buildings

The *English Heritage Monitor* notes that at the end of 1997 the computerised database held by the Royal Commission on the Historical Monuments of England included over 17,000 listed places of worship (Hanna 1998). At June 1996, there were some 8,500 pre-Reformation Anglican parish churches, the largest proportion of the medieval building stock in Britain, also containing many of the finest works of medieval architecture and art. Their distribution is heavily biased towards the more sparsely populated parts of the country, though many important nineteenth-century churches and chapels stand in what are now economically deprived and socially fragmented inner city locations. There is a great range of scale between the small buildings scattered around town and country, and most of the sixty-one cathedrals, major heritage attractions in historic cities more accustomed to managing modern tourism. Additionally, many stand with chapels, vicarages and schools or in wider precincts; churchyards contain valuable monuments and ecosystems.

Churches and cathedrals occupy semi-detached pockets in late twentieth-century secular consciousness. The report of the Archbishops' Commission on Cathedrals, *Heritage and Renewal* (1994), began with the rhetorical question, 'What is a cathedral for?' The answer included otherwise unarticulated perceptions of holiness and eternity, insights into fellowship with past believers and into historical processes, artistic and cultural achievements, education, evangelism and witness to the presence of God. For the large majority, who do not use them for worship, these buildings may be little more than poorly understood but reassuring exteriors, townscape or landscape symbols of permanence and continuity with the past. For those who like going to look at interesting old buildings, they are a reliable item on the list. For an unquantified minority they are a source of deep interest and endless fascination. For numbers that are even smaller (but are said to have stabilised), they are the places where nothing less than the significance of life can be understood in fellowship with like-minded believers.

The obviousness of the case for the historic and spiritual significance of churches must not conceal an increasingly widespread lack of understanding about their purposes and uses. For two generations, active religious involvement on the part of most people has rarely gone beyond formal school assemblies. Those who visit churches may not be able to recognise functions and meanings, past or present, such as the whereabouts and significance of the chancel. Ensuring that the experience moves beyond unengaged cultural grazing may require some very basic explanations.

The legal context

The general systems of control over change to churches cover matters of preservation and presentation. Listed churches in use are 'exempt' from secular listed building and scheduled monument controls, although planning permission is required for ordinary development and alterations to external appearance that would otherwise have required listed building consent. This is not the place to rehearse either the history of the 'ecclesiastical exemption' or the debate about its future (but see Newman 1997). The Church of England's ancient system of faculty jurisdiction, its own equivalent of planning control, is now embodied in the *Care of Churches and Ecclesiastical Jurisdiction Measure 1991*, and the *Care of Cathedrals Measure 1990* administered by the Cathedrals Fabric Commission for England (CFCE). Faculty jurisdiction has a more detailed level of control over uses and fittings, including those of interpretation and tourism, than is available for non-religious buildings covered by the secular system.

Secular listed building control exercised by local planning authorities respects a general requirement to reconcile the need for economic growth with the need to protect the natural and historic environment. Within it, there is a general presumption in favour of the preservation of listed buildings, except where a convincing case can be made out for alteration or demolition. The best way to preserve a listed building is to ensure its continuing maintenance and repair through keeping it in its original use (DoE 1990; DoE 1994). The ecclesiastical Measures of 1990 and 1991 require due regard for the use of the historic building as a centre of worship and mission. In this context, the case of St Luke's Maidstone was a landmark judgement by the Church of England's appeal Court of Arches. It stressed a strong presumption against permanent changes to a listed church that would adversely affect its character as a building of special architectural or historic interest. It indicated that, in order to determine such proposals, a balance has to be struck between, on the one hand, the clear gain of benefits for worship and mission and, on the other, undeniable losses from adverse impacts. The benefits must at least be substantiated by demonstrations of compelling necessity and by the lack of any alternative solution' (Mynors 1995, 32). Time and case histories will show how far this approach to managing architecture of outstanding quality is sufficiently analogous with what happens in the secular system.

Presenting continuing and evolving uses

Worship and mission have presentational aspects, to affirm religious purposes within the community of believers, and to attract others to share in faith and liturgy. These aspects incorporate attitudes towards the building, changing down the years, and now fitting variably with the special architectural or historic interest of the places where they find themselves.

At ends of the spectrum, attitudes place either great store on the beauty of holiness, expressed through architecture, decoration and liturgy, or little store on the church building by giving primacy to the preached word and the occupying congregation of the faithful. Catholic or 'high' Anglican congregations have a particular interest in the aesthetic and didactic qualities of their historic buildings, especially fine medieval survivals and those built or extensively altered during the more florid architectural episodes of the nineteenth century. Non-conformists usually focus upon the people, the congregation and their worship; the building is the means to the end of their fellowship, the shell where it takes place; the life and purpose of the meeting need not be devalued by moving to another venue. Redundancy followed by demolition or reuse has been much higher amongst chapels than Anglican churches. Between 1985 and 1992, there were over 100 applications to demolish listed non-Anglican buildings, mostly affecting chapels, which have been identified as the second most threatened historic building type in England, after barns (Freeman 1995, 7).

It is in the broad centre of the spectrum that tensions between mission and conservation most easily arise, when approaches to the presentation of worship change in a building regarded as an important part of religious expression. This is not new in the history of the church: major alterations to fabric, fittings and furnishings followed changing ideas of how to celebrate the liturgy, arising from church reforms after the Norman Conquest, the Reformation, as part of the nineteenth-century Oxford Movement, and with this century's Liturgical Movement. The latter has been described as 'a renewed emphasis on the Christian assembly as a community of faith' which 'gives rise to an increasing pressure to re-order liturgical space to give clear architectural expression to the basic elements of liturgical action – font, ambo and altar' (CFCE 1998).

There is a range of approaches to the practical implications. The exhibition at the magnificent, largely fifteenth-century, town church of St Mary Redcliffe in Bristol includes a balanced statement:

> Put baldly, the dilemma we face is this. We are the inheritors of a treasure which is not replaceable. That treasure belongs to everyone, Christian or non-Christian – it is part of what the past has given us, in a sense as a gift of love. Many people are drawn there by that gift from the past. But we must never lose our sense of proportion and start to worship the building, because however difficult it may be for the twentieth century to grasp, this building was always intended to point beyond itself, to a reality of which it is merely a dim reflection.

A more radical and provocative approach is taken by Canon Richard Giles in *Repitching the Tent*. He answers his own question, whether Christian communities should have a building at all, with a wary affirmative. Un-reordered churches may fail in their missionary task because the 'buildings have ceased by and large to speak clearly of a present reality, and instead convey a mumbled message of a glorious, though faded past'. Those that contradict, in their layout and design, the Church's own message and theological understanding are fit only for the heritage trail. He castigates 'gothic clutter', those who resist change 'when their precious church-museum is threatened with "desecration"', and 'preservationist constraints imposed by those who have no understanding of the Christian vocation' (Giles 1997, passim). The most must be made of a building: a medieval tympanum marking the entrance can be emphasised and cherished, but pews and furnishings should be cleared for gathering spaces built around a kitchen, large enough to accommodate the whole community, under the same roof as the place of liturgical assembly.

The key concept here is 'sacred space' which can be used flexibly in the service of the liturgy. Positive architecture can enhance it; measures should be taken to counteract negative aspects, such as intricate Victorian parish church design that focuses attention towards a remote high altar at the east end of the church. In the words of Bishop Michael Marshall, 'all reordered liturgical space is not an end in itself, but should be seen rather as an empty board on which the people of God paint the icon of Christ in their liturgical formation and movement' (Marshall 1996, 177).

The pressure for change is not just about liturgy in action; it is also about making the buildings more welcoming and helping to sustain local church communities. Lack of facilities and flexibility threatens the continuing viability of many parishes limping on with regular congregations in only one or two figures. Congregations undergoing evangelical expansion may put pressure on the use of medieval buildings or in rare cases outgrow them altogether. The desirability of encouraging liturgical change that may have architectural impacts on individual historic churches can sit uneasily with the corporate concern of the Church as an institution to retain its exemption from secular listed building controls. Tensions can become acute in churches of architectural merit already beholden to the state for substantial repair grants intended to ensure continuing use without radical physical change.

Many of these factors came together in a fairly exceptional recent case involving proposals to alter the church of St Mary the Virgin at Yielden in Bedfordshire (Figure 7.1), as part of a Community Building Project. They sprang from the need for a new village hall and a proposal to provide these facilities in an adapted church whose congregation, like so many, was so small that it used only part of the available space. The church is medieval, listed Grade 1, and, apart from the chancel, possesses an accumulated patina largely untouched by the hand of the nineteenth century. Its fine interior has sixteenth-century pews, wall paintings, carved stonework details, monuments and a worn but attractive flagged and tiled floor. The scheme's proponents took the view that their proposals were an expression of faith and community that justified the impacts upon the historic building. They included de-pewing, inserting a wooden floor and several partitions, and subdividing the south aisle into meeting rooms. The nave would have become a flexible, multipurpose space, to be used as a village hall, as overflow from the chancel where services would normally be held, and for games such as badminton and other social activities. The proposal, supported by the Diocesan Advisory Committee, was opposed by English Heritage and the local planning authorities. A section of the village, though mostly not members of the congregation, preferred to retain an evolved and relatively unaltered medieval building. A Church Consistory Court

Figure 7.1 St. Mary the Virgin, Yielden in Bedfordshire: view west along nave; south aisle to left

Source: David Baker

hearing was narrowly averted when the weight of opposition became clear. Over two years later, alternative solutions are still being worked out.

Presenting the architecture of religion

Churches and cathedrals represent such vastly different scales of problems and opportunities that it is tempting to treat them as two different categories of buildings, despite their common underlying purposes. Instead, the following discussion tries to separate issues arising from presenting the architecture of religion and its religious purposes – which concern all churches – and the management of visitors, balancing consequential impacts upon fabric against financial and spiritual benefits – which largely affects cathedrals.

The standard of presentation in many fine and interesting churches has not yet caught up with the era of the tourist as customer. Booklets are often over-technical, archaic, and difficult for non-architects to understand; some are misleading, fondly repeating a compendium of attractive errors and groundless traditions; others, with the best of intentions, swamp explanation of the building with glowing evocations of uses and purpose or excursions down historical by-ways. A growing number of local publications do successfully combine explanation and exhortation, but there is a need for wider guidance that supports without discouraging local ownership. Public grant-giving bodies could usefully develop a scheme that linked the review of appropriate presentational facilities with the provision of funds for repair: it must surely be within remits to promote public enjoyment of heritage.

Poor explanatory literature will probably not affect preservation, but good material can greatly increase its basis of support. It can also meet the needs of visitors by engaging them in exploring and understanding the building, rather than expounding it academically or liturgically on a take-it-or-leave-it basis. Ways of satisfying three sets of customers might be envisaged. The transient experience of the casual visitor can be orientated through a short leaflet with basic information, clearly and simply expressed for a relatively young reading age. It should cover matters such as the age of the church, why it is there and not somewhere else, how it has been and is now used, what is its extent and how it is organised, what are the most notable elements, and in what order they are best seen. It can also make an appeal for funds to help projected conservation and repair programmes. The more purposeful visitor or student could have a more technical product for a lasting and structured recollection: this might incorporate the pictorial souvenir, or visual needs could also be met separately by postcards. With the needs of the local community in mind, and in conjunction with teachers, educational resource packs could be devised, dealing with one or a group of churches.

Another form of written presentation is point-located captions or notices explaining the significance of particular tombs, paintings, carvings or other special features. These may not be too much of a visual intrusion in large cathedrals, but even discreet, well-designed and well-placed notices have overtones of museum rather than living building: the feeling intensifies as the overall space becomes smaller.

The written word is not the only medium: voices and music can also be used. The standard device here, mainly in larger buildings and cathedrals, is the portable, pre-recorded, often multi-lingual, tape which acts as a personalised guide. Once it is accepted that there will usually be numbers of visitors moving around inside a building, it is only a small visual exacerbation for several of them at any one time to appear to be listening to over-sized portable telephones. The other approach, providing generally available rather than personalised sound, has its drawbacks, exemplified at the magnificent, largely twelfth-century collegiate church of

St Aignan-sur-Cher in the Loire valley. Here, attached to an arcade column at the west end of the nave, is a panel with a row of buttons for a tour of the church and its predecessor, now a crypt. Press one for the language of choice, and speakers and lights draw the visitor from one part of the building to another, illuminating and explaining superb sequences of carved capitals and wall-paintings. Only one language can be played at a time. It was fine during a May lunch-time in a deserted building, but this internal mis-application of the '*son-et-lumière*' approach must be a recipe for chaos at busier times.

A continental habit that may not yet have reached Britain is the provision of ecclesiastical *musak*, often plainsong. On first encounter in a good acoustic, the innocent secular ear may experience a pleasurable goose-pimple; by the tenth occasion it has become a degrading sound-bite. A reserved English mind might find it at least an unnecessary distraction from the special solitude of the place, and more centrally from the purposes of the building. Visits can gain greater meaning from the routine sounds of the building in action, such as organ or choral practice, or a service in a temporarily closed chapel. York Minster takes a more proactive approach: at set times in the day, a priest leads short prayers from a microphone in the nave; all the staff and some visitors participate where they stand; others continue to perambulate with varying degrees of guilt or incomprehension.

Two topics, bells and floodlighting, the church audible and visible, deserve special comment. Both enjoy a higher profile as the end of the second Christian millennium approaches. Nothing is more English in the general imagination than the sound of bells across countryside or townscape, speaking to the wider population of services in progress, happy or sad events, or the healthy exercise of ringing peals. The preservation of medieval oak bell-frames and early sets of bells is hindered by their unsuitability for post-medieval full-circle ringing, or by decayed frame-ends in loose masonry. Conservation policy now usually seeks to retain old frames of good quality, repairing them *in situ* rather than replacing them in steel simply because they are old. Conflicts can, however, arise over proposals to increase the number of bells beyond the capacity of historic frames, or to re-tune historic bells so that they conform to the new ring. On one side is the argument that ringing is a living activity that needs to grow and change; on the other is the view that the antiquity of what survives is an intrinsic part of its value, and must be allowed to set reasonable limits upon change.

The peculiarly modern practice of floodlighting can benefit the local community and act as a wider signpost for tourism. Like bell-ringing, it is also an expression of pride in a church. At a time when light pollution is a recognised environmental issue, however, each proposal needs justifying on its merits. The Churches Floodlighting Trust is aiming to guide up to 200 churches of all denominations towards grants from the Millennium Commission. The schemes have to demonstrate visual appeal, energy efficiency, avoidance of light pollution, low costs of installation, maintenance and running, and compatibility with church architecture and fabric. Only six had been fully completed by May 1998, but it seems to be a good way of guiding local initiatives towards better conclusions than might otherwise be obtained.

Accommodating visitors

Churches as objects of tourist interest raise several inter-related topics, including basic availability, the impacts of visitors and presentational strategies, and the extent to which those impacts are exacerbated by links between visiting and fundraising. Visitor management has to reflect the level of demand to see the building, the quality and vulnerability of what is there, and the resources that are available, voluntarily, through existing budgets or from making charges.

Those churches that stay locked outside the times for normal religious services represent an extreme clash between the most basic form of presentation – simple availability – and preservation, in this case from theft, vandalism, arson and desecration. The Ecclesiastical Insurance Group reports an average of 5,300 claims annually for 1993–7 in Anglican parish churches. Post-war decades have seen an increasing proportion of buildings kept locked, against the risk of losing art treasures like paintings, furniture such as parish chests, and even carved stone details. With the increase in drugs-related crime, urban churches have become particularly vulnerable to theft of unattended boxes for donations and sales of publications. Some porches have a notice saying where a key can be obtained; others remain silent. Though public access is a condition of grants received from English Heritage, realism has dictated that it can be satisfied through a key-holding arrangement. As a reaction to this deteriorating situation, the Open Churches Trust was founded in 1994 by Andrew Lloyd Webber, with an ultimate objective of enabling 'anyone at any time to wander in and out of fine churches at will'. Grants are provided to help in cases where churches can be opened outside hours of worship only with someone present as an attendant or guide (Gurdon 1997).

Visitors make direct impacts through, in order of severity, their feet, hands and breath. The time-worn hollows in steps and stone flooring have been greatly increased by later twentieth-century tourism: a recent study by the Building Research Establishment found average wear of about 1 mm/decade on pavements at heavily used places in Westminster Abbey and St Paul's Cathedral (Fawcett 1998a, 121). There is serious wear on newel staircases up to towers and galleries, and sometimes on ledgers and tomb slabs set into aisles or cloister walks. Grit on hard shoes causes major damage; the frequent use of floor cleaning equipment adds its own abrasions. At Peterborough Cathedral, a section of J. L. Pearson's 1890s floor was replaced due to excessive wear on vulnerable materials. At Winchester Cathedral, people are now able to walk over the repaired medieval floor in the retro-choir. The options seemed to lie 'between barricading certain areas and increasing the load on others, or leaving the space free to spread the load of tourists' (Bird 1998, 119). Yet if concentrated or distributed access continues in the longer term, 'the tiles, which are extremely vulnerable, will be destroyed' (Fawcett 1998b, 221). Touching with hands may seem less erosive, but the effect is repetitive and cumulative, usually affecting particular things like details on monuments, or places where passing crocodiles of coach trippers steady themselves on the tour guide's regular route. The effects of visitors' exhalations, on a larger scale than any pre-twentieth-century building will have encountered, is more difficult to assess, and is part of the wider issue of environmental control and heating in contexts where there are delicate assets such as painted surfaces or ancient fabrics.

A specialised aspect of touching is brass-rubbing, another activity whose historical, aesthetic, spiritual and physical benefits have to be balanced against cumulative damage to the brasses themselves. It is now increasingly prohibited, with people redirected, especially in cities, to where replicas can be rubbed. Ironically, the brass-rubbing centre and shop in the north cloisters at Westminster Abbey is setting up problems of wear to historic floors with ledger memorials (Fawcett 1998b, 220).

Such centres are part of directly provided visitors' facilities, a topic to which the issue of signage is a logical introduction. Unless it has been positively designed and managed for maximum visibility and minimum visual impact, a large building may accumulate several different types and standards. Lack of strategic planning has led on occasion to three sets, some coming with the monuments themselves, some explaining the building and its contents, and others directing people to tower, toilets and tea-room.

Signage connects with access, which is an issue in buildings never intended to take the volumes of people and the standards of facilitation required today. Different floor levels can result from successive building periods, rebuilding or liturgical requirements. Ensuring or improving access for people with disabilities can be technically challenging. Some access problems are insoluble: long newel staircases must exclude people entirely unused to physical exercise, with weak hearts or prone to vertigo. The defence of some well-intentioned but unimaginative solutions, like the huge ramp in the north-east corner of the cloister walk at Hereford, may be that they are laid on existing surfaces and are reversible, but that does not reduce their obtrusiveness. Even imaginative solutions can be controversial, as in Sir Giles Gilbert Scott's Liverpool Cathedral, where an open glass lift in the body of the building has been successfully proposed as a way of providing access to exhibition space created at gallery level. Proponents applauded the opportunity for high-level views across the building giving an enhanced experience of its vast spaces and monumental verticality, whilst opponents saw it as a distractingly mobile, visual intrusion jarringly aping the secular arrangements in the atrium of a modern office block.

Access connects with charging for admission. Only at the lowest level and in the most informal mode can the activity of visiting be truly 'free', without cost to visitor or what is being visited. Even the smallest parish church will usually have a notice inviting contributions to the fabric fund, and for decades cathedrals have tried to encourage giving by confronting people with the mathematics of hourly running costs. There are mixed issues here. On the principle of charging for admission at all, the major cathedrals find themselves caught in the cross-fire of conflicting social and cultural messages. For some, entry into the house of God should always be unfettered; for others, payment is both necessary and reasonable in today's economic circumstances, even for the genuine spiritual pilgrim. The transition from one position to the other can be painful: Canterbury Cathedral hoped that its annual total of 2.25 million visitors could be persuaded to accept the charitable ethos of the institution and donate £2 each voluntarily, but obtained only an average of 13p: admission charges were therefore introduced. On the practicalities of charging admission, much depends upon the pressures of tidal visitor flows. At Ely, a simple table manned by stewards seems to suffice, providing an informal foil at the entrance to the magnificent vista of the nave (Figure 7.2). That would not work at St Paul's Cathedral, where the visual intrusion of payment points inserted

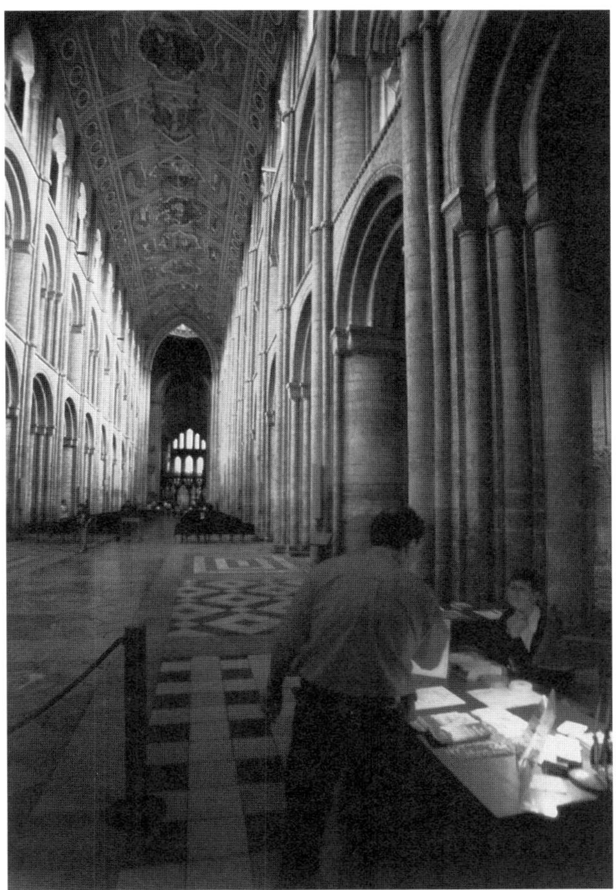

Figure 7.2 Visitors' welcome to the great space of the nave at Ely Cathedral

Source: David Baker

at the west end of the building is sometimes concealed by the sheer numbers of tourists and visitors.

Visitor facilities are mainly an issue for cathedrals, though some larger urban churches also have them. A distinction can be drawn between traditional *ad hoc* approaches, fitting in bookstalls, tea-room and toilets on-site wherever possible, and attempts to combine them, sometimes in off-site visitor centres. That strategy has a different set of problems but is now perceived as more realisable with the advent of the Heritage Lottery Fund.

There are instructive contrasts between the on-site facilities at the adjacent cathedrals of Worcester and Hereford. At Worcester, the tea-room is discreetly accommodated in the parlour next to the Chapter House, and the bookstall in the passage adjacent to the west end of the south aisle; both obscure historic fabric and potentially restrict circulation. Their location within ancient compartments makes no wider visual disruption, but is somewhat cramped and has little scope for expansion. At Hereford, the bookstall is crammed into the bays of the cloister walk next to the church. The tea-room is a long-lived 'temporary' Portakabin sitting in the space south of the church formerly occupied by the Chapter House, its incongruity compounded by the addition of a large access ramp (Figure 7.3)

Moving to a visitor centre that combines previously separate functions is a major step that needs careful planning if controversial impacts are to be minimised.

Figure 7.3 Portakabin tea room and ramp, Hereford Cathedral

Source: David Baker

Basic issues that do not always get considered fully at the earliest stage are whether one is actually needed, and, if so, on what scale or capacity. If multi-disciplinary professional consultants are not brought in at the outset, poor strategic planning can create unfortunate situations that become difficult to unpick. Crudely, tourism managers seeking unfettered optimum solutions might argue for location immediately outside the west front, with drastic impacts upon architecture, archaeology and setting in many cases.

The few internal solutions represent special opportunities amidst crowded urban environments. St Paul's Cathedral was fortunate enough to have a large, ready-made crypt which is incorporated into a managed flow of visitors. At York Minster the bookshop is fittingly sited in the late medieval Library building, but this is clearly cramped even under moderate pressures.

Where precincts are more extensive, the reuse of former monastic buildings becomes an option. At Norwich, there are advanced proposals for providing exhibition space, shop, meetings rooms, classrooms, café and lavatories by rebuilding within the footprints of the largely ruined main west and south claustral ranges. Whilst on many sites these would be left as monuments, the proposal is to replace the form of what was probably there originally in order to meet presentational and other needs. The project has been developed through several rounds of negotiation and redesign: the main challenges have been to produce designs that make their own statement whilst respecting a highly specific context, and minimising archaeological damage. These matters figured in the debates of the 1970s at St Albans. The Visitor Centre built over the site of the Chapter House placed a large modern building on the medieval footprint against the cathedral, and occasioned an archaeological excavation that would not otherwise have been required.

Neither of those options was available at Southwell Minster, where the limitations of both the cathedral and adjacent buildings were recognised. No attempt has been made to compromise the majestic austerity of its twelfth-century nave and transepts with more than temporary visitor information facilities, nor to rebuild within the shell of adjacent ruins. Instead, the visitor centre, with bookstall and cafeteria, sits unassumingly just inside the northern boundary of the churchyard, adding definition to the townscape rather than intruding upon the setting of the Minster. In similar vein, this kind of wider solution, with visitor facilities providing a link between cathedral and town, is one of several options being comprehensively considered at Ely, after the rejection of an initial proposal for a new building on an architecturally and archaeologically sensitive site.

Getting a good framework does not automatically solve problems, but it does make it easier to be clear-sighted about them. St Mary Redcliffe at Bristol has some of the architectural quality and scale of a cathedral, but not the pressured location of Canterbury or York. The already quoted text of its interpretative display continues: 'Many of our greatest churches . . . see tourism as one possible way to survive. And yet this often destroys the very peace and quiet which used to be such a rewarding feature of a church at the centre of a city.'

There are intractable problems facing those cathedrals where the tourist pressures are greatest. For significant periods of time each year, pressures increase to levels that must be intolerable to the majority of visitors and a huge distraction from primary religious activities, let alone the quiet personal contemplation that great architecture can support. Global tourism is driven by demand and market forces, not by any natural subliminal rationing of the kind that prevents fish from over-breeding in a pond: it is heavily promoted as an income-provider by the same governments that dispense conservation grants. Nettles may have to be grasped here, jointly by state and Church authorities. The only credible route towards controlling and reducing these pressures may have to follow the example of prehistoric cave paintings (see, for example, Clottes and Chippendale 1998), and develop more effective means of presentation and interpretation off-site, all explicitly justified and geared towards sustaining precious historical, cultural and spiritual values.

Conclusion

The idea of a comprehensive approach to managing primary uses, conservation, development and arrangements for visitors, within a cathedral and its precincts as a whole, is a fitting note on which to end this short study. Peterborough Cathedral has been setting an example through the preparation of a Strategic Plan, and other cathedrals are now considering the preparation of Conservation Plans (Heritage Lottery Fund 1998) for entire precinct areas. Such a framework is essential for places of outstanding significance on the national or international scale (see discussion of World Heritage Sites in Chapters 1, 2 and 10). Only thus can difficult decisions, some involving clashes between preservation and presentation, be made in the secure knowledge that all foreseeable factors have been taken into account and all options considered.

Tailored to scale and circumstances, this approach can be applied to all historic ecclesiastical buildings, even the smallest parish churches and chapels. Its strength derives from its starting point, a statement of significance whose compilation ought to engage those responsible for the building, improve their understanding and its explanation. It helps to deal systematically with problems arising from haphazard correlations between architectural interest, presentation, overall condition, size and vigour of sustaining congregation, prevailing churchmanship or liturgical outlook, cohesion of community context, and pressure for enhanced facilities. Behind the interaction of these factors are wider forces, often divisive social and economic conditions, and arguments about the priorities for allocating resources between social renewal and conservation of historic fabric. The way to avert over-simplistic and confrontational attitudes, such as that people must always take priority over old buildings or vice versa, is to show the links between the elements. Promoting awareness of this wider context, as part of preserving and presenting, may also head off perceptions that only an inturned minority interest is at stake, and can help these buildings act as one of several focuses in healing divisions and promoting regeneration.

■ ■ ■

Acknowledgements

This chapter has been informed by valued experience of membership on St Albans Diocesan Advisory Committee and English Heritage's Cathedrals and Churches Advisory Committee. Conversations with Jonathan Goodchild, Penny Gardner, Paula Griffiths, Richard Halsey, Michael Hare, Jane Kennedy, Julian Limentani and Christopher Pickford have been particularly helpful, though the writer is responsible for views expressed and residual errors.

References

Archbishops' Commission on Cathedrals (1994) *Heritage and Renewal*, London: Church House.

Bird, P. (1998) 'Winchester Cathedral, conserving the retro-choir pavement', in J. Fawcett (ed.) *Historic Floors, their History and Conservation*, Oxford: Butterworth-Heinemann.

CFCE (1998) 'Preservation and Alteration of Cathedrals: Balancing Conflicting Requirements', *Consultation Draft Guidance Note*, Cathedrals Fabric Commission for England.

Clottes, J. and Chippendale, C. (1998) 'The Parc Pyrenean de l'Art Prehistorique', in P. G. Stone and P. Planel (eds) *The Constructed Past: Experimental Archaeology, Education and the Public,* London: Routledge.

DoE (1990) *Planning Policy Guidance Note 16: Archaeology and Planning*, London: HMSO.

DoE (1994) *Planning Policy Guidance Note 15: Planning and the Historic Environment*, London: HMSO.

Fawcett, J. (1998a) 'Use and abuse: management and good practice in cathedrals and greater churches', in J. Fawcett (ed.) *Historic Floors, their History and Conservation,* Oxford: Butterworth-Heinemann.

Fawcett, J. (1998b) 'Appendix: Cathedral floor studies – identification of areas at risk and location of historic features', in J. Fawcett (ed.) *Historic Floors, their History and Conservation,* Oxford: Butterworth-Heinemann.

Freeman, J. (1995) 'The work of the Historic Chapels Trust', *Context* 45, 7–9.

Giles, R. (1997) *Repitching the Tent*, Norwich: The Canterbury Press.

Gurdon, A. (1997) 'The Open Churches Trust: frustration reaps its rewards', *Churchscape* 16, 15–16.

Hanna, M. (ed.) (1998) *English Heritage Monitor 1998*, London: BTA/ETB.

Heritage Lottery Fund (1998) *Conservation Plans for Historic Places*, London: HLF.

Marshall, M. (1996) *Free to Worship*, London: Marshall Pickering.

Mynors, C. (1995) 'M'Learned Friend', *Context* 45, pp. 32–3.

Newman, J. (1997) 'A Review of the Ecclesiastical Exemption from Listed Building Controls', Department for Culture, Media & Sport and the Welsh Office.

Chapter 8

BRODSWORTH HALL
The Preservation of a Country House

Martin Allfrey

When English Heritage acquired Brodsworth Hall in 1990, it faced a daunting challenge to arrest years of progressive decay without destroying its special character. The approach taken was to tell the story of the house, including its gradual decline and subsequent conservation. This developed from a desire to retain something of the unique quality of the place, which had evolved over 120 years, rather than to restore it to its Victorian splendour. Central to the philosophy adopted at Brodsworth was the acknowledgement that what we now see is not something preserved from change, or a complete picture from any period, but the outcome of a continuing process, which includes the programme of works to open the site to the public. This chapter considers the strategy adopted by English Heritage for the conservation and presentation of the Hall in the context of current perspectives on the interpretation of historic places.

Brodsworth Hall was built and furnished between 1861 and 1863 by Charles Sabine Augustus Thellusson. It is Italianate in style, and designs survive by an Italian architect, Chevalier Casentini (Girouard 1963, 1971). The house is set within a landscape of formal gardens, surrounded by shrubberies and woodland. Although changes were made by later generations, many of the original decorative schemes with elaborate cornices, marbling and wall hangings survived, as did much of the original furniture, textiles, sculpture and paintings. The house also contains many rooms that had fallen into disuse, particularly in the servants' wing, which were used for storage. Consequently, Brodsworth contains not only the fine furnishings and fittings from the principal rooms but also many of the more mundane items that were an essential part of any country house (Whitworth 1995a). The house had been identified by Mark

Girouard as exceptional, and he described it as 'the most complete surviving example of a Victorian country house' (Girouard 1985). The real significance of Brodsworth, however, is that it demonstrates the evolution of a country house, not a complete picture from any one period, but a palimpsest, with evidence of changes through time. By understanding the way in which each generation has adapted the house for their own use, as well as people's changing attitudes towards the place, it is possible to consider not only the functional aspects of the house but also the cultural meanings embodied by the building and the collections it contains.

Sylvia Grant-Dalton, the last family member to live at Brodsworth, was keen that the house and its contents should be preserved. Recognising its historic significance, Sylvia was the force that had kept Brodsworth intact, struggling doggedly against enormous problems of mining subsidence, leaking roofs and a general lack of maintenance. By the time of her death in 1988, the house and contents were in a perilous state of decay and desperately in need of a programme of conservation and repair. Clearly, there was ample justification to preserve the house and to make it available to the public, and the only practical way to achieve this was for it to be taken on by a public body with the necessary experience and resources, such as the National Trust, English Heritage or the Local Authority. Any other solution would have jeopardised the essential character of the house. If the building had been acquired by a private owner, it is highly unlikely that the interior of the house or the collection would have survived intact. What is important at Brodsworth is the association of the objects with the building for which they were bought. Away from their context, the collections have little interest or significance.

Following Sylvia Grant-Dalton's death in 1988, the family entered into lengthy negotiations to find a new and appropriate owner for the Hall. Although the National Trust would probably have been the preferred organisation to take the property, there was no endowment to generate the funds needed for the repairs and maintenance of the house, which the Trust as an independent charity requires. In 1990, therefore, very much as a last resort, Brodsworth came into the care of English Heritage. The house and gardens were given to English Heritage by Sylvia Grant-Dalton's daughter, Mrs Pamela Williams, and the contents were purchased by the National Heritage Memorial Fund for £3.36 million and transferred to English Heritage.

Developing a philosophy for Brodsworth

The philosophy adopted by English Heritage for the preservation and presentation of Brodsworth evolved gradually in the early stages of the project as our understanding of the building and its contents grew. Many people saw Brodsworth only as a rare survival of a Victorian mansion and assumed that the approach would be to restore it to its former glory, removing the later accretions, which were initially thought to have little or no significance, and replicating the missing elements. Whilst the Victorian core remained, albeit in a much faded condition, however, the house contained an eclectic collection spanning 120 years of family life. Selecting an arbitrary date to represent the most significant period of the house's history would have been difficult, and there was a growing desire not to lose the spirit of the place and its inhabitants.

Before agreeing any policies or embarking on any programme of repair or presentation, it is always essential to *understand* a building, as the results of thorough research will inform every subsequent decision made about that building. The principle of assessing the importance of a site and establishing long-term policies for balancing the requirements of users against the need to retain significance has been greatly developed in recent years and is now embodied in the widespread adoption of conservation plans for places of cultural significance (Kerr 1996; Heritage Lottery Fund 1998). Brodsworth did not benefit from a conservation plan and although many of the aspects required in a conservation plan were undertaken, an agreed set of policies for the whole site would perhaps have helped to resolve some of the difficult decisions and conflicts that arose during the project. The main thrust of the work in the first stages of the project, apart from the emergency repairs to make it wind and watertight, was directed towards researching and recording the building as fully as possible. Rectified photography and architectural surveys were undertaken to provide an 'as found' record, and a full computer-based inventory and photographic record of the 17,000 objects was completed. The inventory, together with conservation reports on the condition and possible treatment of types of material, and ongoing research into the original appearance and subsequent changes to rooms helped to formulate the conservation and display policy for the interiors and collections. Documentary research into the many different aspects of the building and its past inhabitants was also carried out, and an oral history project was set up to record the personal histories of people associated with the Hall in more recent times. The project produced an archive of tape recordings of people who had lived and worked at the Hall, as well as family members. Some 5,000 photographic images were gradually discovered and became an important archive, which has recently been more thoroughly catalogued to provide a usable resource for exhibitions, education and research.

From the outset, it was considered important to formulate a policy that took account of the views of not only academics but also other potential users of the property. Research was commissioned on people's attitudes to the Hall amongst a cross-section of potential visitors, locally and nationally, as well as through the help of amenity groups such as The Victorian Society. As part of the research, a seminar and focus groups were set up to canvass opinion as to how the house should be treated. We wanted to ensure that Brodsworth would continue to be valued and that it had a viable social and economic use.

The philosophy eventually agreed upon was that we should attempt to tell the history of the house, including the undeniable effects of time and neglect, rather than to try to recapture the appearance of its earliest years (Whitworth 1995b). The research demonstrated the importance of preserving the mark that each generation had left on the place, repairing, redecorating and modernising. This layering of features, similar to an archaeological excavation, was an important aspect of the house and it needed to be recorded, interpreted, and wherever possible, preserved. What had survived was not a complete picture from any one period, but the evidence of a complex and changing pattern of social and cultural meanings from the 1860s to the 1990s. Whilst the 1860s survive most coherently in the main hallways with their original decoration, textiles and sculptures, the over-riding impression given is of the house in the later days of its last inhabitant, Sylvia Grant-Dalton. This is in general what is being aimed at, although it is not strictly 'as found' by English Heritage; the record photographs taken in the 1990s show many rearrangements by the family and valuers during the period of the negotiations for ownership, and are not therefore an accurate record of how the house was when it was lived in. Brodsworth cannot claim to be the first proponent of this 'it's all part of the history of the house' approach; a similar stance had been taken by the National Trust at Calke Abbey, which influenced the way Brodsworth was tackled (Jervis 1997). It is also part of a general movement away from restoration and recreation of historic interiors towards the conservation of as much historic fabric as possible (Brereton 1995). It may be relevant that, although the curator, Caroline Whitworth, had a fine art background, most members of staff involved in the project came from an archaeological and buildings conservation background.

The conservation programme

Preserving the essence of Brodsworth and giving it a sustainable future involved a massive conservation programme, both to the building and its contents. Unlike the interior of the hall, which no longer has to function as the living space for an affluent family, the building itself still has to function as it was intended: keeping the contents secure, dry and at the correct temperature and humidity. Years of inadequate maintenance had resulted in the need for substantial repairs to solve the problems of leaking roofs, rising damp and unstable stonework. A temporary roof was constructed over the building while the roof was reslated and large areas of the soft magnesian limestone walls were cut out and replaced (Figure 8.1). New electrical installations and heating systems to control the environment of the building were installed, and it was also considered vital to incorporate the most effective fire detection systems available, in the light of disasters at Uppark and Windsor Castle (Fidler and McCaig 1992; Fidler 1993; Thorneycroft 1993). During the works on site, the contents of the house were removed to a 1,500 sq. m. (16,000 sq. ft) environmentally controlled warehouse, and a rolling programme of conservation of the historic interiors and collections was initiated. The basic aim was to slow the process of decay and to make the objects and decorative finishes stable

Figure 8.1 The exterior of Brodsworth Hall showing the temporary roof that prevented further damage to the interiors while the roof was repaired. It also illustrates the extensive damage to the stonework

Source: English Heritage Photographic Library

enough to be shown to the public, not to restore them. In many cases, this was achieved simply by gentle cleaning to remove harmful dirt, whilst the more unstable objects needed greater intervention. The house and collections were also suffering from rampant infestation from a variety of insect pests, and thorough cleaning was necessary to eliminate this and the dirt in which the pests thrive (Figure 8.2). There are always difficult judgements to be made about how far to take the conservation of an object, and inevitably some objects will appear to be 'as good as new' after a gentle clean whereas others will have suffered more damage and will look faded and worn. At Brodsworth, no attempt was made to present the house as 'untouched'; the aim was to retain as much information as possible, allowing the complex meanings and history of the objects and house to show through, whilst conserving them for the future. Visitors see the effects of lack of maintenance or inappropriate repairs in the past, and no attempt has been made to disguise damage or reproduce missing sections, although the visual impact of major losses was lessened by infill or support materials of a colour close to the surviving original, for example to the marbled paintwork, or in dyeing the net used to support the

Figure 8.2 Loading curtains into a deep-freeze unit. All the textiles were frozen in several batches for seventy-two hours to kill all stages of insect life. This was a relatively new technique that reduced the need for fumigating with chemicals

Source: English Heritage Photographic Library

deteriorated silks. Wallpaper damaged by rising damp, leather upholstery repaired in the past with hessian and gloss paint, as well as old nail varnish repairs to painted surfaces, have all been conserved where possible and left for visitors to see (Figure 8.3). Anything that was causing continuing damage and was removable, such as clear adhesive tape, however, was removed (Babbington and Hughes 1992; Berkouwer and Church 1993).

Managing the conflict

The greatest challenge facing those who manage historic properties is to strike a balance that allows access whilst eliminating, or at least minimising, the damage caused by visitors: making the place available for people today, whilst safeguarding it for future generations (see Riddle 1994). To achieve public access at Brodsworth it has been necessary to make changes to the house for practical purposes, including

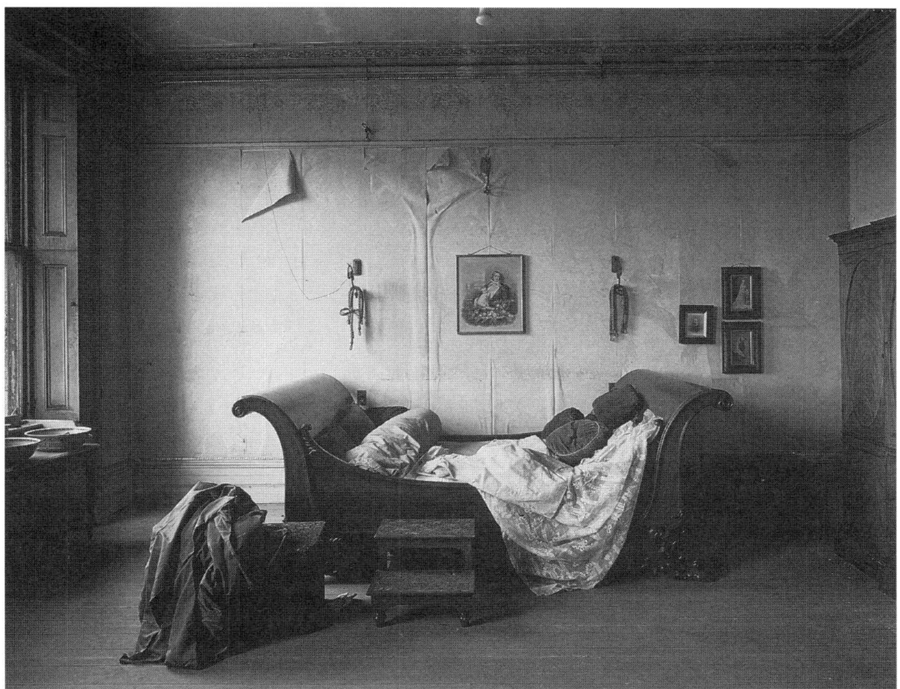

Figure 8.3 Bedroom 8 with its peeling wallpaper and fragile furnishings in 1990 before conservation. The wallpaper had been held up by steel tacks which were left 'as sound' after the paper was conserved

Source: English Heritage Photographic Library

the health and safety of staff and visitors. The general principle has been to retain and display everything, if possible, as it was found when the house was taken on by English Heritage, whilst recognising that in some areas this would not be feasible for a combination of conservation and practical reasons. The net result, therefore, differs from, but is informed by, the record photographs of the house in 1990.

Some of the essential elements of transforming a historic house into a visitor attraction, such as the public toilets and the ticket office, have been provided outside in new, purpose-built structures. The shop and catering facilities have been incorporated into the servants' wing, which has caused a number of difficulties. The most significant of these was the increased fire risk, which has to be carefully managed, and the consequent loss of the integrity of the servants' wing. Offices and storage space have also been created within the house, necessitating the introduction of additional services and fire escape routes into historic fabric. Even in these areas, attempts have been made to ensure that all works are as reversible as possible and that historic surfaces are retained and protected. In the kitchen and servery areas of the tea-room, historic wall surfaces have been recorded and remain protected behind hygienic, wipe-clean cladding.

The most striking introductions to the house are the replica carpets in the main thoroughfares where the original carpets were most damaged and too fragile to withstand the traffic. These new carpets serve a partly practical and partly interpretative function. They allow free access and give the visitor the chance to experience something of the grand public spaces without the need for rope barriers. They also hint at the original richness of the interiors, without trying to recreate its exact colours (if these could be known), since they copy the brightest surviving colours of the now faded historic carpets. Visitors are also encouraged to contrast the replica carpets with the worn original examples nearby.

There is a need to control the movement of visitors through the building to minimise the damage to historic fabric and for the security of small objects on open display. Here custodians and room stewards have a dual role to help with interpretation while providing security cover. Visitors are guided through the rooms between ropes and stanchions, and in areas where visitors walk across the conserved historic carpets these are covered with protective druggets. The druggets, ropes and stanchions were specially designed for the Hall, and although they are obviously modern, they are made of materials that are sympathetic to the house. The barriers in the family areas of the house are made of crimson rope supported by highly polished wood stanchions, reflecting the heavy mahogany furniture found in these areas, whereas the barriers in the servants' areas are of brown rope supported by light oak coloured stanchions, which reflect the servants' furniture. In some areas they are visually intrusive and they do change the feel of the house, but where there are large numbers of vulnerable small objects on display and very fragile carpets underfoot there is currently no other option. The circulation routes around the house for visitors are designed to give almost complete access for people with impaired mobility as Sylvia Grant-Dalton, who used a wheelchair herself in later life, had a lift installed in the main part of the house. Only the top floor of the servants' wing is not accessible to wheelchair users. The lift itself is of historic interest, as Sylvia had made a collage of pictures and family photographs on the inside of the lift shaft, only visible when the lift passes between floors.

Light levels in historic houses are a constant source of conflict, and Brodsworth is no exception. Meeting the needs of visitors who want to see rooms in bright light and view the garden from the windows, is often at odds with the conservation requirements of the objects. At Brodsworth, all windows have filters to cut out damaging ultraviolet light, and new holland blinds have been installed, and yet light levels are still damagingly high from the huge Victorian windows. The only way we will be able to win the public over to accepting the reduced light levels is by demonstrating how damaging the effects of light can be. We intend to do this by showing examples of light-damaged fabric alongside pieces that have not been subjected to light.

Visitors inevitably want to establish a relationship with the past, not just by seeing it, but by actually touching the historic fabrics and surfaces. It is difficult to deny them the right to do this without explaining that by doing so they will eventually destroy that fabric. We do not want a house littered with signs saying 'Please Do Not Touch', but we do want people to understand why they should not touch. We hope that people come away from Brodsworth with an understanding of some of the processes of decay. At the point of entry, they are given information about the need to protect the collections and some of the causes of damage that can be avoided, such as excessive light and stiletto heels on fragile carpets. There is a board where visitors can look at different types of decay and they can contrast pristine fabrics and surfaces with those damaged by constant wear and tear. The final section of the guidebook explains the way in which Brodsworth was repaired and looks at how the interiors were treated.

The house is open only during the summer season to minimise the hours of exposure to sources of damage. Inevitably, there is some damage caused by the throughput of 50,000 visitors to a house designed as a family home. There is a constant need to monitor wear and tear and to prepare mitigation strategies to achieve a sustainable use of the house as a visitor attraction. Specially trained conservation cleaners complete a daily circuit of the house to keep it clean and to monitor damage from visitors. They are also responsible for ensuring that insect pests are constantly monitored and that the necessary action to control any outbreaks is quickly taken. During the winter months the house is 'put to bed'. This entails a thorough clean and an assessment of the condition of everything in the house. Small items are packed up and larger pieces are covered with dust sheets, each with a large label to enable easy identification in the event of an emergency. The closed season also allows any repairs or conservation treatment to be undertaken.

Managing groups of children in a fragile historic environment has its difficulties, but one of English Heritage's statutory duties is education and we are committed to encouraging people to use the house as an educational resource. A Teachers' Guide for the site has been produced which gives a brief introduction to the house and shows examples of how teachers can make the most of a visit. Teachers are encouraged to use the house as a source for learning not just about history but also about many other subjects in the National Curriculum. There is an education room which can be booked by educational groups for use during weekday mornings while the house is closed to other visitors. It not only contains information about the house and the people who lived there, but also gives children information about the conservation of the building and the collections. There are examples of the materials used and albums of photographs showing how the work was done. During normal opening hours the education room is open to all visitors.

The Brodsworth project has been judged a success, not only in terms of the pioneering conservation work but also in the eyes of its visitors, which was demonstrated recently by its placing as Best Overall Property in the NPI National Heritage Awards 1997. This consistent achievement of high standards across all the key areas is due to a genuine commitment on the part of all the staff, who are working towards a shared vision for the site.

Conclusion

The over-riding aim of the Brodsworth project was to preserve the tangible remains of the Victorian house, complete with the many layers of changes made by later generations whilst at the same time making it available to the public. Ironically, there has been more intervention during the conservation programme than it saw in a hundred years of life as a family home, but its future has been assured. It has been transformed and given a new role as a historic resource and a visitor attraction to enable it to survive. Arguably, nothing authentic remains and what we now have is a contemporary representation of the past created by conservation professionals. We have accepted this and have attempted to incorporate it in our interpretation of the site. All stages in the conservation process are apparent and open to challenge, and we have attempted to empower rather than dominate the

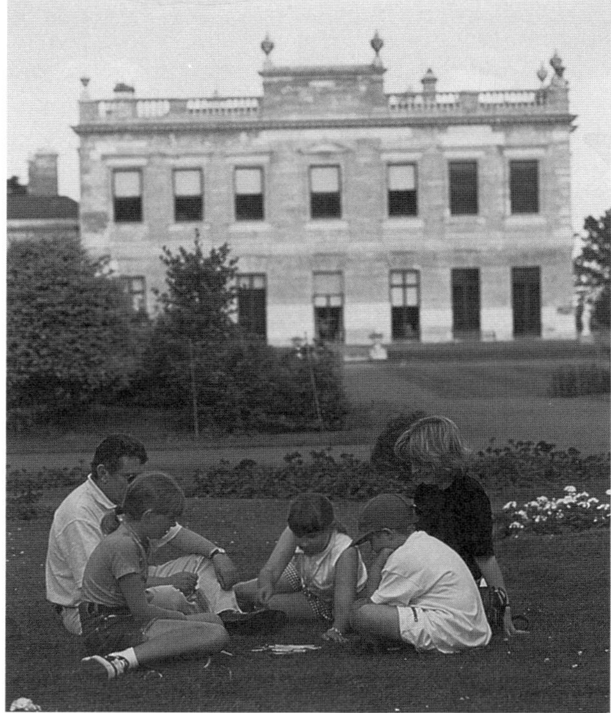

Figure 8.4 Visitors enjoying the formal gardens

Source: English Heritage Photographic Library

visitor, acknowledging the subjectivity of the processes and making them visible to others. Visitors are encouraged to think about the past and to consider how they relate to it. The past is a cultural resource that belongs to everyone, and as Robert Hewison has remarked, it is 'not the past that matters as such, but our relationship with it' (Hewison 1987).

The strategy for Brodsworth's long-term survival is based on collaboration. Our stakeholders are many and varied, ranging from academic researchers to those wanting a good day out. A sustainable future for Brodsworth is dependent on our ability to serve these different people, managing the conflicts and balancing the needs of each group with the need to preserve the property for future generations.

■ ■ ■

Acknowledgements

I would like to thank the staff at Brodsworth for their help with this chapter.

References

Babbington, C. and Hughes, H. (1992) 'Conservation of the painted decoration at Brodsworth Hall', *English Heritage Conservation Bulletin: Scientific and Technical Review Supplement* 1, 3–6.

Berkouwer, M. and Church, D. (1993) 'Textiles at Brodsworth', *English Heritage Conservation Bulletin* 19, 12–14.

Brereton, C. (1995) *The Repair of Historic Buildings: Advice on principles and methods*, 2nd edn, London: English Heritage

Fidler, J. (1993) 'Fire Protection Measures', *English Heritage Conservation Bulletin* 21, 20–1.

Fidler, J. and McCaig, I. (1992) 'Disaster mitigation for historic buildings', *English Heritage Conservation Bulletin: Scientific and Technical Review Supplement* 1, 8–10.

Girouard, M. (1963) 'Brodsworth Hall', *Country Life,* October 3 and 10.

Girouard, M. (1971) *The Victorian Country House*, Oxford: Clarendon Press.

Girouard, M. (1985) 'A Victorian Masterpiece at Risk', *Country Life,* October 24.

Heritage Lottery Fund (1998) *Conservation Plans for Historic Places*, London: Heritage Lottery Fund.

Hewison, R. (1987) *The Heritage Industry*, London: Methuen.

Jervis, S. (1997) 'Far From Uniform', *S.P.A.B. News* 18, no. 4, 12–15.

Kerr, J.S. (1996) *The Conservation Plan: A Guide to the Preparation of Conservation Plans for Places of European Cultural Significance*, Sydney, Australia: National Trust of Australia.

Riddle, G. (1994) 'Visitor and user-services', in R. Harrison (ed.) *Manual of Heritage Management*, Oxford: Butterworth-Heinemann.

Thorneycroft, J. (1993) 'Windsor Castle Fire', *English Heritage Conservation Bulletin* 19, 32

Whitworth, C. (1995a) *Brodsworth Hall,* London: English Heritage.

Whitworth, C. (1995b) 'Remembrance of things past', *English Heritage Conservation Bulletin* 27, 3–4.

Chapter 9

TIME TO 'LEAP THE FENCE'
Historic Parks and Gardens

Krystyna Campbell

'He leaped the fence and saw that all nature was a garden . . . ' (quoted in Hadfield 1960). These famous words written by Horace Walpole describe William Kent's breakthrough which, in terms of the English landscape, was equivalent to Archimedes' revolutionary discovery when bathing. William Kent (1685–1748) was a painter; his patron was Lord Burlington. It was Kent who realised the importance of the surrounding English landscape which, if thoughtfully adorned with architectural ornament, could be seen as the living, English equivalent of the classical landscape compositions portrayed by landscape painters like Claude (1600–82) and Poussin (1615–75) (see Hussey 1967a). Kent himself did comparatively little new garden design, in the main reworking the designs of others. What was important about his activity, however, was the new perspective that he brought to the existing highly formal styles of garden and landscape which were strictly delimited by strongly contrived boundaries.

In parallel, all the boundaries of more than 400 ancient monuments and historic houses of national importance in the care of English Heritage have been delimited very tightly. When taken into government care – or guardianship – the boundaries of the monuments were often drawn so that only the known standing or buried structures were preserved. In the past, there has been relatively little awareness of their setting within the wider landscape. Contemporary appreciation of their value stemmed directly from an 'antiquarian' approach, where recording and archaeological investigation were the basis of understanding a site's history and the development of the property. Thus at many sites today, the approach in presentation and interpretation frequently starts from the perspective of the building or monument itself. There is a need to 'leap the fence' that defines the accepted curtilage of preservation and protection around these sites and to examine them in their surrounding landscapes. Doing this can aid or even redefine the basis of the presentation of a site, so that a monument is seen in a social, artistic or economic context and not as an isolated survivor (see Williamson 1995 for the political and economic aspects of the importance of certain landscapes).

Such an approach is critical where designed landscapes or parklands are concerned. The problem does not relate to properties in state guardianship alone, for many buildings are alienated from their associated landscapes through separate ownership or through differing management regimes which obscure their relationship. The problem is exemplified at English Heritage properties, however, and is the more acute in the case of important houses, or ruins of houses, deemed to be of national importance where, on acquisition for the nation, associated gardens or land were frequently disregarded and the property acquired was limited to the immediate vicinity of the buildings or monuments. This has sometimes been the consequence of the limitations imposed in the difficult process of compulsory acquisition. In other cases, guardianship has been applied to ruined castles or abbeys to ensure their continued survival, although their associated picturesque, eighteenth-century landscapes have gone unrecognised for their own intrinsic value. The majority of these land holdings continue to be managed by private individuals without reference to the focal picturesque or romantic ruins integral to them. The relationship between the historic buildings, the focus of landscape views and vistas, or the inter-visibility of sites has been lost.

This approach has led to the majority of historic properties in public ownership being 'isolated' from their surrounding lands and original contexts. In turn, these lands may be in multiple private ownership, so that the management of once uniformly designed and managed areas are disrupted, for example, by the intrusion of fence lines between arable, the positioning of new woodlands, and the subdivision or loss of pasture. New ownership boundaries may disrupt views, original drives and access routes, and neighbouring new development may intrude and further fragment the landscape. Public access to sites is limited to formally negotiated routes that are not always historic routes, and thus the original design concept for public appreciation of the composition may be limited or hindered.

At all sites, land-uses within the parks have changed. The problem has been exacerbated by alterations resulting from modern farming practices, which have frequently been to the detriment of designed parkland. A change from pasture to arable not only alters the nature of the landscape but, with unsympathetic management, trees are frequently lost through plough damage, hedgerows can be uprooted and farm buildings sited unsympathetically.

The Register of historic parks and gardens

Since 1986, English Heritage has been empowered to compile the *Register of Parks and Gardens of Special Historic Interest*, which identifies parks and gardens that are of national or international historic significance. The main purpose of the *Register* is to draw attention to the best historic parks and gardens, and in doing so to encourage and help authorities to appreciate, maintain and enhance sites, whilst providing adequate protection for them. Whilst all sites on the *Register* are considered to be of special historic interest, their individual importance varies. Like historic buildings (see Chapter 11, pp. 158–60), each site is accorded a grading, as a comparative assessment, dependent on a knowledge of their landscape history. Sites of exceptional historic interest are assessed as grade I, those of great historic interest as grade II*, and those of special historic interest as grade II. Of over 1,250 sites on the *Register* to date (1998), 10 per cent are classed as grade I, 30 per cent as grade II* and the remaining are grade II.

Table 9.1 shows thirty-five historic properties on the *Register* that are in the care of English Heritage, together with some additional sites known to lie within historic designed landscapes. They have been included because they were houses set in parkland, or sites that were incorporated into parkland (as at Waverley Abbey). In each case, their architectural and archaeological history is strongly linked with their surrounding designed landscape. By divorcing the two, the important relationships between the landscape and the building are ignored. By concentrating the available but scarce resources into the conservation of historic buildings, landscapes may be pushed further into decay and may consequently be more vulnerable to development.

Table 9.1 English Heritage properties on the *Register of Historic Parks and Gardens of Special Historic Interest*

Grade I	*Grade II**	*Grade II*	*Unregistered Parklands*
Audley End	Bolsover	Acton Burnell	Bishop's Waltham
Belsay Hall	Kenwood	Appledurcumbe	South Wingfield
Chiswick House	Kirby Hall	Battle Abbey	Sutton Scarsdale
Hardwick Hall	Marble Hill	Bayham Abbey	Waverley Abbey
Rievaulx Terrace	Osborne	Bishop Auckland	
Studley Royal	Roche Abbey	Boscobel House	
(Fountains Abbey)	(Sandbeck Park)	Eltham Palace	
Wrest Park	Sherborne Castle	Gorhambury	
	The Grange	Hill Hall	
	Wardour Castle	Kenilworth Castle	
	Witley Court	Lulworth Castle	
		Rufford Abbey	
		Wenlock Abbey	
		Walmer Castle	

The value of designed landscapes

Designed landscapes are as important historically and archaeologically as ancient monuments or buildings. In themselves they can, by their very design, express the political and social attitudes of their owners and designers, as well as containing more purely functional elements of agricultural and economic patterns of exploitation. They are important elements of the historic landscape because they document people's changing attitudes towards their environment. Their importance extends into wider landscape considerations involving aesthetics, appreciation of the surrounding countryside and the variety of habitats found, with their associated ecological and wildlife values.

Agricultural/silvicultural systems

The modern landscape reflects past patterns of agricultural management and silvicultural (woodland) systems. At some sites, the layout and make-up of the landscape are themselves of importance to the interpretation of the monument, for example the monastic landscape at Rievaulx Abbey with its field patterns, woodlands and fishponds. The development of the landscape at Belsay Hall over a period of some six centuries is complex, from its medieval origins as a fourteenth-century castle, subsequent development as a manorial centre until its culmination as one of the most important neo-classical houses in Britain set out amidst extensive gardens and parkland. At each period, the existing landscape influenced the decisions made in remodelling or managing land, a point that can sometimes be discerned only through studies that reveal the earlier antecedents of a design.

Landscapes of association and memory

A number of the properties are the remains of earlier buildings that were incorporated as focal features into a designed landscape because they were valued for their historic associations. These are frequently defensive or monastic sites, historically significant and revered as the remnants of previously established orders. Monastic ruins set in picturesque layouts served as memorials of the Dissolution. The ruins of castles reminded Royalist families of the political and social upheavals of the Civil War and the loss of Kingship. Some significant examples managed by English Heritage include the ruins of Fountains Abbey, which were incorporated as the culmination of a natural and picturesque experience begun by John Aislabie at Studley Royal. Imaginative use of vistas and viewpoints make use of both Fountains Abbey and distant Ripon Cathedral in a picturesque and Romantic landscape. Similarly, the ruins of Rievaulx Abbey inspired the making of the hilltop Terrace at neighbouring Duncombe Park in 1745–58. The remains of fourteenth-century Old Wardour Castle became incorporated into the views seen from the New Wardour Castle built to the north-west in 1770, designed by James Paine.

Their significance lay beyond pure Romanticism, however, and made a contemporary political point: the castle had been defended with heroic courage by Blanche, Lady Arundell, who, with a household of only twenty-five, withstood a siege of 1,300 strong Parliamentary forces in May 1643 for eight days.

All this highlights the importance of a sense of place and an appreciation of the continuity and significance of the local landscape and tradition. In the main, with the passage of time, our increasingly urban-centred population has lost touch with the meaning and significance of these landscapes. The need to extend and foster their appreciation and understanding is one of the main challenges faced.

The antiquarian approach and picturesque landscapes

The eighteenth-century landscape movement, which gave rise to many of the important designed landscapes recognised in the *Register*, grew out of an earlier interest in antiquities in the countryside ranging back to William Stukeley's activities. Currently, amidst a wide range of archaeological and academic interests centred on Stonehenge, few realise the status of Stonehenge within the group of 'antiquarian' curiosities engrossed or built into the landscape at Amesbury Abbey, Wiltshire, in the early eighteenth century. There, a complex geometry of rides through a wooded area are aligned with Gays Cave, built into a steep hillside; Vespasian's Camp was included in the landscape after being acquired in 1734, and from the highest point of a wooded area on the west side of the landscape, views over to Stonehenge were included. Victorian photographs of the Amesbury Estate include views of Stonehenge.

In the distant, and not so distant, past, ruined sites were often plundered for architectural fragments. Netley Abbey, near Southampton, a ruined Cistercian Abbey and one of the latest to be founded in England, was relieved of parts of its north transept in 1770. It was re-created at Cranbury Park, Hampshire, by Thomas Lee Dummer. Erected as a sham ruin and christened 'The Castle', the north transept now functions as an eye-catcher in his picturesque landscape creation. Dummer is also known to have managed the woodland around and inside the Abbey ruins. From the mid-eighteenth century onwards, Netley was a frequent stop for those on a picturesque tour; it was used as the subject for painting, poetical and lyrical prose compositions (Sambrook 1980). This culminated with an opera composed by William Pearce and performed at Covent Garden in 1794. The management of the landscape around the ruin at this period is significant, for it effectively created an atmosphere and strong sense of mystery. This is in striking contrast to later management, which sees a different approach to the control and presentation of the landscape, arising from purely archaeological and architectural considerations, with the need to control a *cordon sanitaire* of mown grass around the ruins. Although Netley Abbey is not registered as a 'designed' landscape, it is important in the development of the picturesque landscape tradition. It is a major example of how antiquarian and picturesque attitudes blended together and influenced appreciation of landscapes.

Allegorical landscapes

Of equal challenge is the presentation of some of the experiences that owners and designers of landscapes aimed to induce in spectators and visitors. Without doubt, the visitors to many of our great eighteenth-century designed landscapes were led through a contrived design piece calculated to give an 'experience' far removed from the modern 'visitor experience' today. The set route that had to be followed at Stourhead revealed an allegory, where a series of classical references set in inscriptions, direct views, the grotto, urns, buildings and statuary relate to incidents in Virgil's *Aeneid* (see Hussey 1967b). This idea of infusing a landscape with meaning can also be seen in later periods, as at Mellor's Gardens, Cheshire, where in the mid-nineteenth century, the visitor could trace Christian's journey to the Celestial City in *Pilgrim's Progress* (Turner 1987).

Parkland landscapes

A basic theme within traditional parkland landscapes is that the viewer's sight of the main house at the focus of the landscape was controlled from the moment of entrance, until a view was opened up as a surprise. With the original entrances and formal approaches in separate ownership, it can be difficult to re-establish the eighteenth-century experience of anticipation, surprise and approach connected with the passage through a designed parkland.

Other routes led around, delighting the eye with grand vistas, terrifying heights, dark groves, grottoes or tunnels – it was the physical and emotional senses that were as much part of the experience as the visual and aesthetic. Where the traditional conservation perspective relating to the major building on the site prevails, by concentrating on an archaeological and architectural study of its features, these more ephemeral aspects will more easily be lost. With our modern concerns relating to health and safety issues, commercial and transport needs, these are aspects that are increasingly difficult to accommodate or are frequently ignored in site presentation.

The design piece

Although historic buildings are important architectural designs in themselves, if presentation of them is completely divorced from their designed landscapes, the authenticity of the original concept and composition can be lost. It is inappropriate if these historic buildings and ancient monuments, recognised as nationally important, are not considered alongside the surrounding countryside and landscape valued by earlier generations. It is even more drastic where the landscape, gardens and historic buildings are all parts of a significant architectural composition, and each is an integral component. The traditional view of the 'buildings as the focus and landscape as the context' can serve to debase the architectural value of the whole.

The most striking and contrasting examples of design compositions among the English Heritage properties on the *Register* are Northington Grange and Witley Court. They contrast with one another in that at one property the parkland is integral to the design importance of the place, and at the other it is the gardens. At The Grange, Northington, Hampshire, the grade I classical mansion was taken into guardianship in 1974, in recognition of its outstanding importance in the neoclassical revival. In 1805, William Wilkins (1751–1815) was commissioned by Henry Drummond to remodel an eighteenth-century house that had originated as a seventeenth-century hunting lodge, encasing it with immense porticoes. The positioning and effect of the resulting 'Temple' was accentuated by placing it on a formal, high podium. These steep, stone-dressed terraces cut out of the ground fell sharply down to a series of lower terraces. Slightly later, in the 1820s, C.R. Cockerell added a Corinthian portico, a large conservatory and other alterations in the classical style by Wilkins. He constructed a formal terraced garden with fountains and balustrades. Cockerell's diary for May 1823 describes the scene:

> A steady sunshine upon the building, as clear a sky, the lights and shades and reflections, as to Greece, the rocks and jackdaws in the lime tree avenue sailing and cawing in the air brought home recollections of the Acropolis, the bussing of the blue flies and flowers something of the aromatic scent of Thyme, nothing more satisfactory than the line of the terrace building terminated by the two great piers, the gravel walk beneath the sloping bank, the inclination to the water and tufted trees, fine and more luxuriant than ever on the banks of the Illissus.
>
> (Quoted in Land Use Consultants 1987)

Although The Grange, when remodelled, was set within an existing mature park, Drummond extended it and laid out further sections during the mid-1800s; open fields were laid out to pasture and groves of trees were planted. Contemporary illustrations and written accounts show the house sitting within its classical landscape. There can be no doubt of the original classical inspiration in architectural terms, which can still be appreciated today. This Greek temple should, however, sit within an Arcadian landscape, also originally part of Drummond's concept, for he was responsible for planting cedars near to the lake and at focal points around the mansion.

The important landscape structure of the planting belts, lake, parkland trees and copses with accent planting, form the composition integral to the designed 'set piece' embracing both building and landscape. The area taken into guardianship, however, lies tightly around the mansion, whilst the important landscape integral to Drummond's concept lies outside the curtilage. The Victorian ornamental flower gardens, which have not survived, are not fundamental in themselves to the intrinsic architectural concept and important composition. Whilst in general the condition of many historic parks or gardens is slowly deteriorating, some, as at Northington, have now reached a critical point that makes their survival as recognisably 'designed'

Figure 9.1 The Grange, Northington: main facade from north of the lake, late nineteenth-century view

Source: Krystyna Campbell

landscapes unlikely (Figures 9.1 and 9.2). This will be a loss to the heritage, the more poignant as it is avoidable, for replanting and lake dredging could still be undertaken within modern economic management. The large capital costs remain the obstacle.

This contrasts with Witley Court, where the landscape is included on the *Register* in recognition of important work by one of the most influential garden designers during the mid- to late nineteenth century, William Andrews Nesfield (1794–1881). As at Northington, the house is in guardianship and conserved as a ruin; it has been open to the public since 1990. Although ruined, the mansion still retains its grandeur and an imposing presence. It is listed as a grade II* historic building as well as being scheduled as an ancient monument, and the gardens and surrounding parkland are registered grade II*. There is no public access to the parkland, which is now mainly arable, but which in part contains earlier field systems and a Jacobean parkland layout. Within the guardianship area protected and managed by English Heritage, there remains the 'ruins' of the garden laid out by Nesfield (Evans 1997).

These gardens were designed to be a 'perfect foil to the Italianate mansion, encompassing the south and east fronts of the house. The grandest design was to the south, where a flight of steps with a curved balustrade led down from Nash's portico' (Evans 1997). The ruins of the mansion as seen today are the remains of the grand mansion remodelled by Samuel Whitfield Daukes (1811–80) for William

Figure 9.2 The Grange, Northington: main facade with remnants of cedars, 1984

Source: Krystyna Campbell

Humble Ward, first Earl of Dudley, and designed in the Italianate style made fashionable during the late 1840s by the royal works at Osborne, Isle of Wight. Due to the inclusion of this relict formal garden in the guardianship area and within their control, English Heritage is able to conserve and repair the structural elements of the gardens, to complement the ruins themselves. In terms of its historic landscape significance, the parkland at Witley Court is not as significant to the composition as is the parkland at Northington, whilst the gardens are. The Grange and Northington park together were an Arcadian ideal exemplified in the English countryside, whilst Witley Court and its gardens epitomised the *joie de vivre* of the more eclectic Victorian garden.

Repair and restoration schemes

The designed landscapes we have inherited date from different periods. Just as with historic buildings, careful decisions have to be made about the emphasis that should be given to different phases and how historical and landscape considerations can be reconciled with ecological, current economic or practical concerns (Forestry Commission n.d.). It is rarely possible, let alone desirable, to repair and restore a landscape to one particular period, for landscapes evolve and were seldom laid out completely without reference to existing or previous features. There can be no standard prescription for the repair of a historic park or garden, but broad principles can be applied to generate a suitable solution for a particular problem.

The principal problem facing the specific sites in English Heritage's care, as well as many sites in private ownership, arises where multiple ownership of these landscapes exists, resulting in different forms of landscape management and control. This can be detrimental to the presentation of the site, to the preservation of the designed landscape and to the complex of experiences that were meant to be associated with visiting them. In order to secure the resources needed for their repair and management, there must be a strategy that unites the separate landowners, managers and decision makers who are responsible for the different parts of these once unified sites.

Restoration schemes have an important part to play in establishing well-balanced strategies that are sustainable in the longer term. Experience has proved the value of preparing restoration management plans for historic designed landscapes, especially where private estates and landowners are involved. They can present a comprehensive and integrated approach to the repair and management of the historic landscape based on survey, assessment and the definition of aims and objectives. By providing a more balanced and considered framework for the treatment of the historic landscape, benefits of investment and the implications for future management and maintenance can be judged objectively.

The methodology used in preparing a landscape restoration and management plan relies heavily on an initial stage of survey and assessment. A series of specialist studies covering the archaeological and historical development of a site, a field survey covering the location and survival of features, the site ecology and current land-uses, including public access, and the planning contexts provide the base data needed to discern what survives, and its condition, and enables its importance to be evaluated. Indeed, this type of 'conservation plan' approach – which starts with assessing why a historic place is significant and how that significance may be vulnerable to change – is rapidly becoming a prerequisite for conservation programmes in all aspects of the historic environment (Kerr 1996; Heritage Lottery Fund 1998).

A restoration management plan serves to highlight the specific factors of importance that need attention. Thus, any available finance or management measures may be given consideration directly related to the priorities raised. The diversity of sites, their condition and special site-specific factors do dictate that a brief for the preparation of a restoration management plan is imperative, and that this should be tailor-made to each site. The state of knowledge regarding the survey material is varied, and as the amount and level of information required will vary, so will different levels of specialist surveys be needed.

A co-ordinated approach

Provided that owners agree on the objectives of preparing such a plan, it provides a useful forum for discussing disparate issues and concerns. Careful negotiation and decision can result in a restoration and management plan that embraces diverse interests, establishing common interests and concerns to the benefit of all the landowners. Consequently, the landscape may benefit if adjacent landowners who control it can use their limited resources to agreed and common objectives. An effective restoration plan will enable a designed landscape to be managed once again, within an agreed and unified strategy.

Unfortunately, whilst many examples of repair and restoration plans, or of management plans, exist for designed landscapes in single ownership, it proves harder to provide examples where they are a vehicle for joint decision making, and an agreed management regime. Although this plan-based approach, based on research, survey and analysis, has now become an accepted prerequisite for historic landscape conservation, it has still to prove its maximum potential in providing the framework for the conservation of landscapes in multiple ownership.

Nevertheless, some examples do exist, and where these have been based on thorough research and survey they have been successful in effective conservation. At Staunton Country Park, near Havant, Hampshire, a local authority partnership was formed in conjunction with other key stakeholders such as Portsmouth Water Authority, who had acquired a major part of Leigh Park, a historic parkland, as a future reservoir. The Country Park was formed out of all the historic estate as well as surrounding fields and woods. Registered grade II*, the park also has eleven listed buildings and structures, and lies within a Conservation Area. This joint partnership has been successful in uniting the interests of the two local authorities within which the park falls and in funding a restoration programme.

The design and layout of the estate was the personal vision of Sir George Staunton and has survived largely untouched by subsequent owners. The pleasure grounds, with walks, specialist gardens, follies and buildings, all centred around Sir George Staunton's life and achievements. Had the partnership not been formed and the restoration project not started, there is little doubt that further parcels of the land would have been developed. The pleasure grounds and part of the parkland, which had been retained for public recreation grounds, would have seen a steady growth of formal, recreation facilities that would have evolved at the expense of a more rural landscape. Without doubt, the traces of Staunton's design would have deteriorated further.

The National Trust as landowners find themselves in a more fortunate position regarding land management and ownership. Frequently, bequests have included the major tracts of a designed landscape. In recent years, the Trust have made considerable advances in restoring areas of parkland that had been put into profitable arable production. A prime example of their approach is at Ickworth, where the whole of the South Park was ploughed up post-war. Hundreds of trees between the River Linnet and the parkland perimeter, which was formed by woodland belts, were removed. Currently, this is being reversed and, with the assistance of incentives over a ten-year agreement through the Countryside Stewardship scheme (run by the Farming and Rural Conservation Agency on behalf of MAFF, and see

Grenville 1999), this area of the park is being returned to grazing. Although this does not involve the co-ordination of multiple owners, it does involve tenant farmers. The objectives of the landscape restoration plan rely, for their successful implementation, on finding a tenant farmer sympathetic with the objectives and aims. These must be understood and farming practices harnessed to the landscape objectives (Grenville 1999).

Repair and restoration or reconstruction and restoration-in-spirit?

'Repair', in conservation terms, expresses the intention to safeguard the survival of important features within important landscapes. This may include like-for-like replacement or the reinstatement of vanished features, but these aspects of restoration remain distinct from speculative reconstruction or recreation. It is important to recognise the distinction, as this will have a bearing on the presentation and interpretation of a site. At Witley Court, extensive examination of the historical sources combined with archaeological investigation can enable repair of the Nesfield design, with its carefully considered spatial layout and the integral structural elements of the paths, ground-modelling, grass areas and parterres (Figure 9.3). More difficulty comes in reinstating the individual planting elements within the design compartments, for over a period of some sixty years the individual plants within elaborate parterre schemes were changed, grew over-mature and were replaced, or reconsidered as horticultural fashion or practical considerations changed.

In contrast to the 'repair' of the Nesfield design, it is not feasible to 'restore' the gardens because of the resources needed for their subsequent upkeep, as well as the fact that they would look incongruous around a ruin. The adopted approach is to reinstate the basic structural elements that form the South and East parterre gardens. This means that components like the paths and areas of gravel, and the topiary and clipped standard trees, which form the design structure of the parterres, will be reinstated. The topiary and specimen plants can be replanted where missing; those that remain, although overgrown, can be pruned back and managed into some semblance of formality. They are important to the scale of the parterres and were used by Nesfield in manipulating the perspective from the house over the great South parterre, which focused on the gigantic Perseus and Andromeda fountain.

The restoration techniques of reinstatement and repair are distinct from 'reconstruction', which often involves speculative replacement. Sometimes the extent of replacement is such that it can be said to constitute re-creation rather than repair. Where reconstruction involves the removal of sound fabric, it can be both undesirable as well as of dubious historical value. Reconstruction is likely to be justified only where records exist to enable replacement on the site of the old, and where the work would bring positive benefits to the integrity of landscape design as a whole.

Restoration-in-spirit, involving the re-creation of gardens with limited knowledge of the original structure, can devalue the genuine historical interest of a site;

Figure 9.3 Witley Court: aerial view looking north showing Nesfield parterres which are integral to the historic importance of the property, October 1993

Source: English Heritage Photographic Library

straightforward maintenance and repair may be preferable. The creation of 'period' gardens, relying on the study of authentic features and flowers from historical texts, illustrations and parallel information from other sites, however, has a role to play in site interpretation and education but lies outside current considerations here (Harvey 1988).

Careful research and survey using a variety of techniques and including field archaeology, as well as historical texts and topographical works, are an essential basis of landscape conservation. It is only by understanding the landscape around our national sites and monuments, and the resource that exists, that we will be able to present and manage them in an appropriate manner. This must involve partnerships between a variety of owners and land managers. The creation of period gardens and restorations-in-spirit, where they are applied to significant historic landscapes, can be justified only as a last resort. Uniting and managing a divided landscape should be a primary objective in heritage management where the landscape is of special historic interest. Just as the hidden fence, or ha-ha, provides an invisible but effective boundary, so partnerships and agreements with common objectives can remove the artificial fences that divide an important building or ruin from its landscape.

■ ■ ■

References

Evans, S. (1997) 'The gardens of Witley Court', in *Witley Court*, London: English Heritage.

Forestry Commission (n.d.) *Forestry Practice Advice Note 3: Woodlands in Designed Landscapes*, Edinburgh: Forestry Commission Environment Branch.

Grenville, J. (ed.) (1999) *Managing the Rural Landscape*, London: Routledge.

Hadfield, M. (1960) *A History of British Gardening*, London: John Murray.

Harvey, J. (1988) *Restoring Period Gardens*, Princes Risborough: Shire Garden History.

Heritage Lottery Fund (1998) *Conservation Plans for Historic Places*, London: Heritage Lottery Fund.

Hunt, J.D. and Willis, P. (eds) (1975) *The Genius of the Place: The English Landscape Garden 1620–1820*, London

Hussey, C. (1967a) *The Picturesque: Studies in a Point of View*, London: Cass.

Hussey, C. (1967b) *English Gardens and Landscapes 1700–1750*, London: Country Life.

Kerr, J.S. (1996) *The Conservation Plan: A Guide to the Preparation of Conservation Plans for Places of European Cultural Significance*, Sydney, Australia: National Trust of Australia.

Land Use Consultants (1987) *The Grange. Summary of the Historical Review of the Gardens and Parks*. Unpublished report to English Heritage.

Sambrook, A.J. (1980) 'Netley and Romanticism', in *Netley Abbey*, DoE handbook, London: HMSO.

Turner, A.C. (1987) 'Mellor's Gardens', *Garden History* 15 (2), 157–66.

Williamson, T. (1995) *Polite Landscapes: Gardens and Society in Eighteenth Century England* London: Sutton.

Chapter 10

PRESERVATION, RESTORATION AND PRESENTATION OF THE INDUSTRIAL HERITAGE
A Case Study of the Ironbridge Gorge

Marion Blockley

Introduction to the issues

The Ironbridge Gorge provides a fascinating case study in the development of conservation and presentation philosophy over the past thirty years. The international significance of Great Britain's role as the first industrialised nation was symbolised by the inscription of the Ironbridge Gorge on the World Heritage list in 1986. The pioneering work of the amateur industrial archaeologists of the 1950s (Rix 1955), and the demolition of Euston Arch and other iconic industrial structures in the early 1960s, generated a wave of concern for the protection of the industrial heritage (Raistrick 1972). This culminated in the impassioned plea by Michael Rix to establish national parks of industrial archaeology, in which he stated that 'Ironbridge Gorge is a prime candidate for such a designation' (Rix 1964). This sense of urgency to conserve the physical evidence of early industry, however, led to an over-emphasis on the concept of the industrial monument. One of the main criticisms that has been levelled at the practice of industrial archaeology by historians and archaeologists alike is that it has been substantially descriptive rather than analytical, without a broader research agenda regarding the origins and social and economic effects of industrialisation (Riden 1973; Trinder 1982; Gould 1995, Palmer and Neaverson 1995, 1998). Henry Hodges in *Artefacts*, his classic text on the history of technology, makes the following disclaimer: 'the study of technology must always be, to the archaeologist at least, of secondary importance, for a history of technology, no matter how complete, cannot pretend to describe more than a single aspect of mankind' (Hodges 1971, 13).

Despite an apparent lack of protection until recent years, there is an embarrassment of riches of resources surviving from the last 250 years in comparison, for example, with the material culture of the entire prehistoric or early medieval periods. Uniquely, the industrial heritage resource also includes documentary footage, company archives and the testimony of the surviving workforce to illuminate and inform our understanding of industrial processes and working practices. The lack of a clear research agenda has, until recently, hampered a strategic approach to the selection of buildings, landscapes, townscapes, machinery and other artefacts for conservation and public presentation. Indeed, should our limited resources be more effectively targeted on the preservation of company archives, oral testimony of the workforce, documentary film footage and aerial photographic survey, rather than on the presentation of building shells and entire landscapes of extraction?

For the purposes of this chapter, industrial archaeology and industrial heritage will be taken as referring to the material culture of the last 250 years. There is an argument, however, that without a clearly defined research agenda regarding the social relations and symbolic meanings of the structures and processes of 'industrialisation', the descriptive catalogue of 'industrial monuments' should also include those of the Roman Empire: massive civil engineering projects (Boethius and Ward-Perkins 1970), ironworks (Cleere and Crossley 1985), extractive industries (Burnham 1997), potteries and brickworks. Further, the worldwide development and distribution of techniques of manufacture, such as bronze casting in the prehistoric period, is surely of equal if not arguably far greater significance than the developments of the eighteenth century in Europe (Singer *et al.* 1954–7). Similarly, the remarkable developments in science and technology within early medieval China, some six or seven centuries before the Industrial Revolution of the eighteenth century (Needham 1965), also emphasise the somewhat narrow chronological focus of industrial archaeology in Europe and North America.

From the 1960s onwards, the lobby for the preservation of industrial monuments, without any established criteria for the selection process, led to the preservation of a random sample of industrial buildings, often containing waterwheels and steam engines or associated with key people or events. The relatively recent establishment of research and survey programmes by English Heritage to create national inventories has belatedly made the selection process more representative of the whole range of industries (Cherry 1995; Stocker 1995). There is still an emphasis, however, on the preservation of monuments rather than the scientific study of industrial buildings and structures to learn about their technological and social context. Unlike mainstream archaeology with its various research agendas, industrial structures are largely still viewed as 'objects', icons of early industry. The recent designation of the Ironbridge Gorge Museums amongst the non-national museums housing collections of national significance was dependent on its claim that the structures and monuments of industrialisation were a significant element of its collection (Museums & Galleries Commission 1994; Ironbridge Gorge Museum Trust 1997).

The meaningful analysis of industrial complexes requires the use of archaeological concepts such as function, context and typology. The assumption that form follows function is often used in the development of typologies; industrial structures, however, are particularly susceptible to adaptation according to the availability of capital for investment, market forces or the introduction of new technologies. The current development of listing criteria for industrial buildings attempts to take into account these specific problems (Cherry 1995). The flexibility to apply both scheduling and listing legislation to industrial structures, buildings and landscapes can be very beneficial in protecting machinery *in situ*. The machinery housed within industrial buildings is fundamental to the understanding of industrial processes, and, in the past, listing alone has not provided an effective means of protection for it: often at the point of decommissioning, plant and machinery have been shipped out and sold off for their scrap value. The recent scrutiny of the existing Schedule of Ancient Monuments indicated that industrial monuments had been under-represented in the Schedule, and a national research programme, referred to above, has been implemented industry by industry as part of the Monuments Protection Programme (English Heritage 1995; Stocker 1995). The Nuffield Survey of Ironbridge Gorge carried out by the Ironbridge Institute was a pioneering attempt at a detailed survey of an industrial landscape (Clark and Alfrey 1986, 1987a, 1987b, 1988; Alfrey and Clark 1993). The thematic surveys of listed buildings by the Royal Commission on the Historical Monuments of England (RCHME) have enabled the formulation of new criteria for listing industrial buildings. These now recognise their informational and associative value as well as their aesthetic appeal. The criteria also include the completeness of a site, to enable the context of buildings to be considered as well as evidence for the evolutionary change of buildings.

Conservation Area designation provides a useful measure protecting those industrial buildings and complexes that individually do not merit listing, but collectively are worthy of preservation. Thus outbuildings and boundary walls within the Ironbridge Gorge World Heritage site are protected, within the boundaries of the Conservation Area, by Conservation Area legislation, rather than its status as a World Heritage Site, which currently provides no additional legislative protection. At present, the local planning authority is attempting to establish an Article 4 direction for the World Heritage site to provide it with additional powers of protection (see Ross 1996 for an outline of statutory provisions and policies).

Legislation alone does not provide adequate protection, unless it is effectively administered by central and local government, with the informed, active interest of the local community. The lime kilns along the Wharfage in Ironbridge are a salutary reminder of this point. Despite being designated as a Scheduled Ancient Monument within a World Heritage Site, planning permission was granted by the local planning authority for a bungalow to be built on top of the kilns. By contrast, the building shells of the former lead-mining complex at Snailbeach in the south Shropshire hills were imaginatively protected using Conservation Area legislation (Hampson 1997). The empty, fragmented buildings, scattered amongst the slopes of a bluebell wood, form a romantic if largely unintelligible set of ruins for ramblers and hill walkers. Access to the site has been kept low key so as not to conflict with the needs of the local residents in this remote rural community. Yet ambiguous trail leaflets, inadequate signage and way marking already generate additional confused visitors who trespass inadvertently on private property. Within the Ironbridge Gorge, the blast furnaces at Blists Hill and the Bedlam furnace along the river frontage remain mysterious and unintelligible ruined elements of the landscape for visitors, compared to the enhanced heritage product presented in the museums. Undoubtedly, ruins generate their own sublime romance, yet visitor surveys carried out annually indicate considerable confusion or complete lack of awareness: 'a medieval building' according to one visitor (Horne 1997). The Darby furnace itself in Coalbrookdale is viewed by many as a shrine, or 'the cradle of the industrial revolution'. Yet stripped of its waterwheel and bellows, and shrouded by a massive cover building separating it from its landscape context, its significance remains unrevealed. Undoubtedly the cover building provides a good weatherproof cover for the ruined structure; elsewhere in the Gorge the excavated incomplete structures are vulnerable to water penetration and root or frost damage. Repointing and waterproof caps for the ruined walls allow these structures to be maintained as monuments but add little to their visual appeal or context as a wildlife habitat. A solution adopted in Finland and the USA has been to create a cover building in the style of the original profile of the complete kiln from surviving depictions, incorporating an element of reconstruction and interpretation as well as conservation.

Traditionally, large machines such as steam engines were displayed as sculptural objects in splendid isolation in the science and technology galleries of museums, with no reference to the structures that originally housed them (Horne 1984, 110–15). Whilst an understanding of industrial processes is best provided by working exhibits, the conservation implications of this are considerable. 'Unique' machinery – such as the Newcomen-type engine at Elsecar, for example – may be placed at risk of irreversible damage by demonstration running, whilst heavily restored and repaired machinery can be used for these purposes with less concern about incidental wear and tear. Conversely, some machines and structures, such as kilns or cooling towers, if not used regularly, will suffer permanent damage as a result. Within a museum gallery it is not generally feasible to provide an authentic power source such as steam or water, and working exhibits are usually powered by a quiet, odour-free electrical motor which itself creates a completely false impression. Individual working machines cannot convey the noise and smell of an entire factory floor. Modern health and safety regulations ensure that the working looms at sites like Styal Mill, Helmshore textile mill and Calderdale Industrial Museum are run for only short periods and that demonstrators wear ear protection.

Industrial collections within museums are also particularly difficult to manage because of their sheer bulk. Only relatively recently has the need for a more strategic approach to the development of collecting policies for industrial museums been fully appreciated (Ball and Winsor 1997).

Relocation or preservation *in situ*

Viewed with hindsight, the decisions that have been taken over the siting of the open-air museum of relocated buildings at Ironbridge are of particular interest. When it was accepted that the currently fashionable (in 1965) Scandinavian concept of an open-air museum would be an appropriate choice for the Gorge, the question was where to site it. Two options were put forward. The first was an area of derelict industrial land of low amenity and historical value at Blists Hill at the west end of the Gorge. The second was around 'the cradle of the industrial revolution' at Coalbrookdale itself, where many of the most significant eighteenth-century monuments, workers' housing and ironmasters' houses survived *in situ*. A Colonial Williamsburg scenario was considered, where the historic landscape would be 'socially engineered' to present Coalbrookdale in its eighteenth-century prime. Late twentieth-century buildings, including council houses, which detracted from the 'purity' of the presentation, would be removed, and 'appropriate' eighteenth-century properties would be imported to fill the 'gaps' in the landscape (Madin *et al.* 1965). With hindsight, this is an intriguing prospect and would clearly have led to the destruction of the vibrant community based around the still-functioning Glynwed Foundry, successors to Allied Ironfounders who claim their proud pedigree from the eighteenth-century ironmasters of Coalbrookdale. How different the landscape of Coalbrookdale would have been with tight controls over traffic, signage and access, and controlled ownership of property.

One of the fundamental conservation versus presentation debates that has been addressed over the years at Ironbridge is the choice to relocate monuments and buildings to an open-air museum or to preserve them *in situ*. In the early years of the museum, there was a clearly stated assertion that it was perfectly acceptable to 'cherry-pick' the most significant monuments depicting developments in industrialisation throughout Shropshire and to relocate them to the Blists Hill Open Air Museum (Morton 1968, 41–3). Thus, the value of these surviving structures could be fully realised only when placed within a museum framework to explain the curator's perception of the development of industrialisation. The world's first iron aqueduct, designed by Thomas Telford in 1796 and still situated on the derelict Shropshire Union Canal at Longden-on-Tern, was an item for relocation to Blists Hill. The bridge at Cound, near Cressage on the A458 Bridgnorth to Shrewsbury road, was designed by Thomas Telford. In the late 1960s it was argued that the bridge could no longer support road traffic and should, therefore, be relocated to Blists Hill. Again, fortunately (with hindsight), it remains *in situ* in its original landscape setting and measures are planned to control traffic use. Similarly, the charcoal furnace at Charlcote would have been removed from its remarkably complete south Shropshire industrial landscape context to illustrate the development of ironworking.

The beam engines 'Samson' and 'David', built by Murdoch Aitken of Glasgow for the Lilleshall Company's Priorslee ironworks in 1851 and still active until 1952, were relocated to the original entrance to the Blists Hill Open Air Museum in 1971. They were intended to form the centrepiece of a concourse building at the entrance to the museum, but have remained for the last twenty-seven years beneath the 'temporary' protective canopy built of a steel frame. The removal of 'Samson' and 'David' was very expensive, and would have been much more so had it not been decided to remove the condensers. Without the condensers, it will be impossible ever to steam the engines again, although it should be possible to turn them over by an electric motor. The intention of the curator at that time was to re-erect them in the engine house of the Blists Hill blast furnaces. Unfortunately, they were too large to be accommodated in the existing engine house, and to display them in a truly 'authentic' setting would have involved the building of a new engine house and the relocation of blast furnaces to be blown by the engines. The Museum Trust therefore decided that since the engines could not reasonably be displayed in an authentic setting, they should be separated from the rest of the museum exhibits, where it was hoped to achieve 'a high degree of authenticity' (Trinder 1984). In the cover building, visitors could explore 'Samson' and 'David' at close quarters to admire their Doric ornamentation, to see in detail the mathematical beauty of James Watt's parallel motion, but no attempt was made to suggest that they were working exhibits. It may be viewed as somewhat incongruous that these relocated structures are listed grade II.

The wrought ironworks at Blists Hill Open Air Museum is an interesting example of the dilemma of working exhibits. As an open-air museum of relocated buildings, the potential existed to illustrate authentic working processes, authentically powered. The rolling mill came from the Atlas works in Bolton, the last surviving wrought iron rolling mill in existence. The building housing it is in fact only part of a structure from Woolwich Royal Naval dockyard. The process of the wrought iron rolling is spectacular and dramatic when working, particularly at night. Initially it was envisaged that there would be a market for the wrought iron produced at Blists Hill in restoration projects for historic buildings and structures, such as Clevedon Pier. In practice, it proved impossible to combine the production of wrought iron with the needs of the market. Surpluses accumulated at certain times and the process itself, archaic and perhaps inherently flawed, proved difficult and unreliable to operate on a regular basis, despite optimistic projections (Smith 1979). The costs of regularly operating the machinery as a working exhibit for the general visitor proved prohibitive. Now the exhibit remains static and unintelligible, although the layers of corrosion and dust clothe it with a false air of authenticity next to the *in situ*, authentic and tidily restored, but confusingly Gothic, ruined

Figure 10.1 Blists Hill Open Air Museum: relocated Stirchley school and Sampson & David Beam Engine – appropriate juxtaposition in a convincing environmental context?

Source: Marion Blockley

blast furnace, the early twentieth-century fairground and a relocated Victorian school (Figures 10.1 and 10.2).

As a result, the open-air museum at Blists Hill, in common with other open-air industrial museums, displays working processes with the use of exhibit demonstrators, but on a small-scale, craft level. This, of course, leads to the criticism of nostalgia and sanitisation. The attractive, quaint aspects of craft production are presented at the expense of the reality of the twelve-hour working day in the steelworks, coal-mine or textile mill (Trinder 1984 and 1986; West 1988; Stratton 1996). One good solution to this problem is the approach adopted at the Jackfield Decorative Tile Works, where a commercial business is housed demonstrating the process of producing encaustic tiles, within the former pattern store of Mintons, Maw and Company, adjacent to the Jackfield Tile Museum (Herbert 1979; Stratton 1996).

The Decorative Tile Works at Jackfield Tile Museum is a commercial venture that has the huge benefit of allowing visitors to experience some of the atmosphere, sounds, smells and mess of a real factory rather than merely a museum exhibit. As with all working factory tours, there have to be compromises to accommodate visitor flow and health and safety requirements. The processes

Figure 10.2 Blists Hill Open Air Museum: picnic tables, period fun-fair and *in situ* blast furnace – authentic setting?

Source: Marion Blockley

of manufacturing with production streamlined for efficiency helps the Museum to interpret the 'division of labour' ethic that dictated the original layout of the Craven Dunnill model factory that occupied this site before conversion to the Jackfield Tile Museum. As with the original Victorian factory, production is laid out following a logical progression: clay preparation and biscuit production, including both pressing and slip-casting, are concentrated in Craven Dunnill's original press shop; biscuit firing is carried out next door, where originally tiles were dried prior to being loaded into the coal-fired biscuit kilns; next to this is the decoration area where screen-printing and tube-lining takes place, followed by the final glaze firing. Production is linear, a small-scale version of what originally happened in the factory, progressing from the raw material at one end of the site to the finished product at the other. As a commercial operation, certain activities have to be batched for the sake of efficiency, however, so it is not always possible, for example, for people to see tube-lining. This commercial enterprise enhances people's insight and understanding of the principles fundamental to any large Victorian enterprise, and guides showing visitors around draw attention to the way in which the current commercial operation reflects the original Victorian concept.

Effective presentation of industrial heritage

Why do open-air museums work?

Despite the critiques of cultural historians regarding authenticity, industrial open-air museums like Blists Hill remain popular with visitors. Partly, this is because they aim to recreate an entire 'way of life', using relocated buildings and collections as stage sets for their costumed interpreters. Visitor research carried out by McIntosh at Rhondda Heritage Park indicates that the main motivation for visiting was 'a significant desire to experience past ways of life and work and to retrace industrial heritage, especially that of nostalgic and emotional significance' (McIntosh 1997, 16). It is easy to criticise nostalgia, but it does allow visitors to relate to past and present lifestyles. This recognition of the way in which intellect may be engaged, through emotional responses to sensory perceptions, is fundamental to interpretative theory (Tilden 1957; Ham 1983). Drawing on cognitive theory, Sam Ham identified three principles for effective communication with 'non-captive audiences' – that is people who do not suffer the additional incentive of academic assessment. First, the information presented must be entertaining to retain interest; second, it must be ordered into meaningful 'chunks' so that it is easy to process; and third it must be relevant to them and their own experience (Ham 1983, 12).

Ham agrees with Freeman Tilden (1957), the father of heritage interpretation, that people relate to things that are relevant to them and retain memory of these rather than others. Ham also identified that verbal participation was a significant element in visitor enjoyment. Further participation by observing and doing was even better. These activities are known as 'active' rather than 'passive' learning, and underpin the popularity of the open-air museums using costumed demonstrators. A dialogue with a coherent interpreter involving questions and answers is 'active learning', whereas reading a text panel, guidebook or listening to an audio tour is passive. The former is more likely to be successful and is termed by Hein as 'discovery learning' (1995, 220).

McIntosh's research, partly carried out at Blists Hill, indicated that 72.2 per cent of visitors to industrial heritage sites visit for 'learning related reasons', although only 14.6 per cent came specifically for 'child-related reasons' (McIntosh 1997, 76). She also found that just over half the visitors surveyed at industrial heritage sites came for 'generalist reasons', 'somewhere for a nice day out' or 'sight-seeing', rather than a specific interest in industrial heritage (McIntosh 1997, 11). This has serious implications for the presentation of industrial heritage. These findings are borne out by research into heritage site visitors carried out for the National Trust (BDRC Consultants Ltd 1995).

The use of costumed interpreters at open-air museums like Blists Hill can stimulate the visitors' interest and imagination. It is also *a responsive mode of communication* and, done well, can communicate on a series of different levels. It is less effective with large groups where the museum may lose control over some of the interpretations presented (Risk 1994).

The social context of industrial heritage presentation

Industrial heritage museums have been criticised for their focus on nostalgia and failure to engage with contemporary economic realities (Hewison 1987; West 1988). The author has great difficulty acknowledging the tangible benefits of detailed research into industrial archaeology in regions currently struggling with the reality of mass unemployment. Others have criticised the elitist/capitalist interpretation of eighteenth- and nineteenth-century British history. Industrial archaeologists have tended to focus on developments in technology and the processes of industrialisation, emphasising progress rather than negative impacts. At Ironbridge, the curator of Coalport China Museum has gone some way towards addressing these issues with the installation of a social history gallery in a museum of china, displayed in the decorative arts tradition. Certainly, there has been a refocusing of the interpretative themes at various industrial heritage sites and museums over the last few years to look at social reform and the social and economic impacts of industrialisation.

It has been argued, nonetheless, that the revitalisation of former industrial districts, such as the Lace Market in Nottingham (Daniels and Rycroft 1993), has effectively disenfranchised the indigenous workforce. Former industrial areas are regularly recreated to present 'establishment' perspectives and to memorialise elite individuals (Tunbridge and Ashworth 1996). In the London Docklands, Short (1989) describes the tension between 'yuppies' (young urban professionals) and 'yuffies' (young urban failures).

In the past, retention of industrial structures was often a result of local enthusiasm rather than a clear strategic approach. One of the main challenges for the selection of industrial sites for conservation and preservation is the assessment of their long-term maintenance. A purely academic case can be made for the historical significance of many industrial sites and landscapes, but the scale and complexity of industrial sites, landscapes and even whole townscapes make their long-term maintenance particularly costly. Over the last fifteen years, the lobby for conservation and public presentation of the industrial heritage for its intrinsic historical significance has adopted a high profile, citing Ironbridge as a successful model for emulation (Liddle 1989; Butler and Duckworth 1993; Goodall 1993; Ball and Stobart 1996). Market forces dictate, however, and there are clear indications of an over-supply of industrial heritage attractions in the domestic tourist market. How many Ironbridge Gorge-style museums can we realistically expect the tourist market to support? The origins, development and financial model for the Ironbridge Gorge Museum Trust are quite specific and do not necessarily transfer easily to other, less scenic locations.

It is a commonplace amongst conservation professionals that objects and structures seldom retain their original cultural meaning. The uninteresting damp pile of stones and brick under a large glass and steel pyramid viewed from my office window in Coalbrookdale is, for some, literally a shrine to one of the Great Men of the Industrial era. Yet to Abraham Darby and his workforce, the furnace was a tool, and no doubt an uncomfortable workplace. Industrial structures are viewed by many as icons of an innovative industrial past rather than as functional structures in a manufacturing environment, shrouded by dirt, waste and noise and considerable effort. William Lipe, in his seminal and often recycled paper (Lipe 1984; Darvill 1993), defined the various values and historical frames of reference used by academics and conservation professionals; these include cultural, intellectual, psychological and historical frames of reference. Importantly, he referred to the associative or symbolic value of monuments which underpin the criteria for listing. Industrial structures have been selected for preservation by virtue of their association with the pioneering engineers Abraham Darby (I, II or III) or Thomas Telford, or other great heroes such as Richard Trevithick. It is not entirely frivolous to note the apparent absence of great heroines of the industrial age. Where is the public presentation of the significant role of the Darby women in Coalbrookdale or Philippa Walton at the Royal Gunpowder Mills, Waltham Abbey, Essex (RCHME 1994, 31–2)? Industrial structures selected for their associative or symbolic value often tend to be innovative or spectacular at the expense of the typical or representative. Less spectacular sites can still have an informational value as an excellent education resource, but generally this can be fully realised only when the site itself has been augmented by the addition of appropriate interpretative media to make the full informational value accessible (Goodey 1993).

Finally, industrial heritage 'assets' can have an economic value to justify their continued existence in contemporary society as heritage attractions for tourism or with a viable adaptive reuse (Binney *et al.* 1990; Prentice *et al.* 1993; Streeten 1995). The selection of structures for their economic benefit is ultimately subject to aesthetic values. Furthermore, the success of heritage attractions is ultimately bound up with public perception and the acceptance of certain elements of past culture in the contemporary landscape (McIntosh 1997). Sites selected for conservation and preservation *in situ* on the grounds of historical significance often run into financial difficulties, due to a dependence on visitor income. Competition for leisure time is intense, and unless industrial heritage sites are imaginatively presented and their significance revealed in a way that engages with a wide range of varied audiences, their long-term survival is threatened, and the considerable costs of conservation and maintenance cannot be justified. There is a strong case to be made for 'preservation by record' for many large industrial complexes in order to retain their informational value. Furthermore, the importance of company archives, documentary film, oral and photographic records of large industrial complexes prior to decommissioning could be considered a more informative and economically sustainable resource for the retention of information regarding former industrial processes. It is worth noting that the obsession with the survival of original, 'authentic' fabric is a preoccupation of European and North American conservation professionals. In the Asia-Pacific region, it is the continuity of tradition or a set of skills embodied in an individual that is important, rather than retention of original fabric *in situ* (Larsen 1995). Thus individual craftsmen can be designated as national heritage assets for the skills that they retain, whilst total rebuilding of historic timber structures *in situ* is entirely acceptable.

Sites need to be chosen for their continued relevance to the local community. Local enthusiast-driven initiatives have led to the creation of a number of preserved steam railways and stationary steam engines all over the country. They struggle to find the recurrent costs of maintenance, however, unless integrated into local authority economic development strategies (Alfrey and Putnam 1992). It is interesting to note that the original proposal for the creation of an open-air museum at Ironbridge was made to the Dawley (later Telford) Development Corporation, on the grounds that paying homage to their industrial antecedents would improve the corporation's strained relations with the local community (Madin *et al.* 1965). Local authorities frequently select industrial heritage sites as a catalyst for economic regeneration, for exploitation as a tourism product or to enhance local pride (Barker and Harrop 1994; Gold and Ward 1994). The danger in this approach is that local economic development and competition between local authorities drive these choices for development, rather than the intrinsic merit of the site and appropriateness of the development proposed. The intense competition between local authorities has led to duplication of tourism products and stagnation in the market (English Tourist Board 1993; Green 1994; Ball and Stobart 1996).

With the benefit of hindsight, concern is now being expressed about the economic benefits generated by many industrial heritage developments. Inflated claims have been made in support of European Regional Funding applications regarding the creation of employment in former industrial regions. A good example would be the repackaging and selective presentation of the South Wales deep mining industry (Prentice *et al.* 1993). These claims need to be tested against the diversion of capital investment from other activities and allowance made for jobs displaced from other sectors.

Designation of a site as a scheduled ancient monument or listed building does not mean that development as a museum or tourist attraction for public presentation is necessarily, even on a World Heritage Site, the only or the most appropriate conservation option. The site may be so incomplete as to remain unintelligible unless some form of reconstruction or simulation is attempted, whether *in situ*, via computer-generated graphics or a conventional site interpretation panel. Preservation by record may be a more realistic response, or a portfolio of alternative uses may be appropriate. Too many industrial heritage sites have been turned into industrial museums emulating the example of Ironbridge, Beamish or the Black Country Museum (Figure 10.3). All current surveys indicate that visitor levels cannot be maintained and there is an oversupply (de Haan 1997). Furthermore, the influx of National Lottery money for the creation of new capital projects will lead to still further over-supply and market congestion. There needs to be a long-term model for the management of industrial heritage sites, with a clear strategy for their imaginative public presentation and the effective management of visitors.

Figure 10.3 Black Country Museum: relocated buildings, workshops and backyard walls – a convincing environmental context, perhaps 'too authentic'

Source: Marion Blockley

At Ironbridge, this model is currently being developed by the Strategy Group of partner organisations for the World Heritage Site as part of the development of a Management Plan for the World Heritage Site (Interagency Group 1997). The current way forward for the conservation and presentation of the Site is exemplified in the process of creating a workable management plan. Drawing on the principles of the Burra Charter (Australia Icomos), the process moves from a tripartite assessment of the Site's significance, condition and development options, through a stage of stakeholder and interest group review, to the final agreement of a management plan. (For further discussion of this process for the World Heritage Sites at Avebury and Hadrian's Wall, see Chapters 1 and 2 respectively). It remains to be seen how effective this current approach – which aims to place emphasis on cultural significance and value, public consultation and long-term sustainability – will be. No doubt, in thirty years' time, colleagues will be reviewing this approach with benign amusement in the electronic heritage media of the new millennium.

■ ■ ■

References

Alfrey, J. and Clark, C. (1993) *The Landscape of Industry: Patterns of Change in the Ironbridge Gorge*, London: Routledge.

Alfrey, J. and Putnam, T. (1992) *The Industrial Heritage – Managing Resources and Uses,* London: Routledge.

Ball, R. and Stobart, J. (1996) 'Promoting the industrial heritage dimension in Midlands tourism: a critical analysis of local policy attitudes and approaches', in M. Robinson *et al.* (eds) *Tourism and Culture: Towards the 21st Century*, Conference Proceedings – University of Northumbria, Newcastle, September 1996. Sunderland: Centre for Travel & Tourism, 2, 21–38.

Ball, S. and Winsor, P. (ed.) (1997) *Larger and Working Objects: A Guide to their Preservation and Care*, London: Museums & Galleries Commission.

Barke, M. and Harrop, K. (1994) 'Selling the industrial town: identity, image and illusion', in Gold, J.R. and Ward, S.V. (eds) *Place Promotion: The Use of Publicity and Marketing to Sell Towns and Regions*, Chichester: John Wiley.

BDRC Consultants Ltd (1995) *Visiting Houses and Gardens Review for the National Trust.*

Binney, M., Machin, F. and Powell, K. (1990) *Bright Future: The Re-Use of Industrial Buildings*, London: SAVE Britain's Heritage.

Boethius, A. and Ward-Perkins, J.B. (1970) *Etruscan and Roman Architecture*, Harmondsworth: Penguin.

Burnham, B. (1997) 'Roman mining at Dolaucothi', *Britannia* 28, 325–36.

Butler, D. and Duckworth, S. (1993) 'Development of an Industrial Heritage Attraction: the Dunaskin Experience', *Built Environment* 19 (2), 116–36.

Cherry, M. (1995) 'Protecting industrial buildings: the role of listing', in Palmer, M. and Neaverson, P. (eds), pp. 119–24

Clark, C. and Alfrey, J. (1986) 'Coalbrookdale', unpublished Nuffield Survey Report No. 1, Ironbridge: Ironbridge Institute.

Clark, C. and Alfrey, J. (1987a) 'Coalport and Blists Hill', unpublished Nuffield Survey Report No. 2, Ironbridge: Ironbridge Institute.

Clark, C. and Alfrey, J. (1987b) 'Benthall and Broseley Wood', unpublished Nuffield Survey Report No. 3, Ironbridge: Ironbridge Institute.

Clark, C. and Alfrey, J. (1988) 'Jackfield and Broseley', unpublished Nuffield Survey Report No. 4, Ironbridge: Ironbridge Institute.

Cleere, H. and Crossley, D. (1985) *The Iron Industry of the Weald,* Leicester: Leicester University Press.

Daniels, S. and Rycroft, S. (1993) 'Mapping the modern city: Alan Sillitoe's Nottingham novels', *Transactions of the Institute of British Geographers* NS, 18 (4), 460–80.

Darvill, T. (1993) *Valuing Britain's Archaeological Resource,* Inaugural Lecture, Bournemouth University, Poole: Bournemouth University.

de Haan, D. (1997) 'Recipe for success' *Museums Journal* 97 (7), 26–7.

English Heritage (1995) *Industrial Archaeology, a Policy Statement by English Heritage*, London: English Heritage.

English Tourist Board (1993) 'Experience the making of Britain', *Industrial Heritage Year Campaign Evaluation Survey*, London: English Tourist Board.

Gold, J.R. and Ward, S.V. (eds) (1994) *Place Promotion: The Use of Publicity and Marketing to Sell Towns and Regions*, Chichester: John Wiley.

Goodall, B. (1993) 'Industrial heritage and tourism', *Built Environment* 19 (2), 93–104.

Goodey, B. (1993) 'Planning for the Interpretation of the Industrial Heritage', *Interpretation Journal* 54, 5–9.

Gould, S. (1995) 'Industrial archaeology and the neglect of humanity', in Palmer, M. and Neaverson, P. (eds), pp. 49–54.

Green, S. (1994) 'Industrial Tourism: an overview', *Environmental Interpretation: Interpreting Working Industry* 9 (3), 16–17.

Ham, S. (1983) 'Cognitive psychology and interpretation: synthesis and application', *Journal of Interpretation* 8, 1.

Hampson, L. (1997) *Snailbeach Lead Mine: How an unique industrial enclave was formed, survived, then disappeared into obscurity and was then reclaimed*, Dissertation submitted for M.Soc.Sc. in Industrial Heritage, University of Birmingham (Ironbridge Institute).

Hein, G. (1995) 'The constructivist museum', *Journal of Education in Museums*, 16, 21–3.

Herbert, A.T. (1979) 'Jackfield decorative tiles in use', *Industrial Archaeology Review* 3 (2), 146–52.

Hewison, R. (1987) *The Heritage Industry: Britain in a Climate of Decline*, London: Methuen.

Hodges, H. (1971) *Artefacts*, London: John Baker.

Horne, D. (1984) *The Great Museum*, London: Pluto Press.

Horne, M. (1997) *I.G.M.T. Annual Visitor Survey* 1997.

Interagency Group (1997) 'Draft Management Plan for Ironbridge Gorge World Heritage Site', unpublished.

Ironbridge Gorge Museum Trust (1997) *Application for Designation*, January 1997.

Larsen, K. (ed) (1995) Nara conference on Authenticity, UNESCO, ICCROM, Paris: ICOMOS.

Liddle, B. (1989) 'The case for modern industrial tourism', *Area* 21 (14), 405–6

Lipe, W.D. (1984) 'Value and meaning in cultural resources', in H. Cleere (ed.) *Approaches to the Archaeological Heritage*, Cambridge: Cambridge University Press, pp. 1–11.

Madin, J. and Partners (1965) 'A Case for an Open Air Museum Presented to Dawley Development Corporation June 1965', not published.

McIntosh, A. (1997) 'The Experience and Benefits gained by Tourists visiting Socio-industrial Heritage Attractions', unpublished doctoral thesis, Open University, Milton Keynes.

Morton, G.R. (1968) 'The Ironbridge Gorge Museum Trust – Blists Hill Open Air Museum', *West Midlands Studies* 2, 39–44.

Museums & Galleries Commission (1994) *Standards in the Museum Care of Larger and Working Objects: Social and Industrial History Collections*, London: MGC.

Needham, J. (1965) *Science and Civilisation in China*, 4 (2), *Mechanical Engineering*, Cambridge: Cambridge University Press.

Palmer, M. and Neaverson, P. (eds) (1995) *Managing the Industrial Heritage: Its Identification, Recording and Management*. Proceedings of a seminar held at Leicester University in July 1994, Leicester Archaeology Monographs 2, Leicester: School of Archaeological Studies, University of Leicester.

Palmer, M. and Neaverson, P. (1998) *Industrial Archaeology, Principles and Practice*, London: Routledge.

Prentice, R.C. Witt, S. F. and Hamer, C. (1993) 'The experience of industrial heritage: the case of black gold', *Built Environment* 19 (2), 137–46.

Raistrick, A. (1972) *Industrial Archaeology: An Historical Survey*, London: Hodder & Stoughton.

RCHME (1994) *The Royal Gunpowder Factory, Waltham Abbey, Essex: An RCHME Survey, 1993*, London: RCHME.

Riden, P. (1973) 'Post-post-medieval archaeology', *Antiquity* 57, 210–16.

Risk, P. (1994) 'People-based interpretation' in R. Harrison (ed.) *Manual of Heritage Management*, Oxford: Butterworth-Heinemann, pp. 320–30.

Rix, M. (1955) 'Industrial archaeology', *The Amateur Historian* 2 (8), 225–9.

Rix, M. (1964) 'A proposal to establish national parks of industrial archaeology', *Journal of Industrial Archaeology* 1 (3), 184–92.

Ross, M. (1996) *Planning and the Heritage: Policy and Procedures*, London: Spon.

Short, J. (1989) 'Yuppies, Yuffies and the new urban order', *Transactions of the Institute of British Geographers* NS 14 (2), 173–88.

Singer, C., Holmyard, E.J. and Hall, A.R (eds) (1954–7) *A History of Technology*, Oxford: Clarendon Press, 1 (1954), 2 (1956), 3 (1957).

Smith, S. (1979) 'The construction of the Blists Hill ironworks', *Industrial Archaeology Review* III (2), 170–8.

Stocker, D. (1995) 'Industrial archaeology and the Monuments Protection Programme in England', in Palmer, M. and Neaverson, P. (eds), pp. 105–13.

Stratton, M. (1996) 'Open-air and industrial museums: windows onto a lost world or graveyards for unloved buildings?', in M. Hunter (ed.) *Preserving the Past – The Rise of Heritage in Modern Britain*, Stroud: Sutton, pp. 156–76.

Streeten, A. (1995) 'Management and funding for England's industrial heritage' in Palmer, M. and Neaverson, P. (eds), pp. 125–31.

Tilden, F. (1957) *Interpreting Our Heritage*, Chapel Hill: University of North Carolina Press.

Trinder, B. (1982) *The Making of the Industrial Landscape*, London: Dent.

Trinder, B. (1984) 'A Philosophy for the Industrial Open Air Museum', *Proceedings of the Association of European Open Air Museums*, 11th Conference.

Trinder, B. (1986) 'The Open Air Museum as a Reflection of the Industrial Landscape', *Proceedings of the Association of European Open Air Museums*, 12th Conference.

Tunbridge, J.E. and Ashworth, G.J. (1996) *Dissonant Heritage: The Management of the Past as a Resource in Conflict*, Chichester: John Wiley.

West, B. (1988) 'The making of the English working past: a critical view of the Ironbridge Gorge Museum', in R. Lumley (ed.) *The Museum Time Machine, Putting Cultures on Display*, London: Comedia/Routledge, pp. 6–62.

Chapter 11

CONSERVATION OF TWENTIETH-CENTURY BUILDINGS
New Rules for the Modern Movement and After?

Catherine Croft and Elain Harwood

Introduction

The conservation of buildings from the current century is perceived to be difficult and controversial. That is why the topic is included here, though it appears to be so different from the others in this volume. How do we define what is difficult? Our story begins with the first buildings of the Modern Movement, but goes on to encompass a wider range of styles than the unembellished, cubist-inspired blocks of rendered brick and concrete that were defined as the 'International Style' (Hitchcock and Johnson 1932). The conservation movement in Britain has moved ahead of most of those in Europe in recognising the interest of other styles of the period. Whilst the London-based chapter of the international group DoCoMoMo (*Do*cumentation and *Co*nservation of the *Mo*dern *Mo*vement) avow a modernist aesthetic, the buildings for which they have campaigned have ranged from examples of Britain's earliest reinforced concrete structures, from the late nineteenth century, to works of the 1960s and 1970s that might be considered proto-vernacular or 'high tech'. The Twentieth Century Society, which grew out of the British amenity society movement in 1979 as the Thirties Society, was founded with the specific aim of preserving neo-classical and art deco buildings from the post-1914 period, and has since expanded its brief to cover all styles of buildings from the post-1945 era also. This pantheistic approach has been adopted by English Heritage in its research and listing programmes.

This chapter looks at how the process of protecting twentieth-century buildings has developed, what the current situation now is, and where listing policy is going. It recognises that listing is only a first step, based on architectural and historical appreciation, and that a broader philosophy of conservation and repair forms part of the stratagem for the survival of a building thereafter. It also looks briefly at three twentieth-century buildings that have recently been selected for opening to the public, and asks how representative they are of the built heritage. Have they perhaps been chosen because they embody values that we are already happy to assimilate within our cultural heritage, and are there other values and objectives in the built environment whose legacy we should be seeking to preserve and to interpret for a public audience?

The listing process

The first 'lists' were drawn up in 1941 to advise demolition crews which buildings should be shored up and 'salvaged' in the event of an air raid. Such concern reflects a growing enthusiasm for 'olde England' during the 1920s and 1930s – at precisely the time when it was falling victim to the rapid expansion of communications, power generation and suburbia. This romantic enthusiasm for things English can be seen most powerfully in the books, films and art of the 1940s, and it imbued both the content and the style of the Festival of Britain. In these years, there was a consensus for the listing of medieval and Georgian remains, though listing was no guarantee that a building would not be demolished, as was proved by the loss of Philip Hardwick's Euston Arch – built in 1838 and torn down in 1961 despite a grade II listing.

In the 1960s, listing had to handle such massive, technologically advanced – and in their use of alien materials often 'brutal' – Victorian buildings as St Pancras Station and Keble College, Oxford. Nikolaus Pevsner wrote as late as 1968 of the difficulties faced by the Ministry of Housing and Local Government, then responsible for listing, in keeping up with the few historians and enthusiasts who were recommending these buildings:

> The public at large is only just getting over its giggles where Victorian building is concerned. Few still are ready to look with open eyes and open minds, and even the experts who spend their time among buildings of power and elegance have only rarely accepted the duty of seeing and evaluating what is comparatively so near to them in time.
>
> (Pevsner 1968, unpag.)

How tastes change can be summed up by Pevsner's own dismissal, in 1951, of Wallis, Gilbert and Partners' Hoover Factory (1931–5) as 'perhaps the most offensive of the modernistic atrocities along this road of typical by-pass factories' (Pevsner 1951, 130). The demolition of the still more spectacular Firestone factory by the same architects, on an August Bank Holiday as it was about to be listed, prompted the immediate spotlisting of twelve 'art deco' buildings including Hoover, which is now grade II*. The revised *Buildings of England* for the area now accepts that 'forty years on one can enjoy the brash confidence of the façade with more detachment' (Cherry and Pevsner 1991, 191). The 'Thirties' exhibition at the Hayward Gallery in 1979, the reworking of the style by post-modernists such as Piers Gough, and above all television programmes like *Hercules Poirot* have served to make 'art deco' among the most popular and 'collectable' styles of today. The listing and upgrading of 1930s buildings is one of the busiest activities of English Heritage's Listing Branch.

Until 1987, English Heritage could recommend for listing only buildings begun in or before 1939. The first request to list a thoroughly post-war building came in 1984, when the then Thirties Society asked for the listing of the National Union of Mineworkers' building on the Euston Road in an abortive bid to save the remarkable etched glass and sculpture built into it. In 1985, the Welsh Office listed the Brynmawr Rubber Factory at grade II*. In July 1987, threats to James Gowan's Schreiber House in Hampstead, and to Albert Richardson's Bracken House in the City of London, led the government to recognise that building history cannot simply stop. It issued a Statutory Instrument permitting the listing of any building over thirty years old, and the listing of any building over ten years old that was both 'outstanding' and under threat – its age measured from the date when construction commenced. The longevity of some building operations, particularly in the late 1960s, makes this definition an important one. For example, the Alexandra Road Estate, Camden, was first conceived in 1959, was designed in its present form as local authority housing by Neave Brown in 1967, and was finally built only between 1972 and 1978. The term 'outstanding' was defined by English Heritage to mean those top 10 per cent of buildings worthy of listing in grade I or II*; this definition had long been in place for the grant-aiding of buildings. The first post-war building to be listed was Bracken House, ironically an unpopular building with the architectural press when it was erected in 1958 but one that is now recognised for its classical elegance and use of fine materials.

In March 1988, another eighteen buildings were added to the list, including the Royal Festival Hall (1949–51, Leslie Martin, Peter Moro and the London County Council Architect's Department) and Coventry Cathedral (1955–62, Sir Basil Spence). In conjunction with the amenity societies and members of the public, English Heritage had proposed seventy buildings, and to have only eighteen recommendations accepted by Lord Caithness, the Minister of State, was a profound disappointment. Clearly the message that the 1950s was an important period, when Britain's rebuilding programme was among the most spirited in the world, was not getting through to those whom it was most necessary to convince.

Looking at so relatively recent a period also poses questions of research and evaluation. Whilst some buildings were widely published and remain in the public eye, other – often more traditional – buildings were neglected in their day and may now be forgotten. Modern literature is scanty, and the longevity and enthusiasm of some living architects may serve to create their own imbalance. In 1980, Brian Anthony, then head of listing, proposed 'an empirical approach' for the listing of inter-war buildings 'because the thirties period is so unstudied that it is terribly difficult to arrive at critical orthodoxy' (Anthony 1981, 25). This is still more true as one approaches the late 1960s and early 1970s. Yet precisely because we are closer in time, such empiricism is not acceptable, in part because the term itself found such disfavour in the late 1950s; instead the aim has been to provide an informed context for each recommendation. This has led English Heritage to commission its own research, in greater detail than has been attempted before, for the listing of groups of buildings. By setting each recommendation in the context of its building type, with thematic studies of schools, university buildings, churches, public housing and so on, a more rigorous selection and justification can be made. There have been a handful of short publications, and a series of public exhibitions culminated in three shows at the Royal Institute of British Architects (RIBA) in 1996. Before reaching this public domain, all recommendations have to be endorsed by a Post-War Steering Group of specialists in the period, by English Heritage's Historic Buildings and Areas Advisory Committee of well-known architects and historians (or by its parallel Cathedrals and Churches Committee), and by its Commissioners. The process has formed a model for subsequent thematic studies of earlier building types. It has so far paid off: all our recommendations for schools and university buildings were accepted in 1994, and two-thirds of our selected commercial and railway buildings in 1995. In December 1997, four of the five sports buildings recommended were listed. These proposals were for the period up to 1965; work is already beginning on buildings erected thereafter, and on schools and university buildings where we have so far looked only at the years up to 1962.

If listing has always to be one step ahead of popular taste, nowhere has this been more sharply highlighted than with the post-war listing programme. Any such study has first to be educational and encourage popular support for our work. Nevertheless, the last ten years have seen a considerable growth of popular interest in the period; 1950s decorative art and furniture have become extremely fashionable, and there is considerable nostalgia for the Festival of Britain. It has been interesting to watch the increasing enthusiasm now emerging not only for the fashion and collectables of the 1960s but also for its architecture, particularly among those in their twenties, for whom the era is as much part of the historic past as any other.

Differences between the twentieth and earlier centuries

The most fundamental question raised by the conservation of modern buildings is that of uniqueness. Most people presume that modern buildings require a different approach to those of earlier periods, though as more work is carried out this is beginning to be questioned. What are the differences that have to be taken on board?

A useful first step, particularly for large and often repetitive structures such as university accommodation and office buildings, is first to identify what makes them 'special'. This is the philosophy behind English Heritage's recommendation that owners and local authorities prepare management guidelines identifying the most sensitive areas of any building likely to be the subject of an application for listed building consent. This is explained in a free leaflet, and informs a more widely disseminated maxim that listing is about 'managing change' rather than a means of imposing blanket controls on owners and occupiers (English Heritage 1996).

The second issue is that of maintenance. The importance of establishing a maintenance programme for a building from the moment it is completed has been stressed emphatically by Edward Mills, Alan Blanc and others:

> It is often forgotten that buildings need looking after once they have been designed and constructed. Somehow we take for granted that our precious historic cathedrals and churches deserve our care; like the Forth Bridge, medieval structures need constant attention to survive the elements. But what about more recent buildings? Here we tend to overlook the fact that some modern materials like concrete and plastic are liable to decay.
>
> (Lord Palumbo of Wallbrook 1994, viii)

The belief, widely held in the middle decades of this century, that modern materials would be 'maintenance free' has left our generation with not only a repair bill but a disillusionment with these materials because they could not fulfil such wild expectations. Whilst for buildings erected in the 1930s there was a more practical reason for the absence of any building maintenance between 1940 and the mid-1950s, there can be no denying that this legacy of neglect and shabbiness was taken for granted for another three decades.

When English Heritage organised a conference on the conservation of twentieth-century buildings at the RIBA in 1995, Andrew Saint contended that the conservation of modern buildings required an approach subtly different from that established for older structures (Saint 1996). In particular, he identified a change of rhetoric, which emphasised the need to define and preserve *authenticity*, in place of the concept of *truth to materials* established by the Society for the Preservation of Ancient Buildings a century ago. He suggested six potential 'differences' which we find a useful framework for our own ideas:

- numbers of buildings
- technique
- intention
- performance
- viability
- appeal

The closer we look at these perceived differences, the more they can be seen to be ones of degree, rather than of fundamentals. This is especially so when discussing the first on the list.

Numbers of buildings

There are undoubtedly a lot more Georgian buildings than medieval, more Victorian than Georgian, and far more twentieth-century buildings than anything else. The principle of making an increasingly discerning selection was first established for buildings post-dating 1840, which were at first listed with the rigour we now associate with the twentieth century. Related to the reaction to sheer numbers is the uncomfortable realisation that a lot of the key buildings of the twentieth century are physically very large, and may also be very repetitive. The most quoted example of this is public housing, but again this is not a new phenomenon: acres of Georgian terraced houses, and many large hospitals, prisons and barracks, have already been listed. These are all building types that begin in the eighteenth century and multiply in the nineteenth century, but they display many of the characteristics that seem so disconcerting about modern buildings. Despite this, they are accepted as important elements of our cultural heritage.

Technique

Saint identified a philosophical divide between the Ruskinian roots of conservation theory, with its emphasis on preserving a hand-worked surface displaying craft skills, and the machine aesthetic of modernism; but such a development is evolutionary. One can argue that there are classical buildings of the seventeenth and eighteenth centuries where the survival of patina is secondary to that of the legibility of their formal composition, just as there are timber and earth buildings (particularly in other cultures) that withstand constant renewal but remain repositories of traditional techniques. Similarly, there are traditional-looking, brick-clad buildings that hide a modern frame construction, which may be contrasted with buildings that, despite their modern appearance, are built of load-bearing brick, such as the fourteen-storey residential towers at Essex University (Kenneth Capon, 1964–72). In all these cases the need to define and preserve *authenticity* becomes paramount.

The next three criteria of *intention*, *performance* and *viability*, are intrinsically linked.

Intention

An authentic restoration can be defined as one where ‘the original priorities of the building’s authors (all of the building’s authors) are critically heeded’ (Saint 1996, 20). These sometimes plural and contradictory intentions are comparatively accessible for twentieth-century buildings, particularly for those of the post-war period whose creators may still be alive. Never before have we so nearly ‘caught up’ with history that the interview has been a feasible option, just as never before has there been a conservation profession to ask a different kind of question from that of the historian. One example that has recently been the subject of a conservation debate is St John's Church, built on the contemporary Ermine estate in Lincoln to the designs of Sam Scorer, and which was consecrated in 1963. The 'authors', however, also include the commissioning priest and his congregation, with whom Scorer worked very closely over a long development period; the craftsmen who designed the stained glass and metal work; and the local authority planning department who specifically asked for a sheet metal covering to the dramatic hyperbolic paraboloid roof which is the dominant feature of the exterior. The building was listed grade II* when potentially damaging alterations to the roof were proposed. The problem is that the roof cladding has failed, primarily because the fixings were insufficient and wind has lifted the individual sheets. There has since been discussion as to whether it should now be asphalted, covered with an improved sheet metal system, or whether the aluminium standing seam solution should be replaced on a like for like basis. Legitimate arguments can be made in favour of all these solutions.

A second aspect of the intention debate focuses on the lifespan for which buildings are designed and argues that buildings are no longer built to last. Again, however, this is not a new problem: London terraced houses were built to a specification sufficient to last only the length of a 66- or 99-year lease, a period that has long since expired. Whilst the now popular 'prefabs' erected under the 1944 Temporary Housing Act were designed with an intended lifespan of ten or fifteen years, most post-war buildings were required to fulfil mortgage requirements based on a repayment period of sixty years, and are thus at least as permanent as those of other periods. The difference is that we have on record the erroneous expectation of contemporary architects, such as those of the Hertfordshire schools, that a more prosperous age would be able to improve on their austere efforts (Saint 1987, 232). Instead, conservation and economics increasingly coalesce in extending a building's lifespan.

Performance

The architects for the external refurbishment of Sir Owen Williams's grade I D10 factory for Boots at Nottingham (1930–32) won an award for a scheme that included the entire replacement of its continuous glazing. This is something that would not be countenanced in an older building, but here it was justified because of the strict brief that this large manufacturing building had to fulfil. It is argued that buildings now get out of date faster, as a larger percentage of construction costs is spent on 'building kit' rather than on monumental fabric. It is becoming frequently uncertain whether the potentially ephemeral services and 'finishes' are part of the architecture, or part of the furniture. An example on the same Boots site as D10 is the D90 office headquarters by Skidmore, Owings and Merrill with Yorke, Rosenberg and Mardall, built in 1968 and listed grade II*. In a recent scheme for its modernisation and extension, it was readily accepted that the fabric of the building's skin should be carefully conserved, but the architects' gridded light fittings will be replaced and heavy timber carrels (individual working bays) discarded.

Modern buildings may also be more finely tuned than their predecessors and therefore less flexible, particularly if they are a response to very specific and narrowly defined briefs. A most explicit example of this is No. 48 Boundary Road, Camden, built as a home for physically handicapped young adults by Evans and Shalev for the local authority in 1976. Built around a ramped central community space with a swimming pool, it has clusters of bed sitting rooms with shared kitchen areas and private balconies. It is undoubtedly very prescriptive: it is expected that young disabled people should live together, that they should socialise with each other, and that they should all go out during the day. It also presumed a larger support staff than is available today. It would clearly be quite difficult to convert it into anything else, beyond a student hostel or an art gallery (it could be a possible extension to the nearby Saatchi gallery). The rapidly changing nature of our ideas about disability makes this building exceptional. Many buildings of previous eras were also very specific, however, yet we may either be no longer attuned to read their specificity, or the process of adaptation may have obliterated their original distinctions.

Viability

How well the building is functioning is not a criterion that can be considered when a listing decision is made, except for the elimination of those buildings that have failed so spectacularly that they have already been demolished or radically altered. The shorter the time span that elapses between construction and assessment for listing, however, the less chance that the self-selection that has previously held sway will have to operate. These difficulties were spelt out in the press release that accompanied the listing of Keeling House, Claredale Street, Tower Hamlets, a block of sixty-four flats and maisonettes by Denys Lasdun (1958–60) that was a unique attempt at integrating a block of high flats within an existing community (Figure 11.1). In February 1994, the Secretary of State for National Heritage, Peter Brooke, explained that he had listed the building at grade II* for its architectural and historic interest, whilst accepting that it would have to be demolished if it could not be viably refurbished. This was an admirably honest clarification of the listing versus listed building consent process, though it is unlikely that the future of a grade II* building from previous centuries would have been subject to such market-place economics. At Keeling House, listing has been beneficial in encouraging realistic proposals for its refurbishment to be produced.

Appeal

Modern architecture is seen, certainly by most sections of the media, as unpopular with the majority of people. Nevertheless, a MORI poll commissioned by English Heritage found that 65 per cent of those interviewed felt that it was

Figure 11.1 Keeling House, Claredale Street, London Borough of Tower Hamlets, 1958–60 by Drake and Lasdun. Listed grade II*, there are now proposals for its conversion to private flats

Source: Elain Harwood

important to list modern buildings (MORI 1996). A comparison can be made with the many workhouses or prisons, which lack popular appeal, but where we have established the principle of listing for historic and planning interest as well as for aesthetic appeal.

In conclusion, then, the conservation of recent buildings poses questions of likeability, and of scale, but their problems are not necessarily different from those of earlier periods. Architects like John Allan (Avanti Architects) and John Winter are building up a roster of buildings from the 1930s that have been 'conserved', either for their original use or as 'house museums'. They have faced the difficulties of replacing or repairing concrete, and of providing better weatherings than were

Figure 11.2 Bracken House, City of London, 1958 by Sir Albert Richardson, remodelled 1988–91 by Sir Michael Hopkins. England's first post-war listed building shows how a drastic intervention was made with listed building consent – to great acclaim

Source: Elain Harwood

allowed for in the stripped aesthetic of early modernism, and of incorporating new services and functions appropriate to late twentieth-century needs. In these buildings, some of which are described below, the preservation of *authenticity* has been paramount, whilst accepting that alterations and additions should be distinctively of our own age. These approaches offer possibilities for the future preservation of more recent buildings. Listing has ensured that buildings such as Richardson's Bracken House have not been demolished, but has permitted dramatic intervention where this has been carefully considered and is itself of high quality – at Bracken House by allowing the rebuilding of its central core as a distinctive but appropriately proportioned new office block by Michael Hopkins in 1988–91 (Figure 11.2). The result has been considered 'a compromise, but a brilliant one' (Bradley and Pevsner 1997, 445). The practice of conservation of twentieth-century buildings has more frequently been to sacrifice elements of historic fabric, and hence overall reversibility, for a more discriminating analysis of what is of fundamental importance and greater emphasis on the overall quality of the final design solution.

Public presentation

The ultimate form of official cultural endorsement of buildings is their selection for public viewing, when people are prepared to turn up and perhaps pay for the privilege of looking around. The three buildings that have been selected for presentation as examples of modern twentieth-century architecture are in many ways remarkably similar. Two are open already, one will be a legacy to the National Trust.

No. 2 Willow Road, Ernö Goldfinger's house, in Hampstead

This was opened to the public by the National Trust in 1996 (Diestelkamp 1994). In the tradition of the Soane Museum, it is the architect's own house with a collection of objects and art works that inspired him. Ernö Goldfinger was born in Budapest in 1902 and moved to Paris where he studied with Auguste Perret, before finally settling in London in 1934 after marrying an Englishwoman. Construction of a three-storey terrace of three houses began in 1938 and was completed the following year. It was passed to the National Trust through the Treasury in lieu of inheritance tax when Goldfinger's wife died, whilst the contents remain in the house on long-term loan and are due to pass to the Trust as a further tax concession in the future. An appeal for endowment funding was very successful, and included an exhibition at the Fine Arts Society and help from the Twentieth Century Society. Further official endorsement of the building's importance came in the form of a grant from the National Heritage Memorial Fund.

The decision has been made to present the building in its 1991 state, without 'unpicking' post-1930s alterations or removing art works acquired at a later date, although it would have been theoretically possible to reinstate a pristine original form as there were copious records and an excellent set of Dell and Wainwright photographs from 1939. Visitors are taken round in guided groups, principally for security reasons, and a cinema has been installed in the garage. Although the physical impact of the works carried out by Avanti (an architectural firm that has an excellent reputation for the restoration of twentieth-century buildings) prior to opening were minimal, as with the buildings of previous centuries where initially the Trust showed only the 'above stairs' areas, the basement servants' quarters have been refurbished as a self-contained flat that is not part of the tour (for a contrasting approach in a traditional country house context at Brodsworth Hall, see Chapter 8).

Headmaster's house at Dartington School, Devon

High Cross House was built in the grounds of Dartington Hall, Devon, in 1932 (Figure 11.3). The architect was William Lescaze, already famous for his Oak Lane School in Philadelphia. This had been commissioned by its headmaster,

William Curry, who was subsequently invited to Dartington to create a Utopian community based around a new school. When the school closed in 1987, the house fell empty. Maggie Giraud, archivist to the Dartington Trust, proposed using the building to display the Trust's collection of modern paintings and ceramics and to allow the public to see the building (Mead 1993). Once again a full set of Dell and Wainwright photographs was available, and in this case it was decided to recreate the 1932 interiors as far as was practicable. On the wall of each room there is a copy of the relevant photograph and the original plan, and each is furnished accordingly as far as possible. As at Willow Road, the most major alteration has been to the garage, which has become the principal gallery space, and there are offices and a café upstairs. The architect for these works was John Winter, himself a modern architect of considerable standing who is perhaps best known for his own house of 1969 in Highgate – itself considered by many to be a candidate for future listing.

It should be noted that High Cross House had one major advantage in terms of public presentation: there is already an established audience, for people come to the Dartington Glassware Factory Shop, which trades on its twentieth-century design history pedigree.

Figure 11.3 High Cross House, Dartington, Devon, 1931–2 by William Lescaze. The first modern movement house to open to the public

Source: Elain Harwood

The Homewood, Esher, Surrey, Patrick Gwynne

Although not yet open to the public, Patrick Gwynne's house, built initially for his parents in 1938–9, will be bequeathed to the National Trust on the architect's death. At the time he built the house, Gwynne was in the office of Wells Coates, co-founder of MARS (the influential Modern Architecture Re-Search group) and architect of Lawn Road Flats (1932–4), to whom the design was for long jointly attributed. Gwynne subsequently pursued an independent career, which has concentrated on the design of private houses and more ephemeral shop and restaurant interiors. Neil Bingham's analysis of the house demonstrates that 'Early Modernism is Classical in inspiration' and draws a direct parallel with Le Corbusier's Villa Savoye (1928–30). The Homewood (Figure 11.4) has a 'rational, sophisticated and poetic beauty', but despite its pioneering modernism it retains considerable elements of traditional country house planning in that it has two wings, one for family and guests and the other for servants (Bingham 1993).

Selection for public presentation

All three buildings described above are very close in date; all are small private houses, and all house collections of art contemporary with their construction or development. Two have a piano nobile and even Willow Road in Hampstead is essentially a pavilion in a landscape, as it is situated on the edge of the Heath. None of these three buildings deals with issues of urbanism, or with the work or leisure of the vast proportion of the population. They are the homes of a new intellectual elite.

Figure 11.4 The Homewood, Claremont, Esher, Surrey, 1938–9, by Patrick Gwynne

Source: Andrew Saint

Alan Powers, in an article in *Perspectives* in which he recommends ten post-war houses that the National Trust might want to consider acquiring, noted that by taking on the Goldfinger house 'the Trust has broken not only a chronological barrier by moving into the later 1930s but, more importantly, a cultural barrier as well' (Powers 1995). Although the Trust has decided to pay attention to the modern movement, it has, however, chosen an example whose 'ideology shares the Trust's basic values about quality of life'. Powers does not elaborate on what these basic values might be, but one could suggest that the pursuit of beauty, the achievement of a relatively leisured and affluent lifestyle, an interest in art objects that relate to the history of the house and are positioned with care within it, and a comfortable relationship between building and landscape might all figure.

The recent acquisition of a workhouse near Southwell in Nottinghamshire shows how the National Trust is broadening its outlook. Nevertheless, it is still seen as 'the principal purveyor of "the treasure houses" of the aristocracy', which are 'the centrepiece of the English heritage' (Mandler 1997, 5). This phenomenon has recently been usefully reassessed by Peter Mandler, who suggests that the cult of the country house is a relatively recent and non-static phenomenon, influenced by changing attitudes to the aristocracy:

> Until the early nineteeth century, country houses were private homes of the aristocracy, admired as art objects principally by their owners and immediate circle. Their role in the national heritage properly begins in the early nineteeth century when the market for cultural products starts to expand rapidly. . . . In this period the older stately homes were popularised as symbols of the common national history shared by all classes.
>
> (Mandler 1997, 3–4)

There was a fall-off in the popularity of country houses at the end of the nineteenth century and the beginning of the twentieth century, with a low ebb between the wars when the popular conception of what constituted our national heritage was the ordinary countryside of cottages and villages. The country house cult rose again after the Second World War, however, and is being perpetuated by the selection of 1930s houses as examples of twentieth-century architecture to be opened to the public. If the general population is to be interested successfully in the most important twentieth-century buildings, and particularly areas such as public housing, concrete construction, and Brutalism – all of which are seen as hard to like – then it has to be weaned from regarding the country house as being the epitome of architectural style in each age. The need for this repositioning should inform efforts to educate the public about the period.

This raises the impossible question of which buildings are of greatest importance in the twentieth century and, particularly, in the post-war period. Then the public realm was of paramount importance, and the interface between public and private realms was manipulated with enormous care. Such themes must undoubtedly be at the centre of understanding many of the key developments of twentieth-century society and not just of its architecture. They can be seen particularly clearly in public housing, where social and architectural ideas were brought together most ambitiously but which is now especially vulnerable to change and demolition. One excellent example that has already been lost is the Penryn Estate of the early 1970s, built by the London Borough of Lambeth in Kennington, London SE11.

How does one 'open' a housing estate to the public? The selection of a representative example of any building type is always a difficult task, and in practice many pragmatic factors come in to play. One example worth considering would be the Lillington Gardens Estate in Pimlico, the result of a competition held in 1961 by the City of Westminster which was won by John Darbourne. His novel design in load-bearing brick respected the scale of its surroundings whilst establishing a 'modern vernacular style' that became widely fashionable – even a cliché – in the 1970s. The three main phases were built between 1964 and 1972 by Darbourne and his partner Geoffrey Darke, and made generous use of balcony planting and public open spaces. Consideration of how the public could be invited to explore them raises many practical as well as philosophical issues. The flats themselves are small for large numbers of people to visit, and are finished relatively simply; in addition, preserving the privacy and security of residents on the very narrow stairs and balcony 'streets in the sky' requires careful thought. Since the 1950s, estates have become increasingly private places from which the general public have been progressively excluded. The opening of Skinner, Bailey and Lubetkin's Bevin Court, Islington (1952), as part of the Open House events for September 1996, however, suggests one approach. In the popular captivation with visiting country houses, the carefully controlled redefining of public and private preserves provides much of the fascination. Can we not develop a similar pride in the key building type of recent decades, one where, like the country house, Britain has an outstanding international reputation? This is almost certainly a necessary adjunct to the listing process and the management of change under listed building control procedures if buildings of this period are to find popular acceptance.

■ ■ ■

References

Anthony, B. (1981) 'Conference report', *Thirties Society Journal* 1, 25.

Bingham, N. (1993) 'The Homewood, Surrey', *Country Life* 177, (29) (July 22), 84–7.

Bradley, S. and Pevsner, N. (1997) *The Buildings of England, London 1: the City of London*, Harmondsworth: Penguin.

Cherry, B. and Pevsner, N. (1991) *The Buildings of England, London 3: North West*, Harmondsworth: Penguin.

Diestelkamp, E. (1994) 'Interiors and exteriors, acquiring modern buildings for the nation', in S. Macdonald, (ed.) *Modern Matters, Principles and Practice in Conserving Recent Architecture*, Shaftesbury: Donhead with English Heritage, pp. 38–47.

English Heritage (1996) *Developing Guidelines for the Management of Listed Buildings*, London: English Heritage.

Hitchcock, H.R. and Johnson, P. (1932) *The International Style*, Exhibition at the Museum of Modern Art, New York.

Mandler, P. (1997) *The Rise and Fall of the Stately Home*, London: Yale University Press.

Mead, A. (1993) 'Restoring an early modern English house to exhibit art', *Architects' Journal* (September), 32–3.

MORI (1996) *Public Attitudes to Listing Buildings*.

Lord Palumbo of Walbrook (1994) 'Introduction', in E. Mills, (ed.) *Building Maintenance and Preservation*, Oxford: Architectural Press.

Pevsner, N. (1951) *The Buildings of England, Middlesex*, Harmondsworth: Penguin.

Pevsner, N. (1968) 'Foreword', in A. Smithson and P. Smithson, *The Euston Arch and the Growth of the London, Midland & Scottish Railway*, London: Thames and Hudson

Powers, A. (1995) 'Welcoming the new pretenders', *Perspectives on Architecture* 9 (January), 36–7.

Saint, A. (1987) *Towards a Social Architecture*, London: Yale University Press.

Saint, A. (1996) 'Defining the principles of modern conservation', in S. Macdonald, (ed.) *Modern Matters, Principles and Practice in Conserving Recent Architecture*, Shaftesbury: Donhead with English Heritage, pp. 15–28.

Chapter 12

CONSERVING RECENT MILITARY REMAINS
Choices and Challenges for the Twenty-first Century

John Schofield

> The mountain Kohnstein is anhydrite but Dora is quicksand. It sucked its slaves into the earth; it sucked its Nazi guards into the abyss of inhumanity; it sucked its scientists into the blindness of goal without consequence, accomplishment without accountability.
>
> It has continued to absorb all who come to the tunnels. It has trapped the researchers who have come to study; it has trapped the historians who have come to write; it has drawn the visitor who has come to wonder at the wonders and the cruelties that have taken place in this strange and hallowed ground.
>
> Anhydrite can be mined, as history can be mined; the tunnels of Dora go into the earth forever.
>
> (Gilens 1995, 113)

Introduction

Recent military remains are, by definition, a new dimension to the heritage that provide a significant and challenging addition to our historic resource. The cultural value of these remains, and the nature of the challenge they present to those charged with their preservation, presentation and marketing, form the subject of this chapter. Dora is indicative of the chapter's central theme: that recent military sites often evoke a depth of feeling rarely seen on other types of site (excepting perhaps the scenes of industrial disasters). That emotional charge is expressed here by one of the first post-war visitors to Dora's underground world, where slaves from

Buchenwald were brought to work on the V2 rocket. Dora also highlights the conservation dilemma: the tunnels were sealed at the end of hostilities and, although they survive as left, what is regarded variously as a monument and a memorial, a testimonial and a shrine, will soon be destroyed by quarrying.

Although recent military remains[1] have been of interest to amateur archaeologists over at least the past thirty years, a professional concern and popular enthusiasm for the physical remains of twentieth-century warfare has developed only recently. The reasons are becoming increasingly clear, and extend beyond the mere fact that 'heritage now spreads into yesterday' (Lowenthal 1996, 17): the nostalgia surrounding the fiftieth anniversaries of VE and VJ days; the reflective mood that accompanies the approaching millennium; the development pressure placed on military remains, for instance through the Ministry of Defence's disposal programme, made necessary by the reduction in size of the armed forces, and operational changes brought on by technological advances in warfare; and changing perceptions of what constitutes the historic environment, and the view that it should be regarded holistically, a key principle in the notion of sustainability (English Heritage 1997). There are certain considerations, however, some unique to recent military remains, that require that they command special treatment, and it is these considerations that form the basis of this chapter. First, the philosophy of preservation: can we view objectively that which is so recent; and should we be preserving sites that can evoke such painful memories? Second, how should military remains and other structures synonymous with the two world wars and the Cold War, as well as those of civil conflict, be presented to a multi-cultural and multi-national audience embracing both veterans and the very young? Finally, if we should preserve, on what basis can a selection of sites for preservation be made, and what form of protection is most appropriate for conserving, on the one hand, redundant military structures, and on the other, the many buildings that remain in use: the respective roles of listing, scheduling and the implementation of government policy through Planning Policy Guidance Notes (PPG) 15 and 16 will be mentioned (DoE 1990, 1994).

The hallowed ground: principles of conservation philosophy

The recent past is today considered as much a part of our heritage as are more distant periods (Samuel 1994; Lowenthal 1996), and as we move into the twenty-first century, its status as history and its cultural significance will become more obvious and more consensual. This concerns not just the military remains, the industrial and infrastructural legacy, but popular culture also (Schofield 1998 and forthcoming); as Samuel has said (1994), the notion of heritage is serving to modernise and update what constitutes the historical, as well as extending its social base. English Heritage view recent military remains as an important part of this wider heritage. They exist as *the* touchstones of the increasingly global conflict which will come to characterise the twentieth century, described variously as an 'age of extremes', and as the most terrible in western history.[2] These were, after all, momentous events that shaped nations; they made the modern world.

Various arguments are made in favour of the preservation of recent military remains. There is a view that selected remains of the two world wars and the Cold War must be preserved, in order that we 'retain our sense of history', as well as giving character to our towns and countryside – the sense of place and community that held such significance during the war years. Furthermore, these remains play a significant role in 'our island story' – in some parts of Britain, the changing character of defence systems, from the medieval period to the middle of the twentieth century, can be viewed and readily appreciated within their physical and strategic context (but cf. Stocker 1992). Also, and importantly, military remains – combined ideally with the testimony of those involved – give archaeologists (and those charged with presentation and heritage management) the opportunity to 'turn the dead silence into an eloquent statement of experience' (Carman 1997, 2). In this regard, military remains also have a significant role in education. The remains are everywhere – town and country – and it would seem that, increasingly, their educational and recreational value is being recognised (e.g. Planel 1995). In addition, there is economic worth. Military sites and museums, local and national, and in particular the Imperial War Museum at London and Duxford, attract considerable numbers of visitors, including many veterans who return to their wartime bases, of which Duxford was one. Finally, there is an emotional value, connected with bereavement, remembering and commemoration (Tarlow 1997), though arguably this has greater relevance at the scenes of conflict and atrocity (concentration camps such as Auschwitz – designated a World Heritage Site – and the First World War battlefields for instance) than in areas beyond the war zone.

There are contrary views to the principle of selective preservation, however. The first concerns the theory of sustainability (English Heritage 1997), and specifically the role of the 'community'[3] in defining its critical assets. Put simply, sustainability requires some mechanism, independent of the heritage agencies themselves, by which to determine whether items of heritage capital are sustainable (Lowenthal 1996, 21). Where they have neither community support nor passive acceptance, this is unlikely to be the case. There is certainly a view that support for recent military remains is to be found only among special interest groups, though there is growing evidence (referred to later) that appears to contradict it. A second view is that the monuments of war should be removed as unsightly and unstable reminders of a sad and violent past. Although unusual nowadays, this view perhaps has some link to the idea that, whilst continuing to honour the war dead, the millennium may be the time to consider modernising the act of remembrance, perhaps even reducing the central significance of war memorials and the symbol of remembrance – the poppy – in favour of something more forward-looking and 'less triumphal' (McCrum 1997). The largely favourable reaction of veterans to the Spice Girls promoting Remembrance Day in 1997, wider participation in the two-minute silence, and the seemingly greater enthusiasm of the very young, who 'want to know', and who actively participate in the collective act of remembering the war dead, may indicate some support for this view.

Three examples illustrate some of the difficulties military remains present in the years immediately following conflict, occupation or repression, and the first example, the Berlin Wall, exemplifies this as well as highlighting a dilemma between conservation and consumption (Figure 12.1). The Wall was built in 1961 in the stalemate phase of the Cold War, to stop mass emigration from east to west, and, in the propaganda of the German Democratic Republic, as a contribution to World Peace: 'a foundation stone for the success of our policy of relaxation and peaceful co-operation' and as an 'anti-fascist protection wall' (Baker 1993). Prior to its removal in 1989, the Wall was undeniably *the* symbol of the Cold War, its significance and power felt the world over, as well as being the defining feature of Berlin. Within seconds of the first hammer-blow, television showed the world the Berliners' instant reaction – to take physical possession of it, climbing on it, then hacking at it. Watching events unfold, we were experiencing a defining moment of the twentieth century. It is easy to understand the reaction to tear it down: it separated many families. Nevertheless, as it came down, nostalgia combined with a conservation ethic in reaction to the overwhelming consumption of Berliners.

Alfred Kernd'l, Berlin's chief archaeologist, said this in support of preservation: 'It is typical for us Germans that at the end of an historical era we want to rip everything down and forget it ever happened. It occurred with the Nazi sites, now it's happening with the Berlin Wall' (Baker 1993, 726). Arguments for preserving

Figure 12.1 The Berlin Wall, looking east (1983): symbol of the Cold War and the subject of a significant conservation dilemma to those charged with its management

Source: John Schofield

parts of it were also offered by the Green Party on the basis that the Wall was essential for understanding a critical thirty-year period in the city's history, as well as being symbolic of one of the most important periods in world history.

To conclude this example, it was proposed that three main sections of the wall were retained, one of which was controversial as it ran alongside the former Gestapo and SS HQ of Himmler and Heydrich – at one time the most feared address in Berlin – this begging comparison between the horrors of the Nazis and the Stasi. One view was that visitors should be confronted by the interrelationships of German history; another was that preserving a section of wall adjacent to the Gestapo HQ would serve only to relativise and dilute the crimes of the Nazis (Kernd'l, quoted in Baker 1993, 727). It is tempting to suggest that, in the future, the interest in this monument will be as much for its demolition by the people, as for its limited physical presence. Indeed, the heritage management regime could almost be seen as representing bogus interference in historical process – an agency acting on behalf of reactionary forces, and against the community will (Stocker pers. comm.). A further political dimension here is that preservation, especially of Nazi landmarks, can lead to their becoming the focus of modern extremist – in this case neo-Nazi – organisations. The Berghof – Hitler's alpine retreat – is an example: partly demolished by the Bavarian authorities some time after 1945, it nevertheless became a place of pilgrimage. The present and controversial plans to construct a documentation centre on the site, incorporating what remains of the underground bunkers, has the intention of retaining its historic significance whilst having a use that discourages the neo-Nazi presence (Traynor 1997). One part of the complex – the Eagle's Nest – where Hitler received Chamberlain and Stalin, is now a mountain-top café.

A second example is the Channel Islands, under German occupation between 1940 and 1945. Hitler intended to make the islands a new Gibraltar, German for all time, thus committing vast quantities of steel, concrete and labour to their fortification. Immediately after liberation, there were stringent efforts to eliminate or hide these reminders of Nazi occupation; much was removed by the British liberating forces, and that which they were unable to transport was sold for scrap. Once the more moveable features were gone, valuable items sold, and memories began to fade, however, the pace slowed almost to a standstill. On Guernsey, many of the more robust fortifications, such as the observation towers (Figure 12.2), survived, and fourteen of the most significant sites, determined from an island-wide survey, are now protected under Guernsey's Ancient Monuments and Protected Buildings law. These remains now have economic benefits – which are marketed by the Tourist Board under the umbrella 'Fortress Guernsey' – and their physical presence (and indeed that of re-enactment groups in Nazi uniforms Stone pers. comm.) seems not to bother the islanders of today, irrespective of their generation. There is a contrast here with Vietnam, where western visitors are advised not to wear shorts, not because of tropical insects or risk of infection, but because of history: shorts remind the Vietnamese of the French, who wore them during the period of their occupation over forty years ago. Note also the contradiction

Figure 12.2 Naval observation tower at Pleinmont: one of fourteen German fortifications (or groups of fortifications) on Guernsey protected under Ancient Monuments and Protected Buildings legislation

Source: John Schofield

(albeit based on economic expediency): Webster (1997, 164) has reported that, in the Vietnamese language, the word for 'American' is the same as the word 'beautiful'. As a Vietnamese put it: 'We are a practical people, and we remember only what we can use of the past. Now we think the Americans can help us. So . . . we love the Americans.'

Finally, let us consider Denmark. Here a 'special emotional problem' is described concerning the works of the Second World War:

> These are reminders not only of a military occupation but also are symbols of the brutality of the Third Reich as experienced by the Danish people. One can, naturally, choose to ignore them or remove them from sight, but an alternative is to let these works remind us, and coming generations, what Nazism and the Third Reich stood for.
>
> (Ministry of Environment 1994, 41)

In all, the Germans built more than 6,000 bunkers for Denmark's coast defence, yet very few of them are visible today. As on Guernsey, those that are visible are popular as visitor attractions, and are used in education. Many of the remainder were stripped of equipment after the war and covered over; they now survive buried beneath sand dunes (Ministry of Environment 1994, 39).

There appears, therefore, to be a standard sequence of attitudes and motivations following occupation and the cessation of hostilities, and it is interesting to note in this context of time-lapse the current clearance initiative in Kuwait, seven years after the end of the Gulf War: here 112,959 bunkers have been destroyed, 341 km (213 miles) of trenches filled in, and 389 km (243 miles) of earthwork berms levelled by the company employed to clear the war zone (Webster 1997, 229). We hear much about (and applaud) the clearance of land mines, but the clearance of fortifications has a different motivation altogether. By comparison, it appears that clearance of the Gulf's desert landscape was much more systematic than was the case with Guernsey in the years immediately following the Second World War, and much more permanent than the clearance of German sites in Denmark. Indeed, there seems a real possibility that all physical trace of the Gulf War will be gone within a short time. Is there not a case for preserving a selection of these structures as monuments to the latest conflict in the history of this troubled region? As with the Berlin Wall, such a proposal may not have 'community' support, mainly given the recent occurence of the events; but it could be argued that, despite the charge of interfering with the historical process, we (the profession) have a duty to preserve a selection of sites for the benefit of future communities in that region. This is certainly a difficult issue, but one that the profession should address, nonetheless.

'Clear-cut, successful in all respects': presenting conflict as heritage

As we have seen, there is a duty on those charged with presenting recent military sites to balance numerous responsibilities: to remember the fallen; to avoid trivialising contributions to the war effort; but also (I would argue) to ensure some emotional engagement with the subject. David Uzzell (1989) termed this 'hot interpretation', and gives as an example District Six in Cape Town (Ballantyne and Uzzell 1993). The Group Areas Act of 1950 effectively formalised the ethnic segregation of South Africa's residential and business areas. Forced removals of Asian and Coloured people were common in the pursuit of racially segregated cities, and in the case of District Six this experience was particularly horrifying, representing the 'best known example of the destruction of a mixed race community through Group Areas legislation in South Africa' (Ballantyne and Uzzell 1993, 7). How this situation could be reversed and resolved in post-apartheid South Africa was the justification for a 'hot interpretation' centre in District Six (now completed): it was intended to have a mediating role, reconciling the different antagonists and allowing negotiated redevelopment. As Ballantyne and Uzzell state:

> Reconciliation should not allow one group to interpret the history of another. This form of cultural appropriation has been the source of much conflict in Australia, Europe and the United States. If reconciliation and a positive change in attitudes are to occur, then groups must work together to interpret their past and alternative futures.
>
> (Ballantyne and Uzzell 1993, 7)

The controversy that often accompanies interpretation is, however, exemplified by events surrounding the proposed exhibit at the Smithsonian, in Washington DC, to commemorate the bombing of Hiroshima – described by the weaponeer who released the bomb as 'clear cut, successful in all respects'. In his book, Harwit (1996) chronicles, with a combination of dispassion and anger, the long evolution of the museum's plans for an exhibition in observation of the fiftieth anniversary of the bombing, for which the centrepiece was to be the *Enola Gay*, the B-29 aircraft that dropped the bomb. Over ten years, the aircraft had been painstakingly restored, and well satisfied the criterion of historic importance necessary for its inclusion in the museum's Air and Space Collection. Unlike the other hardware on display, however, the *Enola Gay* was there not as a triumphant manifestation of higher, faster or further, but rather because it initiated the age of nuclear weapons, killed some 100,000 people and hastened the end of the Second World War. So, not surprisingly, controversy surrounded the question of what the museum's visitors were to be told about this aircraft and its place in history. On one side of the debate were veterans who felt that the plane should be displayed 'proudly'; they demanded an approving if not celebratory observation of the plane's wartime feat. Harwit, however, wanted to infuse awareness that the bomb had caused damage and suffering. The veterans were incensed by plans to display charred artefacts from the bombing: a child's lunch box; a clock that stopped at the moment of detonation. They and other critics said that the proposed display 'sentimentally ignored Japanese culpability and cruelty in the war'. In the end, the exhibit was cancelled, leaving only the forward section of the fuselage on display with scant reference to its historic role. The balance between critical analysis and honouring and commemorating valour and service, it would seem, is a fine one.

Conservation practice in England

Turning finally to practical matters, and specifically the question of how recent military remains can be conserved, discussion is structured according to the staged approach taken by English Heritage towards the evaluation of recent military sites in England: first, how we assess the resource – how can we begin to appreciate its extent and diversity, and from that the relative importance of its component parts; and second, what options do we have in England for its management? Again, some examples will follow general discussion.

In England, as elsewhere, conservation practice is based on the principles of sustainability (English Heritage 1997 and above): specifically, that not everything can be preserved *in situ*, and that decisions on future management must be based on the best possible information. Some elements of the environment should, of course, be preserved at all costs (these are our critical assets, deemed to be of great value and irreplaceable); some will be subject to limited change; whilst some can be exchanged for other benefits. In dealing with recent military sites (and surprisingly,

Table 12.1 Scope of the archival survey

Site types	*Dates*	*Distributional information*
anti-aircraft artillery	1914–46	complete
anti-invasion defences	1939–45	representative
bombing decoys	1939–45	complete
Operation *Diver* sites	1944–45	complete
Operation *Overlord* preparatory sites	1942–45	complete
coast artillery	1900–56	complete
civil defence	1939–45	representative
radar (incl. acoustic detection)	1920–45	complete
airfields (incl. airfield defences)	1914–45	complete
Cold War sites	1947–68	complete

given the recency and the availability of personal accounts and testimony), our understanding until now has not been sufficient to define an appropriate management strategy; over the last five years we have sought to remedy that by commissioning a national review of the subject (cf. Dobinson *et al.* 1997 and English Heritage 1998 for details). By using archival sources held at the Public Records Office, work has been undertaken and thematic reports produced for all major classes of recent military sites (Table 12.1). Each report contains an account of the historical context relevant to the site type, details of typology, chronology, *etc.*, as well as (with two exceptions, see Table 12.1) gazetteers detailing how many sites there were, where they were (usually to the accuracy of a six-figure grid reference), when they were there, what they looked like (often with ground plans or photographs) and who manned them. For two types of site (anti-invasion measures of the Second World War and civil defence), sites were just too numerous to be accurately recorded through archival searches, so having provided contextual information (e.g. the location of anti-invasion 'stop-lines'), this provides the focus for the Defence of Britain Project whose volunteers are recording all surviving examples. For the majority of site types, however, our understanding has been transformed by this survey: archival sources do give a virtually complete account of sites as built, and we are now using aerial photographs to assess the likelihood of their survival. Finally, for the Cold War period, our archival survey is restricted by the Thirty Year Rule to the period up to 1968, but here work by the Royal Commission on the Historic Monuments of England (RCHME) will be invaluable, recording structures that exemplify the main site types, including missile launch sites, radar and communication installations, military bomb shelters, peace camps, research and manufacturing sites and the 'Little America' architecture of the large US Air Force bases. Archival sources have a significant role in understanding and reinterpreting Cold War history at a global level (Gaddis 1997); in England, however, many such sources will not be available to this generation (and maybe several subsequent generations), so here more emphasis must necessarily rest with the physical remains.

In conserving historic fabric, English Heritage makes the distinction between structures and sites that are best served by their future as monuments, and those for which use, or adaptation for beneficial reuse, is appropriate. In military terms, this corresponds to the distinction between the so-called 'teeth' and 'tail' of the armed forces. Buildings of the support services – the tail – are often generalised structures and as such tend to continue in some form of use, whilst the teeth – including fortifications – are now monuments and beneficial reuse is generally difficult to envisage for such specialised structures.

The development of the scheduled monument and listed building systems has been based around a partnership between these complementary approaches, the distinction being made between: 1) the management needs of those critical assets whose preservation takes precedence over their use, and which may have no use except as monuments (these are covered by scheduling under the terms of the 1979 Ancient Monuments and Archaeological Areas Act), and 2) those whose conservation value is best safeguarded by retaining them in use, whose sympathetic use is, in fact, a form of conservation (for which listing is appropriate, under the 1990 Planning [Listed Buildings and Conservation Areas] Act). This distinction has resulted in two separate sets of management controls, tailored to meet the needs of their respective constituencies. Scheduled Monument Consent, for example (the controls that ensure the care of scheduled monuments), makes the assumption that efforts will be made to preserve the designated structure *in situ* and in more-or-less the state in which it came down to us. Its aim is preservationist. On the other hand, listed building controls are more flexible and are based on the assumption that some measure of alteration and adaptation may be necessary in order that the building can maintain a viable use and will retain its value as a capital asset.

Examples illustrate the extremes. The gas warfare testing trenches on Porton Down, Wiltshire, are a Scheduled Ancient Monument. With an overall diameter of nearly 400 m (1,300 ft), these concentric trenches were dug in 1916 during experiments with gas and other forms of chemical warfare. Their concentric design enables gas to be released from the inner trench and its effects tested on personnel in the outer, irrespective of wind direction. The trenches survive as earthworks. The monument is demonstrably of national importance (it is likely to be unique in Britain), and is clearly one for which the strict controls of Ancient Monuments legislation are appropriate. Few recent military sites are currently scheduled: sixty-six in their own right, and a further thirty-seven as parts of other monuments, generally fortifications of earlier date. This figure will increase as a result of our survey, however, with some of the best preserved bombing decoys, coast artillery and Heavy Anti-aircraft gun sites likely to be added to the Schedule in due course. Military buildings that are best managed through continued use, on the other hand, include many of our best known architectural landmarks, such as Horseguards in Westminster, and the Royal Naval College at Greenwich. Clearly such buildings should remain in use, and for that listing is the appropriate designation. This is

Figure 12.3 Calshot Castle (centre) and the flying boat hangars (to its left and right), now managed through scheduling and listing respectively

Source: John Schofield

also the case for most aircraft and airship hangars. At Calshot, for instance, the First World War flying boat hangars are listed, and now contain one of Hampshire County Council's outdoor leisure centres, with dry ski-slope and cycle track. Calshot Castle, managed and presented as a heritage attraction, is a Scheduled Ancient Monument and Guardianship site (Figure 12.3).

The designations can work together, therefore, and this can be seen most clearly with English Heritage's work on airfields and airfield structures, where – through close co-operation with Paul Francis and the Airfield Research Group – information has been gathered on the relative significance of both the airfields themselves and the structures and sites within them. Designation will be the next stage with the possibility of combining, in a case like Bicester, various designations: listing for the majority of buildings that remain in use on the Domestic and Technical sites; scheduling for the well-preserved defence structures that surround the airfield (including blast shelters, air-raid shelters, pillboxes); and Conservation Area status for the whole site, with the intention of retaining the overall character of arguably the most complete of the RAF's 1920s bomber stations, one of only three in England to have retained its grass field, and the most complete airfield site in Britain to predate the 1930s. Conservation Area status has been used before in this context, at Hullavington, for instance, and Biggin Hill.

Also relevant is the implementation of PPG15 and PPG16 in conservation practice. PPG15, published in 1994, is important as it provides a full statement of government policies for the identification and protection of historic buildings,

Conservation Areas and other parts of the historic environment. It also explains the role of the planning system in their protection and complements the guidance on archaeology and planning given in PPG16 (published in 1990). PPG16 has had the effect of increasing greatly the ability of the planning process to protect and manage archaeological sites, and in these terms the current work on recent military remains is beginning to feed the implementation of PPG16 at a local level. In North Yorkshire, for example, as a condition of planning permission, developers are now required to record military sites. An example of this has been the thorough photographic recording of two RAF camps associated with Scorton Airfield in advance of redevelopment.

Conclusion

Recent military remains are an integral part of the historic environment, and one that appears to have growing community support. The various branches of the Imperial War Museum attract large numbers of visitors, as do many of the locally managed attractions around the country. In England, as elsewhere in the UK, the Defence of Britain Project is proving to be successful in tapping into that resource, and making good use of it in its national recording programme. Schoolchildren seem genuinely interested in the subject and want to know more. The media has covered many items on local and national initiatives. Until now, our understanding of the material remains in this country representing the two world wars and the Cold War has been poor. One of the principles of work being undertaken by the Monuments Protection Programme, as with the Listing Team, however, is that any statutory designations must have a credible basis; our research aims to provide that.

Within the profession, there seems little doubt these days that a selection of these monuments, teeth and tail, and reflecting the changing nature of conflict during the course of this century, should be preserved for the future, to serve as touchstones for what is already being described as a calamitous century, an age of extremes. With wider support, English Heritage is moving towards this position. Other countries, including Denmark, Norway and Finland, France and Belgium, as well as the United States, are doing the same, but it is not an easy subject, either in terms of conservation practice or philosophy. With war and conflict, the choices and challenges are greater than ever, and the pressure on those charged with its preservation and presentation to 'get it right' is prodigious.

■ ■ ■

Acknowledgements

I am grateful to my colleagues in the Monuments Protection Programme, and in particular Graham Fairclough and David Stocker, Jeremy Lake in the Listing Team, and Bill Johnson and Colleen Beck of the Desert Research Institute, Nevada, for comments and discussions on this subject over the past few years. I also owe thanks to those participants at the seminar from which this volume arose, for their comments on the original presentation. Ian MacRae, Secretary of the States of Guernsey Heritage Committee, provided valuable information on their selection policy, whilst Oliver Frankham of English Heritage's Records Office provided information on recent military sites on the Schedule as of July 1997. The archives survey described in this chapter was undertaken for English Heritage by Dr Colin Dobinson of the Council for British Archaeology.

Notes

1 Military 'remains' in this chapter refers only to those items that can typically be described as monumental, thus excluding artefacts and military hardware, the subject of a recent study by Webster (1997).

2 Globally, there have been over 900 separate wars or civil conflicts in the years 1987–97 alone.

3 In the context of recent military remains, 'community' has a broad definition, and is certainly not confined only to factional supporters from special interest groups (retired servicemen, those with interests in technology, re-enactment and other enthusiasts), contrary to popular belief.

References

Baker, F. (1993) 'The Berlin Wall: production, preservation and consumption of a twentieth century monument', *Antiquity* 67, 709–33.

Ballantyne, R. and Uzzell, D. (1993) 'Environmental mediation and hot interpretation: a case study of District Six, Cape Town', *Journal of Environmental Education* 24 (3), 4–7.

Carman, J. (1997) 'Approaches to violence', in J. Carman (ed.) *Material Harm: Archaeological Studies of War and Violence*, Glasgow: Cruithne Press, pp. 1–23.

Dobinson, C.S., Lake, J. and Schofield, A.J. (1997) 'Monuments of war: defining England's twentieth-century defence heritage', *Antiquity* 71, 288–99.

DoE (1990) *Planning Policy Guidance Note 16: Archaeology and Planning*, London: HMSO.

DoE (1994) *Planning Policy Guidance Note 15: Planning and the Historic Environment*, London: HMSO.

English Heritage (1997) *Sustaining the Historic Environment: New Perspectives on the Future*, London: English Heritage.

English Heritage (1998) *Monuments of War: The Evaluation, Recording and Management of Twentieth-Century Military Sites*, London: English Heritage.

Gaddis, J.L. (1997) *We Now Know: Rethinking Cold War History*, Oxford: Clarendon Press.

Gilens, A. (1995) *Discovery and Despair: Dimensions of Dora*, Berlin/Bonn: Westkreuz-Verlag.

Harwit, M. (1996) *An Exhibit Denied: Lobbying the History of Enola Gay*, Copernicus.

Lowenthal, D. (1996) *The Heritage Crusade and the Spoils of History*, London: Viking.

McCrum, R. (1997) 'Goodbyee?', *The Observer* (9 November).

Ministry of Environment (1994) *Fortification in Denmark 1858–1945: A status report (an English unillustrated version of Befæstningsanlæg i Danmark 1858–1945: En statusrapport*, Copenhagen: Ministry of Environment.

Planel, P. (1995) *A Teacher's Guide to Battlefields, Defence, Conflict and Warfare,* London: English Heritage.

Samuel, R. (1994) *Theatres of Memory. Volume 1: Past and Present in Contemporary Culture,* London: Verso.

Schofield, J. (1998) 'This is the modern world: managing "our" legacy for the 21st century', *The Archaeologist* 32, 24–5.

Schofield, J. (forthcoming) 'Never mind the relevance: popular culture for archaeologists', in P. Graves Brown (ed.) *Past and Present: Modern Material Culture*, London: Routledge.

Stocker, D. (1992) 'The Shadow of the General's Armchair', *The Archaeological Journal* 149, 415–20.

Tarlow, S. (1997) 'An archaeology of remembering: death, bereavement and the First World War', *Cambridge Archaeological Journal* 7 (1), 105–21.

Traynor, I. (1997) 'Storm breaks over Hitler's eyrie', *The Guardian* (24 November).

Uzzell, D. (1989) 'The hot interpretation of war and conflict', in D. Uzzell (ed.) *Heritage Interpretation 1: The Natural and Built Environment*, London: Belhaven Press, pp. 33–47.

Webster, D. (1997) *Aftermath: The Remnants of War*, London: Constable.

INDEX

Page numbers printed in **bold** type refer to figures; those in *italic* to tables